NASCAR
CONFIDENTIAL

Stories of the Men and Women
Who Made Stock Car Racing Great

NASCAR
CONFIDENTIAL

PETER GOLENBOCK AUTHOR OF AMERICAN ZOOM

MOTORBOOKS
INTERNATIONAL

First published in 2004 by Motorbooks International,
an imprint of MBI Publishing Company,
Galtier Plaza, Suite 200
380 Jackson Street
St. Paul, MN 55101-3885 USA

Motorbooks International titles are also available at
discounts in bulk quantity for industrial or sales-promotional use.
For details write to Special Sales Manager at
Motorbooks International Wholesalers & Distributors,
Galtier Plaza, Suite 200,
380 Jackson Street,
St. Paul, MN 55101-3885 USA.

ISBN: 0-7603-1483-7

On the front cover: Jeff Gordon on the track. *Nigel Kinrade*

Edited by Lee Klancher
Jacket and Book Design by Rochelle Schultz

Printed in the United States of America

DEDICATION

BETTY CARLAN.

INTERNATIONAL MOTORSPORTS

HALL OF FAME

IF YOU EVER TRAVEL TO THE TALLADEGA INTERNATIONAL SPEEDWAY and visit the International Motorsports Hall of Fame, drop into the library and ask to see the most interesting person on exhibit in the place: Betty Carlan. She may growl at you a little, but don't pay any attention. She's just testing to see whether you're worthy of her attention.

Betty is the keeper of the flame. She is surrounded by memories, dozens of trophies, hundreds of books, thousands of photos, model cars, magazines, and car parts. Her tiny, yippy dog, Ralph Earnhardt, sits on her lap while she works. Dale Earnhardt was her close friend.

No one on this planet cares as much about the history of racing as she does. Few have gotten to befriend as many of the greats as she. The last time I was there, Betty cooked biscuits and gravy for Red Farmer. She has done the same for Dale Earnhardt, Bobby Allison, and many, many others.

Betty has been named the Woman of the Year in stock car racing by the Living Legends of Auto Racing Museum. She has befriended me, allowing me to join her wonderful circle of friends, providing me with most of the great photos in this book. It is with great pleasure that I dedicate this book to Betty Carlan.

TABLE OF CONTENTS

PART III: **THE SOUND AND THE FURY**

PART IV: **THE GILDED AGE**

INTRODUCTION

AT FIRST BLUSH, THE TITLE NASCAR *Confidential* SOUNDS LIKE A steamy Hollywood tell-all, but it's not at all meant that way. Rather what I mean by "confidential" is that the men and women interviewed in this book have taken me into their confidence, that they have trusted me with their revelations of the triumphs and tragedies of their lives. It is a responsibility I do not take lightly. My goal here is not sensationalism—anything but. Rather it is to flesh out the history of this sport in what I consider to be the very best way, through the words of those men and women who participated in and witnessed the events that have made NASCAR stock car racing the great attraction that it has become.

I began my quest to record the memories of this sport's heroes with *American Zoom* in 1993 and followed it up with *The Last Lap* in 1998. This is the third in the series, and I fully expect that it will not be the last. But as the sport continues its incredible growth, I am seeing that less and less time and space are devoted to those men and women who for the last 50 years have made the sport what it is today.

When in the summer of 1992 I began my research for *American Zoom*, Winston Cup stock car racing was as popular as any of the stick-and-ball sports, only few knew it outside the hardcore race fans, because the Eastern media giants like the *New York Times* and the *Washington Post* pretty much ignored it.

Back then, NASCAR didn't get as much ink as professional soccer or America's Cup yacht racing. Half the country loved to watch Dale Earnhardt, Davey Allison, Alan Kulwicki, and the other NASCAR racers, but as far as the other half was concerned, it was a sport for grease monkeys and used-car salesmen and hence wasn't worthy of press coverage. Talk about an Eastern media elite.

It is ten years later, and NASCAR has turned the world of sports on its ear. NASCAR has exploded onto the national consciousness with an impact that has propelled it on a par with any other major sport. Television has discovered that millions of stock car racing fans thirst to watch the races live, so that today you can see Winston Cup, Busch, and even the truck races live. There are cable shows like *Totally NASCAR* and *RPM2Night* dedicated exclusively to the sport. There is even one cable channel, the Speed Channel, that devotes itself to one form of racing or another twenty-four hours a day. I have friends who don't watch anything else.

It is this increased visibility from the one-eyed monster of television that has enabled NASCAR to grow and grow and grow, as smaller tracks like North Wilkesboro lose their dates and superspeedways in Las Vegas, Texas, and California are added. Race teams are now able to charge sponsors as much as $15 million a year for the privilege of putting a logo across the hood and sides of a race car for the millions of viewers to see. Drivers, who often toiled in relative obscurity before TV's seemingly sudden discovery of the sport, today have become among the most famous and celebrated American athletes. When Dale Earnhardt was killed on the last lap of the Daytona 500 in 2001, his chiseled face graced the cover of *Time* magazine. When I asked several old-timers about it, they all had the same reaction: wonderment. They were shocked that the editors of *Time* even knew who Dale Earnhardt was! The sport has come a long, long way.

As it grows, however, there has been a trend toward the obliteration of the past. This has happened in every sport. It is also something that is happening in American society in general, as fewer people read. The Internet is not about the past. It is about the "now." This is equally true of network television, which constantly pushes new, young faces. Youth sells to youth. Old-timers don't, so the obliteration of the past is intentional on the part of the corporate suits in charge of NASCAR's image and product. They want their customers concentrating on the current heroes and not on the old guys from the past. The stick-and-ball sports have done the same thing. If you're going to spend 50 bucks on a souvenir, they want you to forget Dale Earnhardt and Davey Allison and buy what Kevin Harvik, Jimmie Johnson, or Ryan Newman have to offer.

As for Curtis Turner; Tim, Bob, and Fonty Flock; and Junior Johnson, the less said about them by the men who run the sport, the better. Even though stock car racing is a sport that was begun by bootleggers, bootleggers are no longer politically correct. Home Depot, Lowe's, DuPont, and Tide are what you are supposed to be thinking about, not the bootleg whiskey that prompted the earliest racers to soup up their cars.

Except for the exceptional ESPN Classic, which is devoted to the history of sports in America and to keeping the memory of our past heroes alive, you almost never see or hear anything about how our sports got where they did or see or hear about the people who led them into the present day. For many athletes, once they step off the ball field, the ice, or out of the race car, they no longer exist, and to me, that is a terrible injustice. These men and women should be honored and cherished, not forgotten.

Without a sense of history, a race fan cannot fully appreciate a sport's greatness or understand the stops and starts that have brought it to where it is today. Without learning about the men and women whose efforts and contributions built the sport from its infancy, the fan at the racetrack can only see a magnificent structure with no past, no ghosts, no memories.

NASCAR has turned 50, and one need only look at the pages of *The NASCAR Encyclopedia* or Greg Fielden's *Forty Years of Stock Car Racing* to see the records set by the greats: Richard Petty, David Pearson, Bobby Allison, Dale Earnhardt, Fireball Roberts, Joe Weatherly, Davey Allison, Alan Kulwicki, Tim Richmond, and to read about legendary figures such as Red Vogt, Smokey Yunick, Carl Kiekhaefer, John Holman, and Ralph Moody.

In *NASCAR Confidential*, I have sought to interview men and women who were closely involved with these legends in order to better understand who they were and what they did. In several cases, legends such as Ray Fox Sr., Frank Mundy, and Louise Smith—racers who are now in their 70s and 80s—are still alive and able to speak for themselves. Through their stories of NASCAR's fabled past, we gain a better understanding of where stock car racing came from and who was involved in its growth, and we become richer in spirit for it.

At the same time, I have taken care not to forget our most recent racing personalities. When I first interviewed them, crew chiefs Jimmy Makar and Robin Pemberton were still involved in making Bobby Labonte and Rusty Wallace winners. I interviewed Larry McReynolds, not only because he is a friend, but also because he had worked with Davey Allison and Ernie Irvan and was the crew chief for Dale Earnhardt when the Intimidator won the Daytona 500 in 1998. Jimmy Johnson was the team manager for Hendrick Motorsports for 20 years. There is no one better to talk about what was going on behind the scenes with Tim Richmond and Jeff Gordon. Every subject in this book adds to the greater glory of NASCAR.

The goal of this book—and of *American Zoom* and *The Last Lap* before it—is to give you, the reader, an intimacy and immediacy that one can only get from hearing the stories straight from the proverbial horses' mouths. The men and women interviewed in this book did it and saw it and lived it from the days when the moonshiners got together to race their cars, to the very first NASCAR late model race on a dusty Charlotte dirt track in 1949, through the days when Carl Kiekhaefer, Richard Petty, and Holman Moody dominated, to the present day when racers compete on the most up-to-date superspeedways in Michigan; Loudon, New Hampshire; and Indianapolis. They saw victory, defeat, and death and experienced both the roar of the crowd and the loneliness of the forgotten.

NASCAR Confidential, like so many oral histories, can succeed only as a result of the cooperation and kindness of the men and women who have been so supportive, patient, and willing to share their memories. A labor of love, it has been an experience I will never forget. Thank you all. As for you race fans, when you rise up in the vast grandstands as the cars come around the fourth turn to take the green flag, remember the ghosts of the past. They will be all around you.

—Peter Golenbock
St. Petersburg, Florida
November 1, 2003

PART I: **ROUGHING IT**

CHAPTER 1

THE EARL OF MARTINSVILLE

___

Clay Earles

IN THE SPRING OF 1998, I VISITED WITH H. CLAY EARLES, THE FOUNDER AND owner of Martinsville Speedway and one of the men who was instrumental in the founding of NASCAR. Earles was a southern gentleman who had earned his wealth through his own vision and through that of NASCAR's founder, Big Bill France.

Earles was 92 years old when I visited him, and he was just as sharp as the day in 1946 when he began to build the NASCAR landmark out of the indigenous red clay of his beloved southland. I began to talk about what I was attempting to do in this book, to tell the history of NASCAR and how it has changed and grown—in the words of the people responsible and involved. In the middle of my explanation, he stopped me.

"Where are you from?" he asked.

"St. Petersburg, Florida," I told him.

"No," he said. "Where are you really from?"

"Connecticut," I admitted sheepishly.

"You're a Yankee," he said.

"No," I told him. "I'm not a Yankee. I moved to Florida."

"Then," he said, "you're a carpetbagger!"

He laughed uproariously, then became serious. "I was in the navy during the war," he said. "I served most of my time at Franklin Field, about forty miles from Norfolk. They made me master at arms. I was in charge of all the work details, the upkeep of the place. When I was in the navy, I met a lot of boys from the North, from Connecticut and New Jersey, some of the nicest fellows."

H. Clay Earles, who passed away in 1999, was also one of the nicest fellows. He had been there when NASCAR was founded, a right-hand man of Bill France Sr., the founder and visionary who made NASCAR what it is. Earles was one of those men who loved racing so much that he built a track from scratch, not for money at first, but because he wanted to see men and machines race.

"I'm from Martinsville," said Earles. "I was born in L. A.—Lower Axton, that is. I was born on a farm there on August 11, 1913."

He owned three service stations in Martinsville, and he bought and sold real estate. When he saw something he could buy and make a few bucks on, he did it.

Earles first became interested in racing in 1946. There were a few tracks around, but they were nothing special, just areas where men cut out ovals in the dirt by driving around and around until they made a course. Nothing was organized. There was no sanctioning body. If two or three tracks were near each other, they might be running on the same night, so they didn't stay in business very long.

CLAY EARLES
The goose used to peck on
the front door asking for lunch.
MARTINSVILLE SPEEDWAY

"I built this track, but it was before NASCAR," said Earles. "I just thought I could build up this track to where people would come. I felt I could make it interesting enough. I told myself it would be a nice hobby. And I figured I could make a few dollars with it, too. I bought thirty-five acres of land. It wasn't even a racetrack. I just shaped out the place. We'd draw two hundred or three hundred people. The prize money didn't amount to anything."

Earles' inspiration was Indianapolis, the granddaddy of all tracks. Cars had been racing at Indy since 1909. Soon after he built his track, he invited the Indy cars to race. He was going to run AAA-sanctioned races at that time, but then after Bill France began the sanctioning body called NASCAR, he changed his mind and hooked his star to NASCAR and not to AAA. Earles had sound logic for the switch.

He said, "I felt it would be the best for me and best for the other tracks in this area, because if I ran AAA, the Indy cars had a long way to come in order to race here, and we didn't have highways then like we have today. With NASCAR, the drivers didn't have to come as far. Plus it was easier to get NASCAR drivers. Also, AAA races cost more. I only ran one AAA race, and it cost me several thousand dollars more than we had to pay NASCAR.

"Before my first race—I'll never forget—I got a call from Bill. I didn't know him. He had heard I had built this track, and he said he'd like to work with me.

"'What can you do?' I asked.

"He said, 'I'll park cars for you.' So believe it or not, Bill France came up to Martinsville to park cars for me before the first race I had, on September 7, 1947. It's the only race I ever ran that I can remember the exact date: September 7, 1947. We had six thousand thirteen people who paid. That was a lot of people."

Bill France knew the drivers, had contact with the media, and knew how to promote races. He drove to Martinsville and helped Clay Earles get his track off the ground. In exchange, France asked Earles to help him with concessions during his races on Daytona Beach.

Earles erected ten of what were called knockdown stands up and down the beach. He got a soft drink company to make awnings with its logo to go over them. That year, the beach race made money.

France also asked Earles to help him run his sanctioning body. He agreed. Soon after France organized NASCAR down in Florida in December 1947, he told Earles he didn't have a single NASCAR track in Virginia.

"I told him I would help him with it, and it wasn't long before every track in Virginia was a NASCAR track. I held a lot of meetings with other track promoters, and I told them what we could do for them. I told them how silly it was for two tracks close to each other to hold races head to head. I said, 'We don't have enough cars.' I talked them into arranging the dates so they wouldn't run in competition and so they'd be helping one another out.

"I can't rightfully say what it was I liked about Bill France. I thought, 'We can work together and build this thing up, and it will be successful.' I'll tell you, I put a lot of work into building NASCAR, not just for me, but for the other track owners also."

Earles held the first meeting to get the promoters together in Richmond so one promoter wouldn't be taking all the drivers and putting the other promoters out of business. At that time in Virginia, a dozen or so tracks were running weekly races—most of them on fairgrounds. Earles got them together and told them, "You're running in competition with each other. We can arrange this thing and get the dates organized where you won't be bumping heads with one another."

Said Earles, "They liked what I said, and I got them into NASCAR. Most of them—the ones still in business—are in NASCAR.

"Right from the beginning Bill France controlled NASCAR. He was the one who came up with it. But Bill had a lot of help. He needed a lot of help. I became a regional director of NASCAR."

In 1948, Bill France came up with the idea to race only new cars, but it was impossible to run his Late Model series because most of the drivers didn't have enough money to buy new cars and get them ready to race.

"In 1948, France continued to allow Modifieds, and that year Red Byron won the first driving championship," Earles said. "Red won my first race right here. I can't tell you that much about him except that he was from down in Georgia. He lived in several places, and he came here and won our first race. We have a picture of him. His face is covered with a layer of dust an inch thick."

"Back then, these race drivers didn't have *any* money," said Earles. "Today, the drivers are worth millions of dollars. Back then, they didn't hardly have enough money to go from one town to another and buy a motel room."

Earles' policies were geared fairly toward the contestants. His policy was to pay them what he could afford. Sometimes racers who didn't finish well would come to his office and plead poverty, and he would hand them 50 or 100 dollars. Not all track promoters were as generous.

"Back then, fifty years ago, it was hard to make money. Bootlegging was no bad thing, just a way of making a few dollars. Even if you hauled legal whiskey in your car and you hauled it across state lines, that was illegal. You know how the law is. But you had to keep a car that would run good on the highway, and I'd say their highway cars were better than we had on the racetrack."

The bootleggers would take a Ford and put a Lincoln engine in it, or an Offenhauser engine. Those tricked-up cars would run faster in second gear than an average car would in high gear.

"The biggest majority of the drivers were bootleggers who hauled whiskey," said Earles. "I can't say I ever saw the whiskey on them—it was just hearsay—but the moonshiners had a pretty good reputation for being good drivers, and they were the ones who got into racing."

In 1949, the drivers, told they would have to run late-model cars, borrowed money to pay for the new cars. In other cases, a driver would go to a friend or acquaintance who had money, buy a car, and agree to split the winnings. They didn't have to do much to the cars. At the beginning, the race cars didn't even have roll bars.

"I can remember Lee Petty raced back then, and he didn't have much money, but enough to build a car, and he got a lot of help from promoters," said Earles. "We got some pretty good publicity out of him. If there was a driver you wanted in the race, you'd call him up and promise him a couple hundred to enter. And whatever I promised, that's what I gave him.

"There was Lee, Curtis Turner, Joe Weatherly, the Flocks. They drew fans to the track. They had good names, and it didn't take long to build up the names because there weren't that many of them. Today, you have thousands of drivers. Back then, you had maybe a hundred. Fireball Roberts had a good name, and he helped racing a lot. People came to watch him."

RED BYRON
The first NASCAR champion.
MARTINSVILLE SPEEDWAY

In 1949, Bill France scheduled eight sanctioned late model races. The sixth race was held at Martinsville. Scheduling the race was no problem because there was little demand for dates. From day one, France gave Earles permission to pick any two dates and he picked two dates (the fourth Sunday of April and September), and he's been running them for more than fifty years.

"In the beginning, it didn't make any difference at all that it was a NASCAR race," said Earles. "It didn't mean a thing. NASCAR had got a lot of publicity for starting this sanctioning body, but that didn't draw fans to the races. Bill France wasn't known very well at all. For a long while, we didn't make any money even though tickets that first year were two or three dollars, which was a lot of money back then, and for the first race we had we had six thousand thirteen paid, though we had more people than that watch the race. That first race we weren't organized that well. We didn't have ticket booths, just people out front collecting money. We didn't have any fences, and there were people who snuck in. But I wouldn't go up to someone and say, 'I know you came in, but you didn't pay.'

"Now that first race we had six thousand thirteen as my initial paid attendance, but everyone left here looking like Red Byron—they were covered with dust all over them. Ladies had come here that day from church with their Sunday best on, and they stood out there on the loose dirt where I was intending to build some stands—I only had about three hundred seats built. I had more planned. But everyone wanted me to have a race, so I went ahead with it, and we drew six thousand thirteen people."

His next race drew about half that, a handful over 3,000 fans, and it stayed that way from 1947 through 1955. To stay in business, Earles knew he had to do something to attract more fans, especially female fans.

Between the spring race and the fall race of 1955, Clay Earles made a decision that would change racing. He decided to pave his track.

"I always put a lot of thought into everything I do. That's one fault a lot of us have, that we don't do enough thinking. Don't you think so? I called up Bill France and I told him, 'Bill, you know we haven't been drawing any people here. I'm going to pave the track.'

"I can hear him right now. He said, 'Don't you think you'll ruin it?' So help me. At the time, there wasn't any such thing as a paved track. I said, 'I'll tell you this, Bill. If I don't pave it, I'm ruined, so I'm going to pave it.'

"So I paved it, and honest to God, the first race I held after I paved it I drew twice the attendance of the first race! I had over twelve thousand people come. That tells you something. People didn't want to come and get covered with dust. And a lot of tracks that weren't paved went out of business. And from that day until this, our attendance has improved every year.

"If I hadn't paved my track when I did, Daytona would have been the longest dirt track in the world."

Added Earles, "When Bill France talked to me about building the Daytona International Speedway, he offered me a fifty percent interest, but honest to God, I could see down the road how much it was going to cost, moving all that dirt, and I just decided if I invested a big piece of money in it, it would still be a small percentage of the total cost. We were going to start out spending two hundred thousand dollars, but I could see he was going to have to spend a lot more. I was afraid we were going to have to invest in it too fast to make it worthwhile for me. I could envision losing my money, so I didn't take it. I had my doubts whether Bill'd be able to borrow that money or get investors to go in with him.

"But Bill had a vision, and he was able to get the money he needed for the track. And by then NASCAR was getting support from the car manufacturers.

"As an owner I wasn't close to the drivers. I tried to stay out of that part of it. If you're promoting a track, you don't want to own a part of a race car, because the first thing some of the drivers could say is, 'He fixed it.' But I did have some dealings with Curtis Turner, who was from Roanoke here in Virginia. Curtis and Bruton Smith built the Charlotte Motor Speedway in the early 1960s.

"I thought a lot of Curtis. He was a man who made a little money over the years. I hate to say this, but Curtis didn't know how to handle his money. You'd hate to invest money with him. I wouldn't want to be partners with him. He'd have a few dollars this year, and next year he'd be broke. A few times I loaned Curtis money. Sometimes he had a hard time paying me back. But he finally paid me every nickel he ever owed me.

"Stock car racing didn't really begin to grow up until the 1970s. People liked the sport, and it kept growing and growing and growing. There was a demand for more seats, and we had to build more seats. Now we have over sixty thousand seats. I just finished six thousand six hundred sixty seven more of them at turns three and four. Soon we're going to build another fifteen thousand to twenty thousand seats between turns one and two. But as we go along, they cost more and more. These seats cost me almost twice what the seats before them cost, because there is so much more steel in them. The seats go into the ground twenty feet and they go up eighty feet, so it's close to a hundred feet of steel. That's money.

"Of course, a ticket today [1997] costs fifty dollars. When you put a lot of money into something, naturally in order to get a good return on your money, you're going to have to charge more. I don't like the idea of going up on tickets, and that's something that's going to hurt some people. At some tracks, the tickets are a hundred dollars or more. Well, the average working man has a wife and a teenage child or two, and he can't afford to pay that kind of money. They drive a hundred miles to the race, buy a hotel room, and buy those tickets. That weekend will cost between five hundred and seven hundred dollars. The average working man can't afford that, so you have to keep some seats that are affordable, or partially affordable. I'm afraid that's going to hurt racing. And another thing, people keep talking about the big tracks, the big tracks. I hate to say anything that's not becoming, but if you are watching a race at a big track, two miles and a half, and you're in turn one and something happens in turn three, can you see it? There's a big wreck and you'd like to know how it was and what happened, but the only way you're going to see it is to watch it on TV later that night. If you take a track like this one that's just over a half a mile, you see all the action. On a big track you hear about it, but you don't see it. And you're paying close to twice as much for a ticket.

"We were here when the big tracks were built, and we'll still be here after the big tracks are gone. I may not be here, but this here track will be."

CHAPTER 2
QUEEN OF THE RACERS

Louise Smith

THE FEISTY LOUISE SMITH, WHO WAS 87 YEARS YOUNG WHEN SHE SPOKE TO ME, IS one of the true pioneers of racing. She drove sprint cars, Modifieds, and with the advent of the Strictly Stock class in 1949, she bought a 1949 Nash Ambassador and raced in some of Bill France's first scheduled NASCAR events.

Racing back then was on tracks of southern red clay, and as Clay Earles said, most women stayed away because at the end of the race fans would leave covered with a layer of grime and grit.

Smith got her opportunity to race because France, a promotional genius, wanted a woman in the competition in the hopes of attracting female spectators to the races and of arousing interest in the media.

There were few jobs for working women in the Carolinas in the 1940s. The biggest employers were the cotton mills, which often controlled the economy of entire towns. As a teen, Smith worked in the mills, until at age 19 she married Noah Smith, who owned the largest automobile dealership in the area surrounding Greensville, South Carolina.

After Bill France involved Smith in stock car racing, she would tell her husband she was going to Daytona for a short vacation, and she would drive in France's beach race. She hid her driving activities from her husband for as long as she could, knowing he would disapprove. Once he found out about her participation, he expressed his dislike of her racing and refused to watch her compete, but he otherwise supported her efforts by providing cars for her and supplying her with mechanics and machinery.

Smith boasts that she won 38 races in the days before records were kept and complains bitterly that throughout her driving career she was harassed and pooh-poohed by the male drivers. Her bitterness about how she was treated runs deep, and she says she was shocked when she was elected into the International Motorsports Hall of Fame in 1999. Until then, though she campaigned for what she considered her rightful place in the hall, she felt that gender prejudice ran so deep that she never would get in. Louise Smith was born in Barnsville, Georgia, in 1916. "Back in those days, work was scarce, and people would move anywhere in the country to get a job," she said. "When I was four, we moved to Greenville, South Carolina. My dad became boss-man in a cotton mill. I've lived here ever since.

LOUISE SMITH
"The women fans were jealous of me."
INTERNATIONAL
MOTORSPORTS HALL OF FAME

"Back then, all kids started working in the cotton mill when they were twelve. I worked two hours a day at school, came to the mill, and worked twelve hours a day. They would have somebody come in for one hour and take your place while you went to lunch. They learned me to work in the weave room that way. "

When the Depression hit, it wasn't as bad for Louise as it was for most people because her father kept his job. Those who were laid off and couldn't find work had to stand in lines to get the welfare foodstuffs: a pound of coffee, a pound of lard, and a small sack of flour.

"I met my husband [in 1935] when I was nineteen. My brother was trying to work on cars as a mechanic, and he came to my future husband's place of business to buy some stuff. My future husband—Noah Smith, Noah like in the Bible—ran an automotive place, a junkyard. I met him through my brother by coming to the junkyard. But he had to sell the business out when he went to World War II. When he came back in 1945, he had to restart it.

"I've been accused of having run moonshine. I tell anyone who asks me, 'No, I didn't haul moonshine.' I might have ridden with them, but that doesn't mean I was hauling it. It was a way of life at the time and all my friends did it, but I didn't have to. My husband had a good business. He had one of the biggest automobile places, new and used, in this part of the country at that time."

While Noah Smith was away in the service, Bill France came to Greenville to promote a race at the local track. Even though it only cost a quarter to get in, attendance rarely rose above 200 in the grandstand. France told the people who had been promoting the Greenville races that they needed to get a woman driver as a draw to fill the grandstand to make some money. The promoters knew of only one woman who might fit the bill. They knew her because she was a menace on the local roads. They told France, "She can drive, but we don't know whether she can drive on the track or not."

Said Smith, "I had never been to a race, never seen one, never knew what the flags were, but I was a fast driver on the highways around town and I had outrun a bunch of policemen just for the fun of it. They'd follow behind you, and you'd get a chase going. They'd get after you, and you'd outrun them. I always had souped-up cars. Because of my husband.

"So they contacted me, and then people started entering bets that I would go out there and outrun 'em. So I went out, without any experience or any-thing. Fred Mahon was the champion at our speedway."

The track lent her Fred Mahon's car. It was owned by a man named Hickey Nichol. She was told she could go out onto the track and practice, but when she showed up, they chickened out and wouldn't let her onto the track. Since they had advertised that Louise Smith would be racing, they had no choice but to give her her car—about fifteen minutes before the race started.

"They only told me, 'If you see a red flag, stop.' And I didn't see no red flag, and I finished in third place. I saw the checkered flag. I saw all the flags. But I didn't know what they meant, After the race was over, they had to come out and give me the red flag to get me to quit.

"Bill France was there, and when he went back to Florida, he asked me to come to Daytona in 1946. That year, Bill France paid three thousand dollars to the first five racers. The rest of us didn't get nothing. They slept on the beach.

"Back then [we stayed at a motel] way down the beach where we started the race. Another woman and I had rooms in the motel. Bill had people come from New York, New Jersey, Pennsylvania, and everywhere, and he had liquor up in the other room where we stayed. The other lady's job was to give a drink of whiskey to everybody who came in."

Smith says she drove at the Daytona beach-and-road track from 1946 through 1952. The first time she entered, she kept it from her husband, telling him she was going to Florida for a vacation.

"In '46, I raced a Modified Ford down there pulled by another car," she said. "Then in '47 I took a new '47 Ford down there, and I drove on the highway to the race.

"It was a brand-new car—you could not buy a car during World War II, and my husband had a friend of his who ran the Ford Motor Company in Easley, about twelve to fifteen miles from where we lived, and he called Mr. Roper and told him, 'If you get a Ford, save it for me for when I get home.' And Mr. Roper saved him one, and that was the '47 Ford."

Smith had a two-man pit crew. Her car had a new motor that her husband's mechanics had souped up,

"I got to Florida, and there were a hundred and some cars racing on the beach that year," she said. "I qualified thirteenth. Unlucky thirteen. We drawed it because it was raining. I tried to swap that thirteen with someone behind me, tried to trade it off all down and up the line. Buck Baker was right in front of me. And Lee Petty and Cotton Owens. But no one would trade me. Nobody wanted that thing. They were scared about that thirteen. So I had thirteen.

"I wrecked in the north turn—there were seven cars piled up there—I hit the back of the last car, and my car turned top to top—my top was on top of another car—and the policemen came down off the side where the ocean washed off the banks and turned my car back on the wheels. They knocked the top back out, where I could finish the race. I tore that car up.

"My husband had to start rebuilding his business, and he had just got it going, and this was the only car we had. I got the car to Augusta, Georgia, where I knew a man down there—I had raced two or three times in Augusta, and I knew this man and asked him to fix the car up where my husband wouldn't know it was wrecked—I should have had more sense than that. But I didn't have sense enough to know that the news of the race would be in the Greenville newspaper. I caught the bus from Augusta and came on home.

"When I walked in the office, my husband said, 'Where's the car?'

"'You know that old thing weren't no good,'" I said. "'You just bought a lemon, and it broke down on me in Augusta, and I had to catch a bus back.'"

Noah Smith looked at her kind of funny and didn't say a word. He went back behind the counter and brought back a newspaper, spread it out, and at the top of the page was the bold headline: Louise Smith Wrecks at Daytona.

"Gosh, I didn't know what to do," she said. "I was in a predicament, so I just turned around and walked out. Over the years I've been asked, 'What did you do then?' I said, 'After lying like that, I couldn't do nothing except leave.' Which is what I done too. I didn't know if he was going to kill me or what.

"Well, he got over it, not financially, but he got over it a little bit. But then he seen that I was really set on racing. See, I had tried to be a beautician, tried nursing. I trained for several jobs, and I didn't like none of them. I liked racing. I liked speed. That's what drawed my attention to it. And it was all because of Bill France. A long time before he died I called him and I said, 'You sure got me in a mess.'

"My husband didn't go along with it, but he supported me anyway. He had eight men working, and when I'd come in after a race—like when I come in from New York on the way to Darlington in 1950. I was the only woman at Darlington with a 1950 Nash Ambassador. The Ambassador was the one you sleep in. That's the reason I bought it. I had one, Bill France had one, and Curtis Turner had one. I had it so I could sleep in it. We didn't have money for a hotel."

Most women stayed away.
INTERNATIONAL
MOTORSPORTS HALL OF FAME

She had wrecked both cars in New York and had to stop in Greenville to get them fixed before going on to Darlington. Even though Noah Smith didn't approve of her racing, he saw how much she loved to race, and he allowed his mechanics to work on the car all night. The race was on a Saturday, and she arrived in Darlington Friday night.

"When I got to Darlington, I didn't have but four tires, and I blowed them all and didn't have anymore. That's why I . . . didn't get to run in it.

"The night before that race we were in a parade down Main Street in Darlington. They didn't have nothing but a fire truck and a few race cars. Roy Acuff got drunk and fell off. You're not supposed to write that in a book. But he's changed his style of living. He's a friend of mine, but that's true. They had one motel in that town, and friends of ours owned it, but we got throwed out of it before it got dark after they got to fighting. All of them. I couldn't exactly tell you who, but they threw all the racers out of the motel, and me and the Flocks and their wives had to go to another friend's bar.

"We got throwed out of everywhere we went, because we were always fighting. Lots of places. They'd say, 'You broke the party up.' I'd say, 'Shoot, I've been throwed out of bigger and better places than this!' You should have been around in that day. You'd have seen something."

After Bill France organized NASCAR, the drivers had mixed feelings about him because his purses were so small. Louise Smith, however, had no reservations about Bill France. He had given her the chance to race when no one else would.

"I owe him a lot because France arranged for me to race with his promoters up in New Jersey, New York, Ohio, everywhere," she said. "I would go all throughout the country and drive. I'd drive four, five times a week and on Sunday. And if you won a race, you didn't win but a hundred, a hundred and twenty-five dollars. There wasn't nothing. We'd spend more than that trying to get there and back. But like when I went to New York, they gave me a hundred and fifty dollars appearance money plus what you could win. I usually won a little bit. But I got more money than the other drivers, because they didn't get appearance money."

Fonty Flock was another driver who got appearance money, according to Smith. In exchange for their appearance money, she said, they, along with France, would go out before a race and nail flyers about the upcoming race on telephone poles. One time, she remembered, Fonty, Curtis Turner, and she went to Philadelphia with all expenses paid to go on the radio to promote a Langhorne race. She also recalled that being one of the few women competing in NASCAR created some problems.

"The women fans were jealous of me, because they thought I was after their men. And the men weren't fond of me being on the racetrack, so I had trouble both ways."

"For a long time, all the drivers gave me trouble, because as I said, they did not want a woman driver out there. They still don't. Back then, I was low-rated because I was a woman, and I went about it in a man's world. The men would yell things at me, and they tried to wreck me."

Not all were so sexist. One Saturday she was in Asheville, North Carolina, at the Asheville-Weaverville Speedway, and racer Buddy Shuman, a good friend of hers, came over and said, "Louise, I'd like to take you out on the speedway and show you something."

She had been out practicing earlier in the morning, and two or three of the male racers had bumped her pretty hard.

"We went out there, and he showed me how you could hit the back of a car bumper and send a guy into the wall. And you wouldn't have to hit him hard to do it. I had no idea! So I started doing that, and I got pretty good at it. I got almost as good as Buddy. And when I started doing that, they started leaving me alone.

"I knew Curtis Turner real well, and he was a wild one. He would do anything in the world for you, but he loved women. Any woman. That was his downfall right there. My husband got his first Ford from Mr. Malley, who had a place adjoining my husband's place. Mr. Malley and Curtis were friends, and they went in Curtis' airplane, and Curtis landed it over in a churchyard on a Sunday morning so Mr. Malley could go into his house and get some liquor. And they got back in the plane and just rose right back up in the air, and of course everyone in church was screaming and hollering, and the air people took away his license. I mean he was wild . . . but I liked him.

"Curtis Turner also showed me the ropes. Curtis knew how to broadside the turns. One day in 1950 at the Occoneechee Speedway in North Carolina—about ten or twelve miles from where Lee and Richard Petty live—on a mile dirt track, I said to Curtis, 'Show me how you do that.' And he got in my car and he drove, and I squatted down in front, and he said, 'Right here at the end of this wooden fence, give it a swing and put on the gas and straight out, and do the same thing in the second turn.' That was his model of driving. I thought I could do it.

"Well, we went around several times, and he let me take the wheel and he squatted down, and I done tried it. Curtis got out, and I ran in the time trials. They used to give us three laps on time trials and they would take the best of the three laps. I was on my third lap driving a Modified Ford, and I broke the record, and then I got airborne. I went up in the air and I hit four or five trees coming down. The car was smashed about flat. It took them thirty-six minutes to cut me out of there. I'll never forget it."

In 1948, two other women, Sara Christian and Ethel Mobley, began racing. Sara didn't run as much as Louise and Ethel, who was Tim Flock's sister. "She was married to Charlie Mobley, and he died, and then she married a Smith, no kin to me," said Louise Smith.

Ethel Mobley and Louise Smith traveled all over the country together. Ethel hailed from Atlanta, and she would drive to Greenville, and the two would tow their cars one right after the other on their way north to race. Ethel drove her husband's car, and sometimes he went with her.

"Before NASCAR I won thirty-eight races on dirt tracks. I don't even remember most places I won them at. I used to have trophies that told you where, but I had a place at Lake Greenwood and somebody broke in and took everything. My trophies were there, and they took a bunch. Then there's a bunch at Talladega and they got some at Daytona. They're scattered all over."

Louise Smith didn't enter NASCAR's first race at Charlotte in 1949, and she can't remember why, "unless I was off somewhere else racing. Used to be we could run outlaw races. All of us ran them. After Bill France organized, he didn't want us running outlaw races, and he started penalizing the drivers.

"At that first race [at Charlotte in 1949], Bill barred Buddy, Speedy Thompson, and Eddie Samples from racing in it because a couple weeks earlier they had thrown thumbtacks all across the track before a Modified race. They threw tacks, they would put sugar in your gas tank—somebody put sugar in Lee Petty's gas tank one time. They did all that stuff back in them days. Lee was a champion driver, and they wouldn't want him winning the next day, and sometime during the night they'd put sugar in the gas tank, and not only his, but several others. too. They done it. They'd do anything to keep you from winning a race."

Smith raced in NASCAR's second race at Daytona Beach.

"One reason I don't remember much about it, back then we didn't know that racing would amount to a row of pins. When we left the speedway, we left it all behind us. We went home and forgot about it until we went somewhere else.

"But I flipped that day—I did that everywhere I went. Kids would come up to me—used to be kids would come up to me on the racetrack before all these rules were made, and they'd say, 'Miss Smith, are you going to wreck today?' I'd say, ' I don't know.' I drove hard, and I'd flip. I told them, 'I could race better if I had the wheels on top!'

"The Daytona Beach course was tough on you. You go down the sand side going up the beach, and then coming back down you go down [Highway A1A] , and it's like a washtub where you just go up and down, up and down. I remember in one of the writeups after a beach race, Tim Flock told a reporter, 'I thought I was going as fast as I could, but here comes this car fixing to pass me, flying.' He said, 'I looked over to see who it was, and this woman'—me—'was putting on lipstick.'

"I said, 'I'm going to kill you, Tim.' He was always kidding me."

Smith says one reason she didn't get the publicity and the credit she deserved was that she spent a lot of time racing up north at the behest of Bill France when her more famed competitors were racing down south. She says that before NASCAR was organized no one kept any records. If she won in New York or New Jersey, she says, the only way anyone found out was if she got on the phone and called a local Greenville radio announcer and let him know. "That was really all the publicity I got," she said.

Louise was voted into the International Motorsports Hall of Fame in 1999. "I had been nominated three times and failed to get in. I said, 'I know exactly why I'm not in the Hall of Fame. I have proven to all the sportswriters that I was a driver. The only thing holding me back was that some of them didn't want a woman in the Hall of Fame. They treated me just like they did on the speedway. They didn't want me in, and I was beginning to think they would never let me in. I just had to battle it all the way through to this Hall of Fame. Then when I got in, they gave me a man's ring. I said, 'They knew all this time I was going in, and they give me a man's ring and inscribe it Louise Smith?'

"But I'm glad to get in anyway."

CHAPTER 3
HELL DRIVING

Frank Mundy

FRANK MUNDY WAS BORN JUST AS WORLD WAR I WAS COMING TO A CLOSE AND grew up in an orphan's home. He began his career on wheels at age 18 as a daredevil motorcycle rider with Lucky Teeter's Hell Drivers. After driving through walls of fire and doing the "boardwalk crash" in front of thousands of spectators at country fairs across America, Mundy joined Jimmy Lynch's Death Dodgers and performed in front of millions more at the New York World's Fair in 1939 and 1940. He was the first to balance a car on its two left wheels.

In 1938, Mundy drove his Harley to Daytona Beach to watch the motorcycle races on the beach, and it was there that he first met Big Bill France, a gas station owner and sometime race promoter.

After World War II ended, Mundy helped France promote some car races. Mundy was in Daytona in December 1947 for Bill France's annual car race on the beach. After the race, France announced that there was going to be a meeting at the Streamline Hotel in Daytona to organize the sport of stock car racing.

Mundy was there when Red Vogt gave the sanctioning body its name, The National Association of Stock Car Racing, or NASCAR. Mundy saw firsthand the power of Big Bill France. He also saw how ruthless he could be.

Frank Mundy drove a 1949 Cadillac in NASCAR's very first Late Model race in Charlotte on June 19, 1949. He was running up front when his right wheel fell off. The cars were literally stock off the showroom floor, and the spindles weren't strong enough to take the pressure during turns at such high speeds.

In the second race of that inaugural 1949 season, held on the beach at Daytona, Mundy finished third behind Red Byron and Tim Flock. It was a punishing race that left him black and blue. He raced at Langhorne, where he remembered how filthy the spectators got watching the race, and he ran at Martinsville and North Wilkesboro.

In those early days, there was very little money to be won, and the racers were in the sport mostly for the fun of it.

Frank Mundy was born on June 8, 1918, in Atlanta. His real name is Francisco Eduardo Menendez. His father, who was also Francisco Eduardo Menendez, was Spanish, and his mother was Irish.

Frank never knew much about his father, who was born in Spain and like many Spanish immigrants landed in Tampa, Florida, and spread out. His father owned a United Cigar Store at Five Points in Atlanta.

"When I was about thirteen, my father had a heart attack and died," said Mundy. "My mother couldn't support us, and since my father had been a Mason and a Shriner, my sister and I were put into a Masonic orphans' home in Macon, Georgia.

"I had no trouble adjusting when I got there because there were so many kids—had to be a couple hundred. I walked barefoot to school each day. They had a bus that would take the younger kids, and we would start walking, and if the bus completed the trip, it would come back and pick up the stragglers.

"It was the heart of the Depression, but naturally you didn't think it was difficult at all. You didn't have any choice. It made a man out of me."

Among the chores Mundy had to perform were getting up in the morning and milking two cows, and in the afternoon he had to go out and pick turnip greens or whatever crop was growing.

"We tried to be self-sufficient, but as a kid I think of it as more fun than anything else," he said. "A certain amount was work. I had to find those two cows, and they had to be milked twice a day regardless."

The grammar school Mundy attended, Alexander No. 3, was right across the street from the home of William L. Stribling, the world light heavyweight boxing champion. Each morning Stribling would train. He'd run out from his house all the way to the Masonic orphans' home and back, about a mile and a half each way, and in the morning, after Mundy milked his two cows, he would run with Stribling to the Masonic home and then back to school. If for some reason Stribling couldn't make it, Mundy ran the route by himself. Stribling, who became wealthy from boxing, owned an airplane; a Cord, a car with a gearshift on the dash; and a motorcycle.

Mundy told himself that someday he would have all of those things, "and that's what started me out."

When Mundy was 16, he began working as a messenger for Western Union. At first he rode a bicycle, and by the time he was 18, he had saved up enough money to buy a motorcycle. Then one day Lucky Teeter, a millionaire-promoter who staged motorcycle stunt shows at fairs around the United States, brought his Hell Drivers to the fair at Lakewood in Atlanta.

FRANK MUNDY
He performed the "boardwalk crash."
INTERNATIONAL
MOTORSPORTS HALL OF FAME

"One of the fellows hurt himself doing a stunt with a motorcycle," said Mundy, "and since I owned a motorcycle, I applied for his job and got it."

Mundy rode for Lucky Teeter for two years. He would perform the "board-walk crash" at state and county fairs. For the stunt, a 50-foot wall of burlap was erected over a steel frame, gasoline was poured on it and set on fire, and Mundy would burst through it on a motorcycle and ride through the tunnel of flame.

"The secret to going through it was timing," Mundy said. "When you came down, they'd run with a torch on either side of it and set it on fire, and then you'd hit it. You had to hold your breath when you went through so you wouldn't breathe it in.

"I also did a trick where I'd step on the back of a car as it drove around the track, with ropes coming out the back window and a pad on my back and fanny and I'd wear a leather jacket and a helmet, and they would pour gas on the track and set it on fire, and just before I got there I'd hit the ground on my back and slide through it."

His next job was with Jimmy Lynch's Death Dodgers. Mundy performed at the Goodrich exhibit at the New York World's Fair in Flushing Meadows in 1939 and 1940. At the time, Goodrich's slogan was, "Goodrich, remember which," intended to remind customers not to confuse Goodrich with Goodyear.

"Ten and a half million people saw the show in those two years. They'd come in one side of the grandstand and go out the other, and as soon as one crowd left, another would come in, and we'd put on another show. We did seven to ten shows a day."

At the New York World's Fair, Mundy was the first to perform the trick of two-wheel balancing, which the Joie Chitwood gang performs today. The first time Mundy did it was by accident.

He could drive the car on the right-hand side on the ramp and balance it up on the two left wheels. He would set it back down as he went into the turn toward the grandstand. "I could keep it on two wheels until the tires blew," he said.

"One time I was doing that two-wheel balancing at the fair at Charlotte, and when you are doing that, your arm is moving a little on the steering wheel, and my elbow accidentally hit the safety belt release, and since I was up on the two left wheels, I was thrown out of the car onto the track, and as I watched the car come down on its side toward me, I threw my feet and hands up, and the car crushed my pelvis."

Mundy was in a body cast with a broomstick between his knees for nine months. The cast was so heavy it would take a group of people to turn him over from his back to his stomach. From then on, the seatbelt release was moved from the side of his body to the middle.

Because Mundy loved motorcycles, he went down to see the motorcycle races on the beach at Daytona in 1938. He owned a black Indian, the one he had ridden to deliver telegrams. When he arrived in Daytona, he pulled into a service station to get gas, and he was greeted by a "big, tall guy" who came out to collect the money. They started talking, and that's when Mundy first met Bill France.

Mundy next ran into France after World War II. Mundy had spent much of the war in Marfa, Texas, where he met his wife, Mae, who was a college student in Fort Worth. He instructed flying the twin engine Cessna Bobcat. When he got out in 1945, Mundy went back to the stunt show.

Mundy was in Charlotte with the stunt show when he saw that Bill France was promoting a race up there. He contacted France and offered to help promote it with him, and they became co-promoters.

"We wanted to hold the race at the fairgrounds, and to get the grounds we had to play politics, 'cause it was owned by the city, so we got the AmVets to get the track for us, and we gave them the parking and the concessions," said Mundy. "My wife sold tickets.

"The show was scheduled for two o'clock on Sunday. We told the authorities to be prepared for a big crowd. They didn't really believe us. Well, by ten o'clock they ran out of hot dogs and cold drinks. By noon, there was the biggest traffic jam in Mecklenburg County history! The traffic couldn't move, and the police had the most difficult time of their lives."

Among the drivers Mundy recalls competing against in that race were Jack Etheridge and Roy Hall, who drove for Raymond Parks, who was perhaps the most successful car owner at the time. Raymond Park's head mechanic was Red Vogt, who was the top mechanic in the Atlanta area at the time.

Said Mundy, "They claim that Raymond Parks made his money through bootlegging, but Raymond wasn't a bootlegger. He was the money and the brains behind the operation. He paid the guys. Very few people had the kind of money that Raymond had. And they say that Raymond was a hell of a driver himself. He only ran once, at Langhorne. His driver didn't show up, so Raymond drove, since he owned the car. Raymond was a natural driver, but when you had the equipment he had, you didn't have to be too good a driver to win in his cars."

Raymond Parks' driver was Red Byron. Red only had one good leg, but according to Mundy, "he was one of the smartest drivers to ever come along. He knew how to stay out of trouble and how to set up a car." Red was also a mechanic, and that added to his ability to win races.

Red Vogt's garage was on Spring Street in Atlanta, one block toward town from the Varsity restaurant near Georgia Tech. The Varsity sells more hot dogs than any place in the world. According to Mundy, Red Vogt's garage was a meeting place for drivers and moonshiners.

"Red would build the cars for everybody who wanted to race, if they had the money," he said. "He built cars for the bootleggers and he built them for the cops to catch them, so he was collecting from both sides."

Said Mundy, "I remember sometime in the mid-forties Bill France and I and a few of the guys were hanging around Red's garage, and a couple of bootleggers came in and started arguing over stealing booze or taking over territory. France and I were sitting in a car at the entrance to the garage, and they started arguing, and one of them pulled out a gun, and when France and I saw the gun, we ducked down underneath the car."

Mundy went to Daytona for the car race in December 1947. He drove for a man named Bill Ritner, who was from New Jersey. "Ritner owned a couple of cars, and I met him in Daytona, and he asked me to drive for him," Mundy said.

"My mechanic was a fellow by the name of Joe Wolf, who was the Red Vogt of the mid-east. If Red Vogt was the top guy, Joe Wolf was next. Joe was from Reading, Pennsylvania, and if you didn't have one of his engines, you didn't have much of a chance of winning. Joe's shop was in Reading, and people would bring their engines to him. Joe might have six or eight cars on the track, mainly 1939 coupes.

"The secret was to get the right gear ratio for your car so it would peak at the top rpms at the right time and not blow the engine by turning too many rpms."

Mundy finished fourth in the race, and afterwards Bill France announced there would be meetings to organize stock car racing on Sunday, Monday, and Tuesday. The racers took over the Streamline Hotel.

"They had a conference room on the roof, and we met there and we made up the rules, made up the name, and that was the beginning of it," said Mundy.

"They had a picture taken with everybody sitting at the table, and like an idiot I offered to get up and hold the flash for the guy who was taking the picture—so I'm not in the picture. The photographer's name was Jack Cansler, and he was out of Charlotte.

"A guy once said to me, 'I saw the picture. You weren't there.'

"I said, 'I held the flash bulb for the photographer.'"

Early in the meeting Bill France was elected president. They picked France because he lived in Daytona and was more active than anyone in the field of promoting races. With the exception of Bruton Smith, who would only promote races in the Charlotte area, where he lived, no one else worked at promoting races the way France did.

"Bruton had car dealerships," said Mundy. "Bruton is so rich it's pathetic, but nobody gave it to him. He's a smart guy. He went out and earned it. France tried to put a wheel under him, didn't want the competition and tried to knock him out. But Bruton had an independent source of income, his car dealerships. Bruton was the only competition France ever had promoting races.

"Racing wasn't very well known or very popular. If you wanted to be a promoter, you had to find a track—usually it was a fairground—and you had to get the American Legion or the AmVets to help you get the track, and to do it right you had to spend a month in advance of the show to let the people know about the race. You put ads in the paper or you put up signs on telephone poles, and some big cities like Charlotte had ordinances keeping you from putting up posters on poles. The cops almost put my wife in jail twice outside Charlotte for putting up posters. She didn't know it was against the city ordinance.'"

At the time of the NASCAR organizational meeting, most of the cars that were running were Modifieds. The 1939 Fords were the most popular.

"Then in 1949 we went to what we called 'Late Model,' said Mundy. "The first race where we ran Late Model cars was at a track just south of Charlotte. It was promoted by Bill France. He didn't have enough police to keep the crowds out. People were coming from all walks, from everywhere, to see it. They were curious, but most of them didn't have too much money, even if he only charged a few dollars. The people around the Charlotte area for the most part didn't have it, so most of them didn't pay. They climbed the fence to get in. The track was about a three-quarter-mile dirt. And they had to put down calcium chloride to keep the dust down."

Before the race France barred drivers Buddy Shuman, Speedy Thompson, and Ed Samples from entering. According to Louise Smith, they had been barred for putting thumbtacks down at the track in an earlier race. But there was more to it than that, according to Frank Mundy. It turned out that two months earlier promoter Bruton Smith had announced a race to be held that day at a different location. France, trying to knock Smith out of business, announced his own race two weeks earlier. When Shuman, Thompson, and Samples refused to drop out of Smith's race, France barred them.

"France was kind of jealous that Bruton Smith was the only other promoter," said Mundy. "Bruton had already planned his race a couple months in advance, and France didn't like competition coming in, and so about a week and a half before Smith's race, France decided to put on his own. Most of the guys had already signed with Bruton, had already sent in their entry fees. And France came up with the rule that if he had a race, you had to race with him or he would outlaw you. In other words, you couldn't run in any other races but his. One year Tim Flock decided to run for Bruton, and France outlawed him, took away his points, and cost him a championship, which was totally unfair. But France wanted to rule it and dominate it, and he'd step on anyone to get ahead, and that's what he did to Tim, and I felt sorry for Tim, because Tim was making a living and had three or four children to support.

"Bruton had spent money to advertise, but France decided to try to hurt him, and so he came up with his week and a half promotion, with his own advertising, to get a crowd."

I asked Mundy whether it was expensive to race back then.

"Everything is relative," he said. "At the time, nobody had any money to take a chance on taking a car out and wrecking it. It had to be somebody who had money in their business who was a real fan to buy a car and get a driver. Of course, everyone at one time or another thinks he can be a race car driver, so they had no trouble finding a driver."

The very first Late Model or stock car race took place on June 19, 1949. Thirty-three cars entered. Frank Mundy drove a 1949 Cadillac owned by Sam Rice.

"Sam was a bootlegger out of North Wilkesboro, which was the spot where quite a few of the guys either built their car or owned it because of bootlegging," said Mundy. "That's where the money came from. The average person didn't have money to spend on racing. Most people worked and had a weekly or monthly paycheck. I got to know Sam through racing. He needed a driver, and he approached me to drive."

I asked Mundy how much preparation he needed on the car before the race.

"I didn't do any," he said, "because all I did was drive for the owner. I left it entirely up to them."

The Charlotte race was the first NASCAR Strictly Stock main event to take place after World War II.

"Did you realize at the time that history was being made?" I asked.

"I had no idea," said Mundy. "Not the faintest. No one even thought about it. It was just a fun day for me to get out on the track. We were always looking for places to run, and the highway was not it. The police would get you. Any racetrack that was promoted, we'd be there. There weren't enough races to make a living at it, so it had to be something you wanted to do."

Mundy was running up front halfway through the Charlotte race when his right wheel fell off. He ended up finishing 30th. He won no prize money.

"I was running second or third about halfway through that first Late Model race," said Mundy, "and a spindle broke on the front right wheel, which back then was about sixty percent of the problems. The average race fan doesn't know it, but if you took a car that you drove on the highway and you went into the first turn at that track there, you wouldn't even have to go in at full bore and the front right wheel would just twist off. It would come off—period. And that happened to everyone who didn't have the wheels reinforced. In other words, extra layers of steel. You couldn't even run one lap if you didn't have a reinforced spindle. Late Model racing was something new, never had been tried, and some people beefed them up, but if you didn't, you'd hit the dirt and flip the car or tear up the front end.

"The other major problem was getting dirt in the radiator from the track. If you were following a car down the straightaway, you were safe. It was when you went into the turn, broadsiding and throwing the dirt back into each other's face that did the damage by getting the dirt into the radiator coils and blocking the air. The cars would heat, and the engines would blow, and you'd be out of the race—if the spindle in the front right didn't break first. In racing, naturally, they discover the weaknesses, and they started beefing the spindles and making them bigger and stronger."

The winning driver in that first stock car race was Glenn Dunnaway, who drove a car owned by car mechanic Hubert Westmoreland.

"Dunnaway was out of Charlotte," said Mundy. "He lived there, and he was a good driver. The car was owned by Hubert Westmoreland, who I knew. Westmoreland made his living as a mechanic. Dunnaway didn't do much work on it.

Dunnaway was disqualified, but under the rules at the time, you could find anything if you wanted to. You make the rules according to your advantage."

"But these were Bill France's rules, weren't they?" I asked Mundy.

"That's what I'm saying," he said. "If France didn't want him to win, he could disqualify him."

"They said his rear springs were stronger than what was found in a stock car," I said.

"Yeah, well, see, you can call it safety," said Mundy, "or you can call it cheating. If they did something to the springs, it was mainly because they had to, not because they wanted to. They made Jim Roper the winner. He was from out west, Kansas, and that was the only race he ever won, and that was because he was practically the only one other than Dunnaway still running at the end of the race. He outlasted them. He didn't outrace them."

Among the other entrants in that first race was Curtis Turner, who drove a 1948 Buick Roadmaster and finished ninth. Mundy was a big fan of the colorful Turner.

"Curtis was the most natural driver who ever came along," said Mundy. "You couldn't beat Curtis Turner if his car would finish. Curtis was the only driver, if he got ahead of me, who I couldn't catch. He was the most natural driver who ever sat behind a wheel. And he was a real nice guy."

Mundy recalled two other drivers who entered the first race: Lee Petty and Sara Christian, one of the few women racers.

"Lee Petty was one of the few people who owned his own car. Lee was the type of driver, damn, it would take you all day to get by him," said Mundy. "He was all over the damn track. Lee Petty was not a clean driver. And he was pretty tight financially. He didn't want to spend a nickel for anything.

"Sara Christian was in the race mainly for publicity. Her husband, Frank Christian, was a bootlegger here in Atlanta. Sara and Louise Smith were used for ballyhoo. If you listen to Louise, she won this or won that. She never won anything in her damn life. That's delusions of grandeur. You'd lap either one of them on the first damn lap. They were just out there in the way. You could call them racers, but as a racer, they'd make good cotton pickers."

The second race of that inaugural 1949 NASCAR season was held at Daytona on the beach. In that race, Mundy drove an Oldsmobile, and he finished third behind Red Byron and Tim Flock.

"The race on the beach was real wild," said Mundy. "The main thing was to stay out of a wreck at the first turn, where most of the wrecks happened, and to save the brakes for the south turn by getting close to the ocean going north and broadsiding into turn one where it got really rough and a Sherman tank couldn't go through the sand dunes.

"After you came north on the beach, you'd come off turn number three, which was at the south end of the backstretch—onto Highway A1A, which is real narrow and you are bouncing. The car is stiff from the shocks being stiff. Your eyeballs are going up and down, and you couldn't see out because the spray from the ocean and all that sandblasting on the windshield. On every lap when I got to the back straightaway on A1A, I'd put my left arm out the window with a rag trying to wipe the windshield, and I'd rub up and down along the left side of the front windshield. You could only reach about four inches. My arm would be black and blue where the muscles would rub as I tried to make a spot on the windshield to look through to see, and all that did was smear it.

"On A1A I had to use the telephone poles on each side of the highway as a guide. It was all you could do to keep the car on the pavement. It was a real hassle. You were going over a hundred miles an hour, bouncing up and down, and my arm would be black and blue for a month.

"To go into the south turn, you had to hit the brakes. You couldn't broadside because it was so narrow. They banked the track, and if you ran out of room, you'd go over the berm and wreck the car. What you wanted to do was use the bank to keep your speed up and the rpms up so you could head north on the beach, and once you got out there, you had to be careful, because the tide would come in, and you couldn't go too far out. You would broadside into the north turn to save your brakes for the south turn."

"You must have been pleased to have finished third," I said.

"I was pleased to have even finished," he said.

Mundy didn't enter the third race of 1949, held at the Occoneechee Speedway in Hillsboro, North Carolina. "Evidently, I didn't have a car," he said. He did enter the fourth race, held in September at the Langhorne Speedway. Curtis Turner won the race in a car owned by Hubert Westmoreland. Mundy finished in fourth place, four laps back in a Sam Rice 1949 Cadillac. A mob of 20,000 was in attendance.

"Langhorne was probably the toughest track in America," said Mundy. "It was egg-shaped. You'd go down into number one, and it would tighten up—the short end—and more drivers were killed there than on any track in America. It was as fast as it could be, and the groove was against the outside rail, and going into the first turn, being egg-shaped, it would get so rough it would just tear up the car.

"I remember coming off four, looking up into the grandstand, and all I could see were a thousand paper sacks. The people had put a paper sack over their head to protect them from the dust and dirt coming toward them. They'd cut out little eyeball holes and put that paper sack over their head, and I saw a thousand of them, because every person had one over their head. It was a hell of a sight. All that dirt and dust came at you up in the stands, and their only protection was a paper sack. It was kind of funny when you think about it to look up in the grandstands and see thousands of paper sacks!

"I remember after one race the people came down into the infield after the race, and one woman was so damn dirty from sitting up in the stands, I said to her, 'What number were you driving?' She was madder'n hell anyway that she was so dirty and filthy, and she pulled back her pocketbook and was going to hit me with it."

"I'm surprised women even went," I said.

"They went because their husbands and boyfriends tagged them along," Mundy said.

Mundy didn't enter the fifth race at the Hamburg Speedway in New York state, but he did enter the Martinsville race, the track owned by H. Clay Earles, and after skipping a race at the Heidelberg Speedway in Pittsburgh, he raced at the North Wilkesboro track, owned by Enoch Staley.

"Enoch was a bootlegger," said Mundy. "Sam Rice and them were in the same business. The bootleggers were the only ones who had any money, who were able to put up the purses. I don't remember much about Earle, but I do remember Enoch Staley. He was big and tall. In fact, one time Bill France and I were in a hotel room in Greensboro, North Carolina, and we got a phone call, and it was Enoch and his partner, Charlie Combs. They said, 'We own some property up here, and we want to promote a race.' France said, 'Come on down, and I'll talk to you.' About an hour later they came down, and France opened the door, and I have never seen France look up instead of look down. France was six foot four, and they were the only guys as tall or taller than he was. They came in, and we talked to them for about an hour and met them the next day at the track to give them an idea of what Bill had in mind.

"The North Wilkesboro track was round, but it was the only track in the world that when you come off number two, you go uphill. It wasn't in the plans, but that's the way the land was, and it was too costly to clear it out with a bulldozer.

"North Wilkesboro was the last race of the 1949 season. I finished last after a rock went through my windshield."

I said, "Red Byron won the driving championship, and he earned the most money, $5,800."

Mundy said, "If you were driving for Raymond [Parks] you had a pretty sure shot of being up front because nobody else could compete with his cars."

"You made $1,160 in prize money that year," I said, "and in 1950 you entered eight races and won $550. Talk about how tight money was."

"The biggest purse of any race was $500 to win it, and it had to be a big race," he said. "Money always was tight. My wife and I slept in the car more than we did in a motel. A motel was the last thing we were interested in. It was always a question, 'Do you sleep in a motel, or do you buy a tire?' and a tire always won."

CHAPTER 4

WILKES COUNTY, NORTH CAROLINA

Benny Parsons

BENNY PARSONS WAS BORN IN 1941 IN WILKES COUNTY, NORTH CAROLINA. His parents had no connections to make any money in northwestern North Carolina, so they decided they needed to do something to better their lives. Benny's dad decided his best chance of finding work was in Detroit, where the Big Three were making cars. He also decided that with money so scarce, he would leave his older son behind in North Carolina to live with his great-grandmother.

"My brother Phil was about six months old, and I was four," said Benny Parsons. "They were going up there with the uncertainty of what was going to happen. They had to take the baby because he was nursing, and they left me with my great-grandmother, Julia Parsons, who had raised my father. He had gone to live with her when he was a baby, and he stayed with her until he got married and left home. And so I grew up with my great-grandmother. Grandma was born in 1872. She was seventy-three when I went to live with her.

"Life when I was a child was so much different than today. We lived in rural Appala*h*chia. Today, it's Appala*y*chia. Back in the 1800s people had settled along the creeks back in the mountains of North Carolina. As the industrial revolution gained strength, people stopped trying to eke out a living with the soil, and they moved to town and got jobs in the textile mills and the furniture factories. After World War II, the industrial revolution had taken full hold. By the late 1940s, my great-grandmother and I were in the last house on the creek with people living in it, so when the co-op brought electricity to our part of the world, the electric company looked at the situation and said, 'Here's an old woman. We're never going to get our investment back.' So they came to her and they said, 'If you buy the supplies—the poles, the lines—we will run them to your house.' She was seventy-eight years old, and she had never had electricity in her life. What did she need with that?

"So everybody got electricity but us. To take a bath, you went to the woodpile, got wood, built a fire in the stove, and heated water. To cook anything, you had to get the wood and make a fire to heat the stove.

"I remember one day I said to my grandmother, 'I sure would like to have a chocolate pie. Why don't you bake me one?' She said, 'I will show you how to make it yourself.' The point I am making, to bake a chocolate pie, you went to the woodshed to get the wood, you built a fire in the stove to get it hot enough, and then you made the dough to bake, and then you made the filling to go in the pie by cracking the eggs, separating the whites from the yolks, and then you took a beater and beat the whites to make the meringue. Today, it's a whole lot easier to go to the supermarket to buy a chocolate pie.

"We didn't have plumbing. We had an outhouse."

I asked Parsons whether he hunted and fished near where he lived.

"When I was growing up in the mountains of North Carolina," he said, "I never saw any game to amount to anything. A rabbit every once in a while, a covey of quail. I never saw a deer. I never saw a bear. Up in the mountains they had trout, but where we were, down a thousand feet, it was no good for the trout, so we didn't have any. All the streams were fished out anyway.

"It was like this: all the deer were killed and all the fish were caught."

"How did your great-grandmother have any income?" I asked.

"Did you ever read *Cold Mountain*?" Parsons asked me. "The girlfriend of Inman, the hero in the book, was living with another woman during the Civil War. One, a blueblood, didn't know how to do anything. The other, a redneck, knew how the barter system worked. That was in 1865, but in 1950 nothing had changed for us. Everything was on the barter system.

"We had a couple dozen old chickens around, and so we had eggs to trade. The only type of meat we ever ate was some kind of hog meat, and that was for breakfast. We ate bacon, which was called side meats or streak meats. Each year we had a hog that we raised and slaughtered in the fall, and that was our meat."

I asked Parsons whether the hog they slaughtered had become a pet and whether he got emotional when the hog was killed.

"It was survival," he said. "I understand where you are coming from. I would feel that way today. There is no way in the world I could do that today. But back then it was survival."

"Did you go to school?" I asked.

"The school bus came and picked us up and took us to school. Maybe there were two or three kids who were the children of a farmer who might have cattle or who might have made a little money, but basically they were in the same boat I was in: nobody had any money."

"Did you keep in touch with your parents?" I asked.

"Oh yeah," he said. "Each summer I would go to Detroit, beginning when I was in the sixth grade. I spent six weeks, and I enjoyed it, and I did that each summer from then on."

"And your parents didn't want you to stay with them?" I asked.

"That became a sore subject," he said. "For instance, at the end of the seventh grade, my parents wanted me to stay and they put a lot of heat on me. Well, we mentioned it to my great-grandmother. She said, 'Please stay here with me.' Here I was, fourteen years old, and my parents were tugging on my left arm, and grandma was tugging on my right arm, and the middle is what started hurting, and I ended up in the hospital."

The youngster ended up back in North Carolina. Then before he was to enter his junior year in high school, he decided he wanted to leave Carolina and live in Detroit. Grandma even gave her OK. But his father insisted he return to his high school, where he played football and baseball, and tell the principal that he was leaving in person.

"I said, 'I can't do that,'" Parsons replied.

"'Well, you have to,' my father said. So we stopped at the school. We were in the car on the way to Detroit. I went in and said, 'I have decided to go to Detroit and enroll there.'

"They said, 'We were hoping you'd be here. Is there any way to get you to change your mind? Let's give you some equipment just in case.' They gave me brand-new shoulder pads. I was a goner. I stayed in North Carolina."

I asked Parsons if his intention was to go on to college.

"That was my intent," he said. "I took pre-college courses. But I was really searching. For a long while, I did very well in school. Things really came easy, and all of a sudden, for whatever reason, starting my junior year in high school, things stopped being easy. I had trouble focusing on the job at hand.

"I went to North Carolina State, but only lasted one semester because I no longer could focus. I was searching. I was wasting my dad's money, and in February of 1960 I went up to Detroit."

"How did you get involved with car racing?" I asked.

"My dad, Harold Parsons, was a huge race fan," he said. "Huge. I saw my first race in 1949 at the North Wilkesboro Speedway. One Sunday he, my uncle, my cousin, and I went to the races. Gwyn Staley, the brother of Enoch Staley, who owned North Wilkesboro, was in the race that day, and I remember some kid flipped end for end coming off turn four in a 1948 Ford. And during the summer on Friday nights when I was living in Detroit we would go to the Motor City Speedway and watch the races. The Motor City Speedway was on Eight Mile Road. It's no longer there. I'm sure like everything else it's a shopping center."

"How did you jump from going to the races to becoming part of the races?" I asked.

"I had gone to work full time for one of the car factories, Chevrolet Gear and Axle, where they made rear gears and brakes. My dad had a gas station where he maintained three or four taxicabs that he owned and worked on other cars as well. In May of 1960 on a Saturday morning I was at the gas station, and two guys stopped by with a race car, a 1960 Ford, on the back of a truck. With my limited experience with racing, I was impressed. Wow, a race car!

"I asked them, 'Where are you going?'

"They said, 'Anderson, Indiana. Tonight.'

"I said, 'Wow!'

"They said, 'Want to go?' I had to go home and get my toothbrush and a clean pair of underwear.

"Their names were Wayne Bennett and Dick Gold. Wayne was the driver. He was good. He raced at the Motor City Speedway. The three of us jumped in the cab of this truck, and we took off. Anderson, Indiana, is just north of Indy, about two hundred and twenty-five miles from Detroit. We got there and ran that race on Saturday night.

"I was mostly a spectator. I rolled tires. I didn't know anything. I had never been there before. I bought a pit pass, and I was behind the wall seeing all these guys and listening to the conversation. I was absolutely thrilled.

"After the race, we drove to Dayton, Ohio, and we raced there Sunday afternoon. I continued to go with them every weekend I could for the remainder of the year and also through 1961 and 1962.

"In 1963, my father said to me, 'I really need some help at the gas station. Would you consider going in with me here?' It was a difficult decision. I had a steady income and whatever benefits General Motors was paying me at the time. My mother didn't want me to do it because she knew how tough that life was because she lived it every day.

"But I said OK anyway. I quit and went to work at the gas station as a mechanic, maintaining taxicabs and doing work on other vehicles as well."

"Where did you pick up the knowledge to work on motors and gears? I asked.

"By doing it," he said. "When I started, I didn't have a clue. I didn't know a carburetor from a rear gear when I was in high school.

"So in 1962 I was working at the garage. Dick Gold, one of the fellows who took me racing for the first time, also had a gas station/garage. He lived in Royal

Oak, north of Eight Mile, which is the dividing line between Detroit and the suburbs, so he had to drive by our place on the way to work. He would stop in in the mornings, and we'd bench race a little bit. 'Did you hear what happened down South?' 'Did you hear about . . . ?' We just talked racing every day.

"One day he stopped and said, 'You want to try your hand at driving?'

"I said, 'I don't know. Why?'

"He said, 'I just bought a car. You know Ralph Young?'

"'Yeah.'

"'Well, Ralph is building my Late Model car, and Ralph had an old figure-eight car, and he needed money and wanted to sell it, so I gave him fifty dollars for it.' Dick said, 'You can have it if you want it.'

"I had been going with him and Wayne for a couple years, helping them, and he was trying to do me a favor.

"I said, 'Where is the car?' It was only a couple of blocks away, and we went over there. It was in a one-car wooden garage. We kicked the snow away from the door and opened it. There was no light in the garage, no sun, so it was kind of dark in there, and when I first looked at it, I said to myself, 'Man, he got cheated.' 'Cause it was all torn to pieces. But it was a 1954 Ford, and we took it down to Dick's gas station, where he had more room than we had. We put quarter panels, fenders, and doors on it, got some springs for it, and made it into a race car.

"Wayne and Dick were running the local tracks, so I would go and load up their car and hook mine to the back with a tow bar and drag them both to the racetrack. It was a pretty cool deal. I didn't have to buy a trailer. They hooked my car to the back of their truck, and off to the racetrack we went.

"They were running in the half-mile races. I ran the quarter-milers. And that's how I started. Once I ran my first race and felt that adrenaline, I didn't have trouble focusing anymore."

CHAPTER 5

PUTTING FOOD ON THE TABLE

Mike Staley

ENOCH STALEY, WHO IN 1947 BUILT THE NORTH WILKESBORO RACETRACK ALONG U.S. 421 in the shadows of North Carolina's Brushy Mountains, grew up in Roaring River, about 10 miles north of the hamlet of North Wilkesboro. One of the pioneers of the sport, Staley, like Clay Earles, built a "bull ring," a 0.625-mile short track that for 50 years wowed its millions of fans with its tight turns, body banging, and paint trading. Like Earles, Staley allied himself with Bill France and saw his fortunes grow along with France's and NASCAR's. Staley's son Mike recalled his bigger-than-life dad and his Wilkes County roots.

"His dad, my grandpa, owned a country store, like a convenience store today," said Mike Staley. "They sold bread, milk, canned goods. I remember when I was small, they had the big drink coolers, with ice water in the bottom of them. The drinks sat down in the ice water in bottles, and that was real neat. Dad told me that Grandpa, whose name was Ranse Staley, wore a suit and tie every day of his life. Grandpa was a big politician. He wasn't elected to any office, but he was the man behind the scenes. He was actually a boot-legger, and that's how my dad and them were able to eat, and they fed everybody in the community. Dad said that around supper everyone would come around and eat with them. They would feed anybody who showed up. They were the first family in the county to have electricity because they had their own generator.

"Back then, people became bootleggers to survive. There were no jobs. The whiskey was made to sell, not to drink. That was the big deal. It was made to sell, not to drink.

"This was in the 1940s before I was born. Grandpa died in the 1960s, when I was ten.

"My dad was the baby of the family. His brothers were the ones who hauled the moonshine, built the stills, and made the liquor, the ones who were put in jail quite often. I remember they had a secret room at the old home-place where they'd hide when the law was looking for them. I used to play in there as a boy. It was a door behind a dresser. It was upstairs, and when you walked into a bedroom, you had to go behind the dresser to open the door.

"I think my dad became part of Grandpa's operation. He didn't say much about it. 'Cause by the time I was born in 1950, he was doing good on his own, had jobs, and had started the North Wilkesboro track in 1946. Then Holly Farms, a major chicken breeder, came into the county, and now it's ties and suits. That did more to stop bootlegging than anything, because it gave people jobs. People had a place to go and work."

I asked Mike to talk about his dad's decision to build the North Wilkesboro racetrack.

"He and two other guys, John Masden and Charlie Combs, were the original investors in the speedway. John, Charlie, and my dad went to see a race some-where in South Carolina that Bill France Sr. was promoting, and they liked it, and they approached Bill Sr. about building a track. He said, 'If you think you can, OK.' So they built the track.

"They only planned on running one race. This goes back to the bootlegging era. Dad's brother Gwyn for one, and all his friends, had all these fast cars that hauled liquor, and they'd race each other, and they needed someplace to race.

"They had a race one day where you entered anything you had, and Uncle Gwyn won it in a pickup truck. He was that good a driver. Gwyn won several Grand National races. He was killed in 1958 at Richmond in a convertible race. At the time, he was leading the convertible division in points.

"But when Dad built North Wilkesboro, he had no long-range plans. He and his partners said, 'We'll run one race, and if it works, good, we'll do another one.' They didn't know how long it would last." [North Wilkesboro held races through the 1996 season.]

When France called together the movers and shakers for the first meeting of NASCAR in December 1947 at Daytona, Enoch Staley was too ill to attend.

"Dad was sick and missed the first meeting," said Mike Staley, "but he was at the second meeting, where they went over the rules. What NASCAR was formed to do was to make sure the competitors got paid. They used to have trouble with promoters running a race and taking the ticket money, and at the end of the race when the drivers came to collect, they would be gone. Then they'd go someplace where people didn't know them, and they'd do it again. They were con men. NASCAR was started to give the drivers some protection and to make the sport legitimate.

"When it first started out, my dad and his partners knew they liked the racing deal, but they didn't know exactly how to run it, so they had Bill France come up, and he ran the show and worked with them and got them started."

The first NASCAR strictly stock Late Model race at the North Wilkesboro track was the sixth and final race of the inaugural season held on October 16, 1949. Bob Flock beat Lee Petty for the victory and won a purse of $1,500.

"The first race they were expecting two or three thousand people, and ten thousand showed up, and it just floored them," said Mike Staley. "They didn't know what to think. They found out they were onto something good. Bob Flock drove a purple car they called "the Easter Egg.""

"I gather your father and Bill France were close," I said.

"Dad became close friends with Bill France Sr., and he worked for NASCAR his whole life. He was a NASCAR employee. He didn't have a real title, but he had different jobs. He became a troubleshooter for France at different tracks. He worked at Daytona and Talladega, and Bill and him owned a race-track together at Hillsboro, North Carolina. They were partners. It was nine-tenths of a mile dirt, right next to Raleigh. It had a big, long Indian name—a band of Indians [Occoneechee]. Nobody could pronounce it and the writers couldn't spell it, so they changed it to the Orange Speedway.

"I remember going down there as a kid. Dad had to take the grader down there and grade it. I would work down there all summer myself, getting the track in order. I never saw a race there. It became more valuable as a real estate property than as a racetrack. Also, the commissioners, preachers, and city people didn't want a racetrack because it brought too much noise, too much dust, and too many drunks, so eventually it closed down in 1968.

"Dad also owned the Asheville-Weaverville Speedway [a half-mile dirt track considered the fastest in the country, until it was paved in 1958].

The Asheville-Weaverville Speedway closed in 1970.

"I was in my teens then. I never did see a race there. I worked during the summers at the track, doing whatever I was called upon to do. We'd work on the roads, cut the grass, repair the fences."

I asked Mike Staley what he remembered about Bill France Sr.

"I remember him coming to the track in the office at North Wilkesboro," he said. "He was a neat guy. I loved to listen to him talk. He was like Ronald

Reagan. He could mesmerize you when you listened to him talk about racing, what he thought about the future. He had a vision, that's for sure."

I had been told that the North Wilkesboro fans could become pretty rowdy. I asked Mike if he ever saw them get that way.

"I remember fans throwing beer cans over the fence at Lee Petty, after he beat Junior Johnson," he said. "They didn't like it. They were throwing cans *full* of beer over the fence at Petty. It's like when you open a bottle of champagne and champagne is flying through the air. People were cursing and hollering all over the place. It was amazing.

"I remember one time a guy took his car and drove it onto the track during a race. I remember he made my dad so mad, Dad knocked him out. Or perhaps he scared him so bad, he passed out. My dad was six foot five, two hundred and fifty pounds, and very intimidating."

"His partner, Charlie, was six foot five. All the guys were big. I remember one time France saying to Dad and Charlie, 'All you guys in Wilkes County are big, aren't you?' And Bill was six foot five. Back then, someone that size is like a seven footer today."

Enoch Staley was big, powerful, and meticulous. He demanded that his track be kept spotless, and if work needed to be done, he was not afraid to get his own hands dirty doing it.

"When Dad saw that something needed to get done, he did it," said Mike Staley. He didn't wait to say, 'You need to do this or that.' If he had the time and wasn't doing anything else, nobody could do it as good as he wanted it done. He was hands-on with everything."

One time Enoch Staley was mowing the grass in the parking lot when the tractor tipped over and landed on top of him.

"It was on the grandstand," said Mike. "It tilted over and pinned him, hurt him a little bit."

Enoch Staley also was a principled man. He charged what he felt was a fair price for tickets, food, and drink at North Wilkesboro, and with inflation and the cost of living going up, refused to increase it.

"It was hard for him to raise prices," said Mike Staley. "And he wouldn't charge for parking. Parking was always free. He wanted to keep the ticket prices and the cost of concessions reasonable. I've heard him say, 'Bring his family and feed his kids good and not be broke.' He was not out to gouge anybody. His motto was, 'Live and let live.'

"Ken Cheek, who owned Staley's Steakhouse in Winston-Salem, rented half of one of the lounges at the racetrack, and every year he would come to my dad and say, 'You need to go up on your prices. I'm not paying you enough.' Ken had a lot of money, and Ken would make Dad charge him a little more each year. You don't hear that very often. Ken was the kind of guy who would come into the office and fan himself with a fistful of hundred dollar bills and say, 'Boy, it's hot in here, isn't it?' He was funny."

In 1957, Enoch Staley paved the North Wilkesboro track. This was after Clay Earles had paved his track at Martinsville in 1955.

"In racing, it's like dominoes. When one person does something that's good, and you know it's good, you follow suit, and Martinsville is just a two-hour drive away. In fact, my dad worked some at Clay's track. Clay Earles and my dad and Paul Sawyer from Richmond were three of the foundations of the sport."

I mentioned to Mike that Lee Petty had won three races in a row at North Wilkesboro, and then Rex White did it, and Richard Petty did it. Mike didn't remember much about Lee, but he certainly had memories of Rex and Richard.

"I was ten years old when Lee won at North Wilkesboro. I remember Rex, because he was so short and small. Rex was like a jockey in that race car. But he could really drive. I sat with him at a banquet at the International Motorsports Hall of Fame dinner in Talladega last year, and I was honored to be with him because I always thought the world of Rex. He was a great driver. He never got as much press as he should have. And now it's not so much the driver's ability, but how they look and how they talk.

"Richard was a great driver. At that point in time, we would have loved to have seen a little more variety in the winners, 'cause the fans would say, 'Richard is going to win. No use going.' He was far ahead of everyone else in the game.

"The Pettys took racing more seriously than anyone else. It was a living for them. It was the way Junior, Richard, and Bud Moore made their living. For the car owners today, it's a sideline, a hobby. Only a few, like Richard Childress, make their living that way. Back then, to put food on the table they had to win."

CHAPTER 6

RACING IN A RENTAL CAR

Frank Mundy

On September 4, 1950, the first Southern 500 race was held at the Darlington Speedway. Darlington, the first superspeedway, was built by Harold Brasington, who initially planned to race Indy cars. Frank Mundy recalled the history of the Darlington track and what went on behind the scenes of that first Darlington race.

"Brasington went to Indianapolis and saw the Indianapolis 500, and he saw the crowd, and he said to himself, I have the land, and I'm going to build a track," said Mundy. "This was ten years before Bill France built Daytona. Brasington banked his track, and the funny thing about it, when you come off turn four, the turn gets tight, tighter than the other turns. Brasington had a minnow farm. He was raising minnows in that area, and he didn't want to disturb them, so he made the turn a little tighter rather than move the minnow farm to make the track circular.

"Johnny Mantz won that first race [by nine laps] in a car owned by Hubert Westmoreland. The secret at Darlington was tire wear. Westmoreland, who owned the car, was smart enough to balance the car, and being [the Plymouth] he drove was a light car, it didn't wear out the tires. The other drivers had to make ten damn tire stops.

"The tire companies were not prepared for the wear and tear you got on the racetrack. They weren't building them special, and you could wear a tire in one lap, make it blow, because at that speed no tire company was prepared for it. And no testing was done.

"The Studebaker was a good car. You had to find a car's weakness, and the only way to find that out was to drive it on the track. When something would break, we'd correct it, and then something else would break, and we'd fix that."

On April 8, 1951, Mundy towed a Nash out to Gardena, California, where he was entered in a race at the Carrell Speedway.

"Fred Wheat, who was a mechanic and a car owner here in Atlanta, went with me to California," he said. "We relieved each other, drove straight through, and we got there in a little over a day and a half. A man named J. C. Agajanian was the promoter at Gardena. He was a hog farmer. He would get paid to collect the garbage from the restaurants downtown and feed his hogs.

"I'll never forget, we were driving around in Agajanian's Cadillac. He was going behind the restaurants in an alley, and he saw a man lifting up the garbage cans and getting food to eat. Aggie stopped the car, and he said, 'This stuff is mine! Get the hell out of here.' Here he was in his Cadillac telling a beggar to leave his garbage alone!

"I stayed at Aggie's home while I was there, because he had radio and TV shows for me to be on. I had told Aggie I knew Art Linkletter and that I would go on his show and get a plug for his race. I had met Art in Charlotte when I was racing. Art's show was in Hollywood, and I called him up and told him I was in town to race and that I'd like to sit in the audience. He said he would walk down and introduce me, and I was able to get in my plug.

"I liked the Gardena track. Most of the drivers out there didn't have the experience on dirt tracks that we did. Only one driver, Troy Ruttman, could compete with us. Agajanian owned Ruttman's car. Troy was practically unbeatable, even though I was able to win three straight times out there.

"When I arrived at Gardena, the Nash Company told us we couldn't drive the car because it wasn't to be introduced to the public until the following week, so that morning Bill France and I were going out to the track, and we passed a car rental lot, and I figured, Aw, hell, I came all this distance, and I went over and rented a Plymouth coupe. France didn't say a thing. He probably figured I was crazy, but we had come too damn far not to race.

"We went by a filling station, and I got whitewash that was used to paint curbs, and I painted an 'X' on it and went to the track where I got a seatbelt and strapped the doors. I entered the race with my rental car and stayed out of everybody's way. I couldn't go hard into the turns, because if I had gone in at any sort of speed, that front right wheel would have come off, so I had to stay in the soft stuff and work the devil out of the steering wheel to keep the pressure } off that tire."

Mundy finished 11 out of 20 in the race won by Marshall Teague. He won a purse of $25. After the race, he flew home in Bill France's private plane.

The next race was held at the Occoneechee Speedway in Hillsboro, North Carolina, a 150-mile race on a 1-mile dirt track. Mundy finished second to Fonty Flock in his Perry Smith 1951 Studebaker and won a purse of $800.

"What I remember most about that track was that I carried about fifteen pounds in my left front tire because the track chewed up so badly. It was a matter of trying to hit the deepest holes with the left front tire, which didn't have too much air in it to keep from tearing the car up.

"I tried to hit all the bad bumps. The groove, which was the most popular route around the track, would change every five or ten laps, and everybody tried to hit the same groove, so you constantly had to find a new groove and then hit it with the front left tire to get through the turns. Otherwise you would lose speed every time you got bounced hitting those bumps. You had to act like a snake going through the turns."

After going out with bad shocks at North Wilkesboro, Mundy went to Martinsville and finished second to Curtis Turner. Mundy was running behind second-place driver Marshall Teague when Teague flipped his car. Mundy recalled how difficult Martinsville was when it was still a dirt track.

"Like any other dirt track," said Mundy, "Martinsville got extra holey. You had to go in between the holes that the cars would make going into the turns. Then five laps later you had to find another spot because everybody would find that same one and wear it out, and you'd start a new one. So it was a constant battle of remembering where to go into each turn.

"You had to determine how hard to drive. If you drove extra-hard, you would tear up the equipment. If the spindles didn't break, it was the wheels. You would make the radiator vibrate loose or you could break the rear axle."

"Finishing second to Curtis was fantastic," I said.

"Just finishing was fantastic," he reiterated.

"Curtis Turner won that day," I said.

"Curtis Turner and Troy Ruttman were the two best drivers I ever had to run against, and Troy Ruttman was practically unbeatable. I knew Curtis real well. We were pretty good friends. Curtis didn't do a lot of talking. He was a real nice guy and was easy to get along with. Curtis was an introvert, not an extravert. He was busy making money in the lumber business. Curtis had a sharp mind for making money, and he did it mainly in lumber. He'd buy land and clear it, selling the lumber."

Frank Mundy won his first NASCAR race on June 16, 1951, at the Columbia Speedway. It was the first stock car race ever held under the lights.

"The car was owned by Perry Smith, who was a Studebaker dealer in Columbia, and that was the same car we put on the pole at Darlington. Every race we were the most-inspected car because everyone claimed we were cheating and they were trying to get us disqualified,

"There was no cheating. Perry Smith had the car to where it would handle so good where some of the other cars had to back off in the turns. I could just broadside it and go on through. With a car that handles good, you could broadside it, and even though you'd lose a little speed, you could keep your rpms up, and you'd save on your brakes. And hitting the bumps with the left front tire with less air in it helped. That was the combination we used to win races."

It was not only Frank Mundy's first Strictly Stocks win, it was also the first win ever for a Studebaker. The win was memorable for Mundy.

"It was a real rough track, but the car handled so good," he said. "I'd look in the rear view mirror and see Tim [Flock] eight or ten lengths back, and then a few laps later I'd be pulling away from him, so I really didn't try to go any harder. I even slowed down a little, because you might come up to traffic, and if the traffic wasn't to your liking, you had to look far enough ahead to plan your next move to get by the cars in front of you so you could stay ahead of the cars at the rear from catching up to you.

"I remember I kept looking for Tim, because he'd always be there. That day the car was geared right, and I could have walked away with it, but I slowed down to make it interesting and also for safety, meaning I wanted to guarantee I would finish. If you punish the car, it's going to punish you, so I backed off and kept it within a decent distance ahead of Tim at the same time staying out front, because I didn't want all the dirt coming back from the traffic blocking my radiator, plus I didn't want rocks from the ground coming up and hitting the windshield. You had to use your head a little."

A bone-dry dirt track brought its own hazards. On July 15, 1951, Mundy entered a race at the Heidelberg Speedway in Heidelberg, Pennsylvania. The race conditions were hazardous, and there were several bad crashes. Mundy, not wanting to kill himself, pulled out after only 25 laps.

"That track that day was so damn dusty," said Mundy. "After about ten laps, there was a crash with eight or ten cars, and Wally Campbell's face was smashed against the windshield. Wally was fearless. He was from New Jersey. He later got killed in a sprint car.

"A few laps later I pulled out of that race because I couldn't see my hand in front of my face because of the dust. When I pulled out, Perry Smith, the car owner, said, 'What's the matter?' I said, 'I can't see a damn thing. I'm not going to drive in that.'

"The next race was at the Asheville-Weaverville Speedway, and Perry Smith let several of the drivers, including Fonty Flock, Gober Sosebee, and Herb Thomas go with us in our plane. There were so many damn people on board that to take off, we had to stand up in the front end of the plane. It was foolish to take off with such a heavy load, but we made it, and it turned out that Fonty finished first, Sosebee was second, Thomas third, and I was fourth—those were all of us on the plane."

On September 3, 1951, more than 40,000 race fans flocked to Darlington for the Southern 500. So many cars arrived for qualifying that it took nine days for Frank Mundy to be declared the pole sitter.

"I remember at Darlington in 1951 eighty-two cars qualified, and I put my Studebaker on the pole. A hundred and twenty cars tried to get into that race. Eighty-two made it. I won a trophy for winning the pole. I started the race, and I was running too many rpms, and twelve laps into the race my engine blew."

Mundy made about $100 that day in prize money after finishing last. He remembers a young Bill France Jr. selling crushed ice to race fans and making more than $700!

"He made more money than just about any driver," said Mundy. "It was a real hot day, and he was out selling those ice cones. He sold ice crushed in a cup, and he'd pour some syrup on it and sell it that way."

On October 14, 1951, Mundy entered the Martinsville race. He drove an Oldsmobile 88 owned by Bob Flock to his second Grand National victory. After he took the lead on lap 87, he beat Lee Petty and Billy Myers.

Mundy then won his third race of the season on November 25, 1951, in a 1951 Studebaker.

Tragedy struck suddenly on December 8, 1951, when Perry Smith, Mundy's car owner, was killed in an airplane crash.

"Perry was a businessman," said Mundy. "He was a Studebaker dealer in Columbia, right near the state capitol, about two blocks away. He had an Avion airplane, and whenever a person got hurt in South Carolina in a car accident on the highway, his plane would take them to the hospital. If a patient was from Illinois or another part of the country, they would call him to take him home. The patient would be on a stretcher, and they'd put him on the plane.

"He was taking a woman to Chicago to be closer to her home, and a nurse went with her. The control tower operator in Columbia happened to be walking by just before Perry was taking off. Perry said, 'I'm just going to Chicago and back. Why don't you come with me?' So the guy got in, and just south of Indianapolis bad weather came up, and the wings of the plane iced, and he went straight into the ground.

"I went to his funeral in Columbia. His wife showed me the keys to his car in a little leather holder. She pulled them out of her pocketbook and showed them to me. They were bent in that little leather packet."

With his patron gone, Mundy had to scramble to find a ride. He showed up for the Daytona time trials and won the pole, but Bill France disqualified the car. Mundy remains convinced that France disqualified him so that another driver in a Chrysler could win the pole.

"We were running on the beach for the speed trials," said Mundy. "All that was involved was a trophy, no money. France wanted Tom McCahill, who was driving a Chrysler, to win. McCahill sold articles about cars to magazines. If McCahill recommended a car, the public would buy it. He ran a pretty fast time, but not as fast as mine.

"They had me first, McCahill second, and then I heard someone say that France was disqualifying my car. I asked why. He said, 'You didn't have a tire in the trunk of your car.' Which means the car has less weight, an advantage.

"I said, 'The reason I didn't, if I started flipping on the beach and the trunk comes open, the tire will come out and it would kill somebody.'

"France said, 'You're disqualified. If you don't like it, you don't have to run.'

"I said, 'That's right, and before I kiss your ass, I quit.' So I sold my car that day, and it got second in the Daytona Beach race, and I left France. I had to go back to AAA and run wherever I could."

CHAPTER 7

THE WILD ONE FROM ST. CLAIR SHORES

Paul Goldsmith

PAUL GOLDSMITH WON NINE GRAND NATIONAL RACES IN A CAREER THAT BEGAN in 1956 and lasted through 1969. Like Frank Mundy, Goldsmith's father died at an early age. Like Mundy, his racing career began on motorcycles and he too was discovered on the sands of Daytona Beach. Paul Goldsmith is the only racer ever to have won the Daytona Beach race both on a motorcycle and in a stock car.

"I was born on October 2, 1925, in Parkersburg, West Virginia," said Goldsmith. "Let's say I grew up in Columbus, Ohio, and Detroit. My dad got sick and was in the hospital, and he passed away, and my mother could not take care of me and my sisters, so we lived with my grandparents on a farm until I was eleven or twelve. Their name was Henderson. If you are a flyer, there is a Henderson intersection over the farm. It was just farming—corn, wheat, cattle. It was a little different then than it is today. You did it by hand, just a little hand machine you planted the corn with. Today, they drill it.

"They had a little over a hundred acres. We also had a saw mill and a grain mill. We ground up grain for surrounding farmers. My uncle had a funeral home. I was driving ambulances when I was eleven and twelve.

"I'd say it was hard when I moved to Columbus. My stepdad was a mechanic, and I went to work with him in the garage when I wasn't in school. I was in my teens and out of school when my stepdad got a pretty good position in Detroit working for H & H Wheel. He did mechanical work on cars and trucks. Today, it's a pretty good-size firm.

"I lived on the northeast side for a while—East Detroit, they called it, and then I moved farther north to St. Clair Shores.

"I bought a motorcycle in Detroit and started riding a little bit, and I got pretty close to the Harley-Davidson dealer, Earl Robinson. We used to go out and play around with the motorcycles, and I must have impressed him, and then after the war when racing started back up again, he arranged for me to ride a racing motorcycle, and I raced at Marshall, Michigan, a half-mile dirt track.

"Motorcycle racing was classified in three divisions—novice, amateur, and expert. Even though it was my first race, the way I qualified they moved me up into the expert class. I was seventeen, maybe eighteen. Among the other experts were Chet Digrass and Leo Anthony. They had raced before the war, and I was moved in with them, and I finished either second or third, and from then on I remained an expert.

"I had just started racing, and a couple weeks later my phone was ringing, and it was Walter Davidson of the Harley-Davidson Motorcycle Company. I knew Walter through Earl Robinson, the local dealer in Detroit. I knew Bill Davidson. I knew John Harley. I knew them all. They lived in Milwaukee.

"Harley-Davidson was a pretty good-sized company even back in those days. There were only two American motorcycle companies, Harley-Davidson and Indian.

"So Walter Davidson called, and in an in-and-about way he wanted to know if I wanted to race for Harley. I told him, 'I sure would.' Here was a big company calling a snotty-nosed kid to go racing. They provided me with motorcycles and parts, and I was off and running from there on.

"I did all my own mechanical work. I ran in the AMA motorcycle races out of Columbus, Ohio. I ran just about every weekend, sometimes on Friday and Saturday nights.

"The big races were at Langhorne, Pennsylvania, and at Daytona on the beach. You know, Bill France was losing his ass when he started, and what bailed him out was motorcycle races on the beach. There was a motorcycle race run in Savannah on the beach, and Bill saw how many people it drew, so he decided to move the race to Daytona because of the weather, and he convinced the AMA to do it. This was before the war—back in ancient times. Nineteen thirty-seven. He was not making any money with the Modifieds, let's put it that way. So then he got that bike race, and he made some money, and that got him started, and then he went into Late Model stock cars, and he really got going. And I know this because Bill told me that.

"I won the [motorcycle] race they ran on the beach in 1953. There's a marble statue on the beach of about ten to twelve of us motorcycle drivers—it's a pretty big monument by the Adams Mark Hotel.

"Harley-Davidson had not won on the beach. It had been dominated by Norton and Indian for many years. I had help with my bike from Smokey Yunick, who lived in Daytona Beach. He gave me a little hand. He improved the aerodynamics on the bike, made it handle a little better on rough pavement—that back road was quite rough. Little things like that. Wasn't a whole lot. He let me work in his garage, gave me a little bit of advice. That's about it. I got the bike running pretty well, got out in the lead, and stayed there. I won $2,500 and a trophy.

"Up to that point, my wife was working. Going down there, she asked me, 'If you win the race, can I quit?' I didn't figure to win, so I said, 'OK.' So she quit.

"I never considered the races dangerous. I guess I still don't. I'm the only one who has ever won the Daytona Beach race on a motorcycle and in a stock car. Same way at Langhorne, which was a very grueling race. I should have won it a couple of times. Langhorne was the toughest race to run, rough in the way it was laid out, and it was hard on the bike, hard on you physically. I should have won the Daytona Beach race three times, but one time I had motor trouble, and another time I had a little accident, blew all the spokes out from my rear wheel, went sliding down the beach a little bit. That day was over.

PAUL GOLDSMITH

He knew Harley and he knew Davidson.

INTERNATIONAL MOTORSPORTS HALL OF FAME

"I went from motorcycle racing to stock car racing because of Smokey Yunick. The first Grand National race I entered was in a convertible race at Charlotte [in 1956]. I had just finished the Daytona bike race. Smokey had a couple of cars, and he wanted to know if I wanted to drive one of them, and we'd go to Charlotte. Well, naturally I did, so he got approval from Chevrolet, and we pulled the car into the garage and started working on it, and about a week later we went up to Charlotte, and I had the fastest time.

"It wasn't a fairgrounds. It was a dirt track. It was banked a little bit. They ran it only a couple of years. It was rough, dusty, and I had the fastest qualifying time, and the one who was sitting on the outside pole was Curtis Turner. Later on I went into the lumber business with Curtis. Anyway, we started the race, and Curtis took the lead. I was following him, and I hit a hole and broke a shock, and I did a roll. I flipped the car. I never even backed off the throttle, and I landed on my wheels, and I still finished second. And from then on I was 'The Wild One from St. Clair Shores.'"

Despite having had little experience driving stock cars, Goldsmith felt at home behind the wheel. Though he was driving against seasoned vets, from the start he felt he was their equal.

"I had enough knowledge on the motorcycle," said Goldsmith, "and with Smokey's help, I didn't have much trouble beating them. From then on, I raced.

"At the time, we were running against Carl Kiekhaefer. He ran three or four cars in a race. Kiekhaefer was a domineering person. Smokey and him didn't hit it off all the time. Carl Kiekhaefer was a bastard. He was like an army general, that guy. He never knew who was working for him. He knew if they had a white uniform on, they were working for him. The rest of us were a little bit dirtier. We held our own with Carl."

Kiekhaefer won a lot of races, in part because he entered several cars in most of the races. Smokey Yunick, who was a businessman first and a sportsman second, only ran in the big races where he felt the purses were worth his while.

"Smokey was always experimenting with something for General Motors. We proved an awful lot of it on the track. We used to go to what we called 'the Jungle Road,' which we ran on just north of Daytona. Wasn't nothing there, and it was about three miles long. No traffic. No nothing. It was a state road. There was nobody out there. No traffic. I don't think I *ever* saw a car out there.

"Smokey and I were very good friends. We used to travel together, have parties together. We were always together. He was always working on something. He'd come up with an awful lot of good ideas.

"We were busy, and I never paid that much attention to what he was doing, because I was too young. We'd go to Sebring with Zora Duntov to test Corvettes. [Duntov is the visionary who put performance into the Corvette.] For a while, the Sports Car Club of America was racing them, and they had trouble with the fan belt coming off, so we developed a fan belt that stayed on. We worked on pulleys and the belt. We'd run that Corvette up and down that 'Jungle Road.'"

The Chevy cars that raced on the Grand National circuit had problems of their own. On June 10, 1956, Goldsmith went to the Memphis-Arkansas Speedway. The car broke before the end of the race.

"I had the fastest time, and I was leading the race," said Goldsmith, "and we broke a rocker arm on the push rod, and that put us out of the race. The rocker arms were a problem at the time."

I asked Goldsmith about the ferocity of competition among car manufacturers back in 1956.

"It was very important," said Goldsmith. "For instance, Pontiac was seventh or eighth in sales, and when they went racing, they rose to third in sales. Do you know what that represents in sales? [Pontiac president] 'Bunky' Knudsen took the silver stripes off it and made it a nice-looking car and a performing car. He always said, 'Without racing, we never would have gotten Pontiac to third place.'

"Bill France was the one who had the idea of running new cars, so the car companies would get involved. When he got out of the Modified division and into Late Model stock cars, from there racing started to grow. Bill had a vision. I remember before cable television really got started, Bill said to me, 'Look, you got any money? Buy stock in cable television.' And look what cable does for advertising and for car racing—or any sport today."

In 1956, Goldsmith entered the Southern 500 at Darlington. Seventy thousand fans attended.

"You know why Darlington ended up with stock cars?" asked Goldsmith. "The racetrack was built for Indianapolis Motor Speedway cars. Very few people know that, but the Indy cars couldn't race there. They couldn't control their cars on that track. It didn't work.

"At the time, if you went down the backstretch—today it's the front—it dropped off so you had to run right against the guardrail where it was banked, the extra few degrees going around that corner. Well, the Indy cars would lose it there.

"The guy who built the track [Harold Brasington] had all his money invested, and then he tried motorcycle racing. At this time, I was racing a bike. I went there, and it was a chilly, cool day, and I went around the track, oh, a dozen times, and I put my bike back on the truck and I called Walter Davidson. I said, 'I'm not racing here. I'm headed home.' He said, 'You do what you want to do.'

"In practice a few fellows got tangled up in a guardrail and broke their legs, so the AMA cancelled the race.

"Now [Brasington] was stuck with a racetrack he didn't know what to do with. He called Bill France and asked him if he would promote a stock car race there. France agreed to make a deal, and that's what got him started."

Curtis Turner's "Purple Hog" won the seventh running of the Southern 500. Paul Goldsmith finished fifth. Goldsmith next ran at Langhorne, and he won the race by seven laps. He won $4,150.

"I was really running," said Goldsmith. "That was Smokey. We split the money fifty-fifty. Back then, it was a decent amount of money. Maybe not to a car owner, but as a driver, I made a few bucks. Christ, I used to run in a motorcycle race, and if I won $200, that was great! That's also why I quit the motorcycles and went to stock cars."

In nine races in 1956, Goldsmith had six top-ten performances, including his win at Langhorne. I asked him if he was happy with his record.

"I was never happy unless I won," he said.

CHAPTER 8
CARL KIEKHAEFER

Frank Mundy

AFTER FRANK MUNDY QUIT NASCAR AT THE START OF THE 1952 SEASON, HE drove the American Automobile Association circuit mostly in the Midwest, winning the AAA title in 1952, was runner-up in 1953, and winning again in 1955. In 1955, his car owner was Carl Kiekhaefer, who not only won the AAA title that year with Mundy as his driver, but also won the NASCAR Grand National title that year with driver Tim Flock.

Unlike most car owners, Kiekhaefer was very wealthy. His philosophy was to spend whatever it took to win, even if he lost money. He was also a brilliant engineer who was able to make his cars run faster than anyone else's. Frank Mundy loved driving for Kiekhaefer, even though the man could be demanding and autocratic. Mundy won, was treated fairly, and he made good money.

"Carl Kiekhaefer was a farmer," said Mundy, "and he bought this big farm in Fond du Lac, Wisconsin, and in the barn was an outboard engine made by Elco. It wouldn't work, and he started messing with it to find out why it wouldn't work, and that was the beginning of Mercury Outboard Motors. [The Roman God] Mercury was fleet of foot, and that's what he named it.

"Kiekhaefer came into racing at the start of the '55 season. At that time, he picked the drivers who were on top. He called me up and told me he'd pay all expenses, plus all I won, and $1,200 a month retainer fee and, mainly to keep the factories like Ford and Pete DePaolo from his drivers. All he wanted were the trophies. Carl never took a penny out of racing.

"No one was an engineer like Carl. He would run more dyno tests on his Chryslers than the factory. In fact, Kiekhaefer wouldn't let the factories get involved with his cars. He didn't want them in. He was independent. He never took a penny from Chrysler. He bought everything. He did it all on his own. And Chrysler got credit for his winning. But it wasn't them; it was Carl Kiekhaefer.

"Kiekhaefer used to call up Bill France at two o'clock in the morning and go over the rules. He gave Bill France more trouble than he wanted. In other words, France was trying to keep the manufacturers involved in the sport by changing the damn rules all the time. But Kiekhaefer didn't back off from anybody. He called him up at home and curse him out about something.

"Kiekhaefer was just as kind as he could be. When I clinched the AAA championship in Milwaukee, I finished second that day. Jack McGrath won, but I didn't even try to win. I just tried to stay out of a wreck, didn't take the turns too hard so if the tire blew I wouldn't hit the fence. I stayed out of trouble all day and finished second.

"After the race, he pulled his checkbook out and wrote me a check for five grand. 'I said, 'What's that for?'

"He said, 'That's for winning the championship,' and he gave it to me. And then he pulled out a set of keys and held them in front of me.

"I said, 'What's that?'

"He said, 'You have a new Chrysler upstairs.' He had bought me a new car and had parked it in front of the hotel."

Frank Mundy repaid Carl Kiekhaefer with his loyalty. The Ford factory offered Mundy more money to leave Kiekhaefer and join the Ford team. Not only did Mundy refuse, but as soon as he could he told Kiekhaefer about the offer.

"I remember at Darlington after the '55 season I went over for the NASCAR victory celebration where everyone collected prize money and trophies," said Mundy. "I was driving for Carl, and I went, and while I was there Pete DePaolo, who ran the Ford factory team, came over to me and asked if I would leave Carl. He said, 'Frank, name your own price. I'd like you to drive for us.' I turned him down, and I went and told Carl that DePaolo was trying to get me to drive for him. Well, Kiekhaefer cursed him out, and DePaolo asked me why I had told him.

"I said, 'I thought he should know what's going on.'

"'What were you doing? Trying to get a raise?' he asked.

"I said, 'No, I thought he should know you are trying to put a wheel under him.' Pete was just looking out for his job. He was doing what he had to do, and I was doing what I had to do.

"I came back to NASCAR in 1956 because Carl Kiekhaefer didn't want to run but one circuit. He didn't want to have to have two crews and two sets of cars. That year, he had four or five cars."

In the first race of the 1956 season held at the Phoenix Fairgrounds in January, the Kiekhaefer cars driven by Buck Baker, Frank Mundy, and Tim Flock finished one, two, three. Kiekhaefer had won 22 of 40 races in 1955. In 1956, he was intent on winning *all* of them.

"With the Kiekhaefer Chryslers," said Mundy, "if you could drive at all, you could win, because nobody was going to beat him. If we didn't hit each other or knock each other out, we'd win.

"Early in the '56 season Tim and I were on *The Bill Lundigan Show*, the network show that Chrysler was sponsoring in Hollywood. It was an hour. Lundigan interviewed different people. We flew out for the show, and we spent a few days at that ritzy hotel [the Beverly Hilton]. My wife, Tim, and I were walking down the street together, and Clark Gable walked by, and we just stopped. We didn't say anything. We watched him cross the street at the light.

"They had a rehearsal. We were there a day. Tim was gun shy when it came to talking on TV. They'd put a mike in front of him, and he'd freeze. So they had to change it where they had to ask me most of the questions. If Tim could answer yes or no, that was it."

For the 1956 Daytona race, which was held on February 26, Kiekhaefer entered cars driven by Mundy, Tim Flock, Fonty Flock, Buck Baker, and Speedy Thompson. Another member of the team was Charlie Scott, one of the few black drivers at the time.

"Charlie Scott wasn't a race driver at all," said Mundy, "but Kiekhaefer did it because this guy was trying to find a car to race, and Kiekhaefer figured it would be a good publicity deal. We have a picture taken at Daytona alongside the car on the beach, and Charlie is in it with us. We were wearing those Italian white racing uniforms. Charlie was a nice enough guy. He just wasn't a race driver.

"He also had a Midwest driver by the name of Norm Nelson, who never made it to the starting line. Carl found some place to test about twenty miles inland of Daytona that was a long stretch of road with orange groves on either side. They were having a mile run before the beach race, and Carl wanted to win it. There was a fire control tower in the middle of the straightaway, and he had one of his boys climb up and tell the guy in the control tower who was looking out for fires that we were going to run through there. Meanwhile, trucks were going through the orange groves getting the oranges.

"We measured the mile and we would hit it full bore, wide open. Carl had hired Norm Nelson to run with Buck and Tim and myself. Norm had won in the Midwest. Anyway, Norm Nelson took off on his run down this road, and in the middle of the run the control tower guy didn't see a truck coming between the trees, and he came out onto the road and Norm just did miss hitting that truck, and it scared the hell out of him. He left town, and we didn't see him after that. After that, he ran for Carl in races in the Midwest, mainly in Wisconsin. But that was the last we saw of Norm Nelson. He got his outboard engine that Carl had promised him anyway."

Tim Flock, who had won the racing title driving Kiekhaefer's famed Chrysler 300 in 1955, won that 1956 Daytona Beach race. Mundy was involved in one of many crashes and finished far back. Tim Flock won again at North Wilkesboro on April 8, but surprised everyone, including Carl Kiekhaefer, when he announced he was leaving the Kiekhaefer race team to drive for Chevrolet. Flock complained that Kiekhaefer had been too controlling, saying he had become too demanding to work for. Frank Mundy thought Flock ungrateful.

TIM FLOCK

"I did all the talking."

INTERNATIONAL

MOTORSPORTS HALL OF FAME

"Tim said that Carl was too controlling. That's Tim's story. It never was like that. He never did check up on me. He figured we had enough sense not to drink the night before a race, and Tim wasn't a drinker to start with. No, Carl took care of the family, wanted everybody happy. This was a lot of B.S. if Tim said Carl was checking up on him. That's blown way out of proportion.

"Tim felt no allegiance to Kiekhaefer, even though Kiekhaefer treated him like a son," said Mundy. "To give you an idea, Carl saw Tim at Daytona moping around, and he asked him why, and Tim said, 'I'm homesick for my kids.' Carl called his pilot and told him to go up and pick up Tim's kids and bring them down in a plane. And then he had little uniforms made for them. That's the type of guy he was.

"Years later they were taking pictures with Kiekhaefer, and Tim came over to get in the picture, and in front of the newspapermen and photographers, Kiekhaefer said, 'I'm not having my picture taken with this guy.' That night driving back to Charlotte from Darlington Tim had a heart attack."

Even without Tim Flock behind the wheel, Carl Kiekhaefer had Mundy, Speedy Thompson, Herb Thomas, and Buck Baker in his stable. In the first 25 Grand National races of the season, Kiekhaefer cars won an amazing 21, including 16 in a row from March to the end of May. Mundy recalled his talented teammates.

"I never did hang around Speedy too much. He didn't talk too much. He was kind of introverted. I don't think he had much of an education. He had very few friends. To a degree, he was kind of bashful, like Herb Thomas.

"Herb didn't know how to talk either. Herb was a decent driver, but if you had Smokey Yunick's car and didn't win, they ought to shoot you. Herb was real self-conscious because he had no education to amount to anything. He was a pretty nice individual, but he was *so* introverted. You had to do *all* the talking. First of all, his English was not adequate. He had no vocabulary to amount to anything. He was self-conscious about it to, and when he'd look in the mirror he'd scare the hell out of himself. He had a big nose, was ugly as hell. But Herb as an individual was a nice cotton farmer.

"Buck Baker was a bus driver in Charlotte before he became a race driver," said Mundy. "Buck was a mean, ornery son of a gun. If he had a drink, he would look for a fight, and you didn't want to be near him. He just wanted to fight all the time.

"I remember at the Biltmore Hotel, we were on the elevator coming down, and Buck was looking around, looking for trouble. He started talking about this woman's hat, and naturally her boyfriend wanted to fight. Buck was just plain mean.

On July 4, 1956, Mundy drove for Kiekhaefer at the Raleigh Speedway. He led the first 13 laps in a race that brought Fireball Roberts his first superspeedway win. Speedy Thompson came in second, and Mundy finished third. After the race, an unhappy Carl Kiekhaefer protested Roberts' win. Kiekhaefer said that the flywheel on Roberts' Ford didn't meet specifications. NASCAR took the flywheel to a fish market in Raleigh and had it weighed. NASCAR upheld Roberts' victory. Mundy is convinced the protest would have been disallowed no matter what.

"Bill France and NASCAR wanted the factories in. Even though Carl was an independent, he always had to fight so the factories didn't get too much of an advantage, even though he was a better engineer, 'cause France would do anything to see that they won.

"It wasn't that the rules were stacked against Kiekhaefer. It was that they were *for* the factories. They were against anybody not part of the factory teams. It just happened to be Kiekhaefer. France was a promoter and smart enough that he wanted to control it, and the factories were his bread and butter."

In that Raleigh race, Herb Thomas drove his own car. The next week he announced he was quitting the Kiekhaefer team, alleging that Kiekhaefer never gave him the best cars because he wanted Buck Baker to win the driving championship and not him.

"The records say he drove his own car, but it wasn't Herb's car, because Herb didn't have any money," said Mundy. "Herb wasn't a businessman, and he didn't have a pot to pee in. And he wasn't a mechanic either. Give him a wrench, and he'd try to sell it!"

On July 21, 1956, Mundy and the other racers traveled to Chicago to run 100 miles on a half-mile oval at Soldier Field. Mundy finished fifth behind winner Fireball Roberts.

"It was a bullring," said Mundy. "In fact, one deal they had for a novelty was for me to drive in one direction, and one of the top guys there to drive in the other direction for three laps. It was more for publicity than anything. We were headed for each other. We just had to remember whether you were sup-posed to stay to the inside or the outside. Andy Granatelli was the promoter, and he drew quite a crowd. Was it dangerous? Not if you stayed on the inside where you belonged."

The next race was held at Elkhart Lake, a road course not far from Carl Kiekhaefer's race shop.

"Elkhart Lake was the same track they have now. It's roughly four miles long with left- and right-hand turns. It was real interesting, because you come over a hill and then go down a hill and up a hill and under a bridge and back left. In practice and in qualifying I got to where I could put the car into a four-wheel drift at one hundred and thirty miles an hour. The car was so well balanced, where the other guys were backing off. I could just put it into that four-wheel drift and make up time."

After Frank Mundy won the pole, Kiekhaefer asked him if he would switch positions with Buck Baker, who had qualified 23rd.

"I sat on the pole, and Carl came up and asked me to swap with Buck, because he was leading in the points. He offered me five grand, and I hesitated, and he made it ten, and I shook hands with him. I didn't give a damn where I started because I was going to win the race anyway. I drove that track like I owned it. At top speed I didn't even have to back off in the esses. I didn't care if Buck Baker or Jim Rathmann or whoever was in front. I was going to win it, no problem."

Mundy should have won the race, but water got in his gasoline, and as a result Tim Flock, who had become an enemy of Carl Kiekhaefer, won the race. Mundy to this day regrets not having won that race.

"I had that damn race won, but what happened, one of our crew put some-thing in the carburetor—gas that had some water in it, it had been sitting—and it got into the gas tank and the carburetor, and it started spitting and sputtering. Hell, that car was so fast and so well balanced, I could have won that race flirting with the girls in the straightaway and picking my nose in the turns!

"The only reason I stayed out was if other cars wrecked or fell out, I'd get that much more money. I just stayed out of everybody's way spitting and sputtering. I probably wasn't doing more than sixty miles an hour. You could hear it banging and backfiring, and it was all because of that stagnant gas they put in there. They didn't do it on purpose. Of all the tracks, that was the one Kiekhaefer wanted to win the most because it was right in his backyard.

"After the rear end went out of Buck's car, Tim won the race, but it was the only one he won after he left Carl. But he lucked into that one. I remember going into the first turn. I was underneath Tim, and I looked over, and when he looked over at me, his mouth came open and his eyes got big—I'll never forget the look on his face. I was alongside him going into number one by myself. He couldn't believe anyone could be there. He knew he was done. I looked over at him, and then I just pulled away. Hell, I looked in the rearview mirror at the end of the first lap and I was at least ten car lengths in front. About eight or nine laps later, I was a quarter-mile ahead. I could have been further ahead, but I figured, no sense punishing the engine. It was more of a cinch if I didn't stretch it. And then I started spitting and sputtering. It was just one of those things that never should have happened."

Because of Kiekhaefer's overwhelming success, many NASCAR race fans resented the dominance of the Mercury Outboard Motor race team, and they would boo loudly from the grandstands. It was not the kind of public relations Kiekhaefer was looking for. Buck Baker was ready to fight the hecklers.

"I remember the people in the grandstands were either for you or against you," said Mundy. "We were at Raleigh, and some of them were against Buck and me. We were standing in front of the grandstand before the race on the track down near the cars, and some of them were hollering this and that, and I had to hold Buck back. He wanted to go up and knock the hell out of a couple of them. Buck would have been in that grandstand fighting. They'd have ganged up on him. But I told him, 'Don't pay any attention to them.' I got him to go to the other side of the car, so the car was between us and the grandstand."

On September 3, 1956, Frank Mundy, Speedy Thompson, and Buck Baker entered the Southern 500 at Darlington in Kiekhaefer cars. There were 70,000 race fans on hand that day.

"Racing was coming along," said Mundy. "Everybody wanted to go. The car manufacturers were getting into it, the tracks were getting bigger, and the publicity was a hell of a lot bigger. I attribute it to the fact that every guy who was sitting in the stands owned a car, and he was proud of it, whether he owned a

Dodge or Chrysler or a Ford. He put himself in the position of the drivers, so Ford people pulled for the Fords, and Chrysler fans pulled for the Chryslers. They wanted to see their car win, and they had a personal feeling about it."

Mundy finished last at that Darlington race when his engine failed. It was the last NASCAR race he would ever run.

"The engine blew real early, thank goodness. There were too many rpms, and it was a good thing because it was a demolition derby from then on.

"Soon afterward Kiekhaefer offered me a pretty good job as zone salesman for Mercury Outboard in Atlanta. I was getting tired of the road, and I took him up on it because it was an every-week paycheck instead of every six months. I had sixty employees here in Atlanta. I had Georgia, Florida, Alabama, and Tennessee. We had to set up dealerships and give franchises. I had two guys calling on the dealers to see [if] they gave service and [they] sent me to a service school."

Not only did Frank Mundy get out of racing in 1956, but at the end of the season Carl Kiekhaefer also announced he too was leaving racing. The booing of his cars had affected him. Buck Baker did win his championship, but only after a hastily arranged race at Shelby toward the end of the season. Herb Thomas, who had left the Kiekhaefer race team, had taken the points lead, and Kiekhaefer arranged two extra races. In the Shelby race, Thomas crashed and almost died. Baker then won three races of the last five to take the title, but race fans blamed Kiekhaefer for Thomas' injuries. But according to Frank Mundy, the most important reason for Kiekhaefer leaving the sport was that he no longer felt there was any challenge left for him.

"He left because the factories said they were getting out. They really didn't, but they said they were, and to him beating the independents was no challenge. He called the factory teams, the 'dinosaurs.' They had tried to belittle him, and that made him mad, and he was determined to beat them, because they were always trying to get his cars disqualified by saying he was cheating. He was right down to the inch on being legit, because he was an engineer and a mathematician, and he was beating their butts, and they couldn't stand it. They tried to ridicule him, and he had so much vanity that he just declared war on them. He was determined to beat them, and he did it at their own game. It galled him, and at the same time it raised the rivalry and the hatred and the despicable feelings for each other. And when they tried to steal his drivers with money, which he would have matched, that made him angrier. If it wasn't for the factories getting out, he would have stayed. But for him, beating the public was no challenge.

"He had started with nothing as a farmer with that Elco outboard engine, and then after he established himself, Johnson and Evinrude were trying to step on him like a bug, and that's what made him more determined. Any time he would get a dealership, they'd come in and offer the guy their product and help to put them in business to bankrupt Carl. He still came through, and he put out a better product.

"Mercury is still the top dog in the outboard—and inboard—field. He started that too. Naturally that was right in his bailiwick with the car engine stern-drives. He became a multimillionaire, and he started the proving grounds in the central part of Florida, and it's still there.

"Carl was quite a guy. The main thing was that he looked out for his employees. But he wanted their respect in return. One day he came to work, and some guys were sitting around outside the factory after lunch. He walked by, and this guy was eating a sandwich, and he said, 'What's your name?' And he fired him. And the guy didn't even work for him!

"Well, he was paying them, and he didn't expect them to loaf, and that's what he thought that guy was doing."

If Kiekhaefer could be a taskmaster, he could also be considerate and understanding. According to Frank Mundy, "he was as kindhearted as a person can get."

Said Mundy, "He never took a penny from his drivers, and the only other person in racing history who did that was the guy from California who Bill Vukovich drove for. Kiekhaefer went first class and took care of everything.

"Carl was kindhearted and generous, but unfortunately the last year he lived he had a stroke and was in a wheelchair. For such an active man, it was a shame."

CHAPTER 9

ONE OF THE BEST

Ray Fox

RAYMOND FOX'S REPUTATION AS A CAR BUILDER IS LEGENDARY. WHEN CARL Kiekhaefer looked about for top mechanics, Fox was one of the first he selected. After Kiekhaefer got out of the sport in 1957, Fox returned to his business of building race cars, and then in 1962 he himself became a car owner. In a distinguished career that ended in 1974, Fox's cars ran in 172 races and finished in the top 10 in 83 of those races. He won 14 races with such drivers as Buck Baker, Junior Johnson, David Pearson, and Buddy Baker.

Before they teamed up in Grand National racing, Fox had been the mechanic on Junior Johnson's bootlegging cars. Fox settled in Daytona, where he and another mechanical genius, Smokey Yunick, fiercely competed against each other.

"I was born in Salem, New Hampshire, in 1916," said Fox. "Just figure I'm old. I'm eighty-six. My secretary likes to say I'm sixty-eight. My parents split when I was three years old, but my childhood was great. I went to the Golden Rule School for a while, and I left there and went to work. There were plenty of odd jobs available.

"I used to love to go to the baseboard track in Salem that the Indianapolis cars ran on. I saw them from the time I was seven years old until I left there. Barney Oldfield and all of them used to run there, and they would then go to Daytona to try to make records. Sir Malcolm Campbell went to Daytona in the Bluebird and set a world record. That always stayed in the back of my mind.

"When I was seventeen, I got behind the wheel of a midget car. We raced at Topsfield, in New Hampshire. Some [motor] cars had aluminum bodies, and we would take the aluminum from the cars and build the sprint cars ourselves. We would hammer them, make them round across the hood. We did our own bodywork and engine work. And I won sometimes. There was very little prize money in the 1930s. Most of the time we raced for fun.

"During the war I helped take care of all the vehicles that we sent overseas. We put the engines in the jeeps. I was stationed in Fort Devens, Widmore Ordnance in Aire, Massachusetts. It just closed recently. All the German prisons of war were sent there. I can remember them hanging their clothes on the fences after they washed them. It was very interesting.

"The war ended, and the cars still were running on the beach at Daytona, and that was always in the back of my mind, and so in 1946 I moved to Daytona for that, really.

"I had an old '35 with a cracked block. I was a pretty good mechanic. It had gone a little ways, and it had cracked right above where I had welded it, so I kept putting water in it all the way to Florida. I had to stop by the side of the road and pour water into the radiator, so when I got to Daytona, I was pooped. I laid on the beach and got me a *bad* sunburn, and I ended up in the hospital for three or four days.

"I worked in different places, in a Studebaker agency, and then for Fish Carburetor. I worked with Fireball Roberts at Fish Carburetor, and Fish's son, Bobby, and Red Vogt, who was there a long time. Red was out of Atlanta, but he moved to Florida. Red had worked with Ray Parks in Atlanta, and then he came to Florida and worked with me. Red was a fabulous person. Fish Carburetor was on the water. If we had an old carburetor we couldn't do anything with, we'd throw it into the river, and then we'd fish the river. I worked with Red a long time, and I learned a lot from him. He was very smart.

"In the late '40s and early '50s, I was racing myself with Fireball Roberts and Marshall Teague. I had just started, and they had been driving a long, long time. We would go all over the place to race. We used to go to Jacksonville, Savannah. We drove Fords with Fish carburetors in them.

"When I started, I had a Hollywood supercharged Graham, and I was pretty good, but a lot of times stuff fell off of it, and I couldn't keep up with it, so I stopped that and went into building cars working for other people. I built Fireball's engines, all flatheads. Of course, Marshall had a Hudson."

In 1955, Carl Kiekhaefer came into racing and changed the nature of the sport. That year, Tim Flock won 19 poles and 18 races and the driving championship. Not satisfied until he won every race, Kiekhaefer hired the best of the best for the 1956 season, including Ray Fox.

"Herb Thomas, from Sanford, North Carolina, and myself were the only ones who could outrun Kiekhaefer's cars," said Fox. "So he hired both of us, hired me as chief mechanic, hired Red [Vogt] and hired Herb.

"Kiekhaefer paid me well. He was a nice guy. He was the type of guy, if it was your birthday, he'd throw a party for you. A lot of NASCAR didn't think he was so nice at times, but they worked with him because he outran so many people. It was Kiekhaefer's job to check out everybody's cams to make sure they were legal. NASCAR had requirements, and Kiekhaefer used to check them. He had special tools that enabled him to do that.

"He ran automatic transmissions. It did good for a while, but they would get too hot and blow up. So then he went to Dodge transmissions, a stick shift, and we would come back from the race, and even though we were breaking a lot of the transmissions where they bolted onto the housing, he wouldn't allow me to put a bracket on the transmission. So without telling him I put a bracket on the transmission to keep it from bobbing up and down and breaking. And then the cars kept winning races, and after Kiekhaefer found out I did that, he was happy with it.

"I respected Kiekhaefer. He was smart. He was a perfectionist, very demanding. Kiekhaefer bought a house for us all to sleep in in Charlotte. He would check on us to make sure we were in bed by eleven." Fox chuckled. "Especially on a night before a race. No one broke his rules. Everyone liked him pretty well.

"Tim [Flock] was a very good driver. But others won races there too. Herb [Thomas] won some races. Fonty won races. Buck [Baker] won races. Frank Mundy won races. We took care of the cars real well. He had a lot of cars, and if someone dropped out, he had another one that kept going, and he'd win the race. NASCAR had a good thing going with him. Every once in a while Kiekhaefer and NASCAR had problems, but they'd get them fixed. In 1956, Buddy Baker's dad, Buck, won the driving championship, and I was named Mechanic of the Year.

"And then in 1957 Kiekhaefer got out of racing, and everyone who worked for him was out of racing. I started my own race team. I built a record car, and LeeRoy Yarbrough set a record here at Daytona at 182 miles an hour in a plain old Dodge."

Fox didn't stay out of Grand National racing for very long. In 1957, he helped build a Buick for Fireball Roberts to run on the beach at Daytona.

"Mr. [Robert] Fish wanted to run a Fish carburetor, but Bill France wouldn't let them, so they installed a four-barrel carburetor. I built the engine all night long and went to the track on time, and it ran every lap. When they checked the engine, they found that Red Vogt had ground the push rods a little bit because he wanted them all the same height, so they disqualified the car, and

Tim Flock won it. It was terrible. They had a rule you couldn't do anything to the engine. All Red did was make the pistons the same height. It wasn't fair.

"Mr. Fish was involved, and he wanted to take NASCAR to court. I was pretty upset myself, because I had worked so hard. I never had any sleep all night long.

"Mr. Fish paid me so much a week, and then he died, and he left the shop to me, but come to find out he owed somebody a lot of money, and when they came to take the shop over, I asked them if I could pay rent, and I was there for a long, long time, until I moved to Charlotte in 1958.

"In 1960, I built a car for Junior Johnson," said Fox. "I had a business here in Daytona, Ray Fox Automotives, and I used to take care of his liquor cars here in Daytona. He used to come from North Wilkesboro down here, so Junior and I were very good friends."

In 1960, John Mason, who owned the dog track near the Daytona Speedway, paid Fox to build him a car. Fox hired Junior Johnson to drive it, and Johnson went on to win the 1960 Daytona 500 that year.

"I had known Bill France for a long, long time," said Fox, "but I wasn't really involved with him until about that time. France began building the Daytona speedway in the late 1950s. To look at it as it was being built, you wouldn't have thought it would amount to anything. But as it went on, he hired good people. Pure Oil got involved in it, and they just did a bang-up job building it. I even bought some stock in the track. I didn't have a car in the first race at the new speedway in 1959, but I went. At the end of the race, I was standing in the pits, and you could hardly tell which car won it. At first, they said Johnny Beauchamp won, but Lee Petty said he won, and he protested, and then someone came up with a picture to show it was Petty.

"In 1961, I ran a Pontiac. I got a deal through the local Pontiac dealer, a friend of mine, Stephens Pontiac, to get the car. Pontiac seemed to be a good-running racer back in them days. One of my first races was Charlotte, and my driver was supposed to be Darel Dierenger, but he couldn't drive because I used Firestone tires, and he had a contract with Goodyear, so someone suggested David Pearson. Didn't know much about him, except one of the inspectors said I should call him and give him a try. Bud Moore [who came from Spartanburg, South Carolina, Pearson's hometown] also said to call him.

"David was putting a roof on his house, so he got down off the roof and came down to Charlotte and tried out the race car, and he was very happy with it. When he came in, I asked him how it was, and he said, "I don't know. I've never run that fast."

"We ran a lot of laps on the new track practicing. Since David was new to the car, I wanted him to know how it was going to run and how it would handle. I had brought a crankshaft with me and had it balanced in Daytona, so when I wanted to change the crankshaft, I put a bunch of cardboard boxes all around the engine and changed the crankshaft right in the stall where the car was. David had about a three-lap lead in the World 600 in '61, when he blew a tire. He kept limping around, limping around, and due to the fact he had such a big lead, I decided not to bring him in for a new tire. In fact, I was afraid he was going to come in to change tires.

"In those days we didn't have radios to talk to them. We had a chalkboard, and I put up on the board, 'David, try what you got.' He wasn't going fast enough to blow the tire, and he kept limping around, and it turned out we were far enough ahead to win it.

"David and I then went to Atlanta, and David ran away and hid from them. Then we came to Daytona to run in the Firecracker, and we won it. Those were the three superspeedways that David won in 1961. And I was the first car owner to win three superspeedway races in one year."

PART II: **THE AGE OF INNOCENCE**

CHAPTER 10

THE CAR COMPANIES PULL OUT

Paul Goldsmith

IN 1957, DURING THE ERA BEFORE THE CORPORATE SPONSORS, CAR OWNERS depended on the largesse of car manufacturers to keep them in business. Without the car companies, even the most successful cars had difficulty breaking even as costs soared higher than the purses.

Smokey Yunick and Paul Goldsmith entered a Chevrolet in the 1957 Daytona Beach race, and when the engine blew, the team finished 21st. Yunick, who was close to the top executives of all the car companies, learned that General Motors did not intend to continue supporting its race teams, so he quickly sought another manufacturer to sponsor and support him. Pete DePaolo, head of Ford's racing program, was always looking for an edge over the other manufacturer's race teams, and he saw in Yunick and Goldsmith a top team able to win. DePaolo romanced Yunick and Goldsmith, and by April, Goldsmith was driving a Ford to a second-place finish behind Fireball Roberts at Langhorne on April 14, 1957.

"I don't really know why Chevrolet didn't want to race," said Goldsmith. "The excuse was that the American Automobile Association was on their fanny. They didn't think stock car racing was a coming sport at the time, and if you remember, Bunky Knudsen slid in and aced them all out in '58 or '59.

"Pete DePaolo asked Smokey and me if we would run a Ford," said Goldsmith. "And with Chevrolet not wanting to race, we said OK. Fact is, Pete DePaolo put a brand new T-bird in my garage to encourage us to go racing for Ford. And that was a big thing at the time."

Because Smokey Yunick only entered races that paid decent prize money, Goldsmith ran 25 of the 42 scheduled races during the 1957 season. He won 4 races, had 10 top-five finishes, and was in the top-ten 15 times. He won $12,733.68 in prize money that year.

After finishing second to Fireball Roberts at Langhorne, on April 28 he took the checkered flag at the Greensboro Agricultural Fairgrounds. He was second to Roberts at the Cleveland County Fairgrounds and was the winner at the Atlantic Rural Exposition Fairgrounds in Richmond.

"I remember that race," said Goldsmith. "Fireball drove Holman Moody's car. At that time, we were carrying twenty-two gallons of gas, and you could barely make the end of the race if you were careful. I shouldn't say this—NASCAR is going to be watching—but before the race we cooled my fuel. I got in a little extra fuel in my tank by cooling it. Usually we took a barrel of fuel and put a blanket around it and stuffed dry ice down the blanket to chill it.

"And I drafted Fireball for quite a ways—I was following him on his rear bumper for half the way. And at the end I knew I could finish and he had to stop. That's why I beat him."

Goldsmith finished third at the Lincoln Speedway in New Oxford, Pennsylvania, ("A horrible, slippery track") and he was the winner at the Lancaster Speedway in Lancaster, South Carolina. By this time, the Ford race team boasted Goldsmith, Fireball Roberts, Ralph Moody, and Marvin Panch. In addition to having top drivers, the Ford team improved its chances of winning races by hiring John Holman and Ralph Moody to make their cars.

"That [car that won at Lancaster] was a Holman Moody car, a Ford. There was dust and dirt down in a canyon, and I ran an extra three laps after I took the checkered flag before they got me stopped because I couldn't see it. I didn't even know the race was over, and they finally ran out onto the track and flagged me down. It was a horrible place, rough."

Then on May 19, 1957, came a race at Martinsville that stopped the growth of NASCAR Grand National racing cold. Billy Myers, driving a Mercury, crashed and then flew into the stands injuring several spectators, including an eight-year-old boy.

Thursday, June 6, 1957, was a dark day for Bill France when all the major car companies made a joint announcement stating that they were dropping all affiliations with NASCAR and all other racing associations.

Car owners had to pay their own freight. With purses still small, making ends meet would be difficult for everyone. Because the factories had pulled out, Bill France announced that he would pay "travel money" to any owner who didn't win $300 in prize money.

The next race Smokey and Goldsmith entered was the Raleigh 250 on July 4. The winning purse was $4,000. Fifty-three cars were entered including both hard top and convertibles, and Goldsmith was the winner over Frankie Schneider. Joe Weatherly came in third.

"I remember that day," said Goldsmith. "Our tires were not as good as they should have been, but there was water running out of the grandstand onto the racetrack. I would run up against that wall to cool my right-side tires in that water. Everybody else was down a car width where the track was dry, while I ran up there and kept my tires cool enough to where I didn't have any tire trouble. When you race a motorcycle, as I did, you look for every ounce of traction you can get.

"I didn't know Frankie Schneider, but I knew Joe Weatherly very well because Joe used to race motorcycles with me. We raced against each other at Richmond; Springfield, Illinois; quite a few places. He was a talented motorcycle driver. I'd say he was one of the top five motorcycle riders in the country.

"Joe *was* a character. He didn't care much. He had a lot of fun partying. He was always going to have fun.

"I remember a banquet that NASCAR had. He went and bought two suits, a pink one and a blue one, and he cut them in half [vertically] and sewed them together. [The left side was pink, the right side was blue.] He stood out like a sore thumb. Joe would do anything to get a laugh.

"He would always be pulling that mongoose business on Smokey and me. [Weatherly carried a box that he said had a mongoose in it. When he pushed a lever, a coiled fabric object would spring out of it, scaring the bejesus out of anyone who had tried to look in the box and see the 'mongoose.'] He would take that thing to a group of women, and they would wet their drawers. Yes, he was always kidding around."

The last race Smokey Yunick and Paul Goldsmith entered in 1957 came at Darlington on September 2, another fateful day in NASCAR history. It was in this race that the popular racing star Bobby Myers was killed when he crashed head-on into Fonty Flock. Goldsmith also hit Flock's car.

"I was following Myers," said Goldsmith. "I was third. A black car driven by Fonty Flock had spun out in the third turn, where a lot of cars had spun out, and there was cement dust on the racetrack, and it would cover up your windshield a little bit and also get on the rear glass. If you were drafting, you couldn't see through it. I was a couple car lengths behind Myers, and he drove right into Fonty's car that had spun and drove Fonty into the wall pretty hard. Well, I saw the explosion, and I turned the wheel, but I still caught part of Fonty's Pontiac that was backed solid into the wall, and that sent both Bobby and me end over end. Bobby was driving for Lee Petty, and I believe the roll bars broke on that car, and that's why he died. But my car was built by Smokey and it was really strong, and I just got bruised up. I don't remember what happened to Fonty. [He was hurt pretty badly.] But I remember the wreck."

It was the end of a disastrous season for many drivers. When the car companies dropped out in the middle of the 1957 season, many of the former racing stars, including Herb Thomas, Tim Flock, Fonty Flock, Dick Rathmann, Marshall Teague, Frank Mundy, Bob Flock, and Hershel McGriff, were no longer able to compete. Not one of these drivers would win another race.

"When the car companies got out," said Goldsmith, "it affected me too. What did I do? I went into the timber business with Curtis Turner. He needed money, and we went up, and I bought a tract of timber with him. We started cutting it, and we set up a sawmill. And then we moved from one tract to another.

"I flew with Curtis when we were in the lumber business. I had a Beechcraft Bonanza. I flew quite a bit. We'd be out looking at timber tracts, and it would be lunchtime, and we'd land right on the highway and taxi into the city and have lunch. We'd go back out onto the highway and leave.

"At the time, there wasn't much to it. He'd pick a little hick town in North Carolina. Nobody ever thought anything of it at the time. I think I've landed on every racetrack in the whole country in my plane. I didn't want to fool around with a rental car and waste my time.

"I was successful with the two tracts we had cut. Then right after that Curtis started building the Charlotte Motor Speedway, and from there on I went back to Detroit, to St. Clair Shores. I didn't want to live in the South. I had moved my family there, and I just didn't like it, didn't like the timber business, so I left it."

Before dropping out of NASCAR entirely after the withdrawal of the car companies, Paul Goldsmith and car owner Smokey Yunick ran two Grand National races in 1958: the Daytona Beach race in February, and the race at the Langhorne Speedway in mid-September. The Daytona race was historic because it was the last race ever held on the beach. Knowing the days of the beach race were numbered anyway, Bill France was busy building a mammoth two-and-a-half mile oval track near the municipal airport. The new track would not be ready for racing until the 1959 season.

It was Paul Goldsmith who won the final beach race, and he beat legend Curtis Turner in the process.

"I won the race. Yeah, yeah, yeah, in a Pontiac," said Goldsmith. "Smokey and I used to use that Jungle Road to test for the race. We ran it out there quite a bit getting ready for the race.

"And our pit stop was real good in comparison for the time for fuel. Smokey and two other guys, Ralph Johnson and Junior Something, were the crew. We didn't have to change tires. It was just fuel and windshield wipe. And the windshield *was* a problem. We had a special wiper that I could manually use if I needed it, and I *needed* it.

"What I remember is that you couldn't see going down that darn beach. You'd pass another car, and it would spray you with salt water. So Smokey had me pick up a windshield washer and a hand wiper in case the wiper quit, which it did, and that saved my fanny.

PAUL GOLDSMITH
He set USAC records.
INTERNATIONAL MOTORSPORTS HALL OF FAME

"Near the end of the race I passed a car, and my windshield was covered, and I missed the north turn. You go down the beach and then down onto the highway, and going into that corner, I didn't get slowed up enough, and I overshot the turn a little bit. I went straight [up the beach]. A lot of fellows, if they get in that position, they have to make a right-hand turn and come back to the corner. It was the last lap, and I missed that turn, but I got it back into the corner, and I had enough lead on Curtis that I kept ahead of him. Curtis got pretty close, but I took the checkered flag.

"It was thrilling, just as thrilling then as it is today."

If driving a race car made for a speculative financial future, testing for a car company did not, and in 1958 Paul Goldsmith left NASCAR to team up with Ray Nichels to test Pontiacs for General Motors on the USAC circuit.

"It was Ray Nichels and myself and Nichels Engineering," said Goldsmith. "The one who hooked us up together was Bunky Knudsen. After I won Daytona on the beach, he called me, and he hooked Ray and me up together. He said, 'I want you to come up and meet somebody and have lunch with us.' I was a snotty-nosed kid. I was quite impressed to have somebody like that call me to come and have lunch with him.

"I lived in St. Clair Shores at the time. So I went up to the GM offices in Detroit, and Ray was there, and Bunky said, 'I want you fellows to go together and build us a Pontiac race car.' And that's what we did.

"We set up shop in Highland, Indiana, a couple miles from Griffith, where we are today. We built all the Pontiacs there in Highland.

"I was doing a lot of test work," said Goldsmith. "Bunky was looking for sales. Well, the South was covered with Fireball and Smokey. We made a lot of parts and gave them to Smokey.

"Bunky asked me to run USAC. He said, 'I don't care if you finish or not, but I want you to be very impressive.' So I usually sat on the pole, and I would lead the race until I won or the engine blew up."

He won a lot of races. In 1958, he entered 16 USAC races at mile tracks like the Indianapolis Fairgrounds; Du Quoin, Illinois; and Springfield, Illinois; and won 12 of them, a record Goldsmith still holds.

The work that the team of Goldsmith and Nichels did for both Pontiac and for Fireball Roberts was inestimable. In 1958, NASCAR desperately needed a matinee idol to make fans forget that NASCAR had been abandoned by the factories. That year, Glenn "Fireball" Roberts emerged to capture the imagination of the racing world. In the 10 races he entered, Roberts won 6 and finished second once and third once. With Paul Goldsmith driving Pontiacs on the USAC circuit and winning championships in 1962 and 1963, Pontiac climbed from seventh place in sales to third.

"That was a lot of money," said Goldsmith.

And then, as is often the case with big companies, the leadership changed. General Motors gave the order to Bunky Knudsen: Stop your obsession with stock car racing.

"If you look, there were very few Chevrolets running at the time," said Goldsmith. "They had already quit. Pontiac was still working at it. They wanted him to stop building racing Pontiacs.

"So Bunky quit and went with Ford. And then he quit Ford in a hassle with Lee Iacocca, the one who built the Mustang, a guy who had the ear of Mrs. Ford, and Bunky wasn't going to kiss his ass, so he quit. He went to start building a motor home in Cleveland."

At the end of the '57 season, Goldsmith and his partner, Ray Nichels, were hired to test cars and engines for Chrysler and Plymouth. Goldsmith left NASCAR to concentrate on research and development for Chrysler at his factory in Indiana. Among his advances was the development of the Hemi engine. Meanwhile, he raced on the USAC circuit, not returning to NASCAR until 1964.

CHAPTER 11

GLENN

Judy Judge

JUDY JUDGE WAS BORN ON AUGUST 25, 1937, IN DAYTONA BEACH, FLORIDA, INTO one of Daytona's most prominent families. Her father, Billy Judge, was one of the more powerful men in the city. He was a state's attorney and a city judge in the Seventh Judicial Circuit. Bill France was one of his private law clients. Judy's mother, Dorothy "Dot" Judge, was the daughter of one of the founders of the city of Daytona Beach. The Judges were the cream of Daytona Beach society.

"As I look back on it," said Judy Judge, "we grew up in the most wonderful, loving, cherished childhood anybody could ask. My sister, Patty, and I had our own horses at the house. We were loved and taken care of, protected. Our grandparents lived with us for a long, long time. We had wondrous childhoods. And then my mother got cancer and she died a month after I graduated from high school, so that put an end to the wonderousness of it."

Though racing and racers were important to Daytona Beach, they were not part of Judy Judge's world as she was growing up.

"Nice girls in Daytona did not do that," said Judge. "Local girls did not do that. We were not part of that crowd. Some of the guys sold programs at the races, they weren't involved with the racers, who drank a lot and were just wild party guys. None of my girlfriends were either. We were cheerleaders. We were thinking about college. You just didn't do it.

"My father was the district attorney, and I didn't dare do anything that would look badly on him or my family. I don't think any of us wanted to, either. It wasn't a topic of conversation."

Judy Judge was a cheerleader at Mainland High School, and she attended Stetson College in DeLand, Florida, where she got her bachelor's degree. She continued her education at Georgia State, where she got her master's in education. After college, she returned to her dad's home to live.

The 21-year-old beauty loved to dance, and often in the evening she and her friends would go as a group to the Martinique, a dance hall in Daytona Beach. You could go and buy a Coke for 50 cents and dance all night. If you were over 21, they stamped your hand and you could drink. But you could get in at 18.

JUDY JUDGE
"He told me his name was Bobby
Edwards, and I believed him."
JUDY JUDGE COLLECTION

The live band played Fats Domino, and "Little Darlin'" by the Diamonds, and "Sixty-Minute Man," and "Mack the Knife," and "Our Day Will Come" by Ruby and the Romantics. It was 1958, and the age of innocence was in full bloom.

On the Martinique ballroom floor during the summer of that year, Judy Judge met a handsome older man who told her his name was Bobby Edwards.

"He told me his name was Bobby Edwards, and I believed him," she said. "He was a good dancer, fun to dance with, and the band was good, and everybody went. For six months, if I would go down there and he was there, we just danced.

"In February of 1959, I had a date with a friend from North Carolina State, who had come down to Daytona for the big race, the first race at the big track. He asked me if I would go, and I said, 'No, I don't want to.' He said, 'Yes, you do.' He asked my father if he could take me, and Daddy said, 'Yes, as long as you behave yourself.'

"We were in the infield of the track, and my friend said he was rooting for Joe Weatherly. I said, 'Get me a program, and I'll find someone to root for.'"

Her friend bought a program, and she opened it up, and there before her eyes was a photo of the man she knew as Bobby Edwards. Under the picture the name read, "Glenn 'Fireball' Roberts."

"I saw Glenn. If you remember, his name was Edward Glenn Roberts," said Judge. "So Bobby Edwards was his name changed around.

"I was very shocked. I was *real* shocked. I couldn't believe what I was seeing. The idea that someone was called 'Fireball' was just repugnant to me. How could that be?

"I said to my friend, 'I'm for him. I know him.'

"He said, 'No, you don't.'

"I said, 'Yeah, I do.'

"We went to get a Coke, and my friend said, 'You'll just have to prove to me that you know him.'

"I went to the fence, and I saw somebody walking by who looked like he belonged, and I said, 'Tell Fireball Roberts to come over here.'

"He said, 'Yeah, right.'

"I said, 'No, tell him.' And I saw him go up to this guy who was sitting on the pit wall and tapped him on the shoulder, and he turned around, and it was Glenn, and he looked at me, and he came over, and I introduced him to my friend.

"It was cold, and I wore a scarf around my head. He came over. Later he told me I looked like a concentration camp victim hanging on the fence with a scarf around my head. He also told me that nobody had ever said to him, 'Come over here,' but when he saw it was me, he did.

"Glenn sent my friend to get him a Coke, and he asked me where I was going to be later on that night. I told him, 'The Martinique.'

"I met him that night, and we had a long conversation. He told me he had called himself Bobby Edwards because if I knew who he really was he didn't think I would have anything to do with him or dance with him or do anything else with him, and I told him he was right. We sat there, and he had a beer, and we stayed until the Martinique closed at two o'clock, mostly talking.

"We got ready to leave, and I was sure he was going to ask me to meet him at the beach the next day. Instead, he asked me, 'Are you going to the race tomorrow?'

"I said, 'What race?'

"He said, 'Judy, the big race is tomorrow.'"

"When people don't know racing, they don't know racing. The race I had gone to was the Modified race. I thought it was the only one they held. I said, 'I didn't know that.'"

"He called me after that race, and I was hooked. That was it."

There was only one problem: Roberts was married. And Daytona was a *very* small town.

I asked Judge, "Did your father know about you and Glenn?"

"I didn't tell him," she said, "and that was very hard."

"Where did your father think you were?" I asked.

"By then, my father had remarried, and he had bought a house with an apartment in the back, and that's where my sister and I lived, so he really didn't know where I was," she said. "Sometimes we didn't see each other very often. And when my daddy found out, I got my own apartment."

"Was he OK with it when he found out?" I asked.

"Oh no. Oh no," she said. "My father was livid, furious, angry."

"He obviously didn't know Glenn," I said.

"He obviously knew Glenn was married," she said. "That was not something that was done. But I did it. He was not a happy camper. *Not* a happy camper. It was not easy. Daytona was a *very* small town, so that was a hard time. But we got through it."

"How did your father find out?" I asked.

"Glenn won the July 4th race at Daytona in '59," she said, "and after the race Doris [Roberts, his wife] called him up and told him."

In 1959, Fireball Roberts only competed in eight Grand National races. He won one race, the Firecracker 250 at Daytona, and earned $10,000. But Roberts added considerably to his earnings by tire testing and doing public relations work for Firestone.

"Glenn only raced in the big races," said Judge. "When we had a big race, like Atlanta or Darlington or Charlotte, we would drive. They qualified on Wednesday then, and we'd have to leave on Monday so we would be gone a whole week.

"Sometimes he would run a small race just for fun. We went to Tampa and to Jacksonville just for fun, but usually when he was not in a big race, he would tire test. He did very well with that. It was very dangerous though. Sometimes they tire tested at night with headlights. And that was scary.

"I went to lots of tire tests. I remember in '59 he did a couple of tire tests at the new Daytona Speedway before the July 4th race, and he said, 'Judy, if I pull up behind somebody on the backstretch, they suck me along.' Glenn was the one who called it 'drafting.' The first one. He told me that he could do that and that the cars broke the air, and he knew it before anybody.

"She said to Roberts, 'I'm going to kill you.' He was an engineer. And now I hear other drivers saying they knew it, but Glenn is the one who told them all. I know that he knew it in '59, because he told me about it. He said, 'It doesn't work, except on the big track.'

"The next year Glenn drove me around that track in his Pontiac passenger car. He went as fast as it could go, and it scared me to death. Big Bill [France] was chasing us in his pickup truck trying to get us off the track. We went around twice, and he wasn't happy. But he didn't say anything ugly. He said, 'Goddamn, why did you do that?' Glenn said, 'I wanted Judy to see what it felt like.'

"I thought to myself, 'Oh my God, I don't want to do that ever again,' though a couple years later Glenn took me around the Augusta track in his race car.

"You know sometimes you just know you're in trouble? You have a feeling. I was sitting in our car watching Glenn and Joe Weatherly practice, and Joe and Jack Sullivan, the crew chief at the time, Lee Terry, and a bunch of them were standing around Glenn's car, and they would look at me and then go back to serious conversation, and I thought, 'Oh God, I am in deep trouble.'

"A lot of people called Glenn 'Fireball', and a lot of others called him 'Balls,' and others called him 'Ace,' and Jack Sullivan came over to the car and said, 'Ace wants to see you.'

"I said, 'Tell him to come over here.'

"He said, 'No, he wants to see you over there.'

"I said, 'I am not going.'

"Jack said, 'Oh yeah, you are.' And he opened the door, and he picked me up. I probably weighed ninety pounds, and he carried me over to the race car and put me in the passenger window, and Glenn said, 'Hold on to that roll bar over the top and put your feet on the bar on the bottom.' We took off.

"I said to Glenn, 'I am going to kill you.'

"He drove me around this road course, with Joe Weatherly behind us in his race car, bumping us. I had to scream, because the engine was very loud, 'Something is on fire.' Glenn laughed and said, 'We're not even going fast.' Well, to me it seemed like we were going *real* fast. And when we came down the front stretch, he spun it out.

"When he stopped, I tried to move my feet, but my tennis shoes had melted to whatever pipe I had put my feet on. I said, 'I knew I smelled something burning.' Jack Sullivan came over, picked me up and carried me back to the car.

"When Glenn finished and came over, I said, 'Is there a reason for this? Why did you do that?'

"He said, 'I just thought you'd like it.'"

In 1960, Roberts again entered eight races, and this time he won two and earned $19,895 in prize money. The next year Roberts entered 21 races, won two and finished in the top ten 14 times. He was fifth in the race for the driving championship, and he won more than $50,000.

"He was doing *very* well," said Judge.

By 1961, Glenn Roberts and Judy Judge were knee-deep in love.

"Glenn asked me to go duck hunting with him," she said. "In fact, that's when I knew he loved me. He bought me waders for Christmas.

"We went down to some awful fish camp in the mangroves. We went out in this boat with the dog—Glenn had a Chesapeake Bay retriever named Rusty— and he kept telling me not to put my face up because it was white, and the ducks would see the glare. I had to look down.

"He was a very good shot. He could do a triple shot, three ducks, bam bam bam. He had wonderful hand-eye coordination.

"We got into these mangrove trees, and the ducks would fly over, and he would shoot them, and the dog would go get them and bring them back, and sometimes they weren't dead, and I cried. All my life we saved animals that were hurt. I hated it. Hated it. It was cold and yucky.

"We took the ducks back to this camp where we stayed, and they had these big barrels full of boiling oil, or whatever it was, and all these hunters dropped the ducks in there on a string and brought them out, and all the feathers would be burned off, so it smelled awful.

"We went home with thirty or forty ducks. I had to call Glenn's mother, and she had to tell me how to cook them. He ate them, and we had friends over, and they ate them, and I ate hot dogs."

"And you never went again?" I asked.

"Sure I did," she said. "I went wherever he went. I did. I knew I had him when he bought me waders."

"Glenn was quite an athlete," I said. He had been a pitcher at the University of Florida, hence the name "Fireball."

"He was," she said. "He worked out long before it became popular. He had weights, and he worked out. He ran on the beach. We walked on the beach. He had asthma, and he was a smoker, but he was conscious of being fit.

"There was a place in Daytona called the 19th Hole, a little, tiny locals-only bar, and they had a shuffle alley machine, and Glenn could beat anybody at that game. We were the couples champion. He would have a couple of drinks, and he would take his shoes off, and he'd beat people with his socked foot. He was very good. He could do anything.

"Glenn was a real party guy before I met him," she said. "I think I was the last thing in the world he wanted. I don't think he had any intention of falling in love with anybody. But he could not have run me off with a stick. He couldn't have. I just adored him. I just adored him."

CHAPTER 12

A CHRISTMAS MIRACLE

Fred Lorenzen

Breaking into Grand National racing has always been difficult for an outsider. If you were a Petty, a Jarrett, or an Allison and you wanted to race, opportunity was not hard to come by. After the car companies dropped out of racing in 1957, getting a ride became even more difficult. Smokey Yunick ran a car, but he picked top drivers. Holman Moody ran Fords, but with very few exceptions, rookies needed not apply.

Back in the late 1950s and early 1960s if you were an outsider, you were pretty much forced to run your own car if you wanted to race in the big time. As Freddy Lorenzen, a hotshot racer from the Chicago area, found out, racing was a very expensive proposition, and if you didn't have a lot of money, the likelihood of success was slim, no matter how great a racer you were.

Lorenzen twice tried and failed. Only when he was hired by the great Ralph Moody, the mechanical mastermind behind the Holman Moody Ford team did the Golden Boy attain success, winning 26 races during a 12-year career that earned him close to half-a-million dollars.

"I was born on December 30, 1934, at South Shore Hospital in Chicago," said Lorenzen. "I grew up in Elmhurst, Illinois, a small town. When I was ten or eleven, I had a cart, and I put four wheels and a lawn-mower engine on it, and I ran around the streets with it. I went thirty miles an hour. There weren't that many houses on the block, but the cops finally came over to the house and said, 'People are complaining you are coming around the corner, and they can't see you over the high bushes.'

"I always liked cars. We had a '37 Plymouth, and I'd take it over to West Avenue to a cornfield. We kept running around and around that thing and made a circle in the cornfield. We weren't racing. We were just running around and around. I was eleven or twelve.

"I first raced in 1949 at Soldier Field, a demolition derby. I was fifteen. I was a cement laborer and a carpenter making $150 a week. My buddy said, 'Come on down and watch me.'

"Andy Granatelli, a great promoter, ran it. He called it 'the Biggest Dollar Show in America.' He used to pack them in. He'd get sixty to seventy thousand people there.

"Granatelli said, 'The first six guys over the wall with white gym shoes on get the first six cars.' I was wearing white gym shoes. I jumped into an old Plymouth in the front row, and I think I finished second, and the following week I came back and won it. I won $150. That was a lot of money.

"Andy is a racer. You know that just by talking to him. He talks horse-power. He just wants cars to go fast. If you don't lift, they don't last, but that was what he wanted."

When Lorenzen was a teen, he also tried his hand at drag racing.

"I won the World Series of Drag Racing two years in a row in '52 and '53," he said. "I won a couple hundred dollars. I did it because I wanted to do it. I had a '50 Ford with a big Caddy engine and an automatic transmission in it, called a 'Fordillac.' It had eighteen coats of black lacquer, a convertible, and a red-and-white interior—a mean machine. I sold it to go racing. I wish I had it now."

Lorenzen felt a bigger pull from racing stock cars.

"In '52, I was eighteen years old, and I got a call from George Montgomery, who owned Montgomery Oldsmobile. He sponsored me. My car was called 'The Golden Rocket.' I ran it at Soldier Field and O'Hare. It was a big car, hard to race, but we did good with it.

"I was a mechanic as well as a racer. In '56 and '57 I built my own engines. I learned just by playing with them. Bob Chapman, from Chapman Automotive, helped me with the engines. He has a place in Florida now."

When Lorenzen was 21, he bought a '56 Chevy from Grand National racer Tom Pistone to drive on the Grand National circuit.

"Tom used to race at Soldier Field too. I knew him," said Lorenzen. "He's a wheeler-dealer, fast-talking, but a good guy. I bought a car from him, and I ran good with it. I won a championship at Soldier Field with it, and then I took it to the O'Hare track and won a championship, and I went on to Milwaukee with my own car, a '58 Ford, and I won a race up there."

On April 26, 1956, Lorenzen entered the race at Langhorne Speedway, his first try at Grand National competition.

"That was the day I got my feet wet in Grand National," he said. "It was a rough track. It about tore the car up. It was a mile dirt, rough, and I didn't like it because it about ruined my car. The Kiekhaefer Outboards were there, big Chryslers, and they'd come around the corner spitting rocks, and they put dents in my car." [Lorenzen finished 28th after his fuel pump failed.]

Lorenzen earned $25. He entered six more races. He found the competition grueling but was moved by the kindness of a couple of the good old boys.

"I went to Concord, North Carolina, and Tiny Lund was like a brother to me. He said, 'Bring it over here, and we'll fool with it.' In the race I broke a spindle, rolled over, and went out of the track. When I came into the shop the next morning, Tiny and Bob McGee, a big-name mechanic, said, 'We got all the dents out of it, and you got something in case you roll it again. You can roll right out of the joint.' Bob McGee had put a roller skate on each corner of my roof!

"I was just a construction worker trying to race on the side. I poured everything I had into it," said Lorenzen. "I didn't win nothing, and I went broke. I made a couple hundred bucks, and I ended up spending everything I had."

Lorenzen returned to the Chicago area and while racing part-time displayed the talent that enabled him to win the '58 and '59 USAC Late Model championships.

"I did it with the help of County Line Pizza on St. Charles Road in Hillside, Illinois. Jake and Joe Tallarico were close friends. I grew up with them. They were racers, but they wanted me to drive the car. They did the mechanic work with me. The car was built in the back of the pizza shop. It was very exciting. The purses were small, and Boo Miller, the County Line Pizza owner, got most of the money because I worked out of the back of his pizza parlor. Whatever was spent, he'd say he bought it. There was never much money.

"We raced at the Milwaukee State Fair Park and won two of the four races those two years. I ran at Langhorne and Du Quoin, Illinois, and won there too. My competitors included Marshall Teague, a great driver. He was very quiet, like Curtis Turner. He spoke with his foot. Marshall was great, and nobody talks about him much. Jerry Unser was an Indy driver at Milwaukee. Jerry was Al Unser's brother. He got killed at Indy.

"Those were my best days. I enjoyed going into the South and meeting the guys. I was a northerner, but everybody gave me hints what to do. A couple of the guys from the Kiekhaefer team gave me hints, but the important one was Ralph Moody. Ralph raced up north at the Milwaukee State Fair Park. He had his own car, and he gave me hints.

"I'll never forget it. The Kiekhaefer guys arrived in these big vans, like the big race teams do today. Ralph pulled in with a red-and-white Ford, number twelve, late in the day behind a little truck. He took the tow bar off, started it up, ran five laps, and sat on the pole. That guy Moody could run a race car! The race started, and he blew everyone off!

"I just couldn't believe it. I didn't know the guy. After the race, I went up to him and said, 'What is this CP [competition proven] on the side of your car?' He said, 'Holman Moody. That's a place in Charlotte where we build chassis parts. You need a set of springs on that car, buddy, before you break your neck. When you come off the corner, your front left wheel comes almost six inches off the ground. The springs aren't working.'

"I said, 'How much are springs?' He said, 'I will sell you a set of springs, and next week you'll be sitting on the front row.' The springs were $199 for the pair of rear springs.

"'I have to think about it,' I said. So he hooked up his car and left. But he shipped the springs up to me. I put them on and went out to O'Hare, and I sat in the front row and won the race."

In 1960, Ralph Moody offered him a job working at Holman Moody, which was located near the Charlotte airport. Lorenzen moved into a small trailer in a friend's backyard.

"Charlotte was a big, gorgeous southern town," said Lorenzen. "I love Charlotte. At the time, there was only one race shop in Charlotte, Holman Moody. A lot of them were in Spartanburg and in Concord."

Once Lorenzen arrived in Charlotte, he pig-headedly decided he would rather drive as an independent rather than for someone else, even if it was Holman Moody. Lorenzen, who was ambitious, didn't want to have to split his purses. Like many young hotshots who don't know any better, he was convinced he could run his own car and win.

"In 1960, I got Rupert Safety Belts as a sponsor," said Lorenzen. "When I bought my '60 Starliner, Rupert came on. He said, 'If you paint it yellow, I will give you a couple grand.'"

Lorenzen entered the Daytona 500 in 1960. The new two-and-a-half-mile-long colossus was in its second year, and Lorenzen was wowed by it.

"It was spectacular," said Lorenzen. "It was like driving down the freeway. Your car takes a set, and you can put your foot to the board and leave it there. It's such a high bank, and the centrifugal force just held you. The trick to Daytona was learning how to draft. Me and Fireball [Roberts] and Ralph Moody figured out the drafting strategy and how to do it."

Lorenzen finished third in the first 100-mile qualifier, and in the big race finished a respectable eighth. But by the end of the 1960 season Lorenzen was no more successful financially than he was in 1956. Though he won $9,135 in prize money, it all went back into the car. Lorenzen discovered that being an independent car owner without factory support was a very iffy proposition. By the end of the season, he was flat broke again.

"On the way back home from the South, I called my father and told him I was coming home," said Lorenzen. "He said, 'That's good. Someone came by today, and I had to give him $6,000 that you had borrowed to go south.'

"I said, 'Why?'

"'Because there were three guys in a huge limousine,' he said. I had gotten the money from a currency exchange, and they turned out to be Mafia."

"It's a good thing your father had the six thousand," I said.

"Yeah, it is," said Lorenzen. "Darn good. When I came home, I sold my whole rig for seven thousand dollars—the car, the truck. the trailer, everything. I didn't have a car, and I took the thousand bucks, and I bought a dark blue '60 Bonneville from an ad in the *Chicago Tribune*. A guy had to sell it right away and he was asking $1,600, and I got it for $1,200. I loved it.

"I went back to construction, to being a laborer, and then I got a miracle call on Christmas Eve of 1960."

The call came from Ralph Moody. He again asked Lorenzen to drive for his Ford-backed race team. Ford had been officially out of racing in 1960, and it was returning with a vengeance for the coming season. Lorenzen was all ears.

"Ralph said, 'I want you to fly to Detroit tomorrow. We're going to have a meeting. We're thinking of going back to racing next year. Ford wants me to get the pilot. And I picked you. They never heard of you, and they want to meet you.'

"'I don't have any money to fly up there.' I said.

"'We'll send you a plane ticket and pick you up at the airport,' he said.

"I flew to Detroit, and they picked me up. Moody was up there. We went over to Ford and sat at a big, round table. Everybody was all dressed up in suits. I was in my Levi's. I didn't know anyone else there. Jacques Passino was there and Charlie Gray, who ran the Ford racing division out of Detroit. Moody ran it out of Charlotte.

"They threw a contract across the table. They said, 'Take a look at the contract. Show it to your attorney.' I began reading it. It said, 'You're going to quit your job back home. You'll be an independent contractor with Ford. You'll get $2,000 a month, all expenses paid, and forty percent of what I win the first year and fifty percent thereafter.'

"I looked at it and said, 'Looks good to me. I'm my own attorney.' And I signed it.

"They said, 'Go to your local Ford dealer and pick out a car you like and tell them to call us, and it's yours.' I drove home, and I chose a '60 Galaxy.

"It was a miracle."

CHAPTER 13

THEY STOPPED THE UNION COLD

Clay Earles and Others

In 1961, Curtis Turner began building the Charlotte Motor Speedway with his partner, Bruton Smith. All was going well until the drillers hit solid granite underneath the topsoil. The track was going to cost an additional million dollars because of the hard bedrock, and Turner didn't have the money to pay for it.

A man with imagination and nerve, Turner contacted the Teamsters Union and proposed a deal: the Teamsters would loan him $800,000, and he would unionize the drivers and work to allow pari-mutuel betting on the races. Turner was desperate, and he was making a deal with the devil. Only one man—Bill France—was powerful enough to stop him, and this France did, threatening to ban any driver who joined the union and forbidding Turner and his sidekick Tim Flock from ever racing on the NASCAR circuit again.

H. Clay Earles, owner of the Martinsville Speedway, saw firsthand what Curtis Turner was attempting. Along with Bill France, Earles foresaw the dangers that Turner's union would bring to the track owners.

"Curtis was in NASCAR with us, a member when I was still a regional director, and then after he began building the Charlotte racetrack he decided he was going to do something to take over part of the money himself," said Earles. "He got with the Teamsters to organize the drivers, and these union people came in and worked with Curtis, and they had about seventy-five to eighty percent of the drivers signed up.

"Well, I knew at the time that we could not run racetracks under a union. I'll tell you why we couldn't: Say we had sold a bunch of our tickets, maybe all of them, before the race, and then on race day the union comes up with something they didn't like and say, 'We're going to strike.' The people who bought the tickets would be there. They wouldn't stand for that. They'd stop going to the races if that happened, and I knew that.

"While Curtis and the Teamsters were organizing, I went to every race, but I'm going to tell it like it was—the Frances were afraid to go to the races. Back in that day the Teamsters Union had a real bad name. They had some rough people. And so I went to every race fully dressed [Mr. Earles patted his side to indicate by fully dressed he meant he was packing a gun.] though they never did confront me.

"I talked to these drivers and I told them, just like I'm telling you now, I said, 'We're in the racing business and we want to stay. And the way I see it, it's going to be a business that's going to grow and grow.' And I said, 'We cannot afford to run under the union. We can't afford to have a race scheduled and have you people strike on us. That's going to put us out of business. And if it puts me out of business, it puts you out of business.'

"I said, 'We think a lot of you, and we want to deal with you and help you any way we can, but if you want us to race, you must get out of the union, because we're not going to run if there's a union.' And I said, 'I'm not only speaking for myself, but I'm speaking for the other promoters. Every one of them is on my side, and they all agreed. If you don't pull out, we're going to lock our gates.'

"One night I went over to the Starkey Speedway in Roanoke, a little weekly track. I knew Curtis was going to be there, and that night Curtis was talking to the other drivers about his union stuff. I suspended him. I sure did. I wrote his suspension in longhand. I wrote, 'Curtis Turner is suspended indefinitely for conduct unbecoming to racing.' That's the way I worded it. He couldn't drive nowhere where there was a NASCAR race. He didn't enter another track for two years.

"After about two years, Bill France let him come back in. But I'll say this now: I've always liked Curtis, but he was doing the wrong thing there, and I couldn't go along with him. This could have been good for him. He would have made some money out of it, but he was going to make it at my expense and everyone else's. It was going to hurt racing. We stopped him."

Fireball Roberts became involved in Turner's plan to unionize the race drivers, and before he knew it, Roberts found himself suspended by NASCAR head Bill France.

"There were many drivers who were afraid of the Daytona track," said Judy Judge. "It was very fast and very dangerous. Marshall Teague had been killed there. And the purses were not always what they thought was fair. Curtis was in trouble with the Charlotte track, and he thought a union would make it more fair for the drivers. They had no medical insurance. Curtis and Glenn talked about it, and they thought this would be the way to go. And then Big Bill France said, 'No, no, no, that's not the way it's going to be.'

"NASCAR was becoming a force to be reckoned with, and Glenn was very, very protective of his name and his reputation. He was an introspective, self-confident man. And Bill just explained to us in no uncertain terms that Glenn would not drive if he joined the union. France went to a meeting of all the drivers and he told them, 'If you join the union, you will never drive in another NASCAR race.' I didn't go, but Glenn told me about it. And at that point he resigned from the union. Glenn wanted to try to make a living as a racer in NASCAR. He wanted to make motorsports his livelihood.

CLAY EARLES
"I suspended Curtis Turner. I sure did."
MARTINSVILLE SPEEDWAY

"He just thought it would never work with Bill France having total control over NASCAR, and that a union would not be feasible. And Glenn was going to do what was best for the sport and for himself. He decided people would follow his lead, and that he owed it to the other people."

In August 1961, Glenn Roberts resigned from the union as did all the other drivers.

"I gather Glenn was mightily impressed by Bill France's response?" I asked.

"Yes he was," she said. "Yes, he was."

I asked Judge whether the union effort improved conditions for the drivers.

"I think it became more fair," she said. "Yes, they upped the purses, some."

"Were there any other improvements?"

"Not that I recall. It was a promise that the purses would get bigger and that they would take care of their own. But I didn't see much of their taking care of their own."

Another of the drivers Turner sought to sign for his union was Rex White, the 1960 champion. It was the weekend of August 9, 1961, at Bowman Gray Stadium, Rex White recalled, when Tim Flock approached him to join the Teamsters Union.

"Tim wanted me to sign with the drivers to form a union and get better purses," said White. "They had a big picture painted, and it sounded good. Tim was working with Curtis Turner, and I said, 'Let me think it over.'

"In the meantime, two people, Ernie Moore, a flagman who worked for NASCAR for years, and Alf Knight, the superintendent of the Atlanta Motor Speedway, came to me at Bowman Gray Stadium on the night Curtis was having his union organizing meeting, and they said, 'Rex, you don't want to be involved in a union. The Teamsters Union is not good for automobile racing. Curtis and them are only looking to get the union to loan them money and help them get out of debt and get the infield fixed up so that it's raceable at Charlotte.'

"I never signed. I backed out, and I don't regret that one bit today. And then, of course, Curtis and Tim got barred from racing for years."

"I understand that Bill France called a meeting of all the drivers to discuss their union activities," I said.

"He did," said White.

"Did you go?"

"Yes. I can't remember his exact words, so I will tell you what he said in so many words: 'You join and you will not be in NASCAR.' He put it bluntly. He said something like, 'If you want to go with them, you go, but you will not run another race car in NASCAR the rest of your life.' Bill had some pretty choice words. He was determined to break it up, and believe it or not, he had the power to do it. Luckily enough, I had already made my decision."

After the meeting that for all intents and purposes ended all union talk, NASCAR appointed an advisory board to discuss some of the issues raised by Curtis Turner in his attempt to unionize. Among those named were Ed Otto, Pat Purcell, Lee Petty, Rex Lovette, Clay Earles, Enoch Staley, and Rex White. They held one meeting in September 1961.

"We talked about all these things, maybe to get better insurance, more money for the drivers at the back of the field, and to my knowledge we never had another meeting after that."

"Did anything come of the meeting?" I asked.

"Not really," White said. "He didn't change the purses or do anything more at that time. Of course, the death benefits I wasn't worried about anyway. Basically what the big man did was squash the whole thing.

"One thing I can say about Big Bill, he was good for his word. If he said, 'I'm going to give you fifty dollars for showing up,' he never forgot. He was a strong man as far as knowing which direction he wanted to go and how he wanted racing to go. His record still shows today.

"Maybe somebody could have done a better job, but he did a pretty decent job organizing racing to where when you ran a race, he always had your purse money waiting, and he had some insurance if you got hurt. You got paid a little something. He had good dates and paid more money than other racetracks. Basically, if you raced on a NASCAR track, you were going to get a reasonable cut of the purse. I have nothing but praise for the guy.

"I've had my ups and downs with NASCAR, but if it wasn't for NASCAR, you wouldn't be talking to me today."

CHAPTER 14

SMOKEY CONQUERS DAYTONA

Judy Judge

IN 1962, GLENN "FIREBALL" ROBERTS WAS HIRED TO DRIVE BY SMOKEY YUNICK. Both were Daytona legends. Fireball had been a star racer since the late 1940s, and Smokey had built fast race cars for NASCAR, Indy, and even powerboat racing. Smokey, who was close friends with a who's who of automotive big shots, was John DeLorean's best friend. [After Smokey died, DeLorean narrated his book on tape.]

In 1962, Glenn "Fireball" Roberts dominated at Daytona, winning one of the 100-mile preliminaries at Daytona, the Daytona 500, and in July, the Firecracker 250. His Pontiac with the number 22 became the most famous car in the land and Roberts the most famous driver. Everybody in the South and those around the country who followed stock car racing knew the name Fireball Roberts.

Nineteen sixty-two was a magical year for Yunick and Roberts. It was also a great year for Judy Judge and her sister, Patty, who was three years her junior. While Judy was involved with Glenn, Patty met Yunick, and they began dating. Because Yunick was 22 years older than Patty, Roberts predicted Smokey would never marry her. He was wrong. They wed in 1963, and their marriage lasted until her untimely death in 1981.

"My sister worked at a men's and women's shop on Seabreeze Boulevard [in Daytona Beach]," said Judge. "Smokey was a creature of habit, and he came across the bridge every day for lunch, and he had lunch at the same place my sister did. And they met. She was tall and blonde and freckle-faced, and she was

101

beautiful. She was young, and she needed a daddy, and Smokey filled that bill. In the beginning, I was not happy about that relationship.

"And my daddy was *really* not happy about it. But he was happier about that than he was about me and Glenn. Smokey was divorced. Glenn said, 'Smokey will never marry her. She is too young.' And of course, he married her.

"Smokey and Glenn had not raced seriously together before '62," said Judge. "Smokey's cars were either 20 miles an hour faster than everything there and they broke after ten laps, or they'd beat everything. If they lasted, they won.

"Glenn was young [born in 1929, he was only 33 in 1962], and their paths did not cross very much, and then when they did, it was like it was made in heaven, because Glenn was so talented and Smokey's engines just seemed to hold together, and he was there to do it. But they had a tenuous, feisty relationship.

SMOKEY AND PATTI
TRISH BROWN COLLECTION

"Everybody fought with Smokey. Everybody. Smokey had that big helicopter, a Jet Ranger. His house is almost directly across the river from the shop, so he would fly the helicopter across the river and land in his backyard for lunch. Well, these are expensive houses on the river, and the neighbors objected a lot, because their pool furniture and landscaping would be flying through the air.

"When the city council voted that you could only land a helicopter at the pier or at the airport, Smokey thought that was a direct hit at him, which it was. So

Smokey would fly over to his house, but instead of landing, he would hover. We'd all run over in the backyard and wave hello, and then he would fly off. He wasn't allowed to land, but he did more damage than ever, and that was on purpose."

"I gather you didn't want Smokey as an enemy," I said.

"Big time," she replied. "He had guard dogs around his shop. You couldn't get in there unless you were the President of the United States. He was always doing secret testing, and nobody worked for him longer than six months, because he ran everybody off.

"Going out with Smokey was no fun either, so we didn't socialize. He'd go out and eat, and he wouldn't talk. He would not say anything."

"He was probably thinking about his cars," I said.

"Probably. But you have to say, you could fault Smokey for a lot of things, but nobody worked harder and nobody put in more hours and nobody was more dedicated than Smokey. He was there working, and he expected you to work too.

"Smokey was a genius, and he had no tolerance for anybody who made a mortal error of any kind. He thought Glenn was lazy. But Glenn didn't want to be over there with him. Glenn said, 'It's his job to fix the damn cars so they can run.' Glenn's job was to drive it and tell Smokey what was wrong with the chassis."

"They did OK at Daytona in '62," I said.

"It was very important to him to win the Daytona 500," said Judge. "He really wanted to win that. He was a local boy. A hometown hero. We couldn't go anywhere—he was very popular. In 1960, he was fourteen laps ahead, and some stupid little part fell off, so he didn't win, and he was crushed. He had won all the qualifying races, all the Fourth of July races. He really wanted to win that race.

"I remember thinking then that the crowd was huge [58,000]. His main competitors were Freddie [Lorenzen], Junior [Johnson], Lee Petty, Nelson Stacy, and of course, Curtis [Turner]. There were a lot of good ones."

In a Daytona 500 that was run with no cautions, Roberts took the lead from Lee Petty with 50 laps to go, and held off Richard Petty to win by 27 seconds.

"It went fast," she said. "I remember thinking, I can't think he's going to win. If I do, I will jinx him."

But Roberts did win, beating Richard Petty, as Joe Weatherly finished third, followed by Jack Smith, Fred Lorenzen, David Pearson, and Rex White.

"It was *something*," Judge said. "When Glenn won, he was just—quiet. Just quiet. He was teary and quiet. It was very important to him, and to Smokey too. Smokey was thrilled. They got what they wanted. That was the biggest one, and it was really wonderful."

At the end of the race, Lee Petty filed a protest, saying that Roberts' crew used more than six crewmen during a pit stop. Judge remembered never taking it seriously.

GLENN
"He did not like Lee Petty."

"You thought it was nonsense?" I asked.

"Yes," she said. "I don't think he did. Pit stops back then were three minutes long, you know. They were not real organized. I can't remember when it was dismissed [three days later], but it was.

"Glenn did not like Lee Petty. Glenn told me that Lee needed to walk around with a huge wrench in his back pocket. 'Cause he said, 'Somebody is going to beat the heck out of him.' Glenn did not like Lee. No."

To complete his perfect year at Daytona in 1962, Roberts won the Firecracker 250 in July by 12 seconds over Bobby Johns. Judge didn't recall the race as much as what happened afterward.

"After the race, Glenn finally got down from the press box. We went out to get our car to leave, and he locked the keys in the car! I had his wallet, but the keys were in the car so we couldn't get in.

"Everybody had gone. And just as Glenn was getting ready to throw a stone through the Pontiac window, a cop came rolling up. The cop didn't know who he was. He screamed at Glenn, thought he was stealing the car.

"Glenn said, 'I won this race.' The cop ended up asking for an autograph and unlocking the door with a tool. That was funny."

CHAPTER 15

THE GOOD TIMES

Curtis Ross Turner

CURTIS TURNER WILL ALWAYS BE BLAMED FOR TRYING TO UNIONIZE THE DRIVERS in 1961, but he should be remembered for so much more than that. Turner, the Babe Ruth of stock car racing, has been called by many the greatest driver of them all. Some say only Dale Earnhardt Sr. was in his class.

Turner was a hard charger both on and off the racetrack.

On the track, he won more than 300 Modified and Late Model races in a career that began in the 1940s and ended in 1968. Turner didn't believe in saving his car. He wanted to start the race out front, stay out front, and finish out front. If ever he was behind, he had but one goal: to get to the front as soon as he could. Turner kept his foot heavy to the floor, even if the strain proved too great on the engine or if the result was a crash. Turner was determined to always go top speed or no speed at all.

Off the track he lived life the same way. In business he won and lost millions of dollars. He was the brains behind the Charlotte Motor Speedway, but when the cost of building the track escalated beyond his ability to pay for it, Turner in desperation tried to unionize the drivers in order to get an $800,000 loan from the Teamsters Union. When Bill France stopped him, he and Bruton Smith went bankrupt and lost their ownership in the track. (Smith would later return and buy it back.)

Turner's oldest son, Curtis Ross Turner, is a minister living in Raleigh, North Carolina. As a child, he adored his dad, who taught the teenager the intricacies of golf and how to woo women. During his childhood, life was a whirlwind of fun and adventure.

"I grew up in Roanoke, Virginia, about forty-five minutes east of where my dad grew up in Floyd County, which is very rural," said Turner. "Roanoke is the closest urban center in southwestern Virginia. Dad was born in '23, and he went in the navy when he was seventeen just before the war. After he got out, rather than go back to Floyd, he wanted a more contemporary environment. He flew a plane, and there's an airport in Roanoke, and he could fly from there to wherever. It was a hub for him."

According to Ross Turner, after his dad got out of the navy he was involved in running moonshine. In the mid-1940s, Turner was running fast on dirt roads to deliver whiskey from the mountains of Virginia to the big cities, all the while fine-tuning a lot of his racing skills.

"Good people ran moonshine," said Ross Turner. "It wasn't just for lower-class people. It was people who were just trying to make a living. Moonshining was very, very lucrative. But it *was* illegal.

"My favorite story Dad told me was one in which he was being chased by police in Floyd County where he drove on steep mountain roads. This night he was kicking butt, going down the road, with two police cars coming behind him, and Dad drove onto a bridge and did a 360 and passed them in the other direction as they were coming onto the bridge. That was impressive.

"I'm sure Dad was chased on more than one occasion, but I don't believe he was ever caught. I remember him telling me the police were on the lookout for his car. My dad told me that they started tailing him whether they thought he was guilty or not. He said he then started changing cars. And all this time he was preparing his motors and strengthening the shocks, because you have to have a good getaway car."

Curtis Turner married in 1944. His daughter Sue was born in 1947, and Ross Turner came along in 1955. The Turners later had another daughter and son.

"I can remember taking trips as a family. This would be the late '50s, early '60s. Dad loved to play golf, and we went to Pinehurst and to Myrtle Beach. In Myrtle Beach we stayed at a place that was a couple stages below Holiday Inn. It was a party hotel. Every night there was a big party. Of course, any place there was going to be a party, Dad was going to be there.

"For the most part, Dad was not a hands-on father. I don't recall Dad ever saying to me, 'This is how you do it, Son,' that kind of thing. When I was fourteen, I learned how to smoke and drink and chase women with my dad, and I was glad to have had that. It was fun. And I also learned to play golf just to be with my dad. I got to where I shot some pretty good golf as a junior higher. That meant a lot to me.

"We always had a home in Roanoke, but around 1959 we lived in Charlotte while Dad was building the speedway. When the track was being built, it was a mess, mounds and mounds of red clay, a young boy's dream. I would ride my bike up and down the mounds of dirt in the infield, just got completely filthy. And I was always looking for the Coke machines. I would play and drink Cokes. I was a pretty-well overweight kid. It wasn't until I was ten years old before I realized, 'I'm kind of fat. I need to do something about that.' It was from drinking too many Cokes and from eating too many pastries our maid Odelia made us."

CURTIS TURNER

JACK CANSLER

When Bill France banned Turner from racing in 1961 after he tried to start a union, Turner barely had enough money to feed his family. The Turner family began moving from house to house, leaving when they couldn't pay the rent.

"I was too young to make the connection that those crises were dictating our moves," said Ross Turner. "But at that point we left our home in Charlotte and moved back to Roanoke for a short time, and then we started moving around—we moved to Fort Lauderdale for the summer, then to Clearwater for half a year, then to Denver, and then to Indianapolis. I hit the third grade in Indianapolis.

"While he was banned from NASCAR, Dad won the Pikes Peak race while he was driving USAC.

"Dad would drag race anybody. We had one of those Lincolns with the suicide doors, the ones that opened the wrong way, the kind President Kennedy was in the day he was assassinated. In fact, we were living in Indianapolis when that happened. Anyway, we were driving on the streets of Indianapolis when someone in another car recognized Dad, and we got to racing faster and faster and faster. Both cars just started racing double breasted down all of these two-lane roads. I was sitting next to my dad. He was having a blast. I just rolled around inside the car like a beachball. Cars didn't have seatbelts back then. I remember hubcaps flying off the car flying out into the woods. I was thinking, 'This is cool. This is fun.'

"Dad was the same way with his plane. One time we were getting ready to land in a field to pick someone up, and Dad told me it was going to be too muddy to stop the plane in time. He said, 'Ross, I'm going to have to do something here. Hang on.' He didn't tell me what he was going to do. He set the plane on the muddy ground, and as soon as he did, he spun the plane around so it was pulling against itself. He used the reverse action of the propellers to stop the plane. When we stopped, we had been going in reverse. Again, I thought to myself, 'That was kind of cool. I enjoyed that.'

"When we'd fly, my dad liked to say hi to people on any street. We would buzz people's houses all the time all over Roanoke in Dad's big plane. Whenever we flew out of Roanoke, he would fly very low over the Blue Hill Golf Course and buzz the clubhouse to say hello to Clarence King, the pro. Meanwhile, all the men on the putting green would throw their putters in the air and drop to the ground. Then Dad would have to pull the plane into a really steep ascent because Tinker Mountain was right past the golf course. We had to go up in a very steep vertical to clear that next mountain. That was cool. That was another day. My dad was a party waiting to happen. He always was.

When Bill France lifted the ban, Turner was back on the NASCAR circuit. He was greeted warmly in his seventh race after coming back, the American 500 at Rockingham. "He drove the Wood Brothers' Ford, and I can remember when the announcer said, 'We're glad to have Curtis Turner back in NASCAR,' there was an enormous reaction. And then when he won it, no one could believe it. It was what I call a 'Cadillac day,' because Dad always drove Cadillacs. That was a great day."

The Turner house was a meeting place for many of the drivers. Richard Petty came over often. Bobby Allison would sleep in Ross Turner's bedroom. The boy and Allison would play cards. Donnie Allison, Pete Hamilton, and Fireball Roberts often dropped by.

"Fireball's wife Doris and my mom are still friends," said Turner. "Junior Johnson's wife was a friend of my mom.

"Dad's best friend was Joe Weatherly. Joe was always playing practical jokes, like cutting off a pants leg and sewing it on a different suit. He did crazy things. I have pictures of Dad and Mom and Joe and his wife when they took a trip to the Bahamas together. They were best of friends for many years, until he was killed in a crash at Riverside in 1964. I was with Dad when he got the news. I remember him caving, like he just couldn't believe it. That really hurt my dad. And when Fireball died at the Charlotte track later that year, that was really hard. Dad had built that track, and Fireball was the first one killed there. It was a dark day all over Charlotte and for all of us.

"In '66 and '67 Dad went with Smokey Yunick and drove a black-and-gold Chevelle," said Turner. "It was definitely the fastest car Dad ever drove.

SMOKEY YUNICK AND CURTIS TURNER
Riding in style.
TRISH BROWN COLLECTION

"Meanwhile Dad was starting to get into more companies.

"Dad also had a race car driver's school. One week I met James Garner, Dick Smothers, and Dan Blocker, who was a star on *Bonanza*. It was fun to be around them, and the rest of the regular people who took the course were such showoffs that they wrecked an enormous number of cars that week.

"He also owned the Galax Mirror Company, and he also had a trucking firm. And I remember he made a trip to South America to expand his timber business there.

"During this whole time Dad was in the timber business. He owned the Carolina Atlantic Timber Corporation, and sometimes I would fly with him when he went on his trips. We would leave Roanoke and fly pretty much over the eastern half of the United States. We'd go someplace and pick up executive-looking people, and I would sit in the back of the Aerocommander, which had three sets of seats. I could sit in the back and not be in the way.

"And then we would start flying into the fruited plain. There were no roads, nothing, just mountain ranges and, of course, heavy forests. Dad was flying the plane, and he would identify the tracts of land and talk about the specific types of timber on them. He'd be explaining, 'The property goes to this line . . .'

"The timber business is what gave Dad his cash. He would work for three days a week, and the rest of the month he'd go back to being a famous race-car driver."

Ross Turner didn't know it, but his life soon would become a soap opera. Divorce, deprivation, and the death of his high-living dad in a fiery plane crash would change his life forever.

CHAPTER 16

KING OF THE WORLD

Fred Lorenzen

Driving for Holman Moody, Fred Lorenzen was afforded one of the best rides in stock car racing. When Ford pulled out of racing, it sold its inventory of car parts and engines to John Holman and Ralph Moody. In an era when few car owners had decent equipment to work with, Holman Moody had several years worth of racing parts and pieces. From 1961 through 1971, Holman Moody was among the dominant race teams in NASCAR.

John Holman was the business savvy. Ralph Moody was the racing brains. Though the two men often fought bitterly, they made an exceptional team.

"John Holman was the financial man," said Lorenzen. "He put the deals together. He got the equipment ready to go out in the shop and got the Holman Moody parts ready for sale. Ralph was the mechanical man. They had a good combination. Ralph didn't get along with John, and I didn't get along with him either very much. They didn't get along very well, but they produced, which Ford liked."

Being trained by Ralph Moody, himself a great racer and one of the best mechanics and car builders in the business, gave Lorenzen a huge advantage. Lorenzen wisely hung on Moody's every word.

"I was his protégé," said Lorenzen. "When I went south, Ralph gave me all the tips. He was sharp. I give him the credit. He taught me a lot of things I didn't know. If you want to get good, you have to have help, and you have to listen to other people.

"Ralph told me, 'You don't race five Joe Weatherlys and five Curtis Turners and five Fireball Roberts for five hundred miles, when you can only race one at the end.'

"A car to me is like a human being. It has an engine under the hood like you have a heart in your body. If you don't treat it good, it isn't going to last long. The same with the body: If you don't take care of it, your heart is going to give out. So you have to take it easy, run the right gears. Races are won with the brain. The brain controls the throttle.

"Curtis Turner was a great driver, but he didn't finish a lot of races because he punished his cars. You can't run something to death. They don't last. Cars are not magic. They have to breathe, like a human.

"Ralph was one in a million. I was his robot. He told me what to do, and I did it. We got in very few arguments. Ralph Moody was unbelievable! Ralph sort of invented me."

The 1961 season began slowly for Lorenzen.

"I brought my own car down. Ralph said I could work on it at Holman Moody. But he said, 'If I let you work on your car, you have to work on all the cars.' He had ten new Fords he had to get ready by Daytona. My car was the last to be worked on, and it wasn't done by the time we went to Daytona, so that's when I drove for Tubby Gonzalez. I was upset my car wasn't done, and Tubby didn't want to give up his ride, and all of a sudden there was a brand new white Ford stationwagon out in the parking lot, and Tubby was handed the keys, and someone from Ford said, 'If you put Lorenzen in your car, you can have the wagon.' I drove it in the Daytona 500 and finished fourth."

By the Atlanta race on March 26, Holman Moody competed the preparations on Lorenzen's car.

"I was leading [the first 106 laps] when I blew a tire. I had a great car, a great crew, great engines, everything. I came from my own little saddle to the best saddle in the world.

"The Holman Moody cars were the best, but the driver had a say-so in building the car. Nowadays the drivers don't even turn a wrench. I used to turn a wrench myself. In my crew was Herb Nab, Wayne Mills, Freddy McCall, and Bobby Skyler.

"And I would have my own pit crew. I trained them. We held practice almost every other night in one of the Holman Moody shops. Some guys said, 'Man, I don't want to be in your crew.' I said, 'Then don't.' They were paid good, but they had to produce. We were down to twenty-two-second pit stops."

Lorenzen, unlike his more famous veteran drivers, Curtis Turner and Joe Weatherly, was a martinet. He didn't party, and he didn't socialize much. He stayed sober and kept his eye on his goals: winning races and making money.

"Fireball and Weatherly and Turner hung around together," said Lorenzen. "They flew planes, partied a lot. I went to a couple of their parties, but they were always the night before a race, and they went on late, and I would go to bed. That's why I did good, because they'd be tired the next day. I would go home at nine o'clock. I wanted to get the money. I never mingled much. All I did was get to the racetrack early, work on the car, and I didn't talk much. I was sort of a loner."

On April 9, 1961, Lorenzen was leading the Virginia 500 at Martinsville, when torrential rain halted the race after only 74 miles. When NASCAR declared the race official, Lorenzen, the new guy from Chicago, was declared the winner.

"It was my first win," said Lorenzen. "I was the Yankee from the North. Some guys would tease me. I said to them, 'I don't care as long as I can get the checkered flag.' They really didn't give me a hard time. I didn't go to parties or mingle much. I stayed to myself. We worked on the car. We would say, 'Get your car ready and go.'

"My philosophy was, 'Perfection to the car. Perfection to the crew.' You have to be perfect. It takes seven guys to be perfect. They have to go to bed at night, and I made sure they did. It's up to the driver. Moody took care of the shop. I took care of the car. The driver had to oversee things—that was years ago. Now the driver just goes to the track. Half of them are prima donnas."

To prove his win at Martinsville was no fluke, Lorenzen won again on May 6 in the Rebel 300 at Darlington in what was described at the time as "the most exciting stock car race of all time." Lorenzen battled the legendary Curtis Turner for the win. For the last 20 laps, they traded paint, trying to put each other out of the race. With two laps to go, Lorenzen tricked the master, passed him, and outran him to the finish line.

"That was my first experience with Curtis Turner, and Moody prepared me for it," said Lorenzen. "He said, 'Turner will put you out of the joint to win it.' With ten laps to go, Moody gave me the board. He wrote on it, 'T-H-I-N-K.' And he pointed to his head.

"I had gotten behind Turner because I had blown a tire. I was ten seconds behind him, gaining a second a lap. Moody was giving me the board each lap, telling me how many seconds I was catching up to him. I was six seconds behind with four laps to go.

"With two laps to go, I went to pass Turner on the outside coming down the front straight. He pushed me up against the wall. I scraped the wall. So I had to fall back, and going down the backstretch I backed out of it, and then I got my momentum up coming into three and four. I let him go fast, and I went high to fake him, and I dove underneath him, got the white flag, went past him in turn

113

one, and I took the lead. The next time I came around the turn the checkered flag was up. We were coming down turn four, I had taken the checkered, and he tried to run me into the wall again!"

"He was pissed?" I asked.

"Oh yeah. I knocked him off his throne," said Lorenzen. "The crowd was going clean out of the stands because they liked this new nobody. I had beaten the King. That was probably my biggest win ever. That was bigger than Daytona, bigger than anywhere."

The win at Darlington was a milestone for Ford as well as for Fred Lorenzen. It was the first major win all season long for a Ford, which announced on June 11, 1962, that it was breaking the agreement made back in 1957 that the major car companies would stay out of racing. Henry Ford II was acutely aware that Ford had been funding Holman Moody, and therefore, he said, the agreement "no longer had either purpose or effect."

Lorenzen, who would benefit greatly by Ford's official return to racing, also won the Festival 250 at Atlanta in July 1961. Though he only entered 15 races in 1961, Lorenzen won more than $30,000 in prize money.

In 1962, Lorenzen moved up to seventh in the points standings. He finished in the top 10 in 12 of the 19 races he entered and earned $46,000 in prize money.

"We didn't run a lot of races," said Lorenzen, "and they weren't ready to run for the title. I was satisfied running what we were running."

On April 15, 1962, Lorenzen went to North Wilkesboro and finished second to 24-year-old Richard Petty in the Gwyn Staley 400. Gwyn, the brother of Enoch Staley, the owner of the North Wilkesboro track, had died in a crash in March 1958 in a convertible race.

"North Wilkesboro was a great racetrack," said Lorenzen. "Some of the new guys today are hurting because they don't have the short track experience of Wilkesboro and Martinsville, which are the two greatest tracks in the South. Bruton Smith bought the dates from Wilkesboro, so he could close it and use the date in Texas.

"I knew Enoch Staley very well. He was a great man. He was a big man, a great man. He was like Clay Earles from Martinsville. The track was gorgeous. He kept the grounds so well you could sleep in the parking lot. It was a little racetrack back in the mountains of Wilkesboro. A great racetrack. A great man."

Lorenzen went to Martinsville on April 22, 1962, and again lost to young Petty, who had the backing of the powerful Chrysler factory.

"Richard was pretty good on the chassis, and he had the biggest car company in the world behind him," said Lorenzen. "They had technical advisors, like I had at Ford when I came up. This makes a big difference. It was multimillion-dollar firms against nobodies running their own cars."

Nineteen sixty-two was another learning year for Lorenzen. During that Martinsville race, Lorenzen was riding behind veteran Junior Johnson. To get Johnson to move, Lorenzen tapped on his bumper, over and over. Johnson, who was quiet and demure until provoked, suddenly and without warning, slammed on his brakes, causing Lorenzen to crash into him.

"He got my grille, knocked my radiator out," said Lorenzen. "I learned not to play with those guys, to go around them, not to keep tapping them. It upsets them. No one had tapped him before, and he got mad. Junior was a great person. He was quiet, didn't speak much to nobody.

"All the time I was learning how to get by them."

At the World 600 at Charlotte in May 1962, Lorenzen drove a Ford sponsored by Lafayette Ford from Lafayette, North Carolina.

"It was a Ford Motor Company dealer," said Lorenzen, "and we ran the car for the dealer. Ford was behind Lafayette. George Pervis, a great man, was the owner of Lafayette Ford. He paid a couple hundred thousand. He paid the bills for the car for the year."

On June 10, 1962, Lorenzen won the Atlanta 500 after a downpour ended it after 328 miles. David Pearson and car owner Ray Fox protested that they had won the race, not Lorenzen. "Freddie never passed me the entire race," said Pearson.

"That's what they all say," said Lorenzen. "He never saw me pass him? Maybe I beat him in the pits. I know I won—legally."

After finishing second to Jim Paschal at Bristol and blowing an engine at Darlington, Lorenzen was third at Richmond behind veteran Joe Weatherly, who would go on to win the racing titles in 1962 and 1963 for car owner Bud Moore.

"Joe was a good man," said Lorenzen. "He was a lot of fun. He was a comedian, a joker. One day he came into the pits at Charlotte, and he had a big bag. He walked around the pits and said, 'Hey, look in this bag. See what I got inside for ya'. It was a live snake.

"A couple weeks later he came out with a rubber snake and threw it into one of the race cars!

"He was a character, a joker who kept everyone laughing. He was quite a person."

On October 28, Lorenzen went to Atlanta and finished fifth behind Rex White. Rex might not have been tall, but he was talented.

"In '58 or '59 I went to Martinsville in my own car. Here was this guy in a white-and-gold Chevrolet, and I said, 'Who is this guy?' I found out. He lapped the field. That guy was nothing but mean on the racetrack. A little guy, but boy, could he go! I'd have to rate him the best short track driver I've ever seen."

In 1962, Lorenzen finished seventh in the points. Looking back, Lorenzen is sure that if his race team had run all the races, he would have had an excellent shot at winning.

"We should have run for the title," he says, "but we didn't. We did run for it in 1963, but it was too much travel. When you run for that title, boy, you are gone from morning until night every day. And I didn't want to go that much I guess."

In 1963, Lorenzen entered 29 races, won six, and finished in the top ten 23 times. Only Joe Weatherly and Richard Petty finished with more driving points. But Lorenzen picked up the most prize money, $122,587, and that was most important to him. By 1963, his race team had become a well-oiled machine.

"We got closer as it went," said Lorenzen. "The crew jelled. They all wanted to win as badly as I did. They all knew the car like I did. They knew every little piece. There were no excuses not to finish races. And the engine crew was proud we had so much horsepower. We had the best of everything.

"Waddell Wilson was our chief engine builder. He was the big honcho. He was the next man down the ladder from Moody. He was an unbelievably smart guy, straight As in college. He was the mastermind of the engine department. Howard Denhart was the engine room manager. He's still down there at Holman Moody at the airport."

Lorenzen finished second to Tiny Lund in the Daytona 500 in 1963. Lund was a sentimental favorite because he had replaced Marvin Panch after Panch was burned testing at Daytona.

"I ran second," said Lorenzen. "Tiny had the Wood Brother's car, a good machine. He was a good racer. The man upstairs helped him out in that race. He deserved it. Tiny was a good man."

On March 17, Lorenzen earned his first win of the 1963 season at the Atlanta 500 when he beat Fireball Roberts by a lap.

"Fireball drove a Pontiac for Smokey Yunick," said Lorenzen. "I knew Smokey very well. He was one of the best mechanics in the South. He invented Fireball like Ralph Moody invented me. He made Fireball Roberts in the Pontiac at the beach. He could build a race car, and they had power, boy."

At Bristol on March 31, 1963, Lorenzen battled Fireball Roberts, who had been hired to drive by Holman Moody. I wondered whether it bothered Lorenzen that such a renowned driver as Roberts was added to the team.

"A little bit, at the start," said Lorenzen, "but then I got over it. You got to roll with the times. You take the good with the bad. I thought to myself, You mind your own business. But I also thought, 'They are getting so big because of me, they are hiring more drivers.' But I wasn't going to worry about it. It never had an effect on me. I decided to do my own thing."

In that race at Bristol, Roberts finished first, Lorenzen second.

"Holman Moody was spectacular that day," said Lorenzen.

I asked whether he and Fireball became rivals since they were driving for the same team.

"Did you want to be *the* guy?" I asked.

"No," he said. "It didn't bother me. That's one thing: I was never jealous of anyone. I felt: prove yourself. That's it. The same with the crew. We had the best crew, and I knew it. But we practiced week nights after we got through with the cars. We'd do pit practice in the old firehouse. Moody had the firehouse for us to work in. We worked a couple hours two or three nights a week. That's what made us the best. Holman liked it, Moody liked it, and Ford liked it. That's what they hired me for, to produce.

"It was my perfection and Ralph's. We talked a lot of stuff over, and he thought it was a good idea."

On June 2, 1963, Fred Lorenzen won a purse of $27,780 when he outran Junior Johnson to win the World 600 at Charlotte. Johnson had the lead late in the race when he blew a tire.

"There's a story behind that win," said Lorenzen. "We were on Goodyear tires, and before the race we switched to Firestones, because the Goodyears were wearing out every ninety-seven to ninety-eight miles. They would not go one hundred and five miles. I thought, 'Geez, if we come to the end, we'll never make it.' And Firestones ran about the same speed.

"So during the race we were running on Firestones, and Junior was running on Goodyears, and with one hundred and ten miles to go, we changed tires.

"We came back out, and Junior and I were running one-two all day. We had enough fuel, and I thought, 'If there is no caution, we will beat him. He'll run out of rubber.'

"Junior was going down into the corner to stay ahead of me, and I could see his right front tire smoking. I knew there was no way he was going to make one hundred and ten miles on it, 'cause the Goodyears wouldn't make it. And I was flying.

"I was a second a lap faster than him, and I was coming up on him, and that tire of his was smoking with him driving it through the corners. With three laps to go, he went into turn three, and the tire blew, and he went into the fence. I slowed down, came around, and won it. And we won it because of the crew's strategy of changing to Firestones."

At Atlanta on June 30, Lorenzen finished second to Junior Johnson, and at Daytona on July 4 he finished second when Fireball Roberts passed him in the final turn and beat him by a car length.

Lorenzen outran Richard Petty at Bristol in July, then won at the Asheville-Weaverville Speedway. He beat Richard Petty and Jim Paschal by a full lap.

"I loved that racetrack," said Lorenzen. "It was a great racetrack. It was banked, and I was brought up on a track like that, O'Hare Stadium in Chicago.

I melted to that track. If you like a track, you sort of melt to it. And the track melts to you."

At Darlington on September 2, Holman Moody entered three cars. Fireball Roberts finished first, Fred Lorenzen was third, and Nelson Stacy finished fourth. Marvin Panch finished second, also in a Ford. The race was run without a caution, and Roberts set a new speed record for 500 miles [at the Southern 500], averaging 129 miles an hour. The old record had been 117 miles per hour.

"I was leading the race," said Lorenzen. I was running like a rocket. I went down into turn one, and there was a wreck, and I bashed the front of my car in. Good chance I could have won that race. I was flying."

At Richmond, he finished fifth behind Gentleman Ned Jarrett.

"Gentleman Ned was a good name for him," said Lorenzen. "He wore suits to the track. I just wore my little white pants and a shirt. He was dressed up. Mechanics did the work for him. I did my own work. A nice guy, though."

At Martinsville on September 22, Lorenzen showed what a year's experience could bring. The year before he had been banging on Junior Johnson's bumper when Junior applied the brakes and caused him to crash, damaging his radiator. This time when Lorenzen banged on his bumper for 11 laps, he waited for Johnson to try the same trick, but this time he was ready for him, and he zoomed right around him. Johnson crashed, and Lorenzen won the race.

The next Johnson–Lorenzen confrontation came at Charlotte on October 13. Junior was driving for Ray Fox, and he defeated Lorenzen by 12 seconds.

"Ray was special like Ralph Moody," said Lorenzen. "Ray was a great car builder and a great mechanic. Ray Fox was one of the best. I'd rate him with Ralph Moody and Smokey Yunick. Ray and Smokey were rivals. Ray built very powerful race cars."

In 1963, Lorenzen had a shot at the racing title going into the Riverside race, but in that race he blew a transmission and finished way back, allowing Joe Weatherly and Richard Petty to take the points leads. Nevertheless, his $122,000 in winnings topped the list.

"But I didn't do it myself," said Lorenzen. "All the mechanics made it possible. I had to finish to get that far, but it took a whole crew, took a combination of everybody jelling together to win.

"Back then, that was a lot of money, I got to keep fifty to sixty percent of it. Yep, back then I was the King of the World."

CHAPTER 17
FIREBALL JOINS HOLMAN MOODY

Judy Judge

AFTER THE 1962 DAYTONA 500, SMOKEY YUNICK INFORMED FIREBALL ROBERTS that he was curtailing his Grand National racing to concentrate on winning the Indy 500. Roberts needed a ride, and he signed with the Ford team of Holman Moody, where he became a teammate of Freddie Lorenzen.

"Holman Moody offered Glenn a really good contract, and really good cars, and more money," said Judy Judge. "Ralph [Moody] was the business end of the business. John [Holman] was the PR-get-the-deal-done guy, and the party guy. I liked John. He was always working some kind of deal, working something. When we were in Charlotte, we were mostly with John Holman, because he was dragging us around to introduce us to people. Ralph was in the shop."

"John drove Ralph crazy," I said.

"I'm sure he did," she said. "I think John would drive almost anybody crazy. But he was very good to me and good to Glenn."

The crew chief for Roberts' car was Jack Sullivan.

"Glenn thought Jack was pretty smart," said Judge. "Glenn and Jack got along very well."

Ironically, when Glenn went to the track, the racer he had to worry about more than any other was Freddie Lorenzen, who also drove for Holman Moody. In 1963, Roberts won four races and $73,000. Lorenzen won six races and $122,000. Three times that season in big races they finished one-two.

GLENN ROBERTS
He was very jealous and controlling.
INTERNATIONAL
MOTORSPORTS HALL OF FAME

I asked Judge about Lorenzen.

"Freddie and I were friends," she said. "He was a golden boy, a hero, but he was young and he spoke brashly—he was from Chicago, and I don't know why, but I felt sorry for him. He wasn't a drinker or a partier. I thought he was lonely, driven, so he and I became friends. And he hated it—for me—that Glenn was married because he knew I loved Glenn, and he knew Glenn loved me. I don't know. He wanted us to be able to be together everywhere, though we were, for the most part.

"We went everywhere together in Daytona. We traveled together, and yet there were still some places I did not go. And Freddie thought that was wrong. Glenn was trying hard to get a divorce, and you have to remember, back then, it was hard to do, especially hard if you didn't want the publicity. It was a very difficult time.

"So if there was someplace in Daytona Glenn didn't want me to go, if Freddie was there, he would take me out to eat, and Glenn hated that. Glenn told him to leave me alone, and Freddie told him, 'No, you're married, so I won't.' And ugh, that was awful. So Freddie and I were friends. Freddie and I never kissed. We never held hands. We just went to dinner and we talked."

"I gather Glenn was jealous," I said.

"Uh-huh," she said. "'Cause I don't think Glenn ever had a relationship like that with a woman. He believed me, but he didn't want anyone to see me with anyone else. Glenn was very jealous and controlling."

"Glenn and Freddie really were not teammates," I said.

"Oh no," she said. "I don't think Glenn and anybody would have been teammates. When you went to the racetrack, it was yours to win."

On April 21, 1963, Roberts crashed early in the Virginia 500 at Martinsville. He injured his coccyx at the base of the spine, but despite his injury, Roberts was back at the wheel at Darlington for the Southern 500 on May 11.

"He didn't miss any races," said Judge, "but they thought he would. They gave him a brace to wear. I spent six weeks with my hand down at the base of his spine so nobody would slap him on the back. That was the only time I had ever seen him hurt, but that was enough for me. I wanted it over. Glenn was talking about retirement, so we could talk about it. He was talking about what was going to happen next.

"They were televising races via a tape delay, and we got to be acquaintances with a lot of the people who did the taping, and Glenn was close to Bob Colvin and other people who were big movers and shakers. Glenn also enjoyed doing the PR work he had done for Firestone and for Pontiac and Ford, so he thought he would be able to do commentary, PR stuff, something with NASCAR maybe, so he was looking ahead to what he would do after he stopped racing.

"In December of '63, Glenn signed a contract with Falstaff to be its spokesman. It was a big-time secret because his divorce was in the works, and he didn't want Doris to know anything about the contract, so we kept it very quiet. We told nobody. At the end of the '64 season, Glenn was going to retire."

CHAPTER 18

CHEVY LEAVES HIM HIGH AND DRY

Ray Fox

WHILE HOLMAN MOODY WAS STOCKING UP ON TOP DRIVERS, THE REST OF THE field, including Ray Fox, was scrambling to survive. In 1962, Darel Dieringer was finally able to free himself from his contract with Goodyear to drive for Fox, and after only three laps in the 100-mile qualifier at Daytona, Dieringer was involved in a collision with Speedy Thompson and Art Brady. Dieringer's—and Fox's—day was over early. After the race, Fox fired Dieringer and replaced him with David Pearson. More than 40 years later, Fox still bristles at what happened that day.

"I don't want to think about it," said an angry Fox. "*You* think about it. That was something in my mind that's passe, because he didn't do no good. When you have a wreck, you don't do no good. Speedy Thompson was a person I didn't much care for 'cause he wrecked Herb Thomas for me in Shelby, North Carolina.

"And that was my last race with Darel. Darel didn't do what I thought he should have done. I decided to replace him."

Though the 28-year-old Pearson finished in the top 10 at Darlington, Charlotte, Atlanta, and Daytona, Fox wasn't satisfied with him either. He replaced Pearson with another former driver, Junior Johnson.

Junior had driven for himself, for Ray Nichels, and then for Cotton Owens. Like Fox, who was rarely satisfied with his drivers, Junior was rarely satisfied with his car owner. Each was looking for the best, and this time each of them found it.

"Junior was very good," said Fox. "He was just brave. And he was good with the bodies. Back in them days the bodies were not as good as they are today. He was good at chassis work, so he did better at the racetrack, and I knew it."

In 1962, Fox and Junior went to Darlington, where they sat on the outside pole and then appeared to have won the race as Junior took the checkered flag. NASCAR, however, gave the race to Larry Frank in the second-place car.

"To my knowledge, Larry Frank was sitting in the turn, out of gas, or his car

had broken down or something," said Fox. "He was just sitting in the turn. He didn't move, and I saw it. When they reshowed the race, it showed Larry Frank sitting there. I hate to say this, but back in those days NASCAR did whatever they wanted. That's the way it was.

"I have no idea why they wanted Larry Frank to win. I wouldn't want to say, because I now belong to NASCAR, and I get a hard-card credential, a life-time card, so I don't want to talk about them, really. But I can say my mood was terrible when they took that race away from me.

JUNIOR JOHNSON

It was hard to catch the Fords.

INTERNATIONAL

MOTORSPORTS HALL OF FAME

"I didn't talk to anyone about it. In those days you couldn't. Other people took care of things like that. You didn't want to bring it up to Bill. He had enough problems of his own. But things like that went on."

Fox and Junior next raced at the Charlotte Motor Speedway on October 14, 1962. They won the race by two full lengths and split $11,155.

"Junior was just good," said Fox. "When he made up his mind to do something, he did it. He won a lot of races. He was a good driver. We split the money. That was a pretty good payday.

"Back then, I figured it cost $7,000 per race to get the car on the track. If it had run in a race, we would have to go through and check it, put it on the mag-naflux, to see that nothing had broken.

"We usually had people to help pay our expenses. One time I had toilet paper people. One time I had K-Mart. I'd pick someone up to help me. Maybe I'd get $3,500 from a sponsor. I tested tires for Firestone, so I got the tires for free.

In 1963, General Motors decided that the mechanical mind it needed to build its cars in order to beat the Fords was Ray Fox. That year, GM supplied Fox with a 427-cubic-inch high-lift engine.

"I had signed a contract to get into racing with General Motors. My deal was $117,000 for the year. When I signed the contract, they supplied me with parts.

"The car ran awful good, and Ford spent a lot of money to try to catch it. Yup. Chevy and Ford were fighting, and Ford gave Holman Moody a lot of money to beat me.

"We had that 427, and I did a lot of work on the heads to port and relieve, grind up the ports to make it smooth, make the valves the right size, where the valves sat on the head—they were fixed. Just did different things to make it work better."

But several months into the season, General Motors announced it was getting out of racing. Midway through the 1963 season, GM left Fox high and dry.

"They had a lawsuit against them that had something to do with used cars and dealers. Someone was suing them, and they didn't want the added expenses of racing in case they lost the lawsuit. The suit was for a lot of money.

"That year, I only paid taxes on $40,000, so it hurt us. After they dropped out, I didn't get any more parts. I had to fix stuff up. Blocks were giving out, and heads were giving out, and I had to fix them all myself. I had to fly engines to wherever Junior was and fly back the other engine."

In 1963, Richard Petty, backed by Chrysler, won fourteen races and had thirty top-five finishes.

"Richard had Chrysler behind him, so therefore he was able to get things we couldn't get. He had total support from Chrysler. I had none from GM. And our stuff was wearing out."

Fox and Junior Johnson suffered frustration after frustration in race after race in 1963. A high point came on June 2 at Charlotte in the World 600 when Junior led with only three laps to go. But a tire blew, and Freddie Lorenzen, who was driving a Ford for Holman Moody, passed him for the win. Junior finished second.

"Junior was lucky to finish," said Fox. "We had a lot against us. Ford had all their stuff, and we had to do more to keep up. It was very difficult to keep up with them."

At the Firecracker 400, Junior won the pole, but the car had engine trouble all day. If Junior was upset about the way things were going, he didn't say anything to Fox.

"I didn't hear him say anything," said Fox. "I definitely was getting upset. Sometimes we were able to bore the engines, but then they just didn't hold up. They were just as fast. They weren't durable."

At Martinsville, Freddie Lorenzen sat on Junior's bumper, and for eleven laps kept tapping him from behind. Finally Junior had enough. He hit the brakes, Lorenzen ran into his rear, and Lorenzen was out of the race. The old vet had taught the new kid a lesson.

"They do that today," said Fox. "I remember they were both upset with each other. Freddie Lorenzen was a very, very good race driver. He could look ahead and see where he could go and where he should be, and he would get there. And he didn't very often get into a wreck. He stayed in pretty good shape. Freddie was kind of a loner—I've sat down in a restaurant to eat with him—but he won a lot of races."

For Fox and Junior Johnson, the frustrations of 1963 continued through the season.

"We started on the pole just about everywhere," Fox said. "But the engines just weren't holding up." Fox was angry. "The blocks would bust, because they were old."

On October 13, 1963, Ray Fox ran three cars at Charlotte. Buck Baker and Jim Paschal were two of his drivers, and Junior was the third.

"Buck was a good driver," said Fox. "Buck won Darlington for me, which was the last race he ever won, and his son Buddy won the first race he ever won for me. Paschal was also a good race driver and a very nice man."

"It was unusual to have three cars in a race," I said.

"I must have had good people to throw in their money in order to do that," Fox said. "I always would say, 'If somebody wanted to put an ad on the car and hand me $7,000 for the race, I'd take it.' 'Cause you needed the money to do what I had to do to the engines and the cars to keep up with going to the races. People knew what I was doing, and they'd get to me. I was with Holly Farms with Junior for a long, long time.

"I got Holly Farms through Junior. Junior knew all the Holly Farms people very well. They were from Wilkesboro, where he lived. Holly Farms paid me, and I paid Junior."

In the National 400, Fox's engine managed to stay in one piece, and Junior beat Fred Lorenzen.

"I just remember I was praying just about through the whole race for it to keep going, because I was afraid it might not," said Fox. "Unless people knew what was going on, they'd just say, 'Ray ain't doin' too good now.'"

"Newspaper reporters and race fans were saying that you had lost it?" I asked.

"Right. Correct. And I didn't want to talk to them and say anything against Chevrolet."

In 1963, Junior and Fox won $67,000 in prize money. But at the end of 1963, Fox knew he could no longer compete in a Chevy, and at first Fox decided to switch to Mercury. But Junior Johnson didn't like the Mercury, and they switched again, this time to Dodge. Dodge gave Fox $80,000 per year.

During the Thanksgiving vacation of 1963, Fox and Johnson went to the Goodyear five-mile course to test their new Dodge. Fox also brought his old Chevy with him. The Dodge execs thought they had a fast car, but Fox proved them otherwise.

"It was Thanksgiving," said Fox, "and we had Thanksgiving dinner right beside the racetrack. We went across the wall to eat. The Chevrolet with the *old* engine in it was fifteen miles an hour faster than the Dodge. So they said to me, 'We're going to build a Hemi and put it in, and you won't have to worry about the Dodge no more.' So the Hemi came out into the Dodge, and the Hemi just raised hell, man. It wiped them all out.

"I was the only car builder involved in that decision."

I asked Fox whether he had recommended the Hemi.

"No," he said, "I didn't have to. They ain't stupid."

Fox didn't send his car to Riverside, California, for the opener of the 1964 season.

"I couldn't afford it," said Fox. "Towing, and way, way out there. It was a long ways away."

During the opener, Joe Weatherly's car hit the wall on the driver's side, his head banged against the concrete, and he died of a brain hemorrhage.

"Joe Weatherly was killed in that race, and it had a real effect on racing. But NASCAR right off the bat did something to stop what happened. When he hit the wall, he didn't have netting in the window, so his head just came out and hit the wall. When you get hit in the head like that, especially that hard, you don't have much of a chance.

"Joe was popular, because he was funny as hell. He joked all the time. He was a nice fellow to get along with. In fact, a *super* guy to get along with.

"We all went to his funeral. It was very solemn because everyone liked him so well."

In the Daytona 500, Fox and Junior Johnson finished ninth behind Richard Petty, who was also driving a Dodge. In 1964, Richard was the fair-haired boy of racing. By April 5 at Atlanta, Junior was complaining that "we can't get the good engines and parts that the other Chrysler teams are getting." In the race, Johnson drove fewer than 100 laps before refusing to continue. Jim Hurtubise took his seat and drove to a fourth-place finish.

Fox agreed with Junior that Petty Engineering was getting preferred treatment from Chrysler.

"We just had to do so much more work on the engines and the heads," he said. "Petty had stuff other people didn't have. I didn't feel bad about Petty, because whatever he could do better than someone else, I felt he should do it. I would have.

"Did anything come of Junior's outburst?" I asked.

"No," said Fox. "I just started cheating a little bit, putting a different head gasket on it to give it more horsepower. I just took it upon myself to do better."

"Was part of that a desire to keep Junior as your driver?" I asked.

"Yeah, yes. Yes. 'Cause I wanted to keep Junior."

In 1964, the driver who was causing a great deal of commotion was Freddy Lorenzen in a Holman Moody Ford. Lorenzen, who only ran in selected races, won five straight races during the spring as he won Bristol, Atlanta, North Wilkesboro, Martinsville, and Darlington on May 9.

"Holman Moody spent a lot of money," said Fox. "They got a lot of money from Ford. They were the only ones who were getting money from Ford, and so they just ran all over everybody horsepower-wise. Money can buy parts, good parts, good head gaskets, good parts to raise the compression in the engine, different things."

"The combination of Ford's money, Ralph Moody's skills, and Freddie's driving ability was a potent combination," I said.

"Yes, it was," said Fox. "They had everything they needed. Ford just spent a bushel with them, and they could do whatever they pleased."

"Couldn't you get the car companies to spread the wealth around?" I asked.

"You know, they were fighting all the time. Ford with Chrysler. In fact, right then was during the time Ford was arguing with Chrysler, and Chrysler was arguing with Bill France, and Chrysler got out of it."

CHAPTER 19

THE DEATH OF FIREBALL ROBERTS

Judy Judge

THE 1964 SEASON BEGAN WITH FIREBALL ROBERTS WINNING THE 139 LAPS AT Augusta International Speedway, a three-mile road course. Judy Judge recalled the added incentive for Fireball Roberts to win that day.

"Banjo [Matthews] was staying down the hall from us at the Holiday Inn, so the morning of the race the three of us went inside to have breakfast, and it was packed, and one of the things Glenn always prided himself in was signing autographs. He would sign autographs for anybody.

"It was very crowded, and everybody was getting antsy, because it was getting late, and our order was late coming. We were going to be late to the racetrack.

"The waitress had just put his eggs in front of him, and he had a piece on his fork leaning over to put it in his mouth, when some guy walked up and said, 'Can I have your autograph?' Glenn never looked at him. He said, 'Do you mind if I finish my breakfast?' The guy walked off.

"I hit him on the leg, and he just gave me that look that said, 'Shut up.' We finished breakfast, and when we got up to leave, Banjo grabbed the ticket, and Glenn said, 'Where is that guy?' I said, 'He's over there in that booth.' We walked over, and Glenn said, 'I'll be happy to sign your autograph now.' And the guy never looked up. He said, 'No thanks, Fireball. I'll wait on the winner.' And Glenn and I walked off.

"He was *so* embarrassed. We got in the car, and I said, 'Well, that was pretty awful.' He said, 'Yes, it was.' And that was it.

GLENN ROBERTS
He rides with Tammy Wilson,
daughter of friends,
the Sunday before the World 600.
JUDY JUDGE COLLECTION

"Well, Glenn won the race, and when he handed me his helmet, he said, 'Where is that son of a bitch? I'm the winner.' It had worried him the whole time. It was the only time I ever saw him do anything like that."

The next race Roberts entered was the January 19 race at Riverside, California. Roberts had made enough money that he could buy himself an airplane, and he and Judy flew out for the race.

"Glenn loved flying," said Judge. "He bought a Piper Comanche. It was wonderful. Seven-seven-four-six-Poppa was the number. He was really a good pilot, and we flew everywhere. I remember one time we flew to Niagara Falls on a PR tour for Ford. We did a little extra sightseeing. It was wonderful. You remember those bridges? [The biggest one is the Peace Bridge connecting Buffalo and Niagara Falls, Canada.] Joe Weatherly and Curtis told Glenn about the time they flew under the bridges. Glenn was talking about putting mud on the numbers of the plane and trying it. I said, 'No, you're not. Not with me in it.' Glenn wouldn't have done it. Weatherly would have. So would have Curtis. And Smokey too. Oh yes, Smokey would have."

Roberts' airplane enabled Fireball and Judy to fly out to Riverside for the race in January 1964.

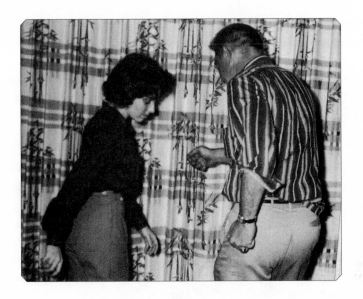

JUDY JUDGE AND GLENN ROBERTS
Twisting the night away.
JUDY JUDGE COLLECTION

"We stayed one night in New Orleans, and then we stayed three nights in Vegas and went on. It was a wonderful trip.

"When we arrived at Riverside, we went to Joe and JoAnne Weatherly's room, and because January 20 was Glenn's birthday, we decorated their room for a surprise party for Glenn after the race."

The party never took place. During the race, Weatherly pitted for repairs, and his car sat idly as the race went on. Because Weatherly was defending the points championship, he decided to go back out and get as many points as he could. On lap 86, he went into the esses, his Mercury wiggled, and the left side of the car crashed against the concrete barrier. Weatherly was killed instantly.

"It was terrible," said Judge. "It was just awful. He went back to finish. It was a fluke. What they told us happened was Joe didn't have a shoulder harness. He just had a seatbelt, and they didn't have window batting, and his head went out and hit the wall. When I went with JoAnne to the hospital to see him, there was nothing—it just looked like he was asleep. So it was a *very* bad trip.

"We flew back. Gene White had an airplane, and someone else—it wasn't Freddie—had one, and the three planes flew together back to New Orleans, and all of us spent the night there, and it was very quiet, very subdued, and very, very sad."

"What do you remember about Joe?" I asked.

"Joe was funny. He was always pulling tricks on people. He would put a plastic snake on a spring and put it in a can, and he'd open the can, and the snake would spring out. He would pull down guys' pants. He would do anything. He was just funny. He and Curtis were best friends. We saw them a lot, but not socially.

"And he drank VO shooters," she said.

"What is a VO shooter?" I asked.

"Just straight shots of VO. He and JoAnne loved to party. They loved to go out and drink. Joe got loud when he drank too much, and that meant we didn't stay. Glenn did not like anything that drew attention to himself, so if you were loud and obnoxious, he didn't like it, and he was out of there.

"Glenn was a college guy. He did not graduate, but he had gone to the University of Florida for two-and-a-half years. He was very bright. Very bright. He liked to read. He liked all kinds of music. He played the stock market. He loved flying his airplane. He did very well in his career. We were very busy those last two years doing PR with Ford and Firestone."

On March 22, 1964, Fred Lorenzen beat Roberts in the Southeastern 500 at Bristol by half a lap even though Lorenzen finished the race with a sputtering engine.

"Glenn could have won, and I thought he was going to," she said. "I really didn't ever care if he won or didn't. I just wanted it over. I just wanted it over."

On April 5, Roberts went to Atlanta, where he crashed on the 107th lap of a 334-lap race.

"That could not have been fun for you," I said.

"No, it was not," Judge said, "but that was early in the race, and that was always better."

Then on April 19, Roberts crashed his car during time trials before the race at North Wilkesboro.

"And that was awful," said Judge. "Ray Fox was from Daytona, and we were friends. Ray and I liked each other. He was somebody to talk to. I was standing with Ray in the infield in the middle of turn two," she said.

Which is right where Roberts crashed through a wooden gate and wrecked the car.

"Before he went out, I said to Ray, 'I want to go between one and two.' He said, 'That's not the place to watch it.' I said, 'That's where I want to go,' and that's where it happened, right in front of me. I don't know why, but I knew. That was not fun."

The next race was Darlington in early May. Lorenzen had won at North Wilkesboro, Martinsville, and he won the Rebel 300. Roberts was convinced that Holman Moody was giving the Golden Boy better equipment.

JUDY JUDGE AND GLENN ROBERTS
They have breakfast together
on May 24, 1964.
JUDY JUDGE COLLECTION

"The period when Glenn thought Freddie was getting better equipment was not pleasant," said Judge. "Freddie adored Glenn. Freddie was a Yankee and brash and Freddie loved me, so he was not Glenn's favorite person. Glenn thought Freddie was getting better equipment because Freddie was there before Glenn, and it was my job to talk to John Holman about that."

"And what did John say?" I asked.

"Not true. Not true," she said. "Not at all true. He said, 'They all get the same stuff. It's the crew's job to fix it.'

It was around this time that Fireball and Judy set a date to be married. Roberts' divorce from his wife, Doris, became final on April 15. Roberts and Judge made plans to have a gala wedding ceremony on June 6, 1964.

"Glenn was a very self-contained man," said Judge. "He loved me more than anybody or anything in this world, and I know that to be true. He changed every way possible. If you talk to Jim Hunter or Max Muhleman, they will tell you.

"Please understand that Glenn was so much more than a race driver. He was so smart, so talented and capable. I felt like he was just beginning to become the man he was meant to be. He loved what our future held for us and was excited about going into the commentary business. He had such charisma, I just know he would have been wonderful. He was happy. His eyes lit up when he looked at me and he lit my world.

"We were together. We were just together. And he told me when he married Doris, he ran away and got married by a woman justice of the peace, and that he did not want that this time. He wanted to be married in Daytona with our families there, and that's what we were going to do.

"We had talked to my daddy, talked to Dick Joslin, a short-track racer, an old, dear friend of Glenn's, and they went back years and years. Glenn had asked Dick to be his best man. He told B. D. Spears and Dick Dolan and John Holman and Bob Colvin. We had bought a house in Daytona. We were going to be married at our house on June 6.

"All I wanted was for him to be through."

I asked Judge, "So Glenn basically had three races to run before his racing career was over?"

"That's it," she said. "Charlotte, Daytona, and Darlington. He had won the Firecracker 400 and the Southern 500 in '63, and he wanted to defend his titles."

The first of the titles Roberts defended was in the World 600 at the Charlotte Motor Speedway on May 24, 1964. He and Judy Judge were scheduled to wed two weeks later, on June 6, 1964. But on the eighth lap of the race, Roberts' famed car with the number 22 on its side spun backwards and slammed into the edge of the concrete wall of the backstretch. His car exploded on impact, flipping and burning him terribly. Ned Jarrett jumped out of his car and pulled Roberts out of the flaming wreck. Roberts screamed, "My God, Ned, help me. I'm on fire." He was burned over most of his body. Roberts was airlifted to Charlotte Memorial Hospital where he was listed in "extremely critical" condition.

Roberts, winner of 33 Grand National races and the epitome of the sport, remained hospitalized from one of the most wrenching crashes in the history of NASCAR. As his stay dragged from days into weeks into months, the racing world prayed that he would survive.

Then suddenly on July 2, he died. Pneumonia and blood poisoning were too much for him to overcome. Judy Judge's life went from fairy tale to nightmare.

"The Friday night before the Charlotte race on Saturday, Max Muhleman, Glenn, and I were sitting in our hotel room looking at paint colors and furniture," said Judge. "Max worked for the *Charlotte Observer*. He adored Glenn. Glenn was a loner who had that kind of relationship with very few people. Glenn and Max were working on a book. We were working hard with Max on it. Max taped his conversations with Glenn.

"Max couldn't get over it. 'I can't believe you're doing this,' he said. But Glenn loved his new house. He was a happy camper. He was *very* happy. He had given me some money—a lot of money—to put in a safety deposit box with my father's name on it in case we were killed in the airplane so Daddy could bury us.

"We had signed the contract with Falstaff. Glenn wasn't going to be racing anymore. We thought if anything happened to us it would probably be in an airplane. Glenn was looking at a twin-engine, but we hadn't gotten that far. He was happy with his life. He was happy with what was going on. I just never thought he would die. I just didn't think it was going to happen.

"I've been very bitter about it," she said. "I think it was one of those safety things."

"You mean lack-of-safety things," I said.

"Right," she said.

I mentioned to Judy that several people had told me they had visited Glenn at the hospital.

"They may have come to the hospital," she said, "but no one saw Glenn. No one, except his mother, his father, Doris, and me. He was burned badly, and you had to gown up, and only the people he called for could see him, and I was the only person he called for. So no one—I don't care what anybody tells you— no one saw him, and they didn't talk to him on the phone. I sent the plane for his mother. They may have come to the hospital and talked to me or his mother or his daddy, when his daddy was there, but no one saw Glenn. It's over forty years, and they may think they did, but they did not. The doctors, of course, the nurses, and the family was all.

"We waited in the waiting room. His daddy was retired from the lumber company, and he owned cottages and rental property right close to Peabody Auditorium in Daytona, and he was taking care of our house too. He came back and forth, but his mother and I would go to the hospital about eight in the morning, and we would leave about eight at night, and I would take her back to the motel, wait till she went to sleep, and I'd go back to the hospital and stay until two or three in the morning and then come back, sleep a little while, and go back.

"There were twelve-hour periods when he didn't call for me, and no one saw him.

"This went on from the twenty-fourth of May to the second of July. He didn't talk on the telephone, and he didn't see anyone—no one. First of all, I wouldn't have let anyone in to see him in the condition he was in, and secondly, they had to put on the garb, and the doctors didn't want any germs in his room.

"Smokey Yunick wrote a book, and we argued about some of the things he said about Glenn. He said that he had come to Charlotte and couldn't see Glenn, which was true. But some nurse told him Glenn's manhood had been burned and if that was the case, Glenn would not want to live. Well, that was just not true. Not true. *Not* true. I told Smokey it wasn't, and he printed it anyway. Smokey also said Glenn was going to quit after the Charlotte race, and that's not true. He said he remembered Glenn telling him that, and I said, 'Smokey, it's not true.' But I couldn't get him to change either one of them. He just wouldn't do it."

I told Judy that Fred Lorenzen had told me that Glenn's death had a great deal to do with his leaving the sport prematurely.

"I think it did," she said. "I kept a diary during the time Glenn was in the hospital, and I wrote down the names of the people who called, and Freddie called every day. Every day. Freddie loved Glenn, and he was also making sure I was all right. And after Freddie got hurt [in a qualifying race before the Firecracker 400], he left the hospital and came to the funeral."

JUDY JUDGE
JUDY JUDGE COLLECTION

I asked Judy whether she ever had an opportunity to talk to Ned Jarrett.

"I have talked to him but not about this," she said. "I called him several years ago to ask him to tell Doris to stop telling people she was Glenn's widow.

"I feel for her, but Doris and Glenn were divorced. She was not his widow. She will *never* be a widow. I don't care for her very much, as you can well imagine, but I don't want to hurt her, and I don't want to hurt Pam, her daughter."

"I've got to think," I said, "that the year after July 2 had to be very hard."

"It was a time I don't like to think about," she said, "'cause I did not do very well at all. Glenn was my whole life, and I just . . . although his parents knew about us, and he had taken me over there and introduced me to them, they had been to our house, they were not very nice afterwards. Within two weeks after he died, I was forced to move out of the house. All our stuff was divvied up. It was very hard. Later his parents begged me to forgive them, and I did, but it's not something you get over. His sister tells me Doris was pulling all those strings.

"My father was furious with me. He was so angry, because he was an attorney, and he said legally I was Glenn's common-law wife and that I needed to sue for the estate. And I wouldn't do that.

"There was nothing common about Glenn and me, and I was an elementary school teacher, and I just couldn't afford to jeopardize my position. Everyone in Daytona knew about it, but I didn't want articles written and didn't want to have to fight. I just didn't think Glenn would have wanted me to do it, so I just didn't.

"I walked away. I figured if I did that, I could pretend Glenn was off racing some place and I could wait for him to come home. And that's what I did."

"You never remarried," I said.

"No," she said, "He is a pretty hard act to follow. So it was a very difficult time, *very* difficult, and leaving Daytona was very hard. It was a very small town, and my family was there, and I left everybody I knew. I was also drinking way, way, way too much, trying to make it through the day.

"I came up here to Atlanta in '65. My high school history teacher was a principal in DeKalb County, and I knew him, and I called him, and he was a family friend, and he got me a job here, and Atlanta was the closest big town that I could get to my sister if she needed me. I taught school for the next thirty-four years. But that year after Glenn died was a terrible, terrible time, an awful time.

"Glenn's sister and I are close friends, and Smokey's children and I are very close. They are too young to know or care about Glenn. Tricia was born after he died.

"Glenn should not be forgotten. He put NASCAR where it is today. He had polish. He did not make mistakes verb tense-wise. He never said, 'He don't.' But I'll tell you what, when we got up to Wilkesboro and he got around Banjo and Junior and that bunch, I would tease him because he would come back and he'd be saying 'tar' for tire and 'far' for fire. I'd say, 'That will sound good over the loudspeaker.'"

I asked Judy whether she ever attended any of the Hall of Fame ceremonies.

"Never," she said. "I haven't been to a race since then. One day I drove over to Talladega by myself on an off day and looked. I want to go to Darlington and look at that. I am close friends with Deb Williams. She wrote an article about me two years ago in the *Winston Cup Scene*. She has a copy of the divorce papers, and has a copy of the letters his sister and I have written to NASCAR from an attorney asking them to stop Doris. But I got no response from NASCAR. You would think they would want its history to be truthful. But Smokey said they don't know from history.

"Until now, I have never talked at length about what happened to me. Max [Muhleman] and I have talked over the years, and he's encouraged me. I just couldn't do it. And I don't know why. I don't know how Deb talked me into it, but it was like opening the floodgates. So many people said to me, 'You have done Glenn an injustice,' and that's the last thing I ever want to do. I never wanted to do anything that would be harmful to him in any way. I said, 'OK, I'm not going to ever deny us again, and for him I will see that the truth is out there.'"

CHAPTER 20

THE DAY THE MUSIC DIED

Fred Lorenzen

THE BEGINNING OF THE END OF FRED LORENZEN'S RACING CAREER CAME IN 1964, when two racing legends, Joe Weatherly and Fireball Roberts, were killed in separate crashes.

"Joe didn't believe in shoulder harnesses," said Lorenzen. "When they came out with them, he wouldn't wear them.

"We were at Riverside, and I said to him, 'Joe, you ought to wear that thing. If you ever roll over in the car and your head gets underneath the side window, it'll kill ya.'

"He said, 'When your number is up, it's up.'

"'Ya.' I said, 'but don't push it.'

"And then during the race we were going into turn six, and he slid into the rail with the left side of his car. Back then, we didn't have window nets and he didn't have his harness on, and his head came out the window, and the car went up on its side, and his head hit the guardrail, which was made out of concrete. And it killed him. It happened right in front of me, about ten car lengths. I saw the car go up. I saw a lot of it happen. I didn't find out he had died until after the race."

Lorenzen continued to win races, winning at Bristol over Fireball Roberts, beating Bobby Isaac at Atlanta, winning North Wilkesboro over Ned Jarrett despite a blown engine, and defeating Marvin Panch at Martinsville. He won his fifth straight at Darlington on May 9, when he outran Fireball Roberts for the victory. It was the highlight of his career.

"We were on a roll," said Lorenzen. "I loved Darlington. One turn was short and quick and turn three and four was a long circle. I would run right up against the fence with my quarter panel. It was my best long track."

After the Darlington race, John Holman fired Lorenzen's crew chief Herb Nab. Holman had wanted Nab to bring Lorenzen in to change tires. Some thought Holman did this so Fireball Roberts could get the win, because Lorenzen was Ralph Moody's guy, and Roberts was Holman's guy. When Nab refused and Lorenzen won, Holman fired Nab.

But two days later Nab was rehired. Ralph Moody made sure of it.

"I don't know why Holman wanted Nab to bring me in," said Lorenzen. "Herb and Holman didn't get along that good. I got him back. I was the driver, and I had a lot of say-so, and I thought Herb didn't make a mistake. We got him back. I considered Ralph Moody my boss. Sometimes Holman tried to be, but Moody was my boss."

Until Dale Earnhardt was killed on the last lap at the Daytona 500 in 2001, the darkest day in NASCAR history occurred on May 24, 1964, when Fireball Roberts was burned badly after a crash.

Roberts had seemed to be on the road to recovery in a Charlotte hospital when on July 2, 1964, suddenly he died. For Lorenzen, who was close to Roberts, his death hit particularly hard.

"I was going down the front stretch when that happened," said Lorenzen. "I saw trouble was coming, so I passed a whole group of cars. I slowed and went around them. There were five hundred and fifty miles to go. I got out of there.

"We didn't have radios then. My mechanics signaled on the board, 'Go around.' We were laying back. That's called pit strategy. A driver can't win by himself. He needs the minds of six or seven mechanics, and they all have to look for everything. The more minds working the better.

"It was a six-hundred-mile race, and after fifty miles these guys were all battling in front of me. I was on the front row for the race, and everyone was battling for the lead with only twenty laps gone—there were three hundred and eighty laps to go—and I thought, 'Geez.' There were three cars in the battle, Junior, Ned, and Fireball, all banging on each other coming off turn two.

"On the board Herb Nab wrote, 'T-H-I-N-K' so I just backed out of it and fell back. And then I was going down the backstretch, and that's when it happened. It was terrible.

"The caution came on, and there was a big wreck coming out of turn two. I came around, and Fireball was upside down and on fire.

"I knew it was pretty bad, but I didn't know it was *that* bad. I heard that a fireman came down with a water bottle, and the trigger didn't work.

"I went to the hospital the next day. I didn't get to see him. They wouldn't let me in. He was bad."

Roberts' crash occurred in late May, and by early July, just before the summer Daytona race all indications were that Roberts' recovery was coming along nicely.

"I talked to Judy on the phone, and she said he was doing better," said Lorenzen, "and the next day I was going to Daytona to qualify. I was still at the motel, and I went to the Volusia Cleaners to pick up my stuff at seven in the morning, and the lady said, 'How is Fireball doing?' I said, 'I talked to his family last night, and he's going to pull through.'

"And when I went to get into my car, the lady came running out of the cleaners, and she said, 'I just heard on the radio that Fireball passed away. Pneumonia.'

"He had died. It killed me. I went out to qualify, and some car spun out of turn four, and I just missed it, and I spun in the infield, and somebody ran into the side of me. I jumped out of my car, and I passed out. My hand was full of blood. It cut all the arteries on the top of my hand and pulled half my foot off, severed my ankle, ripped my ankle bone.

"I had surgery on the ankle and the hand—they put my foot back into the socket and sewed everything back up. I was there two days, and I got out of there to go to Fireball's funeral. They didn't want me to go. I just snuck out of the hospital. I don't remember anything about it. I was on crutches, and I was drugged. My foot was in a cast.

"Then I flew home. The doctor in Elmhurst took care of me. I took the cast off. Dr. Cronin looked at the foot. He said, 'It doesn't look bad.' A couple days later I went back to see him. He said, 'What are you limping for? Walk on that thing no matter how much it hurts. You're lucky you've got it. You shouldn't even be here. Use it. Exercise it.'

"He was a big guy, about six foot five, and he pushed me across the room. And it started working, and it's OK now.

"I returned to Holman Moody. Things had changed a little bit. Fireball's crew just went their own ways. I didn't keep track of everybody. I did my own thing. I didn't mingle with everybody. I kept track of Fred's car, Fred's crew, and that's it. That was all I cared about."

Despite his injuries, Lorenzen returned to race at Bristol on July 26. He didn't ask the doctors if he could. He just did it.

"I was beat up a little bit," said Lorenzen, "but if you want to race, you race, beat up or not."

In the Bristol race on July 26, 1964, Ned Jarrett relieved Lorenzen for laps 276 to lap 443.

"My hand was hurting. I had three severed tendons at the top of my hand. They had to be sewed back together. And I had broken three vertebrae in my back. But I got back in at the end. When you're sitting there watching, everything slowly gets better. You like to drive your own car. And I got back in and I won it."

Richard Petty was leading right to the end when his engine broke a half mile from the finish, giving Lorenzen his sixth win of that star-crossed 1964 season. It was the only lap Lorenzen led all day long.

Lorenzen sat out until September 4 at Darlington, and three weeks later won his seventh race of the season at Martinsville as 27-year-old Richard Petty won his first driving championship.

"We had it down pat," said Lorenzen.

At North Wilkesboro on October 11, Lorenzen finished second to Marvin Panch. Junior Johnson should have won, but he blew an engine with three laps to go. When Lorenzen had to put for fuel with 25 laps to go, Panch was the winner. Lorenzen wasn't happy about it.

"Nothin'," he said. "Second was nothin'. Either I won it, or we figured out why we didn't. We ran very strong at Wilkesboro, Martinsville, and Bristol. The short tracks were what I lived for, really."

After the 1964 season ended, Fred Lorenzen, reacting to the tragedies that occurred, told the press, "The speeds are just too fast. I'll never run another race unless they slow the speeds down."

"When Fireball died," said Lorenzen, "it changed a lot of things for me. I tried to blame everyone and everything. His death affected a lot of people.

"Sure it did. He was a god. He was my Santa Claus, my God, and when he died, it changed everything. And it almost ended my career. It shortened it, way down. Yup, because of what it did to me inside. It was just something. He was a very good friend, and when he died, it was like finding out Santa Claus didn't exist. It just killed Christmas. It killed racing for me."

CHAPTER 21

HE PERFECTS THE HEMI

Paul Goldsmith

BY THE EARLY 1960S, FORD WAS WEANING ITSELF FROM RACING, AND CHEVROLET continued to remain uninvolved. The one car manufacturer who was setting its sights on winning races was Chrysler.

After Pontiac dropped out of racing and his contract with GM was cancelled after the 1963 season, Paul Goldsmith and Nichels Engineering signed to do test work and to race a Plymouth for Chrysler. One of his most important jobs was to perfect the new, powerful Hemi engine.

"I did all the test work for Plymouth and the engines," said Goldsmith. "I had to make different blocks, the spindles. All the stuff came out of Nichels Engineering. Richard had started driving for his dad. He was in pretty good with Plymouth. All the engines and parts in his cars were built in Griffith, Indiana, just down the street here about a block."

In 1964, Goldsmith and Ray Nichels perfected the Hemi for Chrysler. It was powerful, and it proved to be a workhorse that could run all day.

"We proved the car at Goodyear Proving Grounds in San Antonio, Texas," said Goldsmith, "and it was very reliable after we ran it. They have a five-mile circle track, and we went out there and ran the car and checked the aerodynamics and to compare it we had a Junior Johnson–built Chevrolet, and Junior went with us in his Chevy, and when we hit Daytona that year the Ford people were in *deep* trouble."

Upon his return to Grand National racing in 1964, Goldsmith entered the Daytona 500 and sat on the pole.

"I should have won the darn race," said Goldsmith, "but hot dog wrappers coming down from the grandstand got into the grille, and the water temperature was getting quite high. I had to make one extra pit stop or I'd have blown the engine. That put me into third."

Richard Petty, the young son of Lee Petty, won the race, and Jimmy Pardue finished second. Petty, who also was driving a Plymouth, was one of the main beneficiaries of the work Goldsmith and Ray Nichels were doing for Chrysler racing.

"At the start of the season, Ford was still dabbling through Holman Moody, but I don't know how much help they were getting. Holman Moody was being squeezed."

On April 5, 1964, Goldsmith went to Atlanta for the Atlanta 500. He was leading early in the race when his right front tire exploded. Part of the reason: a bet he made with A. J. Foyt.

"You remember [car builder] Banjo Matthews? I qualified third, and Banjo came to me and said, 'I want to bet Foyt $100 that you will lead the first lap.'

"I said, 'You go ahead and bet him, and I will take another hundred.' I knew I was really running well, because I had gotten my car to handle well in practice the day before the race.

"We went down through the first corner, and I got past the second-place car, and on the back straight I passed Fred Lorenzen, and I came around leading, and Banjo held up the sign, '$$$$$.'

"The day was cold, and I didn't realize the tires were going to wear as much as they did. I was leaning on that front tire pretty hard, and after fifty-five laps, it blew, and the car went up and hit the guardrail and flipped upside down.

"Cars were coming at me, but I couldn't see them because of all the dirt. I was down in the infield but I thought I was outside the track."

Goldsmith wasn't hurt, but he didn't race again until May 9 at Darlington. Then on May 24 at Charlotte, Fireball Roberts was killed in a fiery crash.

"We were only a few laps into the race when the accident happened," said Goldsmith. "I was watching in my mirror, and I could see Fireball, and I could see Junior Johnson, and coming onto the backstretch they tangled, and then I went into the corner, and I didn't see Fireball hit the inside guardrail, but when I came around, his car was in such flames—it had exploded—I was on the outside of the track, and the heat from the car was pretty fierce, and we were on caution. After they removed the wreck, we took off again. Fireball was in intensive care, he was burned so bad. He was *really* burned."

After Goldsmith finished third in the Dixie 400 at Atlanta, he was hospitalized because of exhaust fumes. He ran 13 laps at Bridgehampton on July 12 and then did not race again until he entered the Southern 500 on September 7.

"I had to run at Darlington," said Goldsmith. "Curtis Turner and I bought stock in it. Bob Colvin sold us the stock. The best stock I ever bought in my life—Oh, yes. My throttle stuck and I hit the guardrail."

Ironically, after Paul Goldsmith helped perfect the Hemi engine for Plymouth, Bill France banned it for being too powerful. In response, Chrysler ordered its race teams to pull out of NASCAR. Goldsmith, who had a contract with Plymouth, was knocked out of Grand National racing in 1965, as was Richard Petty.

"[Richard] Petty went drag racing," said Goldsmith. "I was testing and building cars." He was also running the Griffith Airport he had bought in Highlands, Indiana. In addition to building cars, Goldsmith and Ray Nichels began building aircraft engines. Among his many customers, for years Goldsmith maintained Bill France's plane. Goldsmith also entered the Indy 500 five times.

"I got a third and a fifth, and the other times I didn't finish," said Goldsmith. "One time it was an accident, the other times the engines blew.

"Indy was more nerve wracking. The tires were not too good. We ran on Firestone tires, and they were like rocks, and there wasn't much traction. Several of the stock car drivers who came up to Indy to try it went home. A. J. Foyt was good here. He came out of midgets and sprint cars and made a pretty easy transition. Cale Yarborough, Bobby Allison, and Bobby Johns tried it, and they went home."

CHAPTER 22

IT WASN'T FUN ANYMORE

Fred Lorenzen

WITH THE OFFICIAL RETURN OF THE FACTORIES TO RACING, NASCAR HEAD BILL France was faced with a serious problem: Each car company began production of new, more powerful engines capable of great horsepower in its attempt to outrun the competition. At the same time, critics like Freddie Lorenzen were campaigning for slower speeds to prevent a repeat of the Fireball Roberts calamity.

France was getting a lot of pressure to do something, and in October 1964 he announced new rules: No engine could be bigger than 428 cubic inches, and hemispherical combustion chambers (Hemis) and hi-rise cylinder heads were banned.

Chrysler immediately announced its displeasure. On October 29, 1964, Chrysler said it was withdrawing from NASCAR. When rival USAC announced it would welcome the Hemi engines on all its tracks, Chrysler made a point to say it would run on any circuit that accepted its engines. Ford, on the contrary, made a point to say it would run exclusively in NASCAR.

Fred Lorenzen, driving for Holman Moody, the pride of Ford, prepared for 1965 as usual, not caring whether Chrysler competed or not. In the 1965 Daytona 500, Lorenzen led the last 15 laps before rain washed out the race after 133 of the scheduled 200 laps. Three hours after the race was called, Lorenzen was declared the winner.

"We planned everything," said Lorenzen. "If the race was going to go caution-free, we had it all planned out. If there was a caution, we had a strategy change. Before the race, Ralph Moody, Herb Nab, Wayne Mills, and I had it all planned."

After the race was over, driver Bobby Johns accused Lorenzen of using an oversized gas tank. Lorenzen scoffed at the charge.

"They said that," said Lorenzen, "but they checked my tank. The tank was all right. You're going to get accused of a lot of things when you're top dog and when you win races. It didn't faze us. Out attitude was, 'Check it if you want.'"

In April 1965, Lorenzen went to Martinsville and led the final 322 laps on his way to victory, and at the Charlotte World 600 he just did outrun Earl Balmer for his 10th superspeedway victory.

"My team was superior over everyone else," said Lorenzen. If you have a good team that clicks, you have no trouble."

But after the Charlotte win on May 23, 1965, Lorenzen went five months without a win. During this time ulcers began to bring him great pain.

Lorenzen finally won again on October 17 at Charlotte, outrunning his Holman Moody teammate Dick Hutcherson. During the race, driver Harold Kite was killed on the second lap. Lorenzen, Hutcherson, and Curtis Turner, whose life-time ban had been lifted by Bill France in July, all fought for the checkered flag.

"We went down the backstretch and came through three and four abreast," said Lorenzen. "I was working so good that I could get on the throttle real early. I did that, and I just got through the corner good, came off the corner strong. I was full throttle three-quarters of the way through the corner. I came off with more power, and I won."

In 1965, Lorenzen entered but 17 races, winning 4 and earning $80,000 in prize money. In 1966, he only entered 11 races, winning 2. The primary reason Lorenzen ran so few races in 1966 was a Ford boycott that began April 18, 1966. Bill France had put a weight limit on Ford's new OHC engine, and Ford pulled out of racing. I asked Lorenzen how he made a living if he couldn't race.

"I had money, endorsements," he said. "I had plenty of money saved up. I still do. All from auto racing. I don't work anymore."

"Did the inactivity bother you?"

"Nah," he said. "Didn't bother me."

"What did you do?"

"I'm an avid water-skier," he said. "I had a Chris-Craft with a big Ford in it, an eighteen-foot ski boat. Everyone wanted to race me with their little ski boats. Coming home from Charlotte one day, I met a boat builder from California. He said, 'Listen, I'll build you a boat.' He owned Howard Custom Marathon. I paid eight thousand dollars for the hull, and I put a seven thousand dollar Hemi in it with seven hundred and eighty horsepower. It had two 780 Hollys. Ray Nichels built the engine and put it in the boat.

"I hung out at Fox Lake, about fifteen miles west of Chicago. I could pull five skiers if I wanted to. I went one hundred.

"When the boycott was on, I spent weekends at home water-skiing. Everyone hung out on a big island called Blarney's Island. It had a beer and hamburger joint where you could buy half-pound hamburgers for a buck. That was my hangout. And we had a ski course. That's how I spent my days that summer."

On August 7, 1966, car owner Junior Johnson entered a Ford in the Atlanta 500. The car's roof line had been lowered. The front window was angled down. Said one reporter, "The car looked like a four-wheel vacuum cleaner."

"They called it 'the Banana' because he cut it in the middle and raised the deck up so it would act like a spoiler. It was a hell of a car," said Lorenzen.

"Junior is very intelligent. He didn't talk much. You didn't know what he was thinking, but when he wasn't talking, he was thinking. He was a *very* smart man.

"The car almost looked normal, but if you had a real sharp eye, no. Junior was big stuff. He was a big drawing card. He was a powerful man in the South, like Curtis Turner.

"And I was asked to drive his car. I don't know why."

Lorenzen was asked to drive because he was the top racer in the Ford stable.

Lorenzen qualified third and was knocked out of the race when he slid in oil and crashed in the wall halfway through the race. But the race was important because Ford was back in racing.

When the 1967 season began, Ford and Holman Moody were doing business as usual. But Lorenzen's heart was no longer in racing.

"I was losing interest," said Lorenzen. "I had won everything, and it just wasn't that much fun anymore, and all my buddies were getting killed. I just wasn't that into it, and when you're not into it, it makes a difference how you drive. You don't drive as hard.

"I might have been spooked because so many had died. It's something you go through in life. All of a sudden it hit me. I decided I was always gone every minute, and I just got tired. I got run down, worn out.

"I would talk to Ralph [Moody] about it. I wasn't sure what I was going to do. Ralph would say, 'Follow what you think.' He was like a father to me."

Lorenzen began the 1967 season winning the second of the twin 100-mile qualifiers at Daytona despite running out of gas just before the finish line.

"That was preplanned," said Lorenzen. "We pulled a 290 gear so it only turned sixty-two hundred, sixty-three hundred, but we could make a hundred miles on fuel. By drafting, I would be sucked along. We weren't using much fuel, so I was able to make the hundred miles on one tank of gas. Everyone else had to stop with ten laps to go. I didn't have to.

"When they stopped, I picked up a lap lead, and when they came back out I was a lot slower—about four miles an hour slower, because I couldn't run as fast by myself—but they couldn't catch me in time for the finish. I won that hundred-miler with *no* pit stops. None. If there would have been a caution, I would have been screwed. That's why Bill France changed the qualifiers to one hundred and twenty-five miles the next year."

It was Lorenzen's last victory on the Grand National circuit. In the Daytona 500, Lorenzen finished second to Holman Moody teammate Mario Andretti. They were the only cars to finish on the lead lap.

Lorenzen entered the Atlanta 500 on April 2, 1967. He qualified third, but after A. J. Foyt blew an engine, oil spilled all over the track, and Lorenzen slid and hit the wall. Three weeks later, on April 24, Lorenzen shocked the racing world by announcing he was retiring from racing.

"Everything got to be too much," said Lorenzen. I decided to hang it up, to forget it. It wasn't fun anymore, and when something isn't fun anymore, you don't do it.

"I just had it. I got what they call 'burned out.' I got sick of traveling and living in motels. I had won everything that was down there, and there was nothing else to achieve, so the interest wasn't there anymore."

Jacques Passino, who ran Ford's racing division, said, "No man since Barney Oldfield has contributed more to the performance image of Ford products than Fred Lorenzen. Over the years, Freddie has shown himself to be a serious dedicated professional who chooses his races carefully, leaves nothing to chance, and gives an all-out effort each time."

Fred Lorenzen was thirty-two years old.

CHAPTER 23

HANGING THEM UP

Paul Goldsmith

AFTER SITTING OUT THE 1965 SEASON BECAUSE OF BILL FRANCE'S BAN OF THE
Hemi engine, Paul Goldsmith and Plymouth returned to racing in 1966 when
France cried uncle and relented. Plymouth wanted Goldsmith to run at
Riverside, California, in the second NASCAR race of the season.

"USAC had approved of us to go out there," said Goldsmith. "The race
was under NASCAR sanction, and the day before we were to qualify, USAC
changed their mind and said we couldn't run. I ran anyway [He finished third
to Dan Gurney and David Pearson.], and USAC banned me from running in
the Indy 500. So I sued USAC and joined the Sports Car Club of America, and
I moved to Mexico for a while."

Goldsmith proved he hadn't lost his touch when he won the first of the
twin 100-milers at Daytona, and in the second race ever held at
Rockingham, Goldsmith outran Cale Yarborough for the win despite having
to make 10 pit stops.

"I won the race in five hours and thirty-two minutes," said Goldsmith.

Goldsmith outran Cale Yarborough for the win at Rockingham in 1966.

"Cale was known to have the fastest pit crew going," said Goldsmith. "We
didn't practice. He practiced. They had fuel cans, and I found out later they
built a little swirl into the big can, and it would drop the fuel in quicker by
swirling, like water going down a drain. If you get it to turning, it's going to
drain quicker.

"Every time we made a pit stop, Cale would be out in front of me, and then I'd get by him again. The last pit stop he was out in front of me again, and I finally was able to get back by him. But he had been in front of me because of his pit stops."

Goldsmith finished one car length behind David Pearson at Columbia, South Carolina, and at Martinsville on April 24, 1966, Goldsmith took the checkered flag, but Bill Ellis, the crew chief for Jim Paschal, demanded the scoring cards be rechecked, and Paschal was declared the winner.

"Don't forget the scoring system was different in them years," said Goldsmith, "and I was from up north. I wouldn't swear to that, but that's how he won the race."

"They figured out a way to take it away from you?" I asked.

"Oh yes," he said. "After that I made sure I had my own scorer. And that never happened again."

On April 30, 1966, Goldsmith finished second to Richard Petty at Darlington. His fondest memories, though, were of his playful young son.

"My son was six, and before the race he had a water hose, and he was hosing down everyone in the infield of the grandstand, and they got pissed off.

"I remember pulling into the pits, and another driver had shut the engine off and coasted right in front of me, and he hosed him down as well. I guess everybody knew my son after that."

The bad publicity brought by the car companies pulling out of racing hurt attendance badly. Ford had announced in April 1966 it was getting out of racing, and Fred Lorenzen, Dick Hutcherson, Marvin Panch, and Ned Jarrett, who were in the Ford stable, were out of action. The fans seemed to be losing interest as attendance at that April Darlington race was a scant 7,000, plus 5,000 Boy Scouts who got in for free.

"What were the Ford drivers supposed to do?" I asked Goldsmith.

"They had to go home and do something else," he said. "It was awfully frustrating for a race driver at that time."

At Bristol in late July, Goldsmith won his third race of the 1966 season when he ran down Jim Paschal and beat Richard Petty and David Pearson for the win. Paschal had had a three-lap lead.

"My car was outhandling everybody," Goldsmith said.

Though few came to the April Darlington race, it was different in September. Sixty-five thousand attended the Southern 500. On the day of the race, Goldsmith couldn't drive his car to the track because of the crush of fans. He had to park it, get out, and walk three miles.

"I couldn't get there because there was so much traffic," said Goldsmith. "They were waiting to buy tickets. I pulled over and parked my car, and I just started running for the track.

"I missed the drivers' meeting. NASCAR had made a ruling that you couldn't pass anybody up to the first corner—the starting line was near the corner, and I didn't know that because I missed the meeting, and when the race started I passed some cars before I was supposed to. They stopped me and set me back a lap, and later I hit the wall, and I fell back a couple more laps." He would finish 16th.

In all, Paul Goldsmith finished fifth in the points standings.

"I never ran for the points," he said.

Plymouth and Dodge dominated early in the 1967 season, but then Ford started winning, and in April Chrysler protested the new rules for Ford, and when NASCAR refused to alter them, in April it pulled out, leaving Petty and Goldsmith on their own again. This time, though, the Chrysler race teams refused to stop racing, as they had in 1965 during the first Chrysler boycott. Petty won 27 races in 1967, including an incredible 10 in a row during a two-month streak.

"Yeah, but what competition did he have?" asked Goldsmith.

With Chrysler no longer supporting his team, Goldsmith and Ray Nichels knew they had to find an alternative means of financing if they wanted to continue Grand National racing. Goldsmith thought if he could get a company to put its name on the car, it would pay him the money he needed to race. Before the 1968 season, it was announced that Frosty Morn Meats and Valleydale Packers would sponsor their race team.

"Frosty Morn/Valleydale Meats are two divisions of the same company," said Goldsmith. "They have the same owner. I went and talked to Frosty Morn over in North Carolina," said Goldsmith, "and then I met with them again at Bristol. They flew up here [Highlands, Indiana] and looked at the shop and sponsored the race car.

"They paid for building the car and transportation of the crew. The year before I had gone to New York and talked to Wrangler Jeans. A week before they had hired Lee Trevino, the golfer, or they would have done it. They had a year or two contract with Trevino, so I walked away from that and went to Valley Meats.

"After they hired Lee Trevino, all his jeans were left on the shelf. They then went and sponsored Dale Earnhardt. They didn't realize how big NASCAR was. But I was the one who opened their eyes.

"The money from Frosty Morn/Valleydale Meats was enough to keep us running in '68, but it was nothing like what it is today.

"Frosty Morn Meats was a sponsor for many years, and then they took their name off the cars and started sponsoring races."

In 1968, Goldsmith had one second-place finish in 15 races. His near-win came at Charlotte, when he was outrun by Charlie Glotzbach.

"Know why? The bad things I remember. I was leading the race, and I had to make a pit stop, and they jacked the car up on the right side, changed the tires, came around to the other side, jacked the car up, and the jack fell down on the tires, and we had an awful time getting another jack to get it back up. That cost me the race."

Goldsmith's final season was 1969. In 11 races, he earned three thirds and a fourth. But he had responsibilities back at the shop in Indiana, and he also had an airport to run, and the dual responsibilities became too much, and he retired.

"I was tired," he said.

Paul Goldsmith quit racing in the latter part of 1969, but he continued in the sport for one more year testing tires for Goodyear. It was during this time that Goldsmith devised one of the most important and controversial innovations in the sport: restrictor plates.

"We were testing tires for Goodyear at Talladega," said Goldsmith. "Goodyear was the only tire company. Firestone had gone. We could run about twelve laps, and the tires would start coming apart.

"We were running at around the two-hundred-mile-an-hour mark in a forty-two hundred-pound car. Goodyear said, 'We're not coming to the race. We quit.'

"I called Bill France, and in a few hours he was there. He said, 'What can we do?'

"'We need to drop a hundred horsepower out of these engines.' I said.

"So Ray Nichels and I came back up here to Highlands, Indiana, and we worked on restrictor plates. You put a plate under the carburetor, making it smaller and smaller, and pretty soon a hundred horsepower is gone.

"We flew back down to Talladega, put it on the car, and we then could run the full distance on a set of tires.

"France said, 'OK, everybody has to have restrictor plates.' The tests occurred in 1970 at Talladega. Beginning with the 1970 Yankee 400 at Michigan International Speedway, restrictor plates became a part of NASCAR racing.

"It was the first restrictor plates ever used. Now I don't want the racers bothering me because Ray Nichels and I did that! The only people who know about that are Goodyear and Bill France, and he's gone. But that was the start of restrictor plates.

"The tires weren't safe. Goodyear was going away. They couldn't keep the tires on the car.

"After I left racing, I then devoted all my time to this airport. I am also involved in nine Burger Kings, and I did one other thing: I owned one hundred and fifty harness race horses. We breed horses. We've had three or four world champions."

I asked Goldsmith whether he ever drove in a horse race.

"I got my license to drive a harness horse," he said. "I drove two races, and that was enough of that."

CHAPTER 24

CALLING IT QUITS

Ray Fox

IT WAS BAD ENOUGH IN 1963 WHEN GENERAL MOTORS ANNOUNCED IT WAS getting out of racing. Ray Fox lost all factory support, so he switched to Chrysler, which had built a powerful Hemi engine so it could compete with Holman Moody's Fords. But Bill France felt that the Hemi gave Chrysler too much of an advantage, and as a result he outlawed the Hemi engine for the 1965 season. When he did that, Chrysler dropped out of NASCAR, leaving the Pettys, Fox, and the other Chrysler teams high and dry.

"I thought it was nuts," said Fox. "But let me tell you what happened: Bill France decided to run less cylinders, so I flew out to California to have some pistons made. I was putting some sleeves in the engines to run with less piston size. I brought the pistons back to my shop, and in the meantime NASCAR changed the rules again and went another route. So I got teed off, and I decided I was through with NASCAR.

Fox ran in only seven NASCAR races after that, and devoted much of his time to other pursuits.

"I decided to do something on my own, to build a car that would set the world speed record on a closed track. I went to see Bill, and he didn't even want to talk to me. France said he didn't want to mess with it at all. 'Cause he thought he'd have to advertise it, and he didn't want to have to do that, because I was running a Chrysler.

LEEROY YARBROUGH

He and Fox set a world speed record.

INTERNATIONAL

MOTORSPORTS HALL OF FAME

"I built it anyway, had somebody come from Cuba to build the scoop on the hood, and he did a good job on it, and we put it together, and we broke the track record. We did it right here in Daytona. LeeRoy Yarbrough was the driver.

"Back in them days we had tires about ten inches wide, and as LeeRoy went down the backstretch at about two hundred and forty miles an hour, he would spin the rear wheels as he would get on the gas, and it would smoke. The spotters thought he blew an engine. So they put the red light on him as he got into turn three, and LeeRoy got off the gas and coasted all the way to the start/finish line, and even then he ran one hundred and eighty-one miles an hour, or he would have run over two hundred. Not too many people know that.

"I couldn't run again. France didn't want me to do it in the first place 'cause Dodge was involved, and he didn't want anything to do with Dodge, 'cause Dodge had pulled out.

"But the next day, France called me into his office and gave me a trophy. I was surprised, but he couldn't do nothing about it because the papers had already written about it.

"Then I was asked to run a couple Chevrolets at Charlotte. Dodge was out and Ford was upset, so the powers that be wanted to run Chevrolets.

"I bought a car myself and set it up. Two or three others also set up Chevrolets. They wanted to get Chevrolet back in because Dodge was out. France wanted individual car dealers to get involved, but there was no money in that, really. But I bought a car, and LeeRoy drove it, and we didn't do any good."

Even though his car had been requested by the powers that be, before the Charlotte race NASCAR officials refused to pass the car, saying it didn't meet the ground clearance requirements.

"Good god, yes," said Fox. "They said you had to have four inches of ground clearance, and I didn't have that much, and in order for me to bring it back up, the whole front end would be out. That was supposed to make it run a little faster.

"But then we got into an argument over it. There was a reason it was that way. Others were that way too. I didn't think it was fair to single me out, to jump all over me. Of course, I was a little bit talkative with what was going on. I was upset and a little bit mouthy. I almost quit, but I didn't. They did let me drop some of it."

Even though the car didn't quite meet NASCAR's requirements, Richard Howard, head of the Charlotte Motor Speedway, let Fox start his car at the back of the field. LeeRoy finished 14th after blowing an engine.

"Not bad considering we had to start at the rear," said Fox.

Fox and LeeRoy went to Atlanta on June 13, where the car led early. On the 112th lap, the engine blew.

"We were in a Chevrolet. I didn't like the Chevrolet anyway. But later I did like it."

Fox went to Daytona with two cars, driven by LeeRoy Yarbrough and Bunkie Blackburn. Neither car made more than 20 laps. At the end of the season, France was forced to backtrack, to allow the Hemi back into racing.

"That's the way NASCAR was," said Fox. "Not that I need to knock NASCAR, but there were things going on, arguing between the car companies and NASCAR and vice versa that was just bad for people who owned race cars."

One of the decisions Bill France made with an eye toward reviving interest in the sport was to reinstate Curtis Turner after a four-year ban for his union activities.

"Curtis was a good driver," said Fox, "brave as hell. He was a nice fellow. He was wild. He would just land his plane in a place like this. I flew with him quite a few times. He wouldn't say nothing. He'd just pick a highway and land. He was crazy. But he *was* a good driver."

In 1966, it was Ford's turn to drop out of NASCAR. Ray Fox went to Daytona with a Dodge driven by Earl Balmer, who won the first of the two 100-mile prelims.

"Earl was someone I knew," said Fox. "I don't know. I was good for any driver."

Balmer, who was from Indiana, had a six-year, part-time career in NASCAR. He won a race in 1966, but then dropped out of sight after 1968 after just 32 races. To replace him, Fox chose Buddy Baker, the son of Buck Baker. Buddy had begun his career in 1959, but he didn't win a race until 1967 under Ray Fox. But Buddy had potential. In August 1966, he finished second to Richard Petty in the Dixie 400 at Atlanta. In that race, Fred Lorenzen, driving for Junior Johnson, raced a funny-looking Ford everyone called "the yellow banana." It wasn't regulation size, but it was an opportunity for Ford to get back into racing, so no one complained too much. Ray Fox certainly didn't.

"I had no reason to complain," said Fox. "What cars I had ran good with Buddy."

With Buddy Baker behind the wheel, Fox's car led the World 600 in 1966, when on lap 51 he blew an engine.

"Buddy was a good driver, but he was overanxious," said Fox. "As he went out of the pits after pitting the car, he would turn so many rpms that it wouldn't take long before a valve spring would break or something else and he'd blow the engine. I just had to get on him every time for the rpms and tell him what it was doing to the engine. We got along good, but I had to get on him *all* the time. When you finally got him settled down, he would win."

Buddy did finally win a race, the National 500 in October. But it would be the only race Buddy and Fox would win in 1967, a year in which Richard Petty became the King, setting a new NASCAR record with 27 first-place finishes.

"He found something that made him run faster," said Fox. "I never found out what it was. You never butted into what Richard was doing. But he had found something that gave him more horsepower.

"Lee was very secretive, but then again, he might have gotten away with something," said Fox. "That year, Richard won ten races in a row."

From August 12, 1967, through October 1, 1967, Richard won at Bowman Gray, the Columbia Speedway, the Savannah Speedway, Darlington, Hickory, Richmond, Beltsville, the Orange Speedway, Martinsville, and North Wilkesboro.

"Buddy and myself stopped his streak with the one we won," said Fox.

It was Buddy Baker's first win after 215 Grand National races.

"I was always happy any time my car won," said Fox. "And Buddy was overly happy when he won a race. He just hugged everybody. Buddy was a good boy."

In 1968, Ray Fox once again had full factory backing. Dodge was paying Fox $80,000 a year again. That year, Cale Yarborough, Richard Petty, and David Pearson won most of the races. In the Charlotte World 600 on May 26, Cale led, then blew a tire, and then Little Bud Moore led, before spinning out. With Buddy Baker in the lead, rain began to fall. NASCAR ran the rest of the race under caution to get it in. Fox and Baker won a purse of $27,780.

"That day I made him stay out on the racetrack," said Fox. "The rest of them pitted, and I made him stay out there, and he ended up winning on a caution. He won it on my thinking everyone else pitted."

In the next race, Baker finished second to Richard Petty. At Islip, Long Island, Buddy sat on the pole, led the first 95 laps, and finished third to Bobby Allison. After the race, Allison was assaulted by Petty crewmen Maurice Petty and Dale Inman.

"It was nothing, really," said Fox. "Back in them days if someone stopped someone from winning a race, or if they thought they were going to win it and you stopped them, you got in trouble. But that was good, good, good for the press. They really hung onto a story like that."

In 1968, Buddy Baker had his one win at Charlotte and sixteen top-five finishes. Buddy ran third at Oxford; second at Fonda; fourth at Maryville, Tennessee; and then on August 24 at the Langley Field Speedway in Hampton, Virginia, he went 166 laps and parked his car.

"It was a bad racetrack," said Fox. "Mud. It was terrible. I probably stopped him. It was awful. You would stand on the track, and you'd go up, because the mud was moving you up, and it was doing the same thing to the cars. It was very dangerous."

Baker finished third at Darlington to Cale Yarborough and David Pearson, running the final 100 miles with no brakes.

"He probably had gotten the brakes hot, and they gave out," said Fox.

Baker was fifth at Hickory, third at Richmond, and then he blew an engine at Martinsville, blew an engine at Wilkesboro, crashed at Charlotte, didn't finish at Rockingham, and that was the season for the Fox-Baker team. Ray Fox couldn't take Baker's lack of patience any longer, and he cut back his racing efforts as a result.

"I just got sick of it all," said Fox. "Buddy was so bad about going out of the pits. He went out too fast, and the valve springs would break. I kept getting on him about that all the time. I had a tachometer. I was the only one who had the key to it. When he would come in, it would say eighty-five hundred. You couldn't do that back in them days. Crankshaft, connecting rods, valve springs . . . I would let him see that, and then I'd turn it off and forget about it.

"I don't know why he was so stubborn. Some people are like that. Some race drivers are like that. I had to get on him all the time about it. And I had had it.

"In '69, Buddy and I weren't getting along at all, because he was screwing up all the time, blowing engines when he shouldn't have. That's what it was all about. I quit Chrysler in '70, and I moved to Daytona from Charlotte."

CHAPTER 25

THE END OF THE PARTY

Curtis Ross Turner

IN THE RACING COMMUNITY, CURTIS TURNER WAS KNOWN FOR HIS PARTIES AND the beautiful women who were always on his arm. But Turner's lifestyle had its costs: But Turner's lifestyle had its costs: During the last few years of his first marriage, his wife, Lillie was sometimes hospitalized from the strain, and his four young children were in the care of servants. His oldest, Ross, continually woke up to female strangers offering to fix the children breakfast and take care of them.

But when the fast-living Turner was killed in a plane crash in October 1970, his 15-year-old boy's world was turned upside down. It would not be long before the dazed youngster would find himself penniless and living alone in an orphanage. Thirty years later, Curtis Ross Turner is still trying to grapple with the mystery of how life could have gone so wrong so quickly for him and his family.

"When Dad was reinstated by NASCAR in '65 we were living in Roanoke and Charlotte on the weekends, and Dad and Mom were not getting along," said Turner. "The house in Roanoke is a long house, a one-floor ranch. The easiest entrance into the house was from Dad's office, where he kept all of his trophies, over a hundred of them. I once counted them one night. Mom and I came back from a trip in town, and Dad was in his chair at his desk, and on the arm of the chair was a beauty queen. I remember saying, 'Hey Dad,' and I waved at the woman, and Mom was with us, and I remember her just walking right past her completely silent. She had *no* reaction. I don't know whether she didn't want to blow up in front of the kids or where she just suppressed it.

"But around this same time, Mom became ill. Mom started taking long drives and not telling anyone. One time she bought a brand-new Dodge Charger—it had that real big sloping back end. She went down to the car dealer and signed Dad's name, drove off and was gone for two or three days. We didn't know where she was. We would find her in West Virginia, find her in Maryland. One time she called from a phone booth 200 miles from Roanoke in a very distraught state. We didn't know this was the beginning of schizophrenia. Periodically, she would have to go to a home to get some rest, and we would be raised by Odelia and her husband, Allan.

"And while she was gone, Dad found his solace in other women. I would like to think he did that because of her illness. I'm an idealist, always have been. But I do think their relationship had been stale for years. Dad was very handsome, and women would throw themselves at him a lot, and he was a red-blooded man. He had the look of a movie star. For years, I'd see James Garner on the TV, and I always thought James Garner looked like my dad.

"While Mom was away, we had a number of caretakers. Dad lived the life of a bachelor. From '66 to '69 we lived in Charlotte on Freedom Drive, which was the house that was photographed in *Playboy* magazine. Dad commissioned an artist to paint a big mural behind the bar with a black light going across it. It was a cartoon version of Dad and several very buxom women. When you turned the black light on, the women's clothes came off. Of course, my guy friends loved that room. 'Can we turn it on one more time?' 'Well, sure.' And Dad had a jukebox in the room with all those cornball country songs on it, Hank Williams and all those guys, and I remember he also had Aretha Franklin's "Respect" on it. Aretha was new at the time, but Dad really liked her music.

"Dad was still married to Mom, but Mom was 'away,' and there were a lot of women. Sometimes Dad would meet them at the racetrack, bring them home, and they'd stay at our house for one night, two nights, and then Dad and the woman would fly back, and he'd drop her off, and so many of them would try to buddy-up to me like, 'We have a future.' I'd look at them and think, 'You are so naive.' I knew better.

"I remember a lot of them would get up in the morning and try to make me breakfast. I'd look at them like, 'Where do you think this is?' One of them, the only redhead I remember—she had huge red hair—seemed to not even know how to make breakfast.

"During this time, Dad got engaged to his secretary, Audrey Meyers. I remember Dad coming into the living room and asking me, 'Ross, I am going to ask Audrey to marry me. Is that OK?' I said, 'I like Audrey. She's nice. What about Mom?' They were still married. And he politicked an answer on me. I was twelve years old. I thought, 'Mom *and* Audrey, sure, I'll take both.' It may have been amoral, but to me it was so common it didn't feel amoral. It was just the way things were.

"Dad and Audrey were supposed to get married. They were a week away from the wedding. I remember she took me to get her dry cleaning. I remember her saying, 'Ross, I really love your father, but I can't do this. I can't marry your dad.' I remember thinking how strange that was. I was only thirteen. She made it sound like there was something wrong with doing it. I really don't know what happened. They were nearly married before she bolted.

"Bunny Vance came after Audrey. I first met Bunny when she was twenty. Dad had brought her home several times, and exactly a week before Christmas of '68 Dad and Mom got divorced, and in January of '69 Dad and Bunny were married. During the summer of '69 I lived with Dad and Bunny, and I have to say that for whatever may have been wrong with it all, Dad was very loyal to Bunny. He called her every night. I really think he played it straight the last part of his life. I remember him saying to me, 'I have to call Bunny every night.' At seven o'clock, I believe. I thought, 'That's kind of nice.' I was impressed by that relationship, and I'll bet you Bunny taught him that.

"Bunny came from a neat family. I thought the world of her mom, a very common-sense, warm-hearted lady, very protective of her daughter. And Bunny must have brought some of those values into their relationship.

"That summer I felt I got to know my dad better than at any other time of my life, and I also got to know Bunny very well. We played gin rummy all the time on the sofa in the living room, and we could talk about anything. I really enjoyed my times with Bunny, and I'm really glad for that last summer. That was very redeeming for me in that I was old enough to know I was with my dad, and he was cool, and I was cool, and he was married to this lady, and I was part of their life.

"Meanwhile, Dad bought Mom a little house across town, a pukey little place, no air-conditioning, hot as hell, and he gave her a '66 pukey-green Impala Chevrolet, and he was paying her two hundred dollars a week child support. My mom is one of the people in my life who I am most proud of. It didn't matter what happened to Mom, she was going to start over, and she started over and over and over so many times when other people would have just stopped. My mom is a beautiful, beautiful lady. She was a very attractive younger woman and had that very elegant Virginia aristocratic kind of air about her in the Jane Seymour way. She is very down-to-earth but elegant nonetheless. My mom is a very intelligent woman. To this day, I'm still impressed by her intelligence and her overall ability to try to think rationally in a life that was very irrational.

"After their divorce, life was manageable. I was planning on going to Yale to become a lawyer or an architect. Things were going along OK. Dad had become extremely close to Clarence King, the local golf pro, and Dad and Bunny and Clarence and his wife, Martha, became inseparable friends. My mom was learning to eke out an existence with the child support she got, and she got a job at a paint store, so she had reentered the work force. Life, nevertheless, took on a divorce tone. I mean, I was in the bungalow with the mom and the kids while Dad and the new wife played in the big house."

Then on October 4, 1970, Curtis Turner and Clarence King took off in his plane, and somewhere in the wilds of Pennsylvania, it crashed, killing the two men.

"It was a Sunday," remembered Ross Turner. "I had gone to bed about nine o'clock, and I had just drifted off to sleep. I was dreaming—this is spooky, but it's the truth—I dreamed that I wondered what it was like to go down in a plane crash. I remember seeing a plane crash in my dream.

"About an hour later, about eleven o'clock at night, there was a knock on the door. I answered it. I remember Mom was sitting in the chair drinking Drambuie and smoking Salem Menthols. I opened the door and looked through the screen at my sister Sue, and I could tell she was very distraught. I could see it in her face, and the first words out of my mouth were, 'Is it Dad?' And she said, 'Yeah.' I said, 'What?' She said, 'He went down in his plane this afternoon in Pennsylvania. And he didn't make it.'

"I remember my mom sitting in the chair, again emotionless. I was overwhelmed with grief. I ran from the woman sitting there seeming not to respond. Of course, I was fifteen and I didn't know what she was feeling, but she was obviously not responding. I pushed the door open, and I ran down the street screaming and yelling. I ran down to a friend's house, and I wailed there until three in the morning. To this day, it is the most traumatic thing that ever happened to me. I'm forty-four, and nothing changed my life more than that did.

"Before he died, I felt Dad was living on borrowed time. The summer before he died, we were driving around, and I asked him, 'Dad, when do you think you'll have enough?' Because he always seemed to be working so hard. I remember him looking at me and saying, 'I don't know.' And I thought that it's not good for a person not to know when they've had enough. I was a young kid who had a lot of discernment, and knew he lived a sensational life, and when he died I knew that the life I had was suddenly and inalterably and completely over. I admitted to myself, Bunny and mom are not going to take care of us. And Dad didn't leave a will, and his estate was a mess. My older sister was named the executrix of the will, but any money that was there went to Bunny and her as-yet-unborn child, and we got nothing. We didn't even get grocery money. And by the end of October we were out of money and out of food.

"I was fifteen, and I remembered some of the people I had been with that summer with my dad, and I decided to call them for help. I remember calling a lawyer friend of Dad's who was from Kentucky, and I said, 'We are hungry and broke, and I need somebody to do something.' And he sent me a check for one hundred dollars, and I went to the bank and opened up a savings account.

"I didn't tell my mom about it, because I could tell my mom was starting to not feel well, I decided to bank the money and try to make it last as long as I could. Every day I would walk the forty-five minutes to the bank and take ten or twenty dollars.

"After about ten days, I got a call from the bank. The check I had deposited had bounced. They said to me, 'Mr. Turner, the check you opened your account with is a phony. The name on it is fictitious. No one has ever heard of that person.' I didn't know. And at that point I couldn't get anymore money out.

"Mom got sicker and sicker and decided to move to Jacksonville, Florida. In November of '70, she took my younger sister, Priscilla, and my younger brother, Tyler, with her. I wouldn't go. I told Mom, 'I realize I'm only fifteen, but Dad's gone and my whole life is different, and I don't want to go to Florida.' She let me stay with her brother and his wife in Roanoke.

"In January, Priscilla called me. She said, 'Ross, we're starving. And Mom is not well.' She had become delusional. One time she was found wandering among moving cars. I got on a bus and went to Florida.

"I ate about once every three days. I did contact one of our relatives, who sent me five dollars. My dad had financed his new business. But for some reason our family has the philosophy, 'You've got to stand on your own two feet.' So we were stuck. There was no one taking care of us, though I just couldn't accept the fact that there was no one looking out for us. I was Curtis Turner's son, and we were going to make it. And badly, we did.

"It was so bad that on a couple of occasions my younger sister and I actually stole bread and milk from a convenience store just to bring something into the house. I learned to eat spaghetti with butter. And I can tell you that I lost all the weight I had gained as a child. I thought to myself, 'This is no way to live.'

"In Jacksonville I attended a horrible school. The year before, students had hung a teacher out the window by her neck.

"I decided to run way back to Virginia in the hopes that Mom would follow me back there, and she did. When she came back to Virginia, she was placed in an institution, where she received treatment for her illness.

"I went to live with my favorite great aunt on my mother's side who baked me chocolate chip cookies. She was a widow, and living with her allowed me to keep going to my junior high school, but she was up in years, and it wasn't long before she decided she couldn't support me any longer.

"At this point, the state of Virginia took custody over my younger brother and sister and myself. We were wards of the state from '70 through '72. The state sent my brother and sister to live with my mother's relatives in Florida. I wound up going to live in the Salem Baptist Children's Home in Roanoke.

"The home was thirty miles from my school, in a different town, but I was determined to continue attending my same school. I got on a city bus and I went to the school board, a fifteen-year-old kid, and I said, 'I'm a ward of the state, my dad was Curtis Turner, my life is upside down, and I don't want to change schools.' And I was able to get permission, and I went on and graduated from that school.

"It was very weird living in the orphanage. I bowled every Saturday, and I asked one of my bowling buddies, 'Please let me come and live with you.' These people loved me and opened their house to me, but they had very meager means, so I asked the state to take me from there.

"I was put in a 'shelter home,' which is a place where kids go after Mom and Dad just shot each other. It was a holding tank in a private home. If you're there for more than sixty days, you automatically go into the foster care system, and once you're in foster care, you no longer have rights as a child.

"I was there fifty-nine days. There were as many as twenty kids in this big house, and my Mom got out of the hospital just in time to take me back. My mom got a room at a Holiday Inn in Salem, and I lived with her and kept going to the same high school, and from there we rented a little apartment on Williamson Road in Roanoke. It had no kitchen, and we ate in a crummy little restaurant.

"Mom got a job with TAP—Total Action Against Poverty—and she learned how to be a secretary. I showed her how to ride the city bus. I worked with her doctors to help acclimate her back into society.

"At this point, I was seventeen. I had had a very long life up until then. From the Holiday Inn we moved to another small apartment down the road, when my brother and sister came back from Florida unannounced. They were just dumped off at our house. I hadn't seen them in a couple of years.

"Through a government program for the poverty stricken, Mom was able to get what was then called a 235 grant, enabling her to get a brand-new town-house in a government project. Mom still lives there today. She is doing well, and I'm so proud of her.

"When I was seventeen, just before my last year of high school, I received Christ into my life. I was in high school, and that was the perfect relationship for me, because He wouldn't die, He wouldn't divorce my mother, He was always going to be there, and He promised He would be not only my friend but my father. It was the perfect relationship. From that point, I began living for the Lord, and my life changed a lot.

"I went to a little Bible college in West Virginia, and then I went to Liberty College, Jerry Falwell's school, and all this time the one thing I kept going for myself was my voice. I had made the all-state and all-regional choir, and as a high schooler I was a sought-after soloist. When I went to Liberty, I made recordings, and I toured all over the country and went to Australia and New Zealand. Today, I sing with the North Carolina Symphony and also sing with a Manhattan Transfer–type group.

"I don't think I realized how abandoned I was until I needed to be a man and realized how incredibly stupid I was. I just didn't know anything. I knew about women. I knew about drinking and Camel cigarettes. But I never held a tool. I had never been fishing. When Dad was around, that was OK. But when I got older, I just felt like, 'Man, I can't do anything.' Except sing. Fortunately, that opened doors for me my whole life.

"After I graduated from Liberty in 1980, I went into the ministry. Over the years I have had churches with several thousand members. I am currently planning to start a new church in Raleigh, where I live. I live on a golf course, and I'm very thankful for the life I have.

"For years, I wondered about what had happened on the day Dad's plane crashed. The FAA put the plane back together, which is what they do. They felt everything was in working order. Around the time he crashed I can remember Dad saying something about the magneto, saying he thought he had to get it fixed. But he wasn't afraid to fly the plane.

"There was some talk that Clarence was at the controls when the plane crashed, which didn't make any sense because Clarence had never flown a plane in his life. There was talk the plane was on automatic pilot, and Dad was asleep in the back. We don't know that. I do know Dad's alcohol content in his blood was pretty high, but we Turners can hold our liquor. I don't know he was too drunk to fly. It's hard to say really. The FAA had no conclusions except to say, 'Pilot error.' They had to say that because the plane seemed to be in working order.

"The one thing I feared was that there had been a fire before the plane went down.

"I lived in Hawaii from '80 to '85, and right before I left I went to visit the Pearl Harbor Memorial. I was there with all these old navy guys, American Legionnaires who were having a convention. I asked this one older gentleman where he was from. 'Punxsutawney, Pennsylvania,' he said. That's the town where my dad's plane went down. I had never met anyone from there. I said, 'I have a question for you. Back in '70 there was a plane crash in Punxsutawney. Do you remember that?'

"He said, 'It happened on my farm.' He said the plane had been bobbing up and down and then just went at an angle into a hill and crumpled. There had been no fire. When I went home that day from Pearl Harbor, I thought to myself, 'There is a God.'"

PART III: **THE SOUND AND THE FURY**

CHAPTER 26

NEIL

Susan Bonnett

I FIRST SAW SUSAN BONNETT SPEAK AT THE INTERNATIONAL MOTORSPORTS HALL of Fame dinner at Talladega in the spring of 2001. Her beloved husband, Neil, who died tragically on February 11, 1994, when during practice his race car turned suddenly and ran head-on into the outside wall at Daytona, was being inducted. When she spoke about him, she had a joie de vivre and a sparkle that reflected their deep love. At the same time, she exhibited an inner strength that I found remarkable. Susan and Neil Bonnett began dating when they were 16. Once they met, they never dated anyone else. During their life together, she acquiesced to whatever Neil wanted to do. Without her understanding and patience, Neil could never have become a racer at the Winston Cup level. He was her whole life. And now he is gone.

When I asked if I could interview her about her husband and her life in racing, this forthright, courageous woman didn't hesitate.

"I was born Margaret Susan McAdams on June 28, 1946, which tells you my age," she said. "I am always the older woman. I am older than dirt. I have a brother who is nine and a half years younger than me.

"I was born in Birmingham. My dad had several different jobs, but he eventually ended up at the steel plant in Fairfield as a fabricator making steel beams. It was a very, very big business and employed a lot of people for many years. It's still in existence, but nothing like it was.

"My mom and dad lived with my grandmother on my mother's side for several years when I was born, and then they bought a small house not too far from my grandmother, so I kind of commuted back and forth from their house to my grandmother's because my mother worked at the telephone company, so she was at work most of the time.

"What I remember about my childhood is mostly no stress. I hear people talk about what a terrible childhood they had. I don't see that in mine. I had a perfect childhood, with lots of cousins. I loved the family get-togethers. That was special to me.

"I didn't go to college. Actually, I quit my last year of high school because Neil and I got married, and when my son was four years old, I went back and got my GED. I'm very unschooled."

She chuckled at the revelation. I asked her how she met Neil.

"On a blind date," she said. "My closest friend, Diane Vallaly, was dating a guy named Bill Green, and Bill was best friends with Neil. Bill and Diane had been trying to get together, but Bill didn't have a car. Neil did. So this was their devious plan to get Neil to go out with me so we could double date and they could have a way to go out."

"Tell me about your first date," I said.

"I was very uncomfortable with the whole thing," said Bonnett. "I was sixteen. And Neil was sixteen. I was uncomfortable because when I asked them about him, Diane said, 'He's a great guy. You'll love him.' But Diane didn't even know him.

"I had heard some things about Neil. He liked to lift weights, and I heard he was wild. I was very leery about the whole thing. He was probably the fourth person I dated.

"They planned it, and we went to a drive-in movie. *The Pit and the Pendulum* was playing. I don't know, but it was kind of an instant thing. We just hit it off, and we were never apart from then on. We never dated anyone else."

"What was it about him that caused the attraction?" I asked.

"I wish I knew," she said. "I don't really know. It was just instant knowing. You know?"

"Was Neil involved in car racing at the time?" I asked.

"His father had always loved racing," she said, "and he had taken him to the old Iron Bowl out at Irondale a lot. At the time, we met there was racing at Birmingham International Raceway, but it was too expensive for us to go, so we would drive up on a hill two blocks above the racetrack where we could watch the third and fourth corners, and we would sit up there Sunday afternoons and watch.

"Neil always wanted to race. He hadn't had a car very long before I met him, and once he got his car, he started slipping off and going to the drag races at Lassiter Mountain and Cherokee Beach in a little place below Bessemer, tearing up the transmission and telling his dad it happened on the street. His dad would believe him and buy him a new transmission. I didn't go with him because there were only certain times I was allowed out, and I couldn't stay out that late."

"His dad was pretty liberal, I gather," I said.

"Neil was an only child, and they pretty much doted on him," she said. "And he didn't blow too many transmissions before his dad figured it out and said, 'No more.' But his dad understood. He had enjoyed the same things all his life. He loved the races. His dad had a boat he liked to take to the river and run fast, and he knew he instilled some of that in his son."

"What was Neil doing at the time you were married?" I asked.

NEIL AND SUSAN BONNETT
"Driving was safer than pipefitting."
INTERNATIONAL
MOTORSPORTS HALL OF FAME

"After we got married, he was sacking groceries at Hills Groceries," she said. "He wasn't making much money, and we were struggling, and his mom and dad helped us out quite a bit. We lived with them to begin with, and then they got us an apartment over in Fairfield, and we moved in, and Neil started checking around about getting into some kind of career. He pursued becoming a pipe fitter, and for five years he went to school two or three nights a week. He passed the test and became a pipe fitter, even though you usually had to have someone in your family to get into the union. He was working all the time, making excellent money, twelve dollars an hour, but it was dangerous work. He was into tall industrial buildings, and he would talk about how scary it was having to walk across the beams, eating up there in the heat."

What scared Neil Bonnett most was having to walk on a six-inch beam 20 stories up. When you look down, you stare death in the face. He lost three close friends to falls. Bonnett sought a profession that was safer: stock car racing. Many years later, Neil Bonnett commented, "When your best friend fell, you didn't wonder if he made it; you knew what happened to him. When somebody crashes [in a race], I can go to the hospital the next day and sit up with him."

Said Susan Bonnett, "He was way up there, and most of the jobs were out of town, and he was working six days a week, but whenever we got the chance, we'd sit on top of the hill and watch them race."

"Was that romantic?" I asked.

"Not for me," she said. "But it was what he liked to do, so I was OK with it.

"While we were still living with my parents, Neil met a guy by the name of Lee Hurley. Lee lived three blocks away. He had been in racing a while, and he had a race car, and every time he would crank that thing up, Neil would hear it. He told me, 'Somebody has a race car.' He kept searching until he found where the noise came from. He went down there and started hanging out with Lee and watching him work, and he picked things up around the shop. He just made himself at home. Lee raced at Birmingham, at Montgomery, at Huntsville, and at the Rocket Speedway at Dothan.

"One day, Lee carried the car out to Birmingham for practice and let Neil drive it, and he was smitten. Lee was driving the car himself, and he had an accident and broke his leg and was not able to drive, and he asked Neil, who had been hanging around for so long, and that was right up Neil's alley.

"Lee was a little bit older, and he was retiring, and he talked two other guys—Anthony Artoli and Bob Guined—who needed a driver, to use Neil. They didn't know Neil, and Neil didn't know them, but they took Lee's word. Lee, Anthony, and Bob built a Cadet car, and that was how Neil started racing, and they had a *long* relationship."

Bonnett began racing on the short tracks around Birmingham at age 17. The first year driving in the Cadet division he won a couple of races, then the following year he moved up to the Sportsman division and won 14 of 18, and the next year he won 19 of 26.

"He did excellent," said Susan Bonnett. "I can remember Anthony saying he was just such a natural. If you saw him back in those days, you just knew it was what he was supposed to do. Which was not too exciting for me. Because the more he got involved with that, the less he wanted to be involved with his pipe fitting, which put food on the table. The wife and the kids worry about that."

"So he would pipefit by day and race by night?" I asked.

"Yeah," she said. "In other words, we didn't sleep a whole lot. We traveled on the weekends, and he worked during the week."

Neil had plans to drive on the Grand National circuit. But first he tried his skill at the big Talladega track in the Sportsman division.

NEIL BONNETT
INTERNATIONAL
MOTORSPORTS HALL OF FAME

"When Neil was driving a Sportsman car for Artoli and Guined, the person who sponsored him was Butch Nelson," said Susan Bonnett. "Butch is a longtime friend who later went into business with Neil in several ventures. Butch was the sponsor when Neil drove his Sportsman car at Talladega. He had to run a last-chance race to get in, and so to make the car go faster they put in some type of fuel, and it caught on fire and blew up. Then he went to Daytona and wrecked there. And that caused him to want to go on further, and that's how he got involved with Bobby [Allison]."

Bonnett's dominance on the local tracks impressed everyone he raced against, including veteran drivers Bobby Allison, Donnie Allison, and Red Farmer, even then known as "The Alabama Gang." Bonnett became particularly close to Bobby Allison, and in 1970 he moved his family to Hueytown to be closer to Bobby and his race shop.

"We moved to Hueytown because that's where Bobby, Donnie, and Red and all the racers were living," she said. "We never even considered living anywhere else. That way Neil could be closer to Bobby's shop and Red's shop and hang around with them. He was forever in and out of those places trying to find out everything he could. At that time, Neil would have paid to drive. He just loved doing it.

"Bobby, of course, was into Winston Cup racing, which was called Grand National, and Anthony and Bob were not able to do that financially. So Neil started hanging around Bobby's shop, and the next thing I know, Neil is helping

175

Bobby and traveling some with Bobby to the Grand National races. He left his pipefitting job and wasn't even employed by Bobby. He just wanted to do it so badly to get his foot in the door, so me and our two children had to make a sacrifice for this to take place."

"Did you ever say to him, 'This is terrible price to pay'?" I asked.

"It wouldn't have made any difference," she said. "But no, it wasn't so terrible, because I knew it's what he wanted to do. He had it in his heart to do it. How could I tell him he couldn't do it? And Neil was a person, if he believed he could do something, he was going to do it. Also, I could see when he started hanging around with Bobby how his attitude about life changed: He was happy. And finally, eventually, Bobby got so involved with his own car and all the things he was doing that he needed extra help, so one day he said to Neil, 'I'll build you a car, and when I can't make an appearance somewhere, I'll send you.' Neil thought that was great. Bobby said, 'You can keep part of the winnings,' so finally some income was going to be coming in."

The promoters accepted Neil Bonnett in Bobby Allison's place because of Allison's fame and reputation. Allison would tell the promoter, "Look for a country hick with his nose in the air and his cold blue eyes on the victory cup."

"I was like a bounty hunter," Neil Bonnett once said. "Wherever I went, I loaded my gun and shot people down. I'd blow in, then blow them out of the weeds."

Said Susan Bonnett, "When people would call Bobby and say, 'We need you. Can you make an appearance and drive at Trenton, New Jersey?' Bobby would say, 'I can't come, but I will send my protégé, Neil Bonnett.' They would say, 'Neil who?' So that's what he put on his car. 'Neil Who?' And the couple of years Neil drove for Bobby, he won something like forty-nine or fifty races, so he was getting known. He would go and run and put on a really good show, and they would remember him."

Bonnett won so often that when a sponsor asked how much he wanted to race, he would say, "Forget about that, my man. What's your trophy look like and how much're you gonna give me for winning it?"

With the winnings, Bonnett built himself a Grand National car.

"Bobby helped him," said Susan Bonnett. "Bobby told him he could slowly take the time and build his own car and his shop. And that's what he did."

In 1974, Bonnett entered two Grand National races. In May, he went to Talladega and finished 45th. At Daytona, he failed to qualify.

"Charlie Roberts, our insurance guy, was piddling a little bit in racing," said Susan Bonnett, "and he asked Neil to drive a car at Talladega, and he went there, and he went to Daytona, but he didn't make the race. They didn't have the money to go any further."

"What was Neil's reaction to driving on a superspeedway track?" I asked.

"He loved it," she said. "Especially Talladega. That was his favorite place. He loved that. Neil made several different tries [at Grand National racing]. He didn't want to go back to Sportsman racing once he did that. He wanted to move on up."

However, it nearly a year for Bonnett to take another crack at Grand National racing. He ran at Nashville in July 1975. In August 1975, he raced at Talladega and finished 35th in a fateful race in which Tiny Lund was killed. Finally, in 1976 Bonnett made the jump to stay. He drove in 13 Grand National races in a car he owned himself. His sponsor, Armor All, made it possible. It was a sponsorship handed to him by Bobby Allison.

Said Susan Bonnett, "Bobby had met some people from Armor All who were looking to sponsor his car, and he told Neil, 'These people might be interested,' and they talked and agreed to sponsor us for three races. The first one was at Daytona, where you have to make the race and finish to make money. We had a certain budget to make the race. Most teams had a motor to qualify and another motor to race. We only had one motor to qualify and to race. And Neil blew that motor, so we had to buy another motor, and we spent seventeen thousand dollars of the money. We were trying to figure out what to do because we weren't going to have any more money for the other races, but he finished fifth —this was the famous race in which Richard Petty and David Pearson crashed at the finish line—and it paid what we needed (fourteen thousand dollars), so we were able to go to the next two races, and after that Armor All gave him more money. And then he met some people from Hawaiian Tropic, so there were several things working there."

Even with sponsorship, Neil Bonnett discovered how difficult and expensive it was to run an independently run team without factory help. In 13 races, he had only one top-five finish. His winnings amounted to $32,275.

"It was really hard," said Susan Bonnett. "He had to get the car where it needed to go, had to work on it and drive it all himself, and he was doing all that. He had the expertise on how to get the car to the track and set it up. He had some people helping him, but basically all the stress fell on him. Plus, he was trying to support his family. And it was pretty stressful on me, because he left all the bills on me."

CHAPTER 27

CLIMBING THE LADDER

Benny Parsons

IN 1963, BENNY PARSONS BEGAN HIS RACING CAREER ON SHORT TRACKS IN THE
Detroit area. In two short years, the talented racer was battling Cale Yarborough
for a ride on the Ford team run by Holman Moody. However, Parsons discovered very quickly that ambition was no substitute for experience.

His first race was on a quarter-mile dirt track. Parsons quickly found out
that you couldn't just get behind the wheel of a race car and win races. He had
so much to learn.

"I lined up for the heat race," he said. "They said, 'Start your engines.' I
pushed the clutch in to shift gears, and my left leg was trembling badly. The
adrenaline was pumping unbelievably. I took the green flag, and I started, and
in the second or third lap coming off turn four, I spun out. I was in a hurry, and I
jammed the thing in gear and stripped all the teeth off the rear end.

"I searched through every junkyard in Detroit to find the gear I was looking
for, a 4-11, that I ran in second gear. I never did find one, but I found a 389. It
came in a '54 Ford sedan delivery, and I put that in the car, and I went out the
next week, and on the second or third lap I spun out coming off turn four. I
jammed it in gear and took off and broke the transmission. I spent another week
looking through all the junkyards for a transmission for a '54 Ford.

"That year, I got to the point where I had a basic idea of what I was doing. I
went to Flat Rock, a paved quarter-mile racetrack one Saturday night. The feature
event that night was a Figure-8 race, and that was the most competitive I had

179

ever been. I was the fastest qualifier, won the trophy dash, won the heat race, won the feature. So the first race I won was actually a Figure-8 race.

"That night I got paid three-seventy-five for my fifty dollar car. I had told Dick Gold, who had given me the car and helped me fix it up, that I would split whatever money I made with him. I kept very explicit records of the money I took in and the money I spent, and when the season was over I gave him one hundred seventy-two dollars."

Parsons moved up to the half-milers in 1964.

"I bought the car that Dick had been using on the half-mile track for fifteen hondred dollars," said Parsons, "and I won the first three or four races I entered.

BENNY PARSONS
INTERNATIONAL
MOTORSPORTS HALL OF FAME

But then I wasn't happy with winning. I wanted to start lapping them, and that's when I became too enamored of myself, started to tear stuff up, but nevertheless, it was 1964, and Ford had lost several drivers—Joe Weatherly was killed, Billy Wade was killed, and Fireball [Roberts] was killed, so they needed some drivers, and they were looking for youth.

"Howard DeHart, who was from Holman Moody, called me up and asked me to go to Asheville-Weaverville, North Carolina, to try out to see whether I had what it took. He said, 'We're supposed to get you a car ready to go to Asheville-Weaverville. We need you to come down here and sit in the seat.'"

I asked Parsons what his reaction was to the phone call.

"I'm a star, man," he said. "But you see, I didn't get enough information. I was a kid. I was twenty-three years old. What did I know?"

The Asheville-Weaverville race was held on August 9, 1964.

"I went up there," said Parsons. "It was a half-mile, high-banked racetrack. I had run on a flat, three-eighth-mile paved track at Ona, West Virginia. That was the biggest asphalt track I had ever run on, and I had raced a Grand National type car a total of once. So the best thing I could have done was to have said to DeHart, 'No, I'm not ready for this.'

"But I thought they were going to work with me and help me out and get me some experience. And when I got there, there was another racer there as well: a guy named Cale Yarborough. And basically it was a contest to see which one of us was the better. And obviously Cale won that contest hands down."

If you looked at the scorecard of the Asheville-Weaverville race afterward, you wouldn't have necessarily thought so. Ned Jarrett was the winner in a Bondy Long Ford. Cale Yarborough qualified 5th and finished 20th with a blown radiator. Parsons qualified 9th and finished 21st when his car overheated. But Yarborough ran with the leaders and impressed everyone while Parsons displayed his inexperience and wowed no one. A month later at Darlington, Yarborough was strapped into a Holman Moody car and finished 8th in the Southern 500 at Darlington, the start of a brilliant career. Parsons returned to Detroit with a better idea of how far he had to go to reach the Grand National level.

"Once it was over and I saw what had happened and how everything shook down, I saw I had no reason for being in the contest," said Parsons. "Cale ran very, very well. He should have been awarded a car to drive, and he was. And I did terribly. My biggest thrill came when I was sitting in the car, and Richard Petty walked up and stuck out his hand and said, 'Hi, I'm Richard Petty.' Like I didn't know. And that was a big thrill, because Richard Petty was a hero.

"When I got home, I called the Ford headquarters in Detroit and said, 'I need help to run in the ARCA series. I think I can do this, but until I get some experience I can't compete at the Grand National level.'

"They said, 'Tell you what you do. You grab the lead in ten ARCA races and come back and see us.'

"By hook or crook, I got an old car. The next race was in Springfield, Ohio, a half-mile dirt track at the fairgrounds, the biggest mess you've ever seen in your whole life, but I did lead the race some. I said to myself, 'That's one.'

"In 1965, I ran the entire ARCA series and went broke. I spent every dime I could get my hands on, and a group of guys in Detroit offered me a job driving their car. Then I met Odie Skeen, a terrific mechanic who worked hard on the old race cars. He loved the race cars. I started working with him. We built a '67 Fairlane, ran a couple of USAC races and some ARCA races, and Ford was doing so well in NASCAR that it wanted to expand, so in December of 1967 Ford had a party in Dearborn for their racing drivers and owners, and they invited me. On the centerpiece at the table, the program listed 'Ford drivers.' And my name was in there! Someone said, 'They are going to give you some help.'

"I said, 'I wish they'd hurry.'

"I kept calling Charlie Gray, the stock car coordinator for Ford. He talked to me occasionally, and finally in January of 1968 he called me up and said, 'What would you do if I told you we had you a car down at Holman Moody?'

"I said, 'That is fantastic.'

"He said, 'We will give you a race car, but you have to build an engine to qualify with. Go down and see Howard DeHart and pick up your car.'

"We had two weeks to be in Daytona for the ARCA race. I jumped in my truck and went to Charlotte, North Carolina, and I picked up a '68 Fairlane that was just a big pile of metal. I went back to Detroit with this thing. We had never seen one of these cars before, much less worked on one.

"I drove it into my dad's gas station, and when I told them I had two weeks to get the car and engine ready, they said, 'You can't make it. It's impossible. You call them and tell them you can't do it.'

"I said, 'Don't you all understand? This is a test. It is *the* test, whether we want to do this or not.'

"My name was on that program in December. They could have given us that car then. But that would not have been much of a test. They wanted to know whether I was willing to stay up all night for two weeks to get that car ready.

"I took that car to Odie's house. He had a one-car frame garage that barely had enough room to get around in. One night we had fourteen people working on that car. We had engineers from General Motors. They were just race fans and they wanted to help out.

"We threw a party and charged everyone five bucks so we had some money for Daytona. We had soda pop and beer and showed racing movies. Three hundred people showed up and gave us five bucks apiece.

"Odie built the engine. We put this car together, and we didn't have a clue what we were doing, and in February of 1968 we showed up in Daytona for the ARCA race, and we sat on the pole with it. We went 180 miles an hour. And Ford gave us a motor. I led the race, but I blew a left rear tire.

"Everybody tried to get me to run Goodyears, but I had always run Firestones. I knew the Firestone people, who gave me some free tires. It was *not* a good deal. That day I blew two left rear tires. And we could not use impact wrenches on the ARCA circuit. We had to use four-way lug wrenches, so I got behind, and I was trying to outrun everybody, and coming off turn four I spun out and backed her into the fence.

"In '68, I spent the year running ARCA, and I won the championship. That was pretty cool. And I won it again in '69."

That year, Parsons went to Daytona to run the ARCA race and also to run the Daytona 500. After he won the ARCA 300, he paid his $50, entered the big one, and finished seventh.

"I almost spun out on the first lap," said Parsons. "I went down in turn three, and I was under Bobby Unser, and he came down the hill, and I was concerned I was going to run into the back of him, so I spun out. I was really concerned about flat-spotting the tires, so I made a pit stop and changed tires and lost a lap or two. And I still finished seventh!"

On December 7, 1969, in the final race of the season, Parsons entered the Texas 500, the inaugural running at the Texas International Speedway—he doesn't remember why he chose to enter that particular race—but he finished a remarkable third behind Grand National veterans Bobby Isaac and Donnie Allison and won a purse of $4,000. The two races made all the Grand National owners looking for some new blood take notice of him. Not that he intended to drive for someone else. Benny Parsons was driving for himself and doing quite nicely, thank you. He and Odie Skeen prepared his car for the Daytona 500 of 1970. That's when he, and the rest of the sport, got the news: Ford was getting out of racing.

"In 1970, I went to Daytona to run the ARCA race," said Parsons, "and while I was down there, I found out that Ford was going to stop racing. So all of a sudden, I was out of business. Without Ford's help, I needed about $50,000. With that, I could still race and not have to work at the gas station.

"I was sick. I was in big trouble."

But Charlie Gray, who was in the charge of the Ford stock car program, knew that Benny Parsons had what it took to be a star on the Grand National circuit, and he thought he knew who needed a driver.

"Charlie Gray said to me, 'Why don't you go over and talk to John Hill?'

"I said, 'Who's he?'

"He said, 'He runs a team for a guy named L. G. DeWitt. They need a driver.'

"I went over and talked to John. Their team had started racing in 1965 with John Sears as their driver, and at the end of the 1969 season L. G. and Sears split up, and they hired a young driver by the name of Buddy Young. They went to Riverside and had one of the worst wrecks that NASCAR has ever seen. Young literally turned over fifteen or sixteen times. He was banged up and couldn't run Daytona. James Hylton had switched from Dodge to Ford, and his cars were not ready, so he went to drive L. G.'s car at Daytona. He went down there and blew an engine coming off turn four and destroyed that brand-new race car. So John and L. G. didn't run the Daytona 500 because their car was junk.

"I talked to John. I had wrecked my car in the ARCA race, and we were crying on each other's shoulders, and I asked, 'Is there any chance of driving that car?' He said I would have to go talk to L. G. So on the way back to Detroit, I stopped by Ellerbe, North Carolina, and talked to L. G.

"When I asked to drive his car, he said, 'We have a driver, Buddy Young, and he says he's going to be able to drive.' I thanked him, and I went on to North Wilkesboro to visit for two or three days before I went back to Detroit and returned to the gas station.

"I was in my uncle's barbershop when Fred Johnson, Junior's brother, called me on the phone. He said, 'Benny, them boys at L. G.'s are trying to get in touch with you, and here's a number to call. Call John Hill at DeWitt.'

"I called, and John said, 'Buddy Young just called. The doctor won't release him to drive. Can you go to Richmond and drive our car this week?'

"I drove to Ellerbe and worked on the car, got it ready, and went to Richmond and ran the race. [Parsons finished 15th.] I broke the rear gear. Rockingham was the next week, and I went there and ran well, and L. G. said, 'We'd like you to drive our car.'

"I went back to Detroit and got what little I owned, and my family and I moved to Ellerbe, North Carolina."

In his very first season, Benny Parsons became a contender for the driving championship. He drove hard, but not too hard, and more often than not, he finished in the top 10. Among his better finishes were a fourth place at Savannah and a fourth at Talladega. He finished the 1970 season eighth in the standings.

"We were just there every week, primarily," said Parsons. "We had a pretty good car, really."

"So you were making a living?" I asked.

"Not a big living," he said, "but enough to get by."

CHAPTER 28

A BRIEF RETURN

Fred Lorenzen

AFTER RETIRING AS A DRIVER, FRED LORENZEN THOUGHT HE MIGHT TRY HIS HAND at running a race team. As Richard Petty and his '67 Plymouth were en route to winning 27 Grand National races that year, Ford was desperate to find a combination that could derail the Petty Express. Ford and Holman Moody gave Lorenzen that chance. Lorenzen was allowed to choose any crew chief and any driver he wanted. Ford wanted his team to be ready for the American 500 on October 29, 1967, at Rockingham. He hired Jake Elder to be his head mechanic, ("Jake was just a smart, quiet, southern boy. He was good.") and he put unknown 29-year-old Bobby Allison in the car.

The way Allison remembered it, Ralph Moody called him and said, 'The answer is yes. You'll be getting a call in two minutes.' Two minutes later, Lorenzen called to say he wanted Allison to drive for him. Allison was about to embark on a career that would lead him to 85 wins and make him one of the legends of racing.

Said Lorenzen, who selected him, "Allison was supersharp in the chassis. I knew Bobby could do it if he had the big money behind him. I had watched him. I knew. You can tell who's a good driver. I knew my car, and I knew if he could drive it he could blow the competition away. Once he had the equipment and the crew . . . there are a lot of good drivers around, but they have to listen. But Bobby didn't have to listen because he already knew it all. He was sharp on the chassis. I give him credit. We got along good. He was a good driver.

"And so we went to Rockingham, and he won the race. It was our first show together. We didn't celebrate much. I didn't. I expected to win."

To prove the win was no fluke, Lorenzen and Allison went to the Asheville-Weaverville Speedway and won for a second week in a row. After the race, Lorenzen told the press, "Bobby Allison has a lifetime job."

But what Lorenzen didn't understand about himself was exactly how burned out he had become. Before the 1968 season Ralph Moody informed Lorenzen and Allison that they intended to get out of racing, and so the two switched to the Bondy Long race team. Long, like Holman Moody, ran a Ford-backed team.

Lorenzen and Allison went to Daytona, where Allison finished third. At Bristol, the car blew a piston and finished last. A crash at Atlanta finished Allison and put an end to Lorenzen's brief stint as a crew chief.

"I didn't want to do it anymore," he said. "I didn't want to drive myself either, so I just decided to get out of it. I had traveled all my life, and I was tired. Tired of that and tired of being around billions of people. You know, if you're at the top, you have to appreciate the public and spend time with them—for free. I signed autographs—that takes a lot of time. Three hours after every race. You can hardly stand up, but that goes with it. You also had to go and talk to sponsors.

"I went home and became a bum. I went water-skiing all summer. In the wintertime, I lived in Fort Lauderdale. I lived a bachelor life. I did sea fishing in the Bahamas. I fished for blue marlin. I had one 300-pounder on for two-and-a-half hours, and he pulled the line before we got him to the boat.

"On the way in, we were dragging this big mullet, and the captain said, 'There's a shark on there. Take him.' So I caught an eight-foot mako shark. I had him mounted. He's in my basement in the trophy room."

Lorenzen stayed away from racing for three-and a-half years. Until he got bored.

"I got tired out from water-skiing. And I missed the cars too much."

On May 24, 1970, Fred Lorenzen returned to NASCAR. He entered the World 600 at the Charlotte Motor Speedway in a car owned by Richard Howard, the track's owner, and built by Ray Fox. Lorenzen was leading the race when the engine blew on lap 252.

"We were flying," said Lorenzen. "We were totally gone. I was driving the wing car. Fox was a good mechanic, and we had a good crew. It takes four or five years to make a great team. But Ray and Smokey Yunick were the best two mechanics in the South. Raymond was an unbelievable mechanic.

"The Plymouth Superbird with the wing you could drive with one finger. The car would steer itself. That wing made it, and the Chrysler was unbelievable! That was the package."

Lorenzen drove in seven races in 1970, fourteen in 1971, and eight in 1972. Though he had some great runs, he didn't win any races.

"I was getting older, I guess. We didn't have the combination. I wasn't winning, and if you're not winning, you're not good enough."

In 1972, Lorenzen drove for Hoss Ellington.

"Hoss was a good man. He owned an insulation company out of Wilmington, North Carolina. He was a racer. He had plenty of money to back the car. He was very smart, very into racing."

After finishing fourth at Talladega on May 7, 1972, and fourth at the Southern 500 at Darlington, Lorenzen failed to show up for his race at North Wilkesboro on October 1.

"I guess I was done. Worn out. The battery was dead."

"At that point, what did you do?" I asked.

"I went back home. I had all my race money in stocks. Later the market crashed and I lost eight hundred thousand dollars, but then an old friend told me, 'Buy the biggest company in the world, and don't look back, and you'll get it back.' I took all my money and put it into the biggest company, Exxon, and I did get it all back.

"I bought my daughter ten shares when she was born, and she is twenty-five, and now she has two thousand shares. I own over a million dollars worth. I live on the dividends, five grand a quarter. That and social security. That's all I need.

"And I got involved in real estate, and I bought a big house in Oak Brook, and my taxes were eight thousand dollars a year, so I left the firm and went to ReMax, where you are your own boss and broker. You pay a monthly fee, and you get all the money, but you have to hustle, and I hustled for about twenty years, and then I quit. I was born and raised in Elmhurst. I did a lot of business in Elmhurst."

Lorenzen, who was married in 1972, has a son who he says is a wildly successful day trader.

"He's the number-one day trader in the state of Illinois," said Lorenzen proudly. "He hit it big. He's making millions of dollars. A good kid. A hard worker. He has seven guys working for him."

I asked Lorenzen if he is surprised at how much money stock car drivers make today.

"I knew everything was going to go up and up," he said, "but I didn't think it would be this high. They're making big bucks. I wish I still did it, but I am too old. The older guys don't have it. Not like the young guys."

"Was there ever a moment when you thought to yourself, I wish I hadn't quit?" I asked Lorenzen.

"Oh sure," he said. "Every day I think about it. Sure. If I had to do it over again, I never would have quit." He sounded wistful.

"It was stupid," he said.

I noticed that over the years that I had never seen Lorenzen at any of the racing functions like the Hall of Fame ceremony at the International Motorsports Hall of Fame at Talladega or at the Legends of Racing dinners in Daytona Beach.

"No," said Lorenzen, "because if you did it all your life—I did it for nine years straight, and I never had any time out, and I just got burned out. I got out because there was too much traveling. I can't take big crowds anymore. That's why I don't go around them. My daughter wants me to take her to Charlotte, but I don't know if I'm going to go or not.

"About a year and a half ago Smokey Yunick called me and wanted to know if I'd go to Sacramento, California, to make a speech for one of his friends who was having a big auto parts meeting.

"I said, 'Smokey, I don't do that stuff anymore. I'm retired. I stay around the house and play with my dog. I flew so much. . . .'"

"He said, 'Lorenzen, what will it take to get you there?'

"'Five thousand and all expenses,' I said. "That's the only way I will go. If they want it, fine. If they don't, I won't bother because the government gets a piece of it, and I hate flying. I just don't like having people around me. I've had it.

"Smokey said, 'I will call you back in an hour.' He said, 'You got a plane ticket. A limo will pick you up tomorrow.'

"I went. I met Smokey in Sacramento at the airport, and we went out to eat. Smokey was a super guy. He died of leukemia about six months later. I didn't even know he was sick."

CHAPTER 29

THE QUIET CHAMPION

Benny Parsons

THE 1971 SEASON BEGAN WITH A SERIOUS PROBLEM FOR EVERYONE. THE SPEEDS ON the superspeedways were so great that the tires would not stay on the cars. This was at the point when Bill France asked Paul Goldsmith and Ray Nichels to do something. The result: restrictor plates to limit the air intake and slow the cars. Benny Parsons understood what NASCAR was attempting when it mandated the restrictor plates.

"The tires would not survive at Talladega," he said. "They put the restrictor plates on, and that way they could keep the cars around one hundred and eighty miles an hour, and finally in '73 Goodyear made a tire that would live."

I mentioned to Parsons that in 1971 David Pearson, driving for Holman Moody, had used what his opponents called a "cheater" plate in a qualifying race at Daytona. NASCAR nevertheless ruled he could keep the win.

"With the restrictor plates there was a lot of gray area," said Parsons, "and Ralph Moody exploited the gray area. He had something that would suck more air through it than anyone else's. It didn't upset me because he exploited the gray area and did a very good job of it."

One thing was clear in 1971. Without factory support, no one could beat Richard Petty or Bobby Allison. That year, Petty won 21 races and Allison 11. Bobby Isaac (with four) was the only other racer with more than one win that year. The difference between the haves—Petty and Allison—and the have nots—most everyone else, was made most clear at Atlanta on August 1, 1971, in the Dixie 500 when Petty and Allison finished first and second, and Benny Parsons came in third—nine laps behind them.

"That was the just the way it was back then," said Parsons. "Petty had the left-over stuff from Chrysler. Bobby had the leftover stuff from Ford, with the expertise of Holman Moody. When the factories left . . . You can go back and look at those race results and realize that racing was in big trouble. That's why Winston was so important to our sport."

It was in 1971 when the R. J. Reynolds Tobacco Company announced that it would spend big dollars to promote itself in NASCAR. But before R. J.

RICHARD PETTY
He was the driver to beat.
INTERNATIONAL
MOTORSPORTS HALL OF FAME

Reynolds' presence could be felt, the sport was dominated by Richard Petty, who in the years between 1967 and 1971, won 27, 16, 10, 18, and 21 races.

In 1971, Benny Parsons won his first Grand National race. It came in the Halifax County 100 at South Boston, Virginia.

"That was one hundred miles, three hundred laps," he said, chuckling.

The crowd for that race was only 1,200, another indication that the with-drawal of the car companies had severely hurt attendance. Parsons noted another factor.

"That might have been the last race NASCAR ever ran on Mother's Day," he said.

The driver he beat that day was Richard Petty. I asked Parsons how hard it was to beat Petty.

"He was tough," Parsons said. "Richard was *the* guy to beat each and every week, because the Pettys knew about survival. By then, Richard, Maurice, and Dale Inman pretty much ran the show. They knew you had to finish to win, and so they finished *so* many times, where the equipment back then was very suspect. A lot of guys could outrun you, but they would blow up or something would happen. The Pettys wouldn't do that."

"Richard had discipline?" I asked.

"Yes," said Parsons, "and a *very* dependable car."

One other important development came in 1971 when Charlie Glotzbach won the Bristol race in a Chevrolet. The promoters were desperate to infuse some interest in the races, what with Petty and his Plymouth dominating. They were hoping to interest the Chevy fans with Glotzbach's entry.

"It was a big deal," said Parsons, "because on the big tracks Chevys were nonexistent. Nineteen sixty-three was the last time Chevy fans had something to cheer about when Junior ran that number 3 white Chevy that had what they called a 'mystery engine.' In '67, Bobby Allison had won a race or two in a Chevelle, but that was the last time. Richard Howard, who was a promoter at the Charlotte Motor Speedway, supposedly owned the car, and Junior Johnson worked on it. They built a very hybrid car. It had a Ford chassis. By then, most all the Fords had a hybrid chassis as well, but NASCAR allowed them to put that Ford chassis under the Chevrolet Monte Carlo. But it did have the 427 Chevrolet engine in it. Richard was trying to awaken the Chevrolet fans who had not had anything to cheer about for a long time."

When R. J. Reynolds put up $100,000 for the top drivers in the points standings starting in 1971, the sport began to grow and change. The tobacco giant agreed to promote races that were 250 miles and longer. Suddenly the owners understood that if they were going to have the dough to pay for their cars, they would have to find corporate sponsors.

"That's when the hunt for sponsorship really took off," said Benny Parsons. "You see, Ford had been giving their NASCAR teams all the parts they needed, all the cars they needed, and $2,000 a race. Ford and Chrysler *were* the sponsors. All of a sudden you take away the $2,000 a race, plus you now have to buy the cars and the parts, and it's not very feasible to do this on your own. That's when car owners started to look for companies to pay it. STP was the first one, on Richard's car. And Purolator on the [Wood Brothers'] 21 car."

"What did L. G. do?" I asked.

"We just struggled along," Parsons said.

"Was he trying to get a sponsor?"

"Oh, yeah. He tried," he said. "But back then almost nobody had any sponsors. Bobby had Coca-Cola in 1971 in that '69 Ford he won so many races with, and then he switched it over to Junior's and Chevrolet in '72. But even if you had a top driver, getting a sponsor still was hard."

It would not be until the races were televised on a regular basis several years later that getting a sponsor became much more feasible.

"When the 1972 season ended, did you ever say to yourself, 'I am going to be the racing champion in 1973?'" I asked Parsons.

"No. No," he said.

But in 1973 the hard-working, modest Parsons, driving for a relatively underfinanced L. G. DeWitt, beat the richer teams and became the NASCAR racing champion despite his winning only one race, at Bristol in the Volunteer 500. Second-place Cale Yarborough, the man who beat him out in his tryout at Holman Moody, trailed him by 67 points. Richard Petty, winner of six races, was only fifth in points that year.

All season long, Parsons had inferior equipment, especially on the superspeedways where Petty, Allison, Yarborough, and Pearson were heavy favorites.

Making Parsons' win less probable was L. G. DeWitt's switch from Ford to Chevrolet at the start of the 1973 season. Usually it takes a couple of years for a race team to get used to a new make of car.

"L. G. had talked to Junior [Johnson]," said Parsons, "and he felt the Chevrolet engines would be easier to come by than the Ford stuff, and so we switched to Chevrolet. Ralph Moody had started an engine company in Charlotte. Waddell Wilson was his head engine builder, so we contracted with them to build us engines."

At the Daytona 500, Parsons blew an engine after 101 laps and finished 30th. At Richmond, he spun out and still managed to finish 10th, then was 31st at Rockingham. But then he ran off a string of top finishes: he was 5th at Bristol, 3rd at Atlanta, 2nd to Petty at North Wilkesboro, and second to David Pearson at Darlington, 13 laps back, in a race marred by crashes. Parsons, in fact, started the worst wreck.

"It was weird. With about thirty laps to go on a restart I was trying to get out of somebody's way," he said. "I moved over and hit somebody and spun him in front of the whole field. I wrecked the whole field, I'm telling you."

Parsons limped around the track at around 40 miles an hour but was still able to finish second. Bobby Allison finished third, five laps behind him.

Parsons then finished sixth at Martinsville and then third at Talladega.

"We didn't have very good equipment down there. We were not good at Talladega." But Parsons finished third because of another stupendous wreck. Ramo Stott's Mercury engine blew in the ninth lap of the race, and after the smoke cleared 21 cars were demolished.

"It was unbelievable," said Parsons, "the biggest wreck you've ever seen in your life. When Stott's engine blew, somebody got in the oil, and it was on."

Earl Brooks broke his hand, and Wendell Scott suffered three broken ribs.

Parsons' consistency for the rest of that 1973 season was amazing. He was second at Nashville behind Cale Yarborough, fifth in the World 600 at Charlotte, seventh at Texas, third at Riverside, ninth at Michigan, and fifth in the Firecracker 400 at Daytona. Then on July 18 at Bristol, a race Pearson and the Wood Brothers didn't enter, Yarborough and Allison were knocked out by crashes, and Petty had to drop out after ignition trouble. Parsons won the Volunteer 500 for the second year in a row, beating unheralded, struggling independent drivers L. D. Ottinger, Cecil Gordon, Lennie Pond, and J. D. McDuffie.

"They were all broke," said Parsons.

Parsons was suffering from neck problems, and so he had to use a substitute driver in the middle of the Bristol race.

"Bristol just killed my neck," said Parsons, "so I got a fellow there, a local guy I knew, a really nice man, John A. Utsman, to relieve me, so we both drove that day. I drove, then John drove, and I drove the rest. And we won the race by seven laps."

Parsons kept his lead for the driving championship even after a 25th-place finish in the Dixie 500 at Atlanta caused by a broken fuel pump, and a 38th-place finish at Talladega when his engine blew. Parsons was confident all along that he would go on to win the championship.

"They had three legs that year," said Parsons. "After ten races, you got ten thousand dollars, and after ten more, you got ten thousand dollars, and at the end of the year you got another ten thousand dollars." Parsons won two out of three of those races that year, netting a cool $20,000.

Going into the final race at Rockingham on October 21, 1973, Parsons led Petty by 194 points and Yarborough by 208 points. But the scoring was so complicated, with half-points being awarded for every lap completed, that no one could figure out where Parsons had to finish to win the title. What the experts all agreed on was that Parsons, Petty, and Yarborough all could win it. I asked Parsons what he remembered about that day at Rockingham.

"You go to the racetrack leading with a chance to win," he said. "I just wanted to ride around all day. I didn't want to see anybody. My plan, if things worked out perfectly, was to finish fifth.

"On the thirteenth lap, I came off the second corner. We didn't have spotters then. I had already passed the caution light in turn one when a guy by the name of Johnny Barnes spun off turn two. On a banked racetrack you can't see around the corner. When you try to look around the corner, all you see is the roof. So I came off the corner, and Johnny was sitting sideways on the racetrack on the exit to turn two. I tried to turn under him, and I caught him right behind my right front tire, and bam!

"I went sliding, though I never did spin out. I came to a stop. A bunch of other cars have crashed. We weren't the only one to crash—by now other cars were wrecking.

"My engine stalled. I fired it back up, put the car in first gear and let the clutch out, and it wouldn't move. I said to myself, 'What in the world?'

"For some reason, I looked to my right, and I saw that I had no right side. I had no sheet metal. I had no roll bars. The right side of the car was gone. Yeah, and when I looked down in turn three, my right spring was laying down there.

"In hindsight, the one thing we didn't do, the one thing we should have done, was have a wrecker on site to make sure we could get back to the garage. John Sears had retired, and he was running a garage in Ellerbe, which was only ten miles from the Rockingham track, and I called him and he came down and he hooked me up and hauled me back to the garage in the infield.

"When we got back to the garage, we said, 'What are we going to do? We don't have any roll bars.'"

What the underdog Benny Parsons never said—and never would say—was that he was so well-liked by the other drivers and crews that not only his crew, but members of other crews, joined together to work on the car so he could go back out onto the track and win the championship.

"Wasn't that unusual?" I asked.

"Yeah, it was," he said.

But ultimately it was Ralph Moody who made the crucial decision that allowed Parsons back on the racetrack.

"Ralph Moody, who was building engines for the car, had been there with a couple who owned a race car," said Parsons. "They had attempted to qualify and had missed the show, and they had not yet loaded up their car. It was sitting at the end of the garage there at Rockingham. And the owners weren't around.

"Ralph said, 'Go down and take the roll bars off that car.' So we did. We took a torch down there, cut them out and brought them back up there and welded them into our car. They didn't like it much," he said chuckling at the memory.

"We had a rear-end housing and trailing arms. We had everything we needed except that roll cage. So we set there and got to work and after an hour and fifteen minutes we were back on the racetrack."

After working in the garage while the other cars ran for 136 laps, the 33-year-old Parsons returned and was able to complete 308 of the 492 laps, coming in 28th, good enough to finish ahead of Cale Yarborough for the driving championship by 67 points.

I asked Parsons what the odds of his winning the racing championship would have been at the start of the season.

"I wouldn't have been the first pick," Parsons said in an understatement. "It's like when the golfer Phil Mickleson picked the St. Louis Rams, the year they won. The odds were an astronomical sum to one. Same deal."

"Was winning the driving championship prestigious in 1973?" I asked.

"No, not really," he said.

"Is that because the races weren't televised?" I asked.

"They weren't televised, and they weren't covered by the dailies anything like they are today."

"But for you personally?" I asked.

"The personal satisfaction was unbelievable," he said. You feel like all the work you've done has paid off. You've won the championship. You've got the trophy."

"Did it affect your life in any sort of material way?" I asked.

"No," he said.

"Did it translate into a better sponsor?"

"No," he said.

"A better ride?" I asked.

"No," he said. "We obviously spent whatever money we won upgrading our team. If I'm not mistaken, we received $71,000 for winning the championship between winning the Winston money and the NASCAR money. My deal gave me ten percent of the Winston money and none of the NASCAR money.

"And I made that deal because if I made five more dollars, that was five more dollars I took out of L. G.'s pocket, and for the team to survive, no one could be greedy; and the team survived. Even if I had had someplace else to go—and I didn't—L. G. had given me my break, and I was not the type of guy to go blow him off and go somewhere else—he was the guy who had given me my shot."

Just as the 1973 racing season came to a close, OPEC decided to reduce the amount of gasoline it produced worldwide, and suddenly the major American gasoline companies didn't have enough to adequately supply their service stations. Long lines of frustrated drivers began to appear at the pumps all across America. Gas prices soared. And if citizens couldn't get enough gas, how would this affect stock car racing? Benny Parsons, the just-crowned NASCAR racing champion, found himself in the grip of a nightmarish scenario.

"No sooner did we win the championship than it seemed like the next day we wondered, 'Was there going to be racing in 1974?'

"I spent so many miserable meals right after winning the championship," he said. "I sat at the dining room table at supper listening to the national news every day, hearing about the oil embargo and seeing the lines and thinking, How are we going to get out of this? As a country, how are we going to get out of this? And where does racing fit in? We certainly are not essential. How are the fans going to get to the racetracks? I just could not believe it. I was literally sick to my stomach."

CHAPTER 30

J. D., HARRY, AND THE WOOD BROTHERS

Susan Bonnett

In 1976, Neil Bonnett found enough sponsorship money to allow him to run 16 races. Despite never doing better than a fifth-place finish at Daytona, he got the sport's attention with his hard-charging driving style.

At the beginning of the 1976 season, driver Dave Marcis was lured from the K&K Insurance team to drive for Roger Penske. To replace Marcis, K&K, owned by Nord Krauskopf and crewed by the legendary Harry Hyde, offered the ride to newcomer Bonnett. The reason Bonnett got the offer was that K&K announced it would no longer sponsor the race team, and veteran drivers didn't want it.

Bonnett and Hyde had to find a sponsorship on their own. The year began with a two-race commitment from Citicorp.

I asked Susan Bonnett how it came about that Neil and Harry Hyde joined forces.

"I don't have a clue," she said, "other than that they were both hardheads."

I asked her what she remembered about Hyde.

"I remember Harry as being pretty dedicated," she said. "And he was kind of a tough guy. But Harry was the sort of guy—however *he* saw it—that's how it was. If you didn't see it the way he saw it, too bad.

"But," she added, "I was crazy about Harry."

With only a two-race sponsorship, times became tough when their attempts were marked mostly by engine failures or crashes. Susan Bonnett recalled that

Neil's career seemed about over before it began when a man by the name of J. D. or Jim Stacy bought the team in mid-April of 1977.

"We didn't know anything about Jim Stacy when he came on board," said Susan Bonnett.

But the arrival of Stacy seemed to change the team's luck and fortune. In July 1977, Bonnett won the pole at the Firecracker 400 at Daytona.

"A day before when they unloaded the car and were practicing, Neil told me, 'That car is unbelievable. It is fast, and I think we are going to sit on the pole.' We were real confident. Harry was real excited about it too.

"But I was wary. I didn't get too excited about it, because I knew how it goes. I found out a long time ago in racing that other teams would sandbag. I was beginning to be conditioned, that's for sure. I said to Neil, 'People don't really let you know what they are going to do in practice. You won't know until pole time.'

"But he did sit on the pole, and he was very excited, and so was Harry and so was Jim Stacy, and of course, all the crew was excited."

Bonnett finished eighth in the race, an encouragement, and then after a couple of races in which the car didn't work very well, he went to Richmond in September and won, the first win for Neil Bonnett, for the team of Neil and Harry, and for Jim Stacy. Back home in Alabama, Susan Bonnett was listening to the race on her car radio.

"I was not there for that race," she said. "I did not get to travel a lot because the children were small. That day I was at a skateboard park with my son David competing in some contest, so I was back and forth in the car listening to the race while my son was on the skateboard doing tricks. It was just me and my son, and I was just ecstatic when Neil won. Of course, your first win is always the toughest. We were real excited about the win, because we felt it would keep the sponsorship going. And the win meant more money than we had in the past."

To prove the win at Richmond wasn't a fluke, on November 20, 1977, Neil Bonnett was victorious at the Ontario Speedway.

"I was there for that one," said Susan Bonnett, "and I can tell you that there were two things that stand out in my mind about that. In the first place, the racetrack was unbelievable, because it was what a racetrack ought to be, friendly, where as a wife I was treated like a queen, not like a dog. I had access to the pits, which was something we didn't have when Neil first started out. I remember when Neil was driving for Hawaiian Tropic, one of the lady representatives pitched a fit, and she was part of the reason we were able to go into the pit area.

"Ontario had a catwalk built over the garage area where wives and kids could watch without being in the way. You could see your husband, see what was going on. And there was a tunnel from the infield over to the grandstand area where they had a restaurant and you could eat.

"The second thing I remember about his winning Ontario, of course, was that it was very exciting and great for us. We stayed there overnight, because we were driving home—we didn't have the money to fly at the time—and the next day we drove past the track. Neil just wanted to look at it again. We parked in an area where we could see in. No people were there. There was debris everywhere, and workers were picking up the paper and trash. Neil said, 'To have so many people there and to have it so exciting one day, and the next day, nothing. . . .' It was almost a letdown. The day before there had been excitement, and then it was like it had left and gone someplace else. We didn't understand all that then."

I asked Susan Bonnett her opinion of Jim Stacy.

"He took us in," she said. "We got close to his family, his children, and he took us to his home. Jim was a laid-back guy. I think he thought the world of Neil."

"Did he get along with Harry Hyde?" I asked.

"As well as you could," she said. "To begin with, yes. Harry could be difficult. I don't want to say that about anybody, but he laid it on the line. He didn't pull any punches. He told it like it was.

"And I know Harry liked to do anything he could do to win a race. I remember one time at Dover, Neil was running pretty good. They had this load of BBs or buckshot—some kind of lead—Harry told Neil when he came in for a pit stop to drop the BBs when he went back out in order to drop some weight from the car. He had rigged up a lever for Neil to pull, and the BBs fell out of the car to lighten it. Well, the BBs fell out all right, and NASCAR saw it, and everybody behind him went sliding. Neil had been in contention to win, and he was penalized, and Neil was really mad at Harry when they got through, because he felt he could have won the race without ever having done that.

"Harry was always trying these little tricks—all of them did—but he got caught on that one. Oh, Lord."

In early May 1977, Harry Hyde and Neil Bonnett determined that the Dodge they were running was no match for the Oldsmobile, so they switched manufacturers. Hyde was between a rock and a hard place, and after the switch the engines blew as often as not. If the engine held up, Bonnett would finish in the top 10, as he did at Dover, Nashville, and Riverside. But when it didn't, as at Charlotte and Michigan, poor finishes resulted. After the Michigan race, Jim Stacy, who had owned two teams and sponsored several others including Bonnett's, got out of racing when his resources finally ran out.

The ones who were between the rock and the hard place, as it turned out, were the Bonnetts, because despite Bonnett earning $122,000 in purses in 1977, for most of the year Neil didn't get paid as Stacy sank into a financial hell.

"Jim started out really big," said Susan Bonnett, "and he found out how expensive it was to be in racing. He was in the mining business, and that wasn't going well. I remember that Neil drove for a long time without getting paid. We struggled. Other people carried their whole families to the races, but we couldn't afford for me to go. I had to stay at home. I would make five or six races a year, and I'd have to drive. Nobody on the team got paid. Neil told me it was inevitable he was going to have to look to go to another team. He couldn't do what he was doing if he wasn't going to get paid. I don't know what happened with Jim.

"Did Neil end up getting his money?" I asked.

"I don't think so," she said.

"That had to be hard," I said.

"It was," she said. "I can tell you this: it was so bad, Neil was at Daytona for the July race, and Donnie Allison went to Neil and told him he was supposed to drive a Modified car for Pee Wee Griffin but that his sponsor didn't want him running anything but Winston Cup and would Neil like to drive for him? He said that Pee Wee would give him *all* of his winnings. That got Neil's attention because he knew he needed to make some money. He went and raced for Pee Wee at Daytona, and Neil finished well, and Pee Wee gave him all the money, and that money carried us over for a while. Pee Wee asked him to start driving for him in what were like the Busch races, the Modified division, and this was also the time when Warner Hodgdon gave him the opportunity to drive an Indy car.

"Bobby had driven for Warner before. Warner had sponsored him, and I'm sure Neil met Warner through Bobby. Bobby was supposed to drive at Nashville for him, and Bobby either got sick or hurt, and Neil drove for him, and that's probably how the relationship got started. I remember going to Riverside and staying in a suite Hodgdon had. Warner talked to Neil about driving an Indy car for him, and Neil got all excited about that because he didn't have a Winston Cup ride at the time. So he practiced the car at Indy—it was an open-wheel car, and of course I was really *very* nervous about that. Neil was used to beating and banging and running up against sheet metal, and I was thinking, 'You can't do that with these open-wheel cars.'

"It was the week before qualifying for the Indianapolis 500, and I got to go, and they treated me like a queen. Neil and Warner got pretty close, and just before he was scheduled to qualify this car for Indy, he got a call from the Wood Brothers. Neil went to Warner and told him, 'I don't want to let you down, but this is what I really want to do.' Warner said, 'Do the Wood Brothers have a sponsor?' And he came in on the deal. He let Neil out of the Indy car ride and got someone else to drive it and he sponsored his car with the Wood Brothers, and that's how Warner Hodgdon got involved with Winston Cup."

On April 22, 1979, Neil Bonnett began driving a Mercury for the Wood Brothers, whose shop was, and is, located in the hidden hills of Stuart, Virginia.

"Have you ever met people who you feel you've always known and been connected with?" asked Susan Bonnett. "That's the way they were. They just took us in as their own. They were a family-oriented operation that included me and the children in everything they did, and that appealed to me. We all hit it off, and Neil and Eddie were very close. They were super people and still are. Always at the races you felt comfortable."

On May 6, 1979, Neil Bonnett went to Talladega and qualified third. He led the race until the engine quit on him with just 40 laps to go.

"Neil must have been disappointed," I said.

"Yeah, we all took the brunt if he was not happy," she said. "As most families do. When he was unhappy, everybody knew he was unhappy."

"Did you give him space until it blew over?" I asked.

"If Neil was upset, you just got out of his way," she said. "He had a quick temper, as quick a temper as he had a quick wit. If he was upset, you better get out of his way. I've got dents in all my doors, and many telephones are down the hill behind my house.

"I have a long wood fence running around the backyard of my house, and I can remember a guy coming to my house to give me an estimate on painting my fence. I had forgotten that two or three days before Neil had pitched a pit and thrown the telephone out the back. Usually when he did that, it went over the fence and down the hill. It's a long way from the deck, where he threw it, and this time it landed on the fence and had wound around it and was just hanging there. And I didn't notice it until the painter came. He said, 'Did you know your phone is hanging there?' I was so embarrassed. I thought, If he only knew how many of those things are down the hill!

"One day Neil bought a chain saw. He worked on it and pulled on it and pulled on it, and it just would not work, and instead of taking it back, he pitched it—down the hill. I said, There is a gold mine for somebody down the hill if anyone wants to find all the stuff he's thrown away."

If Neil Bonnett was frustrated over not winning at Talladega, his fortunes quickly changed when in May 1979 he won the Dover race and followed that up with a win in the Firecracker 400 at Daytona. In that race, he held off Benny Parsons on the backstretch of the last lap for the victory. Dale Earnhardt was third, Darrell Waltrip fourth, and Richard Petty fifth. The wins gave Bonnett his third and fourth trophies and established him among the top drivers on the Winston Cup circuit.

"They came at a good time," said Susan Bonnett. I asked her how Neil Bonnett's success and higher profile affected him.

"I don't think it affected him at all," she said. "except we were able to pay our bills. As far as Neil and his personality, Neil never cared about the fame. He really never did. It was not his thing. The more successful he got, the more in demand he was, and the less in demand he wanted to be.

"He did everything he was asked to do, but as time went on, he had no time to do anything with his family or those things he enjoyed doing, and he finally had to start saying no to something so he could just come home and unwind.

"He did not like going to malls and meeting with people, because he would always say, 'Nobody is coming to see me.' He just felt people would not come. If he had a meeting with his fan club, he'd say, 'Why am I going? Nobody is going to come.' But there would always be a great turnout. He had such a great personality, there wasn't anything he couldn't do if he put his mind to it. But he did not have that confidence in himself. He always struggled with that, though to look at him you never would know it.

"I remember Neil building an old Model A car. He started it and modified it, and when he got to a certain point, he said, 'I'm going to get somebody to finish it.' I said, 'No. You started it, and this is one project you're going to finish yourself.' I kept on him, and finally he did, and he was so glad when he did. Cause usually he'd start something, and he'd either run out of time or he lost interest. I said, 'This is one project you're going to finish,' and so he did, and he did a super job and he was really proud that he did."

CHAPTER 31

MR. CONSISTENCY

Benny Parsons

AFTER WINNING THE WINSTON CUP CHAMPIONSHIP IN 1973, BENNY PARSONS should have been on top of the world. Instead, 1974 turned out to be, as Parsons described it, "a disaster." The gasoline embargo eventually faded into memory, but a reduction in the size of car engines wreaked havoc with L. G. DeWitt's race team.

"It was terrible," Parsons said. "We had won the championship, felt like we wanted to come out and prove ourselves, and that year we switched over to the small block, and we just could not get our hands on the good pieces to save our life.

"We bought the blocks and cylinder heads from Chevrolet, but the problem was with the parts Chevrolet didn't make, the crankshafts, the connector rods, the valves—we just could not get our hands on the good pieces. We blew up engine after engine after engine, and we weren't competitive. It was a disastrous year."

The 1974 championship was won by Richard Petty, and behind him were Cale Yarborough, David Pearson, Bobby Allison, and then Parsons. But his team won no races that year, and for a racer who counted success only by his wins, fifth place was very little consolation and just not good enough.

"Like I said," said Parsons, "it was a disastrous year."

Parsons was so distraught about his poor performance that in the winter of 1974 he called Ken Squier, the anchor for Motor Racing Network radio.

"I said, 'Is there any kind of opening for me with MRN?'

"He said, 'What's the problem?'

"I said, 'I just cannot stand this disappointment anymore, being uncompetitive and all. I need to find something else to do.'

"He said, 'We need you in a race car much more than we need you on the radio.'

"I went to L. G., and I said, 'I just can't stand this anymore. It's just eating me alive.'

"L. G. said, 'Let's try one more year.'

"So I agreed. We went down and won the '75 Daytona 500, and it was 13 more years before I felt strong about retirement again."

His success in the 1975 Daytona 500 was all the more remarkable considering that in the 125-mile qualifier, Parsons finished so badly that he started the race in 32nd place.

"I really don't know what happened to the car (in the qualifier)," he said. "I came off turn two, and the car just turned sideways on me. I went into the pits, because I knew something was broken. We all assumed that the locker in the rear gear broke. So for the 500 we took out the locker and ran an open gear just to get away from that problem."

Parsons ran strong, racing to the front after starting way in the back.

"With about twenty-five laps to go, Coo Coo Marlin, Sterling's daddy, blew up, and there was a caution flag. Pearson was the leader, and I was the only other car on the lead lap. They restarted the race, and I hung with him a few laps, and he got away from me. David pulled out to a six- or seven-second lead. At this point, I was disappointed, because I felt I was not going to win the Daytona 500.

"Richard Petty had the fastest car that day by far, but he had split a seam in the radiator. The water is under pressure, so it would push the water out, so every twelve laps he would have to stop to put water in.

"After his last stop, he came back out on the track right in front of me, and he motioned to me with his right hand, 'Like, if you want to catch this cat, come on.' When I went to latch onto Richard, I couldn't catch up with him, so he waited for me to make sure I kept up with him."

"Why did Richard do that?" I asked.

"I don't know," said Parsons. "Richard Petty was a nice man. He always has been. Maybe he wanted me to win the Daytona 500 more than he wanted David Pearson to win the Daytona 500.

"So we started gaining on Pearson. We came by the line, and there were three laps to go, and we're now in Pearson's mirror, probably a second behind him.

"Something had happened to Cale's car, and he was just making laps, and when we came off the second corner, Pearson misjudged—I've never talked to David about it—I saw this big cloud of smoke—it's pavement now, but it was dirt then—when I came off the corner, I thought, Someone has spun out. And when I rubbernecked the crash, I saw the 21 car.

"Remember, in 1973 David won eleven of eighteen races. You just never saw that 21 car in any kind of trouble. I was just astonished that Pearson had a problem. I said, 'Can you believe the 21 car has . . . ?', and about the time I drove off into turn three, it dawned on me: 'You just won the Daytona 500!'

"I ran two more laps, and when I took the checkered flag, it was by far the most thrilling moment I ever had in racing. You know, when you think back about that fifty-dollar car and all the nights I had spent by myself working on those cars when everybody else was out having a good time, when I was wondering, 'Why am I doing this?' All of a sudden you *know* the reason why you were doing this."

In 1975, Richard Petty won the racing championship. Dave Marcis was second, James Hylton third, and Benny Parsons fourth.

Nineteen seventy-six should have seen Benny Parsons' second win in a row in the Daytona 500. Like the year before, he started way in the back of the pack. In what was arguably the most famous race in NASCAR history, he finished third to David Pearson and Richard Petty. It was in this race that Petty and Pearson crashed on the final lap. Had Pearson not been able to keep his car running, Benny Parsons would have won at the expense of David Pearson two years in a row.

"With thirty laps to go, there was a caution flag," said Parsons. "We changed tires. As it turned out, someone, to get a better view of the racetrack, had stood on the tires and had bent the valve stems on one of them, and we didn't check the tires as well as we should have, and we put a flat tire on the car.

"We restarted the race, and I had to stop and change right sides—it didn't take as long to change tires as it does now because we had no speed limit on pit road—but nevertheless, about the time I got back on the racetrack I broke a push rod, so now I'm on seven cylinders, and I'm by myself. I have no drafting help at all, so it wasn't long before Pearson and Petty came along and lapped me.

"If I hadn't had a flat tire, I might have been able to hang on in the lead lap. So what happened, David and Richard came off the corner and crashed, and if you ever see the video of it, I'm the car going across the line just before Pearson got there. I was two laps down, and I finished one lap down. I made up that one lap, but I was down two because of the flat tire and the seven cylinders.

"Nevertheless, Pearson would have been fit to be tied if two years in a row I had been the benefactor . . . If Pearson's car had stalled somehow, for two years in a row I would have won the Daytona 500 on his misfortune.

"But somehow he kept it rolling," said Parsons.

One of Benny Parsons' best performances in 1976 came at Dover on May 16 after his car was damaged in a crash halfway through. It took Parsons' crew five yellow-flag pit stops to fix the handling problems.

"That was an amazing thing," said Parsons. "We were about a fifth-place car that day. Somebody [Ricky Rudd] spun out in turn three and four, and I came along and hit him and bent my right front fender. Whenever we pit, we tried to beat the hood back in place and get the fender off the tire. But after we did that, the car was beautiful, perfect. We pushed the fender up just enough to give it downforce. After I bent the fender, the car handled beautifully. But we weren't smart enough to realize we had done something extraordinary.

"We won the race, but we should have asked ourselves, 'Why did the car handle so well after we bent the fender? Can we bend this fender every place we go?'"

In 1976, Parsons won at Nashville over Richard Petty and finished third in the points to Cale Yarborough and Petty. It was the first of three straight driving championships for Yarborough. I asked Benny Parsons what made Yarborough so hard to beat.

"He and Junior by then had two or three years together, and the communication had gotten to be pretty doggone good. Junior's cars were very durable, plus Cale finally figured out he needed to do everything he could to finish the races.

"Cale didn't wreck much back then. He came to understand that you needed to finish."

In 1977, Parsons had another terrific season. He won four races, had 20 top 10 finishes in 30 starts. Only Cale Yarborough and Richard Petty finished with more points for the championship. Parsons defeated Petty at Pocono, beat David Pearson at Dover, and his most memorable moment that year came at Charlotte on October 9 when he won the NAPA National 500 after running out of gas.

"That was the dumbest thing in the world," Parsons said. "We might have had the best car we ever had at a racetrack. We were about a half a second faster than anybody. The crew was telling [crew chief Jake Elder], 'We need to pit. We need some gas.'

"Cale was half a lap down. Cale's crew chief was Herb Nab, and Herb and Jake had a rivalry going. Jake said, 'By God, I'm not stopping until Herb stops.'

"I passed pit road, and when I came by the entrance to pit road, I ran out of gas, and I didn't think I was going to make it back. It's a mile and a half, and somehow I coasted back, and it was the longest few minutes. By the time I stopped and got gas in the car. . . .

"We didn't have to gamble. Cale did. That was the frustrating thing. That was just Jake being Jake.

"So we got back on the racetrack a half a lap down, but we were so much faster, and it didn't take me more than a couple of laps to catch him, and I went on and won the race. As I said, that was the best car I ever had anywhere.

"Jake Elder had a very good feel for a race car. He could tell by looking and by talking. He was a mechanical adjuster. We knew nothing about aerodynamics back then. He knew springs and shocks, sway bars, and what have you. That's how he worked on a race car, and he was very thorough, and he was a *very* hard worker.

"Back then, crew chiefs worked on the cars. Today, a crew chief is an organizer. Jake worked very hard and was very thorough and put together a very solid race car."

The year 1978 was another excellent year for Benny Parsons and the 72 L. G. DeWitt car. Parsons finished fourth in the points standings to Cale Yarborough, Bobby Allison, and Darrell Waltrip. In 30 races, he finished in the top ten 21 times. Then at the end of the 1978 season, Parsons and L. G. DeWitt parted ways. As is often the case, money—or the lack thereof—was at issue. Loyalty was still important to Parsons, but the cost of living was rising dramatically, and feeding his family had become paramount.

"In '77 and '78, we were sponsored by First National City Travelers Checks, which is now Citicorp," said Parsons. "The sponsorship had run out at the end of '78, and they decided not to continue in racing. I was making maybe $75,000 a year, so at the end of the year I said to L. G., 'What are we going to do?' He said he didn't know.

"In the meantime, I called M. C. Anderson down in Savannah about my driving the 27 car. Buddy Baker had been released, and I wanted to see if that ride was available, and it was, and I was told if I took the ride, I would make over a hundred thousand dollars a year.

"So my choice was to go down there and make a hundred thousand dollars or to stay with L. G. and maybe not race all the time.

"I went to L. G. and I said, 'I have this opportunity. It's very difficult for me to turn down, and I can't turn it down.' I said, 'As expensive as the business is today, I really, truly think the best thing you can do is shut her down.'

"And L. G. agreed. I called M. C. and took the deal. And for whatever reason, L. G. decided to run one more [full] year [with Joe Millikan driving].

"M. C. was in construction. Our crew chief was David Ifft, who might not have had the mechanical skills somebody else might have had, but he was terrific at getting people to work together. He was very good at keeping the crew together. Which is more important than the mechanical skills. It was a very good two years."

On July 4, 1979, at the Firecracker 400, Parsons finished second to Neil Bonnett, one car length back. Dale Earnhardt was a car length behind Parsons.

"Neil was a great deal like myself," said Parsons. "He was a racer. And he was not above working on the cars. Neil was thrilled to death he could make a living doing what he loved to do."

In 1979, Parsons won two races, the first at North Wilkesboro, near his Ellerbe home, and the second in the final race of the season at Ontario, where Parsons took the lead with five laps to go and beat Bobby Allison for the win.

It was also the year in which Richard Petty won his fifth driving championship, edging a heartbroken Darrell Waltrip, who would have won but spun out and lost his spot on the lead lap. I asked Parsons whether he had resented the Petty Enterprises machine, as some drivers did.

"I did not," he said. "I never did. I felt that Richard Petty *was* stock car racing, that he had been stock car racing for many, many years, that he did all the things I felt were essential to grow the sport, things I thought were essential. It wasn't just that he signed autographs and was warm to the people. For years, Richard carried the sport on his back.

"Richard would go to functions and lend his name to things to help grow the sport, when so many guys were hesitant to do that. I really appreciated Richard doing that and always admired the way he did that, how he lent himself to try to make his sport bigger.

"When STP came along as a sponsor, Richard sold STP as hard as he could. When Winston came along—Richard Petty was not a tobacco user, but he sold Winston as best he could, because he knew that was the lifeblood of our sport. And he was a great, great race car driver."

In 1979, Benny Parsons had an excellent year, winning at North Wilkesboro and Ontario, finishing fifth in the points, and earning $264,929 in purses.

That following year, his second and final year with M. C. Anderson, Parsons was chasing the racing title, which would have been his second. He won the World 600 at Charlotte, the Gabriel 400 at Michigan, and for the second year in a row the final race of the season and the last Winston Cup race ever held at the Ontario Speedway.

"In 1980, at Ontario, for some reason, my Monte Carlo wouldn't run," Parsons said. "I knew I was in trouble when I had to run wide open, just wide open, to keep up with Cale and Darrell down the straightaway.

"You are supposed to be able to run three-quarter throttle and keep up. But I had to run on the mat. And I had a flat tire early on, and had to stop and got a lap down.

"I was a lap and a half down when the caution flag came out. Back then, you could pit at any time. We did not have the rules we have today. So I dove onto pit road hoping to get my four tires and get on the racetrack so I'd be the first car a lap down so I could start up front with the leaders and hopefully beat them back to the line to get my lap back. But guess what, the leader didn't come down pit road, and so now I'm two laps down.

"I was following Darrell Waltrip, and I came off turn four, and I got a terrific run on him coming off the corner. I was drafting behind him, thinking to myself, 'Now if you try to slingshot by and if you don't make it, they are going to train you on the outside and you're going to drop back to sixth.' But for some reason I pulled out and drafted by him anyway.

"No more than fifty yards before we got to the start/finish line, they threw a caution flag, so I beat him to the line by a half a car length. I'm one lap down.

"Now Cale was leading the race. Same deal: I am somehow right behind Cale, and the wind was blowing that day—must have been fifty miles an hour. It was blowing from turn two across to turn four. When you go to turn four, you had to back off early. If you tried to drive the car into the corner, the wind wouldn't let the car turn. He was lucky he didn't crash.

"So the caution flag came out while we were going down the backstretch. Today, they move over and let you get your lap back. I knew Cale wasn't going to do that. He raced me as hard as he could.

"He went into turn three hard to keep me a lap down, but there wasn't any way his car was going to turn. He pushed up and almost ran into the wall, and I just turned under him and went on and beat him to the line by twenty car lengths. Now I am on the lead lap.

"With about ten laps to go, we had a pit stop. We stopped for gas. Cale in Junior [Johnson's] car and Bobby in Bud [Moore's] car stop for fuel only. My guys—David Ifft, Barry Dodson, Pete Peterson, Eddie Thrap, guys who are still around—said, 'With ten laps to go, fresh tires will be worth a lot.' So we changed four tires, because we could change them about as fast as we could put gas in, and it was like taking candy from a baby.

"I went out there, and I was a second a lap faster than they were, because they were on old tires that had been out there 125 miles. With those fresh tires, I drove by them and drove away. And the caution never came back out for them to get back in to change.

"CBS was doing that race that day. I was sitting in the car in Victory Lane, and Brock Yates was the pit reporter. They threw it down to him, and Brock said, 'Benny, here we are in Victory Lane. Sorry, we have to go.' I'll never forget the look on my face. I said to myself, 'That is the story of my life.'"

What made the win remarkable was that despite his excellent year five or six weeks earlier, M. C. Anderson had told Parsons he was replacing him at the end of the year. I asked Parsons how hard it was to drive as a lame duck?

"It's almost impossible," he said. "When the team is going to split up," he said, "the best thing to do is just bust up and go your separate ways, because really and truly, not much is going to get done."

"And yet, despite this, you went on and won at Ontario," I said.

"It was amazing," he said. "It really was amazing."

That year he finished third in the points behind Dale Earnhardt and Cale Yarborough. Though Earnhardt had won Rookie of the Year in 1979 and the racing championship in 1980, most drivers were furious at what they considered to be his reckless driving style. I asked Parsons whether he was also angry at the way Earnhardt drove.

"Uh-huh," he said. "Everybody was. We just were not accustomed to that. If he ran up behind you and was faster, he'd just knock you out of the way. We were really and truly not accustomed to that, and there was nothing we could do about it. We always felt it was NASCAR's position to do something if there was something to be done, but they didn't, so. . . . We couldn't believe anyone would drive that way."

"Did he ever do it to you?" I asked.

"Oh yeah," Parsons said. "I raced with him, didn't I? But he never knocked me out of the way to win a race. No. No. He didn't do that."

In the years between 1972 and 1980, in the points standing for the racing championship Benny Parsons finished fifth, first, fifth, fourth, third, third, fourth, fifth, and third. Over that decade, no one was more consistent. And yet Parsons did not achieve the fame of his more flamboyant competitors like Richard Petty, Cale Yarborough, Bobby Allison, or Darrell Waltrip.

"I didn't go after the ink," said Parsons. "I probably would have liked to have had it. I had my share of interviews. Reporters wanted to talk to me because I was a decent interview."

"You did as well in those eight years as anyone," I said.

"Yes," he said. "It was terrific. I have no complaints at all."

CHAPTER 32

ROBERT GEE AND HARRY HYDE

Jimmy Makar

JIMMY MAKAR HAS A SOUTHERN DRAWL THAT BELIES THE FACT THAT HE WAS BORN and raised in Cedar Knolls, a little town in New Jersey. His dad, Jim, was a truck driver most of his life, working for a paper mill nearby. His dad was also a gearhead who loved tinkering with cars and who dreamed of racing one day on the Winston Cup circuit.

In 1977, Makar's dad decided to make his dream a reality. One of his friends learned that Roger Penske would be selling off some of his cars, parts, and pieces, so Makar's dad took his savings, got a second mortgage on the house, and bought a race car to go run in a handful of Winston Cup races.

Things were different back then. If you had a good car, an independent could make the field in Winston Cup. Travis Carter, who was the crew chief for Roger Penske, prepared the car for the Daytona 500. His dad had been impressed watching a young Morgan Shepherd drive in the Late Model Sportsman division, and he made a deal with Shepherd to drive the car in the race.

It became a community project. Jimmy, several of Jimmy's friends and his brother's friends, guys who hung out together at his dad's shop in town, worked on the car and became the pit crew.

"We went to Daytona," said Jimmy Makar, "and we had some engine trouble." The car didn't qualify for the race. "It wasn't a very good experience. We got our feet wet, ran six races that year. We qualified thirteenth at Atlanta [in the March race], actually outqualifying Roger's cars there, and we ran well in the race.

211

[The car, driven by Jody Ridley, finished 14th.] We went to a few other tracks, Dover, Pocono. Kenny Brightbill drove it there.

"The race at Dover was where I got my start in Winston Cup. Kenny was involved in a big wreck with Jim Hurtubise, Tighe Scott, and two or three other cars. We tore the car up real bad, and we had to send it back to Banjo Matthews' shop to get the chassis fixed. We needed to get a body put on it. Morgan was going to drive the car in the final race of the season, and he knew a guy who could do that by the name of Robert Gee. Robert was well known in this area for body fabrication, so we arranged for the car to go to Banjo's and then to Robert's, and to save money my dad sent me down to do what I could do with the car. Robert's was an independent shop. He took work in from all different places.

"The car got in line at Robert's shop about four weeks before he was ready to work on it. I came down to North Carolina, and he offered to put me up at his house to live with him and work in the shop until he could get to our car. He would teach me the ropes of fabricating. That's how I got started.

"Robert Gee was a fun guy. He loved racing, race cars, loved to have fun. A lot of people have gone through Robert's shop. Looking back at it now, Darrell Waltrip, Jake Elder, and Ricky Rudd were among the people who came through Robert's shop.

"Robert had done some work for Darrell earlier in his career, and he continued to do things for him when Darrell drove the Gatorade car for the Gardners. Darrell had a little Grand American car that Robert built at his shop. Darrell drove it for Robert.

"Gosh, it was a gathering place for guys who have become big names in the sport. It was a place to go hang out in the evening after everyone got done with where they were working and have a good time and talk racing.

"I met Darrell and his wife, Stevie, when I worked for Robert Gee. That was the heyday of the film *Jaws*, in the late 1970s. ["Jaws" was the nickname Cale Yarborough tagged on the controversial, talkative Waltrip.] Four or five of us from Robert's shop went with them to the Snowball Derby down at Pensacola, a Late Model race they have every winter. Darrell won the race that year.

"We all went out to dinner, and afterward we were sitting around on the bed in the motel room—Darrell, Stevie, three or four of us, Frank the dog was laying on the bed, and we turned on the TV to watch the news, and the headline was that there was controversy at the track, that there was a scoring change, and that Darrell was declared *not* the winner.

"We said, 'Wait a minute. The trophy is sitting on top of the TV. We won the race.'

"We got up and went back to the track in the middle of the night to try to find out what was going on. That was a little, half-mile track, a lot of cars, scoring wasn't very good there, a lot of green-flag racing, people pitting and then the caution coming out, and somehow or other, they did something in the scoring where they said we were a lap down . . . typical Saturday night racing. It was horrible.

"They declared someone else the winner, but Darrell took the trophy home. He wasn't giving the trophy back. He still has it.

"I spent the whole day working in Robert Gee's shop. He taught me everything from forming sheet metal to welding—I didn't know how to use a welder when I first went down there—I learned the basics: cutting and forming sheet metal, forming fenders, learned how to build a fender clearance on a piece of sheet metal. I had done a lot of mechanical work and paint and bodywork as a teenager in my dad shop's at the house. We had done a lot of work on street cars. That I could do.

"I spent two to three months there. I did work on three or four cars that had come into the shop before we finally got to my dad's car. We ended up getting the car done for Atlanta and sending it to Atlanta, and before I left Robert, he said to me, 'If you ever want a job, a career in the business, give me a call.'"

Makar returned to New Jersey, and for two or three weeks he thought about what Robert Gee had said. He had always wanted to be involved in racing, and he thought that working for Robert Gee might be a great opportunity to meet people and learn mechanic's skills in a good environment. He called Gee and asked him if he was serious about the job offer. When Gee said he was, Makar packed up everything he owned and moved to North Carolina. Makar worked for Robert Gee for three years.

"My first year with Robert I made nine thousand dollars before taxes doing contract labor. Which wasn't bad, wasn't good. It was enough to get by. I bought a single-wide trailer and lived across the street from the Charlotte Motor Speedway."

Makar would get up in the morning, go to the shop, and work all day. Gee's son, Robert Jr., and Makar also worked on a dirt car that Gee owned, and on Friday nights, Saturday nights, and Sunday afternoons they raced the car at the local dirt tracks. Haywood Plyler drove the car. Gee Jr., Makar, and Plyler won a lot of races in the Concord-Charlotte area. If Plyler didn't win, then his rival, Freddy Smith, did. The two raced against each other all over the Carolinas.

"We had a lot of fun," said Makar. "I learned a lot about Saturday night racing. It was an opportunity to learn fabrication skills and to race on the weekends. It was a great opportunity for me.

"I was very green at it. Seemed like everything I did was new for me. I was trying to absorb all I could. When we were working I'd be around all these people:

Harry Hyde, Buddy Parrott, crew chiefs, and people in the business like Jake Elder and Darrell. It was just a great environment.

"After three years working for Robert, Harry Hyde gave me my first opportunity in Winston Cup racing. I went to work over at his place doing fabrication and body work. Harry had a pretty small operation at the time. This was after Harry's heyday. It was after his lawsuits with Jim Stacy, after everything had gone downhill. It was pretty ugly. Stacy had done everything he could to shut Harry down.

"Harry didn't have a whole lot going on, but he offered me a job in Cup, and that's what I was looking to do. So I took him up on his offer, and went racing with Harry for a couple of years. Tighe Scott was driving for Harry.

"I learned an awful lot from Harry. Like Robert Gee, he was a guy who took you under his wing and taught you everything you needed to know. I can't say enough about what Harry taught me as far as racing savvy, construction of race cars, and how to think during races and make decisions.

"Harry had been around the business a long time. You just absorbed things from him. The things that were mundane and normal for him were very new and enlightening for me.

"I can remember we got talking about race car construction and how stiff a car had to be. A lot of this stuff was just done—there was no science to it. Harry was involved with Chrysler, and he broke out a full-sized blueprint that he rolled out onto the floor of a chassis that Chrysler had done a stress-analysis on and what kind of bars were needed, where they were needed, and where they needed to be placed. The blueprint was from the late '60s, early '70s, way before a lot of people were doing these things in an engineering fashion.

"Most of it was, 'I think it would be better this way or that way.' But when Harry unrolled those blueprints and started explaining it to me, it was like, 'Wow!'

"And bump-steering cars today, you have a toe-pattern gauge to see how the toe changes after it goes over bumps. Back then, Harry would do it with a plumb bob from a wheel and make marks on the wheel and travel the car with floor jacks up through there and restring the plumb bob and mark the floor again and measure the difference between the marks to figure out how the wheel was toeing in and out. It was crude, but very efficient. It got the job done.

"Harry was the first guy I ever heard talking about setting a race car up with a roll couple and trying to figure out what percentages a particular driver liked. Spring rates—how much front spring versus rear springs a driver would like, basically balancing the race car tight or loose for different drivers. This was Harry. He did a lot of little things like that, where he was very sharp, very smart about what he was doing.

"He had been backed by Chrysler and Dodge at the end of his career, but he was just so full of knowledge.

"I just tried to watch everything he did. Harry was very smart and a good guy. A lot of people looked at Harry and saw a hard person, a real strong person, but he cared about people. He took care of me, for sure, and I'm grateful. I had a lot of fun over there.

"It was a short period of time I was there. I wish I could have spent more time with him.

"We didn't have a lot of success. We ran relatively OK—had opportunities to win races at Talladega and Daytona—but it was never a serious effort. Tighe was a lot of fun and a pretty good race driver, but I don't think it was serious enough to run at the Cup level like you needed to.

"Tighe's dad pretty much backed the racing operation. He owned rest homes up in Pennsylvania. But it never amounted to anything, never grew into anything. Tighe ended up leaving Cup racing and going back north where he ran Modifieds for a little while before fading out of the scene.

"After Tighe left, Harry got a deal with a guy out of Ohio by the name of John Rebhan, who built coal mining machinery. The company was Warren Fabricating, and he hired a guy by the name of John Anderson, a real good Midwest driver. We ran John a few races, but we were under a lot of pressure from Rebhan to do real well. I think John had the talent to get there, but there was too much pressure from the sponsor to do well too soon, and it was a short-lived deal.

"What I remember about John, he'd work in the shop every day, work on the race cars, one of the guys, and then we'd go to the racetrack with the guys and drive the race car. He was a hands-on individual, a really neat guy. He had a lot of talent. He just never got the opportunity to prove it, so after that they hired Donnie Allison to drive the car. Donnie was a *real* good driver, had been around a long time, but really never got going very well with Harry.

The partnership got little chance to work out, as Donnie was badly injured in a wreck at Charlotte that took him out of racing for several years.

"After that, John Rebhan pulled out of racing. He decided that was it. He didn't want anymore to do with racing. It kind of shut the door on Harry's operation from that point. We didn't have any racing going on.

"I hung around for two months, piddling around. It was real hard on Harry. He wanted to go racing, but he didn't have any opportunity. I got a job offer, and I told Harry about it. He said, 'Go. Get you a job.' So I left Harry and went to work for Benfield Racing."

CHAPTER 33

A RIVALRY WITH D. W.

Susan Bonnett

In 1979, Neil Bonnett, driving for the Wood Brothers, blazed onto the scene, winning at Dover and Daytona in the Firecracker 400, and defeating Dale Earnhardt at Atlanta in the fall. In the process, the affable Bonnett and his wife, Susan, were making friends. In addition to Bobby Allison, who had been Neil Bonnett's mentor, he also forged a close friendship with a young racer by the name of Dale Earnhardt.

"Neil raced when the competition was very fierce," said Susan Bonnett. "It was unheard of for anyone to come up into those ranks and actually win, because Richard Petty, Cale Yarborough, Bobby, and David Pearson had been so dominant for so long. Neil did well. And we got along so well with everyone. We were the closest with the Allisons, Bobby and Judy and Donnie and Pat, and as time went on, Neil and Dale Earnhardt became very close. I don't even know when they got so close. They enjoyed a lot of the same things, I guess, hunting and fishing, whereas Bobby was not into hunting and fishing. So away from the racetrack, Neil and Dale just had the same interests. They both loved to hunt and they both loved to fish."

I had been told stories of Neil and Dale each buying all-terrain vehicles and racing them at breakneck speeds through the woods.

"Right," she said. "They had a lot of the same goals, and they just hit it off. As he was close to Bobby. Bobby was always there for Neil, and Neil was always there for Bobby. They were not people who would backstab each other. I remember one time people came to Neil and asked him if he was interested in driving a car that Bobby was driving. Neil was very unnerved. He said, 'I think I'm just going to tell Bobby.' I said, 'That's the right thing to do.' And instead of going behind Bobby's back, he went to Bobby and told him. And Bobby was very appreciative."

In 1980, Neil Bonnett blew an engine after leading the Daytona 500 for seven laps. He was able to limp around and finish the race and come in third. That year, Bonnett drove in 22 of the 30 races, winning 2 races and $231,000 in purses.

"Neil was very happy during the [four] years he drove for the Wood Brothers," said Susan Bonnett. "I don't remember any finger pointing. At times it could get frustrating. Any time when you are blowing engines or if there's a wreck when the car is running well, people start looking for excuses or some-body to blame, and that always puts pressure on people. But [with the Wood Brothers] there was never any backstabbing."

Before the race at Riverside on June 8, 1980, Neil Bonnett's first at that tricky road course, he decided he needed some expert instruction, and he attended a two-day driving course taught by the famed instructor Bob Bondurant.

"I remember the first time we went to Riverside, we had a rental car, and Bobby and Judy, Neil and I all went together to the track. Bobby drove the four of us onto the track in the rental car, and he drove us around and showed us how you go through the turns. Neil didn't feel confident, and he decided to take a course with Bob Bondurant. Because Neil was too aggressive, and he needed to have patience, and he really didn't know what to do. When he came back from the course, he did better than he had done in a long time on a road course."

Which is an understatement, to say the least. At Riverside that June, Neil Bonnett was leading the race going into the ninth turn of the final lap when Darrell Waltrip caught him on the long backstretch and won by three-tenths of a second. Benny Parsons finished third.

"Neil had learned a whole lot of patience," said Susan Bonnett. "That was the biggest thing that he learned. I remember him telling me, 'I'm going to try and not be so aggressive, and I'm going to do what I've learned.' And it really paid off."

On July 27, 1980, Bonnett won the Pocono race over Buddy Baker, and the very next week he followed that up with a win at Talladega over Cale Yarborough, Dale Earnhardt, and Benny Parsons. The hometown Hueytown boy sped his Mercury to the lead with four laps to go and held off the trio of contenders.

"Talladega was Neil's favorite place," said Susan Bonnett. "I don't know if it was because it was so close to home, but he loved everything about Talladega, except the fact that everybody who thought they knew him came out of the woodwork that week. Everybody was calling asking for free tickets, wanting Neil to do this, do that, and we always had a lot of company, a lot of people staying with us that week, and it was pretty stressful driving back and forth the hour and fifteen minutes to the track, and you're outside in the hot sun. People pull at you all day long, and you come home and you're worn out, and you have a house full of people. It was his favorite place, and he always wanted to do well, but he always felt there was more pressure on him, but he felt it was a track where he could excel. Knowing that a lot of people he knew all his life were there was important.

"Most of the time he gave the trophy to the sponsor, but after this race he did bring it home. It had a crystal on top of it. The trophy didn't mean that much to Neil. I remember when he won at Ontario, he told Jim Stacy, 'You can have it.' I was thinking, 'Please don't give it away, because it was a silver punch-bowl and twelve cups, and it was beautiful.' Stacy insisted we have it, and I have used that punch bowl until I have about worn it out. But Neil didn't care about trophies, didn't care about fame, didn't care about none of that.

"He had a passion to do what he did, and when you have a passion, you give 100 percent of yourself. It doesn't matter what people think about it. You're going to do it."

In 1981, Bonnett won three more races, nipping Darrell Waltrip by a car length at the wire at Darlington, beating Waltrip again at Dover in September, and winning at Atlanta by a single car length over Waltrip two months later. In a year in which Waltrip won 12 races and earned $799,000, Bonnett did his best but was unable to keep Waltrip from beating his buddy Bobby Allison for the racing championship.

"I don't remember Neil ever saying anything bad about Darrell," said Susan Bonnett. "They had a couple of run-ins at the racetrack, and they had a run-in at the White House. Needless to say, they were not the best of buddies.

"The feud between Neil and Darrell was more a press thing than anything else. Like with Donnie and Cale, the press hyped it up so much that in the next race the least little bump was going to be blown out of proportion. Them ya-yaing back and forth in the paper made it even bigger, and then someone said they didn't know if they could trust them together at the White House, because they didn't want them brawling on the lawn and rolling down the hill at the White House.

"We were invited by Jimmy Carter, who wasn't there. The [Mideast peace] talks had begun at Camp David with Sadat and Begin, so he was not able to be there, but Rosalynn was there. I was so impressed with him and his wife. It was an excellent time. I really enjoyed that."

In 1982, Neil Bonnett won the World 600 at Charlotte, but it was the only race he won, and at the end of the year Bonnett and the Wood Brothers decided it best to go their separate ways.

"They knew when their time together was finished," said Susan Bonnett. "It was time for everybody to move on. And everybody moved on with the right attitude. That's the type of relationship we had."

In November 1983, it was announced that Warner Hodgdon would invest in the Rahmoc team owned by Bob Rahilly and Butch Mock and also in the Junior Johnson team. Hodgdon had hired Neil Bonnett to drive for him at Indy several years earlier, and when Hodgdon bought into NASCAR racing, one of the drivers he wanted on one of his teams was Bonnett.

"Neil was going to drive for Junior," said Susan Bonnett, "but Junior had some contracts to fulfill for a couple of years, so Neil drove for Rahmoc during that time."

In 1983, Bonnett for the first time got to drive in all 30 races. Bonnett in 1983 won 2 races, finishing sixth in the points and winning $453,000 in purses.

"Rahmoc was just the last names of Butch and Bob put together," said Susan Bonnett. "Bob built the motors, and Butch was in charge of everything else. They were two guys in business, and I was—and am—crazy about them. Hard-working. Good guys. They were young, dedicated, and Neil absolutely enjoyed driving for them. They had a real good relationship."

In 1983, Bonnett won the World 600 at Charlotte for the second year in a row and late in the season won at Atlanta after a serious injury.

"If I remember correctly," said Susan Bonnett, "Neil was the only one who ever drove for Rahmoc who ever won a race."

She was right. Rahmoc raced between 1978 and 1991, and Neil Bonnett, with two wins in 1983 and two more in 1988, won Rahmoc's only victories. None of their other drivers won, not Morgan Shepherd, Joe Ruttman, Lake Speed, or even Tim Richmond.

As well as Bonnett did, the celebration at the end of the 1983 season was for Bobby Allison, who after narrowly losing the driving championship to hated rival Darrell Waltrip in 1981 and 1982, edged his rival for his first and only championship. Neil and Susan Bonnett enjoyed Bobby's victory as well.

"We were all excited for Bobby," she said. "He had worked so long and so hard. We had seen the ups and downs, the good and the bad, so it was absolutely just like we had won it. It was meaningful to all of us. Neil and Bobby were close, and if they were excited about something, we were excited about it. They were *for* each other, not against each other. And you don't find that much in racing."

In 1984, Bonnett switched to the Junior Johnson team as planned. With Warner Hodgdon footing the bill, Bonnett drove for Junior's second team. The driver of his other race team was Darrell Waltrip, who Bonnett and buddy Bobby Allison had feuded with over the years. In 1983, Bonnett ran 30 races, won a pole, and had two second-place finishes, while Waltrip had seven wins and earned $767,000—about a half million more than Bonnett.

"Junior had one of the first two-car teams," said Susan Bonnett. "Neil's team was like research and development. That's what they used to call Neil's team, the R&D team, 'cause he was more for research and development.

"Neil was OK with it. He looked at it like it was an opportunity for him. He never got upset with anything like that. He usually just went with the flow.

"The first year Neil drove for Junior, right off the bat at Daytona his crew chief, Doug Richert, was injured. . . . That part was not a good start. Doug getting hurt set off a chain of events, and they didn't have as good a year as they had hoped for."

A bigger problem arose when Warner Hodgdon lost his racing empire after his engineering companies back in California were accused of bid rigging. He was sued for a total of $53 million and was forced to file for bankruptcy. He had owned—and lost—the Nashville Speedway and the North Carolina Motor Speedway at Rockingham. He owned half of the Junior Johnson race team, which Johnson won back in court. By 1985, Hodgdon was out of racing, but ironically that year Neil Bonnett had one of his finest seasons. Though Darrell Waltrip won the driving championship with 3 wins and 22 top-10 finishes in 28 races and purses worth $1,218,274, Bonnett, on the other Junior Johnson team, won 2 races, 18 top-ten finishes, and $530,144. When I asked Susan Bonnett to talk about the relationship between Neil and Darrell Waltrip, she chuckled.

"There is no real easy way to say they didn't get along that well," she said. "Neil could get along with anybody, but there had been misunderstandings. Later we came to know Darrell and we were really crazy about him, but at that time they never got very close because Darrell was the Golden Boy and Neil was second in line."

"And Darrell was very protective of that, wasn't he?" I asked.

"Absolutely," she said. "As a matter of fact, there was a race at Nashville [on May 12, 1984]. There was a caution on the last lap, and Neil won the race. Darrell just pitched a fit over that. He complained that Neil had passed on the caution—we all thought he was ahead when the caution came out anyway—and he pushed NASCAR, and the next day NASCAR took it away and gave it to Darrell, and Neil finished second. And that didn't sit well with Neil, just to be honest. It had never been done before, and he was really upset because he had never heard of NASCAR doing that before. He felt like they should have done it that day when it happened, not to wait until someone threw a fit and then change it. It didn't help their personal relationship.

"And it got me mad at Junior, because I felt he was favoring Darrell, and he was. Darrell had been with him before we ever came. Darrell had won races for him. That's just the way it was."

The last season Neil Bonnett drove for Junior Johnson was 1986. Bonnett won the next-to-last race at Rockingham in October. It had been 17 months since Bonnett's last win. After winning that race, Neil hugged Johnson and thanked him for giving him good cars for the three years. Bonnett, taking his Valvoline sponsorship with him, then went back to Rahmoc.

CHAPTER 34

THE PETTY WAY

Robin Pemberton

ROBIN PEMBERTON WAS BORN AND RAISED IN UPSTATE NEW YORK IN THE LITTLE town of Malta. A local racetrack stood about a mile down the street, and during the 1960s local Modified racers like Pete Hamilton competed, and then in the 1970s the Winston Cup drivers raced there on their northern tour. On the main street was a diner owned and run by Pemberton's dad. When the racers came to town, they ate at the diner, and that's how 13-year-old Robin Pemberton and his friend Steve Hmiel met Richard Petty and his race team. Hmiel left New York and headed for North Carolina, and after getting a job with Petty Enterprises in 1979, Hmiel summoned Pemberton. He has been in the business of building race cars ever since.

"My grandmother and mother used to take me to races when I was six years old," said Pemberton. "They were big fans. They were friends with Pete Hamilton, who went on to drive Winston Cup cars. Pete drove for Petty Enterprises and won the Daytona 500. Those guys worked on my bicycle when I was little.

"I remember in 1970, it was February, and my family and I were on a winter vacation in Lake Placid. My family was in the arena there watching a hockey game, but I was sitting in the car freezing my ass off listening to the radio station playing the Daytona 500 race.

"Pete won the race. I came blasting in the hockey arena shouting, 'Pete won the Daytona 500.' There wasn't one son of a bitch who knew what I was talking about except my mom, my dad, and my brother, Randy. It was really cool to grow up and to be associated with people like Pete and Jerry Cook. And they are *still* good friends.

"When I got older, I had friends who had a retail speed shop that sold parts and pieces for race cars. Malta was centrally located, and if you wanted to, you could drive a few hours to Long Island, Connecticut, and Massachusetts, to Vermont, western New York state, and you could literally race seven nights a week if you were in that area.

RICHARD PETTY
INTERNATIONAL MOTORSPORTS HALL OF FAME

"What would happen, during the summer months guys who raced Modifieds for a living would stay at local hotels and use that as their base, stay in the Malta area, go east, go west. It was Pete Hamilton, Richie Evans, Jerry Cook, all those guys.

"My dad had a restaurant business on the corner of Routes 9 and 67, which everyone had to pass to get to the Malta racetrack," said Pemberton. "They would either eat before they got to the race or after on the way home. It was a family restaurant, seafood and steaks, burgers and french fries and milk shakes. It was in the days before you had chain restaurants.

The Winston Cup series came to Malta in 1971 and 1972, and young Robin got the chance to meet some of the Petty family.

"I was thirteen years old. Richard and his race team came into the restaurant, and I remember Dave Marcis, and it was really cool. I had watched the Modified guys race, and most of them did that just as a hobby, but then here were these Grand National racers who were doing it for a living, and that really got my interest up, even at the age of thirteen.

"Later when I went to work for the Pettys, Richard remembered the group of kids who were hanging around while they were working on their cars during those hot, summer days. So he made the connection, and more than likely I got the opportunity based on that.

"Some friends of mine, including Steve Hmiel, had moved down to the Carolinas in the early '70s. He went away to college, went a couple of years to tech school, and one day just packed his bags and moved to North Carolina to get a job, which wasn't the easiest thing to do, but he got a job working for Petty Enterprises. And Steve and I being friends for many, many years, when the opportunity came up, he gave me a call to see if I wanted to give it a shot.

"There was a long decade between meeting the Pettys in the restaurant and my being able to work for them. Since I was thirteen I worked in my dad's restaurant. I was cook, manager, did hiring and firing, the books, whatever it took. I went to college for hotel management at Paul Smith's, a small school in upstate New York above Lake Placid. So I was really into the restaurant business. But I had worked full time in the restaurant since I was thirteen, and by the time I was twenty, I was ready for a change.

"I had opportunities to go to college—I had scholarship offers. I was a track star in high school. I was a sprinter, ran hurdles. I was ranked in the state and in the country. But I was only seventeen when I graduated, and most of the colleges wanted me to go to prep school for a year. Being from a family-run business, there wasn't a lot of money, and I couldn't afford to do it. They weren't going to pay for me to go to prep school, even though they were giving me a scholarship.

"At the time, I was very disappointed. But I don't get emotional about a lot of things. I take it and let it roll off my back. If I'd have gone to college, I'd have wound up being a track coach or a high-school coach. But missed opportunities in one area led to others. So I buckled down, and I ran the family business instead. I worked from morning until night, similar to what we do now. I was working 120 hours a week, and at the end of a few years, I was so burned out I needed a total change. That was about the time the phone rang and Steve wanted to know if I wanted to move south.

"Steve said, 'It looks like the Pettys are going to hire a few people. You don't need to know a lot. If you will learn, there is a good chance of an opportunity to work there. Are you interested?'

"I said, 'Yeah, tell them I'll come.'

"In April of 1979, I packed my bags and I moved to North Carolina. I moved down with literally fifty bucks in my pocket. I had a '66 Corvette. I had bought it a few years earlier, and I still have it today.

"And when I went to work for the Pettys, it was like living with another family. Back then, it was different than it is now. Teams were smaller. People were closer. Today, teams are huge. But when you were around the Pettys, it was like being at home with aunts and uncles and brothers. And it wasn't just the Pettys. Bud Moore and his bunch were that way. The Wood Brothers. And there was Junior. Those were the only race teams people ever paid any attention to back then. For the people of the '60s, it was still a family-run business. Everyone else was one man who owned the business and ran it.

"When I arrived, Richard was very much the King. In fact, he won the championship that year. That first year, I went with Kyle to the races he ran. We had Sportsman cars to run, Grand National cars to run, dirt, Late Model cars he ran. We did it all out of that shop. I was a mechanic doing whatever anyone told me to do.

"I had a lot of mentors, guys like Dale Inman and Richie Barsz, the fabricator. Richie's roots went all the way back to the old Holman Moody days. He worked for Mario Andretti when he drove at Le Mans. Richie has been at the Pettys off and on since the '60s. He's still there. Dale has retired, but he's still in and out of the place. Richard was there, and his brother Maurice was the engine builder, and if you talk to anyone who's been around Petty Enterprises, they will attribute their success to them, because one of the things they taught you: 'You don't always win, but what's most important is how you carry it off when you lose, to always look good and be professional and behave. '

"We always had a saying, 'There is the right way, the wrong way, and the Petty way.' Which was above and beyond. For example, their cars were nicer than anybody else's cars. Their presentation was a lot better. They had nicer uniforms before anyone had uniforms. They taught you to represent something bigger than yourself, the company, and STP. You tried to behave, but you didn't always do it. They did teach you those things. Today, really, there are a lot of people in racing who need to go through a place like that. Not everyone understands there is more to it than the immediate goal of winning the race.

"Lee was there, but he was always golfing. He was *always* a threat to me. He made me a nervous wreck. I would hide from him. I could have been like some people: When you got done, you'd just hide. But I was from upstate New York. I was the biggest outcast there was, and I just wanted to try to fit in and do the right thing, so as the new guy there, I was always going from one building to another, trying to help out. I'd go see if someone needed a hand doing something, and it didn't matter what time of day it was, morning, noon, or night: It seemed I would always run into Lee Petty head on. As he was puffing on his pipe, one day he said to me, 'Son, you are the walkingest son of a bitch I think I ever met.'

"Later on in life, Lee and I could joke about that, and as I moved on and did better, he paid me a compliment or two. But at the time . . . Man.

"I thought Richard was cool. He was really a cool guy. He's still a cool guy. The problem with a cool guy like Richard was that he couldn't always be cool because there were a million people interrupting him all the time. At that time, it was a regional sport, but the poor SOB couldn't do anything, couldn't go anywhere. I'm sure there were many things Linda and he wanted to do, but they couldn't, and there might have been times when he wanted to let his hair down, and he couldn't do that either.

"In the shop, he built stuff. He worked on cars. The whole time I was there he had some kind of project he was working on. He might have been restoring a pot-belly stove. Richard was really talented. He could do a lot of things. Kyle can do a lot of things. They can build stuff.

"Richard's brother Maurice was a good guy. They worked real hard on their engines.

"Richie Barsz was from Chicago. There weren't a lot of Yankees there at the time. Richie was very hard on me. He'd just pick on me. I would build stuff, and he would get his stuff done before me, and it was a constant competition with Richie about getting stuff done. There were many nights when I went home, and I would just cry. I thought, Man, how could this be this miserable. I was supposed to be having a good time.

"Richie was very talented. His stuff could be beautiful, but he was more functional than anything. At that time, it was more about getting it done than anything. With the experience he had, he could do things twice as fast as anybody and still be better at it than you, even though you tried real hard.

"It took a couple years, and then Richie and I became really good friends. I guess if you made the cut with him, you could make it with anybody.

"I was out of my element, that's for sure. I was 600 miles from home, a New Yorker living in North Carolina, the worst-case scenario, and I probably didn't fit in. But I did have a good relationship with Dale Inman and with Maurice and Richard, and eventually with Richie Barsz.

"There are always guys, and it doesn't matter where you are, guys who just never give you a break or never let up on you, and I see it where I am now. There are guys at the shop who won't give another guy a break, for whatever reason. That's just the way life is.

"As crew chief, you can sit a guy down and talk to him, but I figure it was their mother's problem, and if a guy is going to behave like that, eventually the guy will get what's coming to him. I don't totally believe in the meek inheriting the earth, but there comes a time when things get evened out. You can only babysit adults for so long before you finally give up on them anyway.

"In those days, they didn't have the number of people you have now. In the wintertime, I would hang sheet metal, but I was also a mechanic doing all the suspension work. So at the end of the season you'd roll your toolbox out of one shop and into the other, to work on fabrication or building cars.

"I was getting minimum wage, $2.50 an hour. I lived in an apartment, and I didn't eat very well. I had tomato soup, four-for-a-dollar macaroni and cheese. For two bucks, I'd eat for two or three days. Some days I rode a ten-speed bike ten miles to work because I didn't have money for gas for the Corvette.

"Literally, my take-home pay was ninety dollars a week. That was the going rate. And that didn't change until the mid-1980s.

"And to be honest with you, I wouldn't trade it for anything in the world. I'm not trying to be stupid about this, but there is a bizarre loyalty that some of us have to the Pettys. We didn't always agree on things, but if you look back on it, you wouldn't exchange any of that experience for anything.

"As miserable as I was those first couple of years, the problem just kind of fixed itself. I told myself that being there, making very little money, was no different than if I had gone to college and was trying to learn a profession. I just had to keep convincing myself that this was my college education.

"And then in 1984, when it was time for me to go someplace else, Richard also left."

The 1982 and 1983 season had been less than stellar for Richard Petty. He didn't win a single race in 1982, and Kyle had only two top-10 finishes. In 1983, Richard won three races, but he was embarrassed after the Charlotte race when inspectors discovered his engine was oversize. Robin Pemberton, who saw the operation first-hand, was sure that Richard left for financial reasons as much as anything else.

"The speculation on the part of the people who worked there," said Pemberton, "was that it was really hard running two race cars for Richard and Kyle and trying to make ends meet, and that Richard's going to drive for Mike Curb was the way to alleviate some of the financial pressure.

"This was right before the age of the big sponsors. Teams were starting to have tractor trailers. A lot of money was starting to get spent, more than what the Pettys were used to. There were still teams with open trailers and pickup trucks going to Winston Cup races, and then there were the teams with the tractor-trailers. It was getting to be difficult times for some of them.

"I just kind of knew Richard was leaving. I had friends in the Charlotte area, and they were telling me he was doing something to help himself. I also was looking, and I left, and I went to work for Butch Mock and Bob Rahilly. Neil Bonnett had been their driver, but he left to drive for Junior Johnson.

"We suspected Richard was going to drive for Rick Hendrick, but he was working on a deal with Mike Curb too, and when I told Richard I was going to work for Butch and Bob, he said to me, 'You need to do yourself a favor. You need to work for people who have money and who race for a living. Butch and Bob race for a living, but they don't have any money.'

"I said, 'Richard, I think I need to do this.'

"He said 'OK.'

"That was October of 1983, and sometime during that month, we were at Charlotte, and Richard asked me, 'Do you think Butch and Bob would be interested in my driving their car?'

"I said, 'Hell, yeah. Who wouldn't want you driving their car?'

"I said something to Butch and Bob, and they negotiated, and whatever happened I don't know, but Richard was going to drive the car. We actually tested at Daytona in December of '83 for the '84 season, and then something didn't go too well.

"Something happened between Butch and Bob, and Mike Curb and Richard. We went on a test, we had cars, and Curb was involved. Curb was the guy who was supposed to attract sponsorship—he owned Curb Records. And it went bad, and Richard and Curb started their own team, and Butch and Bob were stuck without a driver.

"I stayed with Butch and Bob, and during that year they had several drivers, Dave Marcis, Morgan Shepherd, Jody Ridley, Jim Sauter, and we did run pretty well with Marcis. We were winning Bristol with twenty, thirty laps to go, and a lap car nailed us. We cut the left rear tire down, and we had to pit, and we finished in the back. That was the only success we could have had. Dave Marcis was a good driver, and to this day we get along great, and we're good friends. I would do anything for Dave.

"At the end of 1984, Gary Nelson called. He was at DiGard. He asked me, 'We might be doing something here. Would you be interested?'"

CHAPTER 35

WORKING FOR JUNIOR

Jimmy Makar

THE EDUCATION OF JIMMY MAKAR CONTINUED WHEN HALFWAY THROUGH THE 1981 season, he was offered a job by crew chief Buddy Parrott to join Benfield Racing. Parrott, a top crew chief, had left the DiGard team where he was crew chief for Darrell Waltrip to help driver Johnny Rutherford.

Said Makar, "Ron Benfield was going to medical school—in fact, he's a doctor today in Cecil, North Carolina, and my dad goes to him. He wanted to get involved in racing, his dad had a little bit of money, and Levi Garrett was a good sponsor, and we had enough money to go racing.

"Buddy Parrott, the crew chief, was another one of those characters who liked to have fun, liked to have things upbeat. But he was a hard racer who liked to do well.

"I watched Buddy, the same way I watched Robert Gee and Harry Hyde, watched what they were doing, seeing why they were having success.

"Buddy was the front tire changer on that car, and I was the rear tire changer. Buddy was excellent and I learned a lot of my skills from him. We had a battle going as to who would finish first, who would have bragging rights. Buddy and I were real fortunate and won the Unocal pit crew contest that year.

"Buddy also taught me about strategy during the race and about setting up the car on race day, how to dial a car in for a race.

"I also got to watch how Buddy dealt with Johnny Rutherford, same as I watched the way Harry related to his drivers. I never really realized the importance of the chemistry between the crew chief and the driver. But I watched how Harry motivated his drivers, got them to do things, and how Buddy was with his. Harry was a little rougher than Buddy. Harry didn't take too much stuff off of them. Harry pretty much told them how it was going to be.

"Buddy had worked for Harry a lot of years, and a lot of Buddy's traits came from Harry. Buddy had a real strong opinion as to how things were supposed to be, but he was more a cheerleader for the drivers and the crew. Buddy did a lot more pumping up of people to try to get them motivated, to get them to realize their potential.

"Johnny Rutherford never won any races, but we ran well in a few races. He was never a threat to win anything. It was a pretty flat experience for us."

JUNIOR JOHNSON
"Junior was just a good guy."
INTERNATIONAL
MOTORSPORTS HALL OF FAME

Rutherford left at the end of that year, and Morgan Shepherd came in to drive the race car. Makar worked as a painter, body man, and fabricator, and he was learning the ropes on chassis work. He also was a tire changer at the races. He was doing Buddy's crew chiefing, telling him what springs to change, what shocks to change.

When Morgan Shepherd arrived in 1982, he ran well in a lot of races with seven top-10 finishes, led some races, but like Rutherford, didn't win any races. There was a personality conflict between Shepherd and Parrott, and things didn't seem to click quite like they needed to.

"Morgan had the same type of personality as Buddy," said Makar. "He believed in his way of doing things. So they never jelled and clicked and got to the point where they could work through things. They didn't grow. And it didn't last very long, and the next year they hired Joe Ruttman, but it still wasn't working very well. Things were starting to fall apart a little bit, and Buddy ended up leaving—or he got fired—and they brought Jake Elder in to replace Buddy. The way things were going, I could see that wasn't going very well, and we were headed down. To me, there seemed to be a lot of conflict and controversy, and things didn't feel like they were getting any better, and I had the opportunity to talk to Jeff Hammond about working with the 11 car at Junior Johnson's, and I thought it might be a good opportunity to talk to them, and so I talked to Junior and Jeff, and they hired me."

Makar began with Junior in 1984. When he went up to Junior's shop, he wasn't sure what to expect. Junior had won several championships with several different drivers, and won lots of races. At the time, Junior Johnson was on top of the sport, and Makar figured by going there he would learn more than at any other race shop. Darrell Waltrip was driving for him, and Junior was just starting the two-car team with Warner Hodgdon and Neil Bonnett. Things seemed bright.

"The shop had been there forever and had been added on to I don't know how many times," said Makar. "It was just a backyard shop. It was right behind Junior's house in North Wilkesboro. You walked out the back of the house across the driveway and into the shop. Not exactly what you expected from a race team that was so successful.

"When I went there, they were building a nice new shop across the creek next to the house. Warner Hodgdon was putting a bunch of money into that, and they were building a nice shop, a parts room, and an engine shop on the other side of the creek next to Junior's house.

"I worked on the 11 car out of the old shop. That was an experience. Junior had chicken coops up on the hill above the shop and behind the shop. Coon dogs were running around everywhere. To me, it was a flashback to the way racing was twenty years earlier, what people call, 'the good old days.' There was still a lot of history there. You'd look around and see neat things. You'd see old parts and pieces from ten years ago that were modified at the time. You could see a lot of history, how racing went from stock cars to where it was in 1984.

"Junior was just a good guy, a country gentleman. He was a nice guy, always. My God, I loved him. I thought he was a lot of fun to work for. Flossie [his wife] cooked breakfast. A lot of times we'd go over to the kitchen and have breakfast with Flossie in the morning before you got to work. A real family-type atmosphere. There were people who had worked for Junior for ten or fifteen years who were still there from days gone by.

"Junior, to me, was like Harry Hyde. There wasn't anything Junior couldn't do. Junior was a hands-on type person. He might come down to the shop and work in the engine room for a day or two, or he might go back and work on the bodies with you for a day or two. He wandered around the shop and put his input in wherever it was needed. He brought an opinion and a lot of experience. It was nothing for him to sit down and weld up a distributor gear, a timing gear, an advance gear, at the welding table. Or he'd go run a dyno. He did a little bit of everything.

"You could go to Junior for advice. Junior was not intimidating. He was a fun guy. He enjoyed having fun. At Christmastime, he'd pull out the moonshine. You'd have a drink during the holidays. For a New Jersey boy, it was interesting for me to see that type of thing going on."

Makar got to see another side of working for Junior Johnson. As serious as he was about racing, if one of Junior's neighborhood farmers needed to repair his manure spreader truck, Junior would have him take it to the back of the shop, and Junior's mechanics would fix it. Junior's men were expected to stop while they were working on the race car and fix this piece of machinery so they could get back to the fields. That happened numerous times.

"I can remember one time we were working in the shop ready to go racing, and Junior came down grabbing people up. We all got in the back of the pickup truck, and they ran us down the road to a field, and we had to herd cattle, had to get the cattle into the trucks so they could go to market. I had never done that before! And I never did this, but I have heard of other guys having to go to the garden between the two shops to pick rocks out of the garden or pick potatoes when they were harvesting. You worked on race cars, but you might do a little farming on the side. That was fun. Those are the type of things I'll never forget from working up there.

"If Junior slaughtered a pig, he'd hang the pig out there in front of the shop to get it ready to make ham. You learned about living in North Wilkesboro and living on a farm. It was a different experience, no doubt about it.

"But we raced hard. Darrell was in his prime. The first races I ever won were with Junior, who won seven races that year in '84.

"Junior was the car owner, Jeff Hammond was the crew chief, and Darrell was the driver. But Junior was an integral part of what was getting done and how they were getting it done. Junior was very much a part of everything that was going on, the race-day calls. He was not a sit-back-and-watch kind of owner.

"Everybody respected Junior. His history spoke for itself. He was successful as a driver, successful as a car owner and as a mechanic. Everything he's ever done in racing he's been successful. You weren't going to question what Junior's thoughts were, although you could have a conversation back and forth with him. He was very open to talk about things. He definitely had opinions, but Junior never ruled with an iron fist. He was not dictatorial by any stretch of the imagination. If you could persuade him to see your side or get him to think the way you were thinking, he would change his mind. He was very smart, and most of the time what he was thinking was the right way to go.

"Again, it was neat to see and get a chance to work with someone who had that much knowledge and so much success.

"When I arrived, Darrell had already had good success with DiGard. His "Jaws" reputation was back in the DiGard days. He had won some championships and was starting to mellow a little bit.

"Darrell was a very talented race car driver, and he was also very smart as far as the race car was concerned. A lot of drivers are great racing the car, but not very good at getting the car dialed in. Mechanically speaking, Darrell was very, very good at that. He could feel a race car very, very well. Darrell was the kind of driver a crew chief loved to have, because he would come in and tell you specifics about his race car. It wasn't just 'pushing' or 'loose.' He'd say, 'It feels like the shocks aren't right.' or 'A sway bar might need to be changed,' instead of a spring. Or he'd say, 'The front of the car feels uncoupled,' versus the rear of the car. He was very detailed, so you didn't have to guess or make a lot of changes until you found the problem. He knew what he was trying to get to. If you look at Darrell's record and career, he won a lot of races.

"I thought I'd be with Junior for quite a long time. It was a good, stable race team that was a great place to learn a lot. I had no reason to leave, except that Buddy Barnes, a friend of mine who I had met and worked with at Banfield's, called me late in 1984. He was working at Blue Max, which was Raymond Beadle's team, and Tim Richmond was driving for him. Tim Brewer had been the crew chief in '84, and the Tims were having problems, conflicts, and Brewer was going to be leaving at the end of the season. They were looking for someone to come in and do the chassis work and wanted to know if I was interested.

"Barry Dodson was taking over as crew chief, and I sat down with him and Harold Elliott, who was building the engines. They said no one had the race car chassis tuning capability, and would I be interested in the job. It was a great opportunity, hard to pass up.

"I talked to Junior. I told him what the situation was, the opportunity being offered me. A lot of people came through Junior's. He understood, knew it was a good opportunity for me to go do that type of work. I had my eyes set on crew chiefing one day, but I knew I needed to learn all the different aspects of racing before I could do that job, and this was a great opportunity to take on a lot of the crew chief's responsibilities without having *all* the responsibilities."

CHAPTER 36

DIGARD

Robin Pemberton

AFTER ROBIN PEMBERTON LEFT PETTY ENTERPRISES, HE JOINED THE RAHMOC team in 1984. The season was a disaster. At the end of the year, Gary Nelson called to see if he was interested in joining the DiGard team, a team owned by the Gardner brothers, Jim and Bill, as well as Mike DiProspero, the Di of DiGard. Bobby Allison was the driver. Robert Yates was the engine builder. Norman Cochamishew was also there, high-profile men thrown together like cocks in a cockfight. Pemberton, who was offered the job of crew chief, quickly discovered he was going from the proverbial frying pan into the fire.

"It was pretty bad," said Pemberton. "But I was leaving a team that didn't have a sponsor. I had gotten married on a Saturday in December, and on Monday joined a team that had gone through five drivers during the year, and they didn't have a sponsor. So even the Gardners appeared to be more stable. That should tell you something.

"When I joined DiGard, they were winners. They were a year removed from a championship. I thought I was going to the top. Little did I know. The saying we used was, 'We're getting into a hot air balloon with holes in it.' We thought we were going up, but no matter how hard we tried, it wouldn't stay up.

"Bobby Allison was an incredible driver. Bobby [had] an incredible feel for the car. Bobby was very good. He had stamina, a lot of common sense, though a lot of times he'd aggravate the mortal shit out of you. He would drag some piece in from Alabama that he needed bolted onto his [street] car—I would kid Bobby and Donnie about it occasionally—you didn't mind doing it, but a lot of times it was at four o'clock in the afternoon of the day you wanted to go somewhere. Like to the racetrack. It was comical at times.

"Bobby was into it. He tried. You try hard for the guys who try hard. If there is something they think they need to go better, then you try to give it to them.

"Bobby was really such a good driver. He could wheel like no tomorrow. I was real fortunate, working with Bobby and Richard. Richard was the same way. Richard could drive.

"No matter what the rules are, it's the same guys who are always at the front. And it's the same guys who are wrecking every week. It's the way it is.

"The problem was that the owners, the Gardners, and the driver, Bobby Allison, didn't get along, and there was a little deceit going on there. Some things that happened were funny.

"We were going to the first Pocono race in 1985. The Gardners had lawyers who had offices in the building, so that should have told me something right there. Nonetheless, the lawyer for the Gardners came to me and said, 'Will you see T. R. this weekend?' As far as I was concerned, T. R. was Tom Roberts, the public relations guy for our sponsor Miller Beer. I said, 'Yeah.' He said, 'Will you give this envelope to him?'

"Well, I went to Pocono, and I handed Roberts the envelope. That was a Thursday, and on Friday morning he came back to me and said, 'You gave this to the wrong T. R.'

"I said, 'What are you talking about, Tom?'

"He showed me the contents of the envelope. It was a proposed contract for Tim Richmond. Turns out it was Tim Richmond who they wanted me to give the envelope to. Tim and I were friends. They knew we went out together and had drinks, had dinner, so their lawyer, as ignorant as he was, he just tried to be real cute and say, 'T. R.' What he didn't know was that our public relations guy from Miller was also T. R. This was while Bobby Allison was our driver. They were going to fire him!

"When I saw the contract proposal for Tim Richmond, I said, 'Ho, shit.' And somehow—imagine this—it leaked out that Bobby was getting the skids put to him.

"Tim Richmond finally did get to see the contract, but he didn't drive for us.

"We went to Daytona for the Fourth of July race. Bobby was our driver. I was his crew chief. DiGard also had a research and development car driven by Greg Sacks. Gary Nelson was his crew chief.

"Late in the race, we were running on seven cylinders, but we were still a top-ten car. If the motor hadn't blown, we'd have won the race. No one figured Sacks would run as good as he was, but he was hauling ass. It came down to a green-flag pit stop, and the Sacks team only had a makeshift pit crew, so all my guys ran down to pit his car. Well, the next lap Bobby came down pit road, and I didn't have anybody in my pit. All the Miller guys were pitting Greg Sacks in his Monte Carlo. There wasn't a single son of a bitch standing in the pits when Bobby Allison came in. Not one.

"I came over to try to change tires. He came on the radio and said, 'Don't worry about it. It's over. Just put gas in it.'

"I didn't have a gas guy. I didn't have anything. One of the guys went over and put gas in it and sent Bobby on his way. And that was the end of it.

"After the race, which Greg won, Bobby told me, 'Hey, I appreciate the effort, Man. I'll be talking to you.' And he said it in a tone of voice where I knew it was not going to be good. The very next race, Bobby started his own team.

"The Gardners didn't treat Robert Yates very well either. They promised Robert part of the business, and rumor had it that as Robert was trying to pay the bills for the engine department to get the equipment paid for, one of the Gardners was mortgaging the equipment back to another bank. There's nothing illegal about that, but it just drove Robert crazy. Even today, Robert doesn't take on a lot of debt. He gets stuff paid off as fast as he can. He just likes to live that way. He's a son of a preacher, and he'll always be that way.

"So it got to be a little edgy. They promised Robert research and development facilities, but the same old deal, they never carried through on their promise. When I signed my contract, they showed me a drawing of this incredible facility for research and development—it was beautiful. But it was never built. They used the promise of it to attract people.

"When Bobby left, he took the number twenty-two. Greg kept his seventy-seven. The win at Daytona was Greg's only top-five finish that year. We made some decent runs with Greg, but we were struggling. We made it through the year, made it through the wintertime attempting to build a car or two, but then there was big money trouble. The checks never bounced, but we knew it was close when you would get paid, because we always got our paycheck two minutes after the bank closed.

"We made it through the wintertime, but some of our people left. They had been there long enough, and it didn't look like we would have a sponsor.

"We signed TRW, the automotive aftermarket, to be Greg's sponsor in '86. We started the season, but we were struggling. Robert Yates was still there. In February of '86, we were at Daytona for the 500, and Dick Beaty, who was in charge of competition for NASCAR, made the announcement at the end of the day, 'OK, guys, put your tools down and go home.'

"The night he made that announcement, Robert Yates said, 'OK, I'm laying my tools down, and I'm going home.' Well, what Robert meant was, he was laying his tools down and going home. He said to me, 'I got you this far.'

"I had the sense something was going wrong, and sure enough, that was his last day at DiGard. He was gone. He took his tools, and he went home. He just had enough. One too many checks didn't go in the right direction. So the next day I have no engine builder.

"We went to Richmond, then we went to Rockingham. By then, we were working from six in the morning until five or six in the morning every day. We didn't have enough men, didn't have enough going on. You would literally leave the shop, drive home, take a shower, turn around, and drive back to work. My wife wasn't doing real good with it. Our child was four months old. This whole thing was insane.

"It was time to leave."

It wouldn't be the last time.

CHAPTER 37

THE BEAN COUNTER

Jimmy Johnson

When Jimmy Johnson first arrived to run the Hendrick Motorsports team in December 1985, old-timer Harry Hyde ridiculed him as a "bean counter." For most of NASCAR history, race teams had an owner, a crew chief, and a driver, but under owner Rick Hendrick's organizational chart, a new layer of bureaucracy was added, the team manager, who ran things and answered directly to Hendrick while he was away building his car dealership empire.

Johnson was needed because Hendrick, who had begun with one car dealership, was so successful with his management style that he proceeded to steadily acquire car dealership after dealership throughout the Southeast until today he owns more than 90.

As an example of Rick Hendrick's extraordinary ability to sell cars, when he took over the Chevy-Honda dealership in Bennettsville, South Carolina, in 1986, the company was selling 25 cars a month. The first year Hendrick owned it, he was selling 1,200 cars a month!

To run his race team, Rick Hendrick wanted someone who loved racing, understood finances, made good decisions, and who was loyal to him. He would also have to work like a dog. Jimmy Johnson, who had worked hard all his life, fit the bill perfectly.

"When I was fourteen, my dad had some money problems, and I couldn't play organized sports because I had to work," Johnson said. "I started out working for a CPA typing income tax returns and doing yard work at his house. I'd get out of high school, run the mile and a half to his house, type returns until nine at night when his office closed, then walk home and do my homework for the next day."

Johnson also worked for a local race team on the weekends.

"I lived in Whiteville, North Carolina, and when I was fourteen, I'd leave home Friday night and travel to races with Monk and Jean Hair and Monk's brother Mickey and return home Sunday night to go back to school Monday.

"I was literally a gopher. We had three stalls in this shop we worked in on Highway eighty-seven just south of Fayetteville. In one bay, we worked on the race car, which was an old, old Ford.

"I just absolutely loved the sport. We raced in the Late Model division against John Sears, Johnny Newton, and Winding Wayne Andrews, big names back then. John Sears went on to race Winston Cup for many years. We raced all over the Southeast.

"We won a lot of races and had a lot of fun. We drank a lot of beer and traveled around the country and made tons of friends. It was one of the best times of my life.

"In the center bay, Curtis Lane and Monk Hair, who co-owned the car, built transmissions. With the profits, they would send Mickey and me to Kannapolis to buy tires. Nobody had any money.

"In the left bay, they stored corn for the hogs. The corn was piled from the floor to the ceiling. Most of the time, my job—when I wasn't bringing them wrenches and parts and water to cool them off when they were welding with a torch—was to sit there with a twenty-two-caliber rifle with rat shot in it and shoot the rats that came out of the corn to keep them away from the workers. That was my first job in racing: shooting rats.

"When I graduated from high school, I took a twelve-month course and graduated from a small business college in Fayetteville called Worth Business College. I got a junior accounting degree in 1965."

For three years, Jimmy Johnson was the comptroller for the 82nd Airborne NCO club. Then he was contacted by George Purvis, who was opening up a new Ford dealership in Fayetteville. Purvis hired him to be his office manager, and he worked at Patrick Ford and then at Lafayette Ford for 10 years.

After a short stint as F&I (finance and insurance) manager at a Chevy dealership, he then went into the business of putting video arcades at putt-putt golf courses and game rooms in malls.

"As luck would have it," said Johnson, "just about this time twenty years ago, a mutual friend of Rick Hendrick and mine called me and said, 'Would you be interested in going to work for the Toyota store in Fayetteville?'

Johnson's first inclination was to say no, because his allegiance was to American cars. But then the friend mentioned that the owner was Rick

Hendrick, who was making a name for himself in the business. Hendrick had taken over City Chevrolet, the largest Chevy dealership in the Carolinas, and Johnson was intrigued at getting a chance to work for him. There was another reason Johnson wanted to work for Hendrick: racing. Hendrick had been the drag boat racing champion three times. Johnson had watched him race on Lake Ocala. And the word was out that Hendrick intended to become involved in Winston Cup racing. Johnson was hired to be office manager of Hendrick's Toyota store.

"My official first day was September first, '83," said Johnson. "I've been with Rick ever since."

That year, Rick Hendrick needed a warehouse for his boats, motors, and equipment, and he rented a building from Harry Hyde, who talked Hendrick into starting a Winston Cup race team. Hendrick began his racing operation. He called it All Star Racing, and with Hyde as crew chief and Geoff Bodine his driver, Hendrick was off to the races.

Bodine was an instant success, winning three races in 1984. Before the Daytona race of 1985, Hendrick called Jimmy Johnson, not to run his race team, but to run his new Toyota dealership in Hudson, Florida, on the Sunshine State's west coast. Since Johnson's girlfriend (now wife) Press lived an hour and a half from there, he quickly jumped at the chance.

Johnson was responsible for overseeing construction of the building, hiring employees, licensing, and paying bills. Oh, and selling cars.

The dealership opened in October 1985. It was a period of great growth for the Hendrick empire. He had opened seven new stores that year and was expanding rapidly. Since racing was still just a hobby for Hendrick, he needed to turn it over to someone he could trust.

In opening the new dealership, Jimmy Johnson showed intelligence, organizational ability, and an ability to work 18 hours a day, seven days a week when needed.

Said Johnson, "I wasn't a superstar and never will be, but I did a good job and I worked awfully hard. I gave him 110 percent. He let me run it like it was mine, and that made it fun, and I loved it."

A month later, Rick Hendrick flew down and asked Jimmy Johnson if he would be interested in moving to Charlotte.

"I was living in a condo on the Gulf of Mexico," said Johnson. "My boat was in my backyard, and I was half a mile from work. The last thing I wanted to do was move to Charlotte. I had it made where I was. Plus, Press was ninety minutes away instead of eight hours."

Hendrick told him, "I want you to take over the racing operation."

Johnson replied, "It will take me about fifteen minutes to get packed."

But first, Johnson had to find a replacement, and in December 1985 he moved to Charlotte to run Hendrick Motorsports.

Johnson had two race teams to service, one with Tim Richmond and crew chief Harry Hyde, the other with Geoff Bodine and crew chief Gary Nelson.

"We had rented a 5,000-foot shop behind BSR on Highway twenty, about five miles from where we are now," said Johnson. "They had one tiny office, and that was going to be mine. I had a desk, and Gary Nelson had a desk, and we butted them together so I literally sat across the desk from Gary.

"If I ever get a chance to thank Gary, I should, because whatever successes I've had I owe a lot to Gary, because he was my mentor. He didn't let my rookie stripe show. I just remember how Gary followed through on everything. He introduced me to the right people, and he taught me the mechanical side of racing."

Gary Nelson had been in the sport for more than a decade. He had been Bobby Allison's crew chief at DiGard, and after they started a second team, he and Greg Sacks won the Pepsi 400 at Daytona in 1985.

"Gary was wonderful, and I needed that," said Johnson. "because on the other side I had Harry Hyde, who I absolutely loved as a father, but at times our relationship was tenuous. At ten o'clock every day, Harry had a break, and if I happened to be there during break time, Harry would say, 'There's Jimmy Johnson. He's the bean counter. Gosh, we're so happy to have him here, and we probably wouldn't be in racing if Jimmy wasn't here.' All that good, goofy stuff. I'd walk out the door, and the guys would tell me he'd say, 'That dumb son of a bitch don't know what the heck he's doing.'

"Harry's favorite line was, 'Racing was a whole lot more fun when I had money in the cee-gar box. But things have changed.'

"But I gradually won Harry over, and he was wonderful. When he left here, I'd see him on the road. We'd always stop, and he'd always tell me a story and put a smile on my face. We all miss that.

"I loved him and respected him, and I wish he were here today. [Harry Hyde died in 1996.] There's a big void missing."

CHAPTER 38

BLUE MAX

Jimmy Makar

AT THE END OF THE 1984 SEASON, JIMMY MAKAR DECIDED TO LEAVE THE JUNIOR Johnson race team and take a job with Raymond Beadle's Blue Max team, an all-star ensemble with racer Tim Richmond behind the wheel.

"When I took the job with Raymond Beadle's Blue Max team, I didn't know much about Tim Richmond," said Makar. "He had driven a race or two with Harry Hyde, and I had run into Tim there during my five or six years there. He was a good race driver, but he had not made a splash, hadn't done anything to speak of.

"Barry Dodson was the crew chief. He took care of all the races. He did more of the everyday running of the race team at the shop. Barry was a real good fabricator, so he fabricated and built race cars, and I worked on the chassis end of it, the springs, shocks, bars, set up, that type of thing. It was a pretty big area to work in. It was a neat opportunity.

"It wasn't a big race team, only fifteen or twenty of us, including the engine room. There were four or five guys in the fab shop, four or five of us in the chassis shop, setting up the cars. Todd Parrott worked there as a mechanic and a tire changer. Harold Elliott, who was there, had previously worked at Junior's for years. So at the time there were not a lot of well-known personalities, but looking back, we had a lot of guys with a lot of talent who nobody really knew about.

"In '85, Tim didn't win any races. He ran up front, led a lot of races, had limited success, did fairly well.

"There are reasons a driver leads races but doesn't win. Sometimes you don't stay up with your race car when the track conditions change. As the race comes toward the end, you don't change your race car enough to be in a position to win. Sometimes you have to run the car harder than it needs to be run for the set-up that's under it, so you lead races, but you use up your race car, use up the tires, before the end of the race. A lot of different reasons.

TIM RICHMOND
"He was a partying kind of guy."
INTERNATIONAL
MOTORSPORTS HALL OF FAME

"Our team was a partying kind of team, and Tim was a partying kind of guy, but I never went with them. Most of the guys were single and always liked to have a good time. Raymond Beadle was the same way. He liked to have a good time, loved to have a crowd of people around him. Things were always fun. That whole crowd loved to play hard and race hard. That was the type of individual we had.

"Tim had a huge amount of talent. He was like a wild Mustang in a corral that somebody needed to calm down, to tame, to harness his energy, to get him focused in the right direction. Looking back at it, he had all the makings of becoming an Earnhardt, a Gordon, the type of person who would have been an integral part of our sport for years to come. At least he started out that way.

"Tim was a very hard race car driver. He needed a Harry Hyde, somebody with experience to help him figure out what he needed in the race car. Jimmy Makar was not experienced enough to do it. Barry and the rest of us were young and learning ourselves. We didn't have what it took for Tim. And Tim was not the type of driver to help you figure out what to do with the race car to be comfortable or to make it go faster. When he was with us, Tim was a diamond in the rough.

"At the end of the year, Tim left Blue Max and went to Harry Hyde, and in '86 he won seven races and started to have success. Harry and Tim clicked when they got together. It was the Old Man and the Kid. They developed a good relationship, and they were able to have a lot of success together. Everybody started seeing how talented Tim was, and how Harry's wisdom and experience were able to take him and put him in the place he needed to be to have success.

"Unfortunately, Tim ran into a situation where his health got in trouble, and once that happened, it was downhill from then. He was in his prime when his health problems arose. Tim was a great guy, a lot of fun, a people person, really loved to be around people, loved to have people around him all the time. When he put his helmet on, you knew he was going to go fast.

"Tim left and went to Harry's, and a young Rusty Wallace came to drive for us in '86. When he hired Rusty, he was driving for a guy named Cliff Stewart. They were in financial trouble. They had a lot of trouble keeping good parts under the car. They blew a lot of engines, really struggled as a race team, and this opportunity came about. Rusty had a sponsor in his pocket that would come with him, an antifreeze, Alugard. When Raymond hired Rusty in '86, they came aboard with him.

"Rusty was a fun-loving person. He loved to go out and have a good time and play hard at night. He fit right in with this group of guys.

RUSTY WALLACE
"He fit right in."
INTERNATIONAL
MOTORSPORTS HALL OF FAME

"Rusty was a lot like Darrell Waltrip in that he had worked on his own race cars, built them, prepared them, took them to the track with one or two guys, made a lot of the changes to the cars, understood why a certain change would get a certain result. He was very chassis-smart. In my whole career, I learned more about chassis setup and chassis work and how to tune race cars from Rusty Wallace than anyone.

"Rusty and I clicked when we started working together. I can remember many, many times coming off the top of the truck with a thought in mind after watching the race car in terms of what we should be trying to do next, and when I got to the car window and we started talking about it, his thought and my thought would be right in line, so things just clicked very, very well. We had a great relationship for several years there at Blue Max, won Rusty's first race, won a lot of races, won a championship there."

The first win was at Bristol. It was hot and humid, as it typically was there. The drivers were pooped, falling out of their seats. Rusty Wallace was tired too.

With Dale Earnhardt pressuring Wallace hard, both of them were about at the point of exhaustion. Rusty did beat him, and after the race he could barely climb out of the car. He sat down next to the car—exhausted.

"It's special when a driver gets his first Cup win," said Makar. "It was a neat experience to see that. Those were real special times for me. They highlight a career even more than some of the bigger races you win. It's the specialness of winning that first race. You try so hard, get close, and finally you see a guy break into the winner's circle—that's a *big* deal.

"I had real affection for Rusty. We had a good relationship on and off the track, a lot of fun. His wife and my wife spent a lot of time together. We went to a lot of places together, did a lot of things together away from the racetrack. We went and did some ASA shows on off-weekends. We'd go up to Milwaukee and run with him up there. We went to the fairgrounds in Illinois north of Chicago. My wife and I and he and his wife would go together and we'd go out to dinner and we'd have a good time. We had a neat relationship. Rusty was a people person who liked being around people. It was fun, and we were having success, so that made it even more special.

"In '89, we won the championship by twelve points. In '88 we had lost the championship to Bill Elliott by only a few points. We were just trying to amass enough points at the end of the year to beat him. We finished second, fell a little bit short."

Going into the final race at Atlanta, Bill Elliott needed to finish 18th or higher to edge out Wallace for the championship. When he finished the race 11th, the title was his.

"[In '88] we went to Atlanta, the last race, led it, got all the points we could," said Makar, "and we still lost the championship. So we really had a lot of fire and determination the next year to go in there and try to win that championship.

"We had a very slim lead going into Atlanta. That Atlanta race is what I remember best about that whole '89 season. If anything could have gone wrong, it did go wrong at Atlanta. We had flat tires, wheels loosening up during the race, vibrations in the car—we pitted for more things than you could imagine. Every time we turned around, a tire would go down or we'd get a vibration or something would happen that we had to pit. At one point, it actually looked like we weren't going to win the championship.

"We had to finish seventeenth or better, and late in the race we were twenty-first or twenty-second, and we were panicking. It was our worst nightmare. Things were going wrong that hadn't gone wrong all year long. You could see it slipping through your fingers."

But Wallace didn't lose it. He finished the race in 15th place, and though his closest competitor, Dale Earnhardt, won the race, Rusty won the championship by a scant 12 points.

"When we finally got it done," said Makar, "it was hard to celebrate. There was more a feeling of relief.

"It was a team that was relatively underfunded. Our sponsor, Kodiak smokeless tobacco, didn't give us a lot of money. The whole six years I was at Blue Max we never had a high-end, well-funded organization. We had to do things on a shoestring, but everybody had a lot of character and a lot of heart, and everybody just wanted to go racing and win. That's why we were able to overcome not having a lot of money—by sheer determination and willpower and desire and a lot of hard work.

"Winning that title ranks right up there at the top of my list of accomplishments. It still does to this day.

"Of course, everything changes, and that's why you have to cherish and really enjoy the good times you have, because nothing, it seems, lasts forever. Kodiak was still there in '90, but they were going away as a sponsor. The next year, we got Rusty hooked up with the Miller Brewing Company, but we were still having a lot of financial troubles. For several years, we were scraping the bottom and barely making ends meet, literally. Even though we had won the championship, Raymond wasn't in a real strong economic way, and things never did get going.

"We were on pins and needles trying to make ends meet, pay the bills, and get by. I remember being at the racetrack on a Friday and Goodyear telling us they weren't going to give us any tires because Raymond was so far behind on the bills. Oh, yeah. In fact, Richard Childress and his organization offered to buy us several sets of tires to get us in the race, but Goodyear wouldn't let him do it! So Raymond ended up scraping some money together and on Saturday handed them a check.

"As a result, we all suffered from undue stress. When you look back, it was kind of amazing we were able to accomplish what we were able to accomplish with all that was going on behind the scenes, all these extra distractions and problems.

"At the end of the 1990 season, the Blue Max team dissolved."

CHAPTER 39

TIM RICHMOND

Jimmy Johnson

IN 1986, JIMMY JOHNSON, THE GENERAL MANAGER OF HENDRICK MOTORSPORTS, not only had to face Harry Hyde's negativity toward him, he also had to mediate the rift between Hyde and his driver, the mercurial and talented Tim Richmond.

"When we started, we bought four cars from Billy Hagan. Terry Labonte had won a championship in '84 driving those cars.

"We got off to a bad start," said Johnson, "because one of the worst things that could have happened to Harry was Geoff Bodine winning the Daytona 500. Harry had said that Geoff couldn't drive, and so we moved Harry over to Tim and gave Gary Nelson to Geoff. Tim had wrecked in the 125s. We had ten guys on Gary's team, and we went to Daytona, and Geoff won the darn race. And boy, that tore Harry up. It almost killed him.

"The first half of the year was horrible," said Johnson. "Tim was so much better than we were. Rick never put any restraints on how much money we could spend, so we had good equipment. We were renting engines from B&R for certain racetracks. Randy Dorton built good engines. We had everything we needed, but Harry was old school, and it took Harry a while to come around. Tim used to tell Harry, 'The car is hunting down the straightaway,' or 'The car is looking up the track in turn three.' And those terms of Tim's used to drive Harry nuts. Harry couldn't stand it. Tim knew what he was talking about, but Harry didn't know what he meant. Harry wanted 'loose' and 'tight.'

"We struggled. We made bad decisions in the pits. We didn't have the best braking system. Harry made Tim run big, old four-speed Chrysler transmissions, which were absolutely bulletproof, when everybody else was running quicker, fancy Jerico transmissions.

"We made it to Charlotte without them killing each other. Rick had wanted me to move over to where Tim and Harry were, so I moved out of Gary's and rented a little office trailer and put it outside Harry's shop, and that was my office, and I hired a girl to help me do some of the accounting, because basically I was doing everything, the accounting and the general manager's job.

"Well, Harry and Tim were in the trailer, and they literally were ready to fight. It got very bad. Tim was accusing Harry of not knowing what he was doing, and Harry was saying, 'You better go back and learn how to drive,' and I stood between them with a hand on each of their chests holding them apart.

GEOFF BODINE
When he won the Daytona
500, it almost killed Harry Hyde.
INTERNATIONAL
MOTORSPORTS HALL OF FAME

"Harry finally told him, 'If you step outside this trailer, I'm going to whip your ass.' Tim was thirty-one. Harry was sixty-two. Tim said, 'You get out,' and Harry busted out the door, and Tim followed.

"Tim stood there a minute, and he said, 'You know, Harry, I would hate to get my ass beat by someone twice my age.' And they laughed. And I'll tell you, things turned around that day. Shortly after that we went to Charlotte, and we finished second to Cale Yarborough. And from there on, we won seven races the second half of the '86 season, and we sat on nine poles.

"We could have won the championship if we had gotten off to a good start, because we finished only three points out of second place. Darrell Waltrip beat us for second.

"In addition to Tim and Harry seeing eye to eye, another positive addition was the hiring of David Oliver, an expert tire specialist. Back then, the race teams controlled whether the car was 'loose' or 'tight' by staggering the tires. Oliver helped Harry Hyde match up the tires.

"For years and years, David had measured the circumferences of tires, so he knew if you put this right rear tire with that left rear tire, it would loosen or tighten the car, and David did a heck of a job," said Johnson.

"That year, Geoff won two races. He won Daytona and he won Dover, and Tim won seven races and finished second four times. If he didn't win, he was right on their butts."

In addition to trying to keep Harry and Tim from killing each other, Johnson also had to make sure that Richmond performed his contracted duties for his sponsor and for the race team.

"It was *bad*," said Johnson. "It was real *bad*. It was really, really, really *bad*. Rick was out building his empire, and I would report to him each day where we were going, and as great as Tim was in the race car—and to me he was the best race car driver who ever lived—but when Tim took that helmet off, he could be a handful. We were always trying to keep him on the straight and narrow with the sponsors and making sure he showed up for appearances, said the right things. That was always a challenge."

"Did you ever sit him down and give him a lecture?" I asked.

"You didn't sit Tim Richmond down and give him a lecture," said Johnson. "You tried to reason with him, but believe me, no one had enough horsepower to sit him down and read him the riot act. That just didn't work with Tim. He was so good as a racer that the good *way* overrode his faults. We tried to manage it, if that was the term. We managed Tim. He was never real good with things like that, but he won so many races, won so many poles that the sponsor absolutely loved him."

The shame of it all was that Tim Richmond had only one great season, the magical year of 1986. By the end of the year, he was suffering from pneumonia, and by the end of '87, he was out of the sport, one of the very first public figures to contract AIDS. Tim Richmond was only around the Hendrick shop a short time, but for Jimmy Johnson it was an experience he will never forget.

"He was so much fun to be around," said Johnson. "Anybody who hung around with Tim, you got an education, believe me. Tim was ten years ahead of his time. If you dropped Tim Richmond into today's world, he'd be as popular as Shaquille O'Neal or Barry Bonds. He would be right there with them. He had that charisma. He had style. Everybody else was wearing cowboy boots and big Harley belts, and Tim was wearing silk suits.

"I remember we had just bought a Learjet, and that was a big step. We were really struggling to figure out how to pay for it. One day Rick said to me, 'Call Jay and Crutch,' our pilots, 'and get them ready. They need to take Tim to New York. It's important.'

"The cost was five hundred dollars each way, and I told Tim, 'It's going to be a thousand dollars.' That was a lot of money. Tim said, 'I don't care. I got to go.' We got the jet ready, and they flew to New York, and when they got there, the pilot said, 'How long are you going to be?' Tim said, 'Not long. I'm going to Manhattan. I've got to get my hair cut.'

"That's what he went to New York for, to get his hair cut! Two hours later, he was back in Charlotte. That's just the kind of guy he was.

"Tim was very impulsive. In '86, Humpy Wheeler and the Charlotte Motor Speedway held the Hayride 500. There was a drought up north, and the crops were barren, and the cattle had no feed. We had plenty of feed in North Carolina. So Humpy got a bunch of NASCAR teams to donate the use of empty freight trailers, and we loaded twenty or thirty tractor-trailer loads full of hay, and Tim Richmond drove one of them himself. All the other race teams furnished transport drivers. Tim said, 'I'm doing this.' And in this case, he did have on his cowboy boots and his jeans and cowboy hat. They had a big sendoff at the Charlotte Motor Speedway, and off they went to Ohio and dumped hay for the farmers who didn't have any. It was impressive that Tim even knew how to drive a tractor trailer. But there was nothing that guy couldn't drive. I don't even know if he had a commercial driver's license, but you didn't tell Tim 'no.' You just kind of managed him.

"Tim was a very, very clean driver, and he almost never tangled with the other drivers. Besides, most of the time he was out front. He didn't have to rough you up. He was so in control. The only driver who really didn't like Tim was Richard Petty. I don't really know why. Maybe it was a run-in in a prior year, but Richard just never really liked him.

"Tim told me a story about a time when he was driving for Blue Max and he got into a beating and banging match with David Pearson. When the race was over, Pearson pulled up beside him, or vice versa, and Tim said, 'I'll see you in the garage area.'

"So they pulled in, and Tim said he jumped out of the car, and here came Pearson, and the next thing Tim knew, he was waking up with smelling salts. It was a one-punch knockout.

"Tim said, 'I didn't know what hit me. All I remember was waking up, and there were smelling salts.' Pearson had knocked him out. Pearson was old school, buddy, old school."

As great a year as Richmond had—seven wins, eight poles, and $973,000 in winnings, by the end of the 1986 season it was clear that something was terribly wrong with Tim's health. Jimmy Johnson and the rest of the Hendrick Motorsports team had no idea what was wrong with him.

"Tim showed up for the end-of-the-year banquet in New York, but he was sick, and he looked terrible," said Johnson. "The last race of the year was at Riverside, and he looked bad there, but we just thought he had a bad cold, and then he got to New York for the banquet, and he was coughing and hacking. He accepted his checks for third place, and that night he looked me up about mid-night, reached into his coat pocket and handed me his checks, and he said, 'Boy, I'm feeling terrible.'

That was the last Johnson saw of him until he returned to racing to run nine races in the 1987 season.

"I had no idea what kind of medical care he was getting. No idea."

Richmond informed Hendrick and Johnson that he was too sick to enter the Daytona 500 in 1988. After getting medical help at the Cleveland Clinic, he was ready to get back in his race car in March. Johnson scheduled a test for Richmond at Darlington.

"Tim and I lived in the same area on Lake Norman," said Johnson. "We had rented Darlington for a private test. I drove about a quarter mile to Tim's house, and I rode to Darlington on Tim's bus. I'd say to Tim, 'I like your bus.' Tim would correct me all the time. He'd say, 'It's a coach. It's not a bus.'

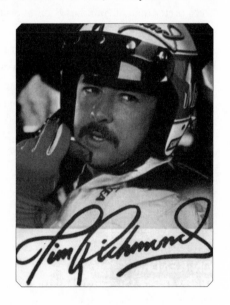

"I jumped in the coach with Evelyn and Al, Tim's parents. Tim was driving. We took off for Darlington, and on the way we stopped at McDonald's for something to eat. Tim was himself. He looked good. He couldn't wait to get there.

"We pulled into the racetrack. They let us in, and we told the security guards there was to be 'absolutely no one coming in here. Period.' They said, 'You can't keep the press out of the press box.' We said, 'The press box is fine.' I don't know how they knew Tim was going to be there, but they did.

TIM RICHMOND
Off the track he was a "handful."
INTERNATIONAL
MOTORSPORTS HALL OF FAME

"We went out and ran the test, and we were fast from the get-go. Before the last run of the day, Harry said, 'We're going to show them something,' and he put four left-side tires on the car, and off Tim went, and we blew the track record away by half a second. It was unbelievable how fast Tim went.

"We went on to Pocono [on June 14, 1987] and won that race, and that was the only time I ever saw Harry Hyde cry. Harry was one of the toughest guys who ever lived. I was around Harry more than I was with my own family for ten years, and I never saw a tear in his eye except when Tim came back and won Pocono. He wasn't the only one. I'm an emotional person. I have an excuse. But when Tim won that race, Harry and Tim and I and everyone else in Victory Lane shed a lot of tears, because it was one of the greatest days of my life, right there with Jeff Gordon winning the first Brickyard. We weren't supposed to win it, and just by the grace of God and the talent of Tim Richmond, he went out and won the race."

But when Richmond went to Watkins Glen for the race, he was weak and he was acting strange. Some drivers thought he was hungover, even drunk.

"He had really gotten out of hand at Watkins Glen," said Johnson. "Some of the things he said in a television interview really upset NASCAR. They were pretty mad at him. Les Richter and Dick Beaty [NASCAR officials] were gunning for Tim.

"We went to Michigan, and Tim wasn't himself. He really didn't look good. And he was acting strange. Apparently he knew he was dying of AIDS. I didn't. I can swear on a Bible that the only thing I knew was that he still had pneumonia, because I knew nothing of AIDS at the time.

"When it came time for qualifying, we couldn't find Tim. Harry told Dennis Connor and some of the other guys, 'Go find Tim.' They went to his coach, which was parked right outside the gate, and they looked in the window and saw him laying on his bed. They beat on the coach, but he wouldn't answer the door. 'Tim, we gotta go. It's time to qualify.' Finally, they got him up.

"Tim was on some pretty heavy medication, and they got him into a golf cart and ran him out to the racetrack. He jumped in the race car, and I ran back to the transporter and stood up on top with a stopwatch while he qualified. Harry Hyde was up there with me.

"We heard him go around the first and second turns, but we didn't see him. He went down the back straightaway, and we didn't see him. He went through three and four heading to take the green flag, and we still didn't see him. Turned out that Tim ran the whole qualifying lap on the apron! Needless to say, we were ten seconds slower than the fastest car. Tim drove straight to the transporter. He jumped out and went inside. I was right behind him.

"I said, 'Are you OK, Tim? What's wrong?' Harry was livid.

"He said, 'What were you doing?'

"Tim said, 'Harry, that's just where it wanted to run.'

"I knew something was wrong. Tim grabbed a coffee pot—Folgers was our sponsor—and he started drinking coffee as fast as he could drink it. I thought, 'Boy, this is strange.'

"Les Richter came up, and he wanted to know what in the world that was all about. I said, 'We're having a meeting. We'll see you after qualifying.'

"Late that afternoon, I started to walk out through the garage area. I was by myself. I was between the garages heading out to get my car to drive back to the hotel, and Les Richter and Dick Beaty stopped me.

"They said, 'What is going on?' I said, 'I don't know. Everything is fine.' Richter said, 'No, things are *not* fine. I want to know what's wrong with Tim.'

"All of a sudden, Tim was standing right next to me. It was like Tim dropped from the sky.

"'You're talking about me, aren't you?' Tim said to Richter, who was a big, intimidating, wonderful guy.

"'Tim, yeah, we're talking about you,' said Richter.

"'I'll tell you what,' said Tim, 'I'm sick and tired of people talking about me. Sick of it. All the people in NASCAR are talking about me.'

"I looked over, and in one corner of the garage area were twenty-five inspectors. They were waiting for Dick and Les to come over and get their last-minute details before they left for the evening. They were over there talking and laughing.

"Beaty turned and looked at the inspectors, and he said, 'Tim, you tell me which one of these NASCAR guys are talking about you, and I'll fire him on the spot.'

"Tim looked over there and said, 'Junior.'

"Beaty looked quizzical and stared at the inspectors, and then he looked back at Tim and said, 'Junior? Junior who?'

"And Tim said, 'Bill France Junior.'

"I thought, 'Oh my God.' I literally grabbed Tim around the waist and started to pull him toward the gate. And Tim was madder than a hornet. He was giving Dick and Les a hard time and pointing his fingers at the inspectors, and I dragged him away and put him in his coach.

"Tim became addled during the race itself. You could listen to his voice and tell there was a big sense of anxiety, and all of a sudden he came off four and came down pit road with smoke pouring from the car. He drove it straight into the garage area without saying a word on the radio.

"Dennis Connor went in and punched the telltale tachometer, and it was pegged. I think Tim had about had it. He figured the only way he could get out of the car was if he had a problem, and it sure looked as if Tim had clutched the engine on purpose to get out of the car.

"My wife and I were standing together, and I started running toward the transporter. Tim never got there. He stopped the race car between the two garages, and when I got there, he had undone his seat belts, and he was running to his coach, and that was the last time I ever saw Tim.

"You'd hear things about him. He never came around the racetrack. Every now and then a rumor would trickle down that Tim had AIDS, and everyone would laugh about it, especially me, saying, 'Yeah, right.' At the time, the only way I knew you got AIDS was gay sex, and from the time I spent around Tim Richmond, one damn thing I knew: he *wasn't* gay. I'd say, 'If there is one person in the world who doesn't have AIDS, it's Tim, because he's not gay.' Nobody had a clue.

"In *American Zoom*, I'm quoted in there saying, 'Tim liked whores.' He did. They were beautiful, and they didn't want anything from him. It was fifty bucks and 'See ya.'

"After the book came out, I was sitting in my office and the phone rang, and the switchboard operator said, 'Evelyn Richmond is on the phone.' I thought, 'Oh, my God.' And I love the lady. She was wonderful. I thought to myself, 'It's time to face the music, Johnson.'

"She always called me 'Son,' and I called her 'Mom.' I got on the phone and said, 'What's up, Mom?'

"She said, 'Son, I need to thank you.'

"For what?" I asked.

"'I just read *American Zoom*,' she said, 'and thank you so much for what you said about Tim, because so many things have been said about him being gay, and he wasn't gay, and what you said is exactly what happened to him.'

"'Tim did love prostitutes. He really did,' Evelyn Richmond said."

When Tim Richmond called Rick Hendrick and told him that he wanted to race again in 1988, Hendrick got in touch with NASCAR, which wasn't about to let Richmond race again after his bizarre behavior the year before. NASCAR ruled that he couldn't run at Daytona because he had failed a drug test. When it turned out that the drugs he was taking were Advil and Sudafed, NASCAR ruled that he couldn't run until Richmond showed his medical records. Richmond sued. The issue became moot when his conditioned worsened. He died on August 13, 1989.

"When Tim died, it was a relief," said Johnson. "By then, we all knew what he was going through. We had resigned ourselves to the fact we would never see him again. So it's not like it was a time to shed tears. It was more of a time to thank God for taking him when he did."

Tim Richmond was 34 years old.

CHAPTER 40

THE END OF AN ERA

Benny Parsons

AFTER BENNY PARSONS WAS RELEASED BY THE M. C. ANDERSON TEAM AT THE END of the 1980 season, he was hired by Bud Moore, who had owned and built race cars on the Grand National/Winston Cup circuit since 1961. Parsons won three races in his only year with Moore, but engine trouble beset his car all season, as he dropped to 10th in the points.

"Bud had a really good team," said Parsons. "He raced out of Spartanburg. He built really good race cars, and he ran his team with an iron fist. He was the boss, which is a lot better than doing it by committee.

"We won three races that year, but God, we had so much engine trouble. This was the early '80s, and they were trying to solve the breaking valve springs and dropping valves problem. It was terrible. And obviously I remember the opening race of the season at Riverside, where I hit some oil going into turn nine, at about one hundred and fifty miles an hour, and just killed the car."

At Daytona in '81, in the second of the 125-mile qualifying races, Darrell Waltrip cut inside Parsons and beat him for the win. It was a dangerous move on Waltrip's part, but there was criticism whispered at Parsons that he should have cut him off, even if it meant wrecking him. Parsons refused to even consider it.

"When Waltrip went down on the apron to pass me, we thought it was a very dangerous move," he said. "Why would anyone do that to win a qualifying race?"

"But that said a lot about Waltrip, didn't it?" I asked.

"That's right," said Parsons. "It did."

259

"So Waltrip was controversial at the time?"

"At the time, he was," he said.

"People wondered why you didn't cut him off," I said.

"Then there was going to be a wreck," he said. "So."

Parsons won over Waltrip and Bobby Allison at Nashville in May 1981. Then on June 7, he beat Dale Earnhardt in a dramatic finish at the Texas World Speedway.

"That racetrack was extremely rough," said Parsons, "on the bottom of the track especially. We qualified well, and I took off, and I went to the top of the track to try to get out of the rough stuff.

"I was cruising along, leading the race, and I looked in my mirror, and I saw this car gaining on me, and pretty soon I realized it was Earnhardt. When he got to me, I discovered he was running down in the bottom of the racetrack, which literally was like a plowed field.

"I said, I'm not going to go down there until I have to, because the previous year in the 27 car [owned by M. C. Anderson], I had gone down there and had shaken the radiator apart, literally apart. But after Earnhardt caught me and passed me, I said to myself, I don't have much choice. I have to go down in all that mess.

"And to this day I'll never figure out how I did it, but I went down there and passed him with four laps to go, and the car held together and I won the race."

In September 1981, Parsons held off Harry Gant to win at Richmond, his third win of the season under Bud Moore, but despite winning $311,000 in purses, Moore dropped Parsons when he had the opportunity to sign the 1980 champion Dale Earnhardt. In addition to acquiring Earnhardt, Moore was also gaining a sponsor with deeper pockets than his current one.

BUD MOORE
Childress sent Dale
to drive for Bud.
INTERNATIONAL MOTORSPORTS
HALL OF FAME

"Earnhardt had been driving for Richard Childress," said Parsons, "and the fact of the matter was that Childress told him, 'You'll be better off with Bud, because I'm still trying to build my team, and Bud has a better team, so you'd be better off.'

"Bud was sponsored by Melling. It was for around two hundred and fifty thousand dollars a year, and he had a two-year contract. Bud was being sought for Earnhardt to drive his car with a Wrangler sponsorship, which I knew was for more money than the Melling deal. I talked to Harry Melling, who I knew and who had become a friend, and I told him Bud was being offered that deal. Harry didn't want contracts. Everything with Harry was a handshake.

"Harry said, 'If Bud can get more money, he ought to quit this and go get it.' So I told Bud, 'If you can get more money from Wrangler, Harry will let you out of his contract.'

"Bud talked to Harry, and he did, and he did."

In 1982, Parsons went to drive for Harry Ranier in one of the cars sponsored by J. D. Stacy. Waddell Wilson, who had been the chief engine builder for

DALE EARNHARDT
Benny passed him with four laps to go.
INTERNATIONAL
MOTORSPORTS HALL OF FAME

Holman Moody during its heyday, was the crew chief. During qualifying at Talladega, Parsons and Wilson teamed up as their Pontiac ran a lap at 200.176 miles an hour, a new speed record for Winston Cup racing. Parsons became the first driver ever to run a qualifying lap at more than 200 miles an hour.

"We knew we had a shot," said Parsons. "We were very close to two hundred miles an hour, so we really went out there and went for it, trying to get that two-hundred-miles-an-hour lap.

"I'll have to give the guys credit, because it was set up about as perfectly as you could have it, so loose that you wanted to back out of it, even though you knew you couldn't, right on the edge.

"And when we did it, all of us were very proud of what had happened.

"Waddell was just a terrific engine man, but the deal with Ranier in 1982 was basically a disaster. They had a financial arrangement with Pontiac that year. The Pontiac LeMans had a superior body to anything out there. The year previous, it had almost won the Daytona 500, but NASCAR didn't want everyone building a Pontiac LeMans, so they placed an inch and a half rear spoiler on it when every other make of car had three- or three-and-a-half-inch spoilers. As a result, the LeMans was so loose, I could not drive it.

"We had the fastest speed at Daytona, sat on the pole, but that was for one lap. In the race it was so loose you couldn't drive it—I couldn't drive it. I ran over some kind of debris in the corner, blew a right front tire, ran into the wall and destroyed the car. But I was not outrunning anyone to begin with.

"We had no downforce in the rear as compared to the competition. And you just could not drive the car. I couldn't, and neither could anybody else, because when I left, they put Buddy Baker in the car, and he was certainly the same as I was. You couldn't drive that car."

In the end, Parsons was let go by owner Harry Ranier midway through the 1982 season in part because of his refusal to wreck a competitor to win a race.

"The biggest disappointment for Harry Ranier came at Talladega [on May 2]. We had a very fast race car, and the rear spoiler did not hinder us there nearly as much as it did at the other racetracks, because you didn't need all that downforce at Talladega.

"On the last lap, I was leading the race, and I did not block Darrell and Terry Labonte, who was behind him, the way I should have, and as a result Darrell won and I finished third, and it made Harry Ranier very angry.

"He said, 'The next race you go to, if it ever happens again, bring back the steering wheel or the trophy.' I just didn't want to drive under those circumstances."

Parsons drove his last race for Ranier at Riverside on June 13. He finished toward the back after a loss of oil pressure.

"There I was, I had nothing to do," said Parsons. "The U.S. Tobacco people were involved with Hal Needham and Harry Gant, and they said, 'We're getting a lot of mileage out of this. Maybe we ought to think about starting another team and advertising some of our other products,' like Skoal, and so they did, and they asked me to drive it, and I jumped at the chance.

"The guy in charge was Johnny Hayes, a really terrific guy. Johnny called a guy in Asheville by the name of Leo Jackson and asked him to be the crew chief, and in August we went to Michigan in a Buick, and we finished fifth!"

At Darlington, Parsons followed that effort with a very respectable eighth-place finish.

"Leo Jackson was just a very, very nice man," said Parsons. "I just absolutely loved my time with Leo. He was terrific, and also, while I was driving that 55 car for Johnny and Leo, I started doing TV on the weekends when I wasn't driving.

"We were running half the races. Ken Squier was doing the TBS shows, and they asked me to sit in sometimes when I had an off-weekend.

"Was the TV money decent?" I asked.

"No, the money wasn't decent," he said. "It paid four hundred a race, which was not a lot of money, but at least I felt like I was trying to get myself some experience for down the road. That's why I jumped at the chance to do it. I did that for several years."

In 1983, Benny Parsons drove in 16 races, and his younger brother, Phil Parsons, drove a second car in 5.

"Phil had been running a Busch car with Skoal sponsorship," said Parsons.

At Talladega on May 1, 1983, Benny watched helplessly as his baby brother's car was demolished in a horrific crash on the 71st lap.

"It was one of the worst moments I ever had in a race car," said Parsons. "I was in the race. I had had a pit stop and had gotten half a lap down, and after they restarted the race, I was on the other side of the racetrack when it happened.

"I came around, and there he sat. Looking at it, it looked about as bad as it can get. It was terrible. I said to the crew, 'Get me out of here. Get somebody in this car, cause I *got* to get out of here.'

"They were looking for somebody, but by the time they found him, they came back with the news that Phil was OK. They had just talked to him in the hospital, and he was OK."

In that race at Talladega, Richard Petty beat Parsons by less than a car length for his 197th win, and then at Charlotte on October 9, 1983, Petty achieved his 198th win. The race inspectors discovered that Petty's engine was too big, and NASCAR let him keep the win, but he was fined $35,000 and 104 cup points were taken away. I asked Benny Parsons, who finished third behind Petty and Darrell Waltrip, what he remembered about that incident.

"It was just disappointing that Richard, after all those years, had to go down to that level to win.

"I'm sure he had been complaining they didn't have the power he needed to win, so they put a bigger engine in the car, but that still was not the deal. They also put left sides on the right for that last little deal.

"A big engine? That's shoplifting, cause you still have to get through the corners. Putting left sides on the right, that's premeditated, number one, murder. I mean, the big engine you can overlook. You could not ever, ever overlook lefts on the right because it's unsafe. Goodyear recommends how you use this tire, that tire. If you use lefts on the right, if you run more than a few laps, you're going to blow the tires, and when you do, you're in the wall."

"I gather Richard was embarrassed by the whole thing," I said.

"You know he had to be," said Parsons.

A few days later, Richard Petty announced he was leaving Petty Enterprises and going to drive for Mike Curb.

"It was a shock," said Parsons. "A big shock."

At Riverside, in the final race on November 20, 1983, Parsons led with five laps to go until Bill Elliott passed him and won the race.

"That was very disappointing," Parsons said, "just very disappointing. You know, it would have been very nice to have won that race."

And so the scoreboard for 1983 read: 16 races, no wins. Parsons won his 21st and final Winston Cup race on March 18, 1984, at Atlanta in the Coca-Cola 500. He beat Dale Earnhardt and Cale Yarborough by a whisker.

"That was an unusual day," said Parsons, "because it was a partly cloudy day. The clouds would move over the sun, and the racetrack would be in the shadows, and then the clouds would leave, and the racetrack would be in the sun. And that was as good a race car as I've had. When the sun was out, the car was perfect. When it went behind the clouds, it pushed a little bit. Luckily, just at the end of the race, the sun stayed out. I just outran them. We had a car that could."

It was Parsons' only win of the year. At Charlotte in May, Parsons sat on the outside pole for the World 600. When the green flag dropped for the race, he made six laps before the car quit.

"I burned a piston on the pace lap," said Parsons. "On the pace lap, I had always kept the tachometer at a steady rpm, 4,000 or 4,500. For some reason, that engine, that carburetor, that camshaft didn't suck any fuel at that rpm, so it leaned out at that rpm, and when they dropped the green flag, I had a burned piston. Oh God, how bad is that? The car was so good, and it burned a piston on the pace lap."

Then on July 4, 1984, in front of President Ronald Reagan, Richard Petty won his 200th and final Winston Cup victory. Parsons finished fifth that day. I asked Parsons whether anyone found it funny that Richard ended up winning this particular race, what with the President in attendance.

"Oh yeah," he said, "everybody did. Yeah, they talked about the 'Presidential restrictor plate.'"

It was Parsons, whose crash brought out the caution, that allowed Petty to gain the win that day.

"With two or three laps to go, I was racing with Bobby Allison for fourth or fifth, and we came up to lap a driver by the name of Doug Heveron. About the time I started by him in the tri-oval, it dawned on me, 'He doesn't know I'm here.' And I don't know what told me he didn't. But he didn't, and I couldn't back off the gas much because Bobby was right on my bumper, and when he came up the hill I caught him in the right rear, and the last time I saw him, Heveron was flipping. It was a terrible deal.

"So Heveron and I caused the caution flag that Cale and Richard raced back to." When Richard reached the line first after the caution flag came out, the victory was his. Said Parsons, "Now you know the *rest* of the story."

In 1984, Parsons had no wins, no top-five finishes. In 1985, another year of frustration for Parsons, Bill Elliott won the Winston Million when he won three of the most prestigious races, the Daytona 500, the Winston 500 at Talladega, and the Southern 500 at Darlington.

"The Winston Million was a big deal," said Parsons. "R. J. Reynolds brought a lot of attention on the sport with that deal. That was T. Wayne Robertson. With Winston now going away, we shouldn't forget him, because what Winston did for the sport was a big deal. T. Wayne died in a boating accident down in Louisiana. He was going duck hunting, and a boat going out to an oil rig ran into him and killed him.

"But after Bill won at Daytona and Talladega, we were all pulling for him to get the Million, though we did not want to be the ones to lose to him."

That year, Elliott won 11 superspeedway poles and won 11 superspeedway races.

"The most amazing thing that Elliott did that year came at Talladega, when he made up two laps on the green. Yep, two laps under the green. It was unbelievable."

In 1986, Benny Parsons limped along with two top-five finishes. In a year in which Dale Earnhardt earned $1,768,000, Parsons, in 30th place in the points standings, still was able to earn $176,940. I asked Parsons whether the money was enough to stay in the game even though he wasn't leading races.

"Yeah," he said. "Also, by then as a driver, you are also getting money from the sponsor. It wasn't just what you were able to earn driving the car. I probably made $50,000 a year from U.S. Tobacco for doing promotions."

By 1987, the sport had become sponsor driven. I asked Parsons how that had changed the sport.

"It makes the driver more of a personality," he said. "He's not the guy who works on the race car anymore. He's a personality. Now all of a sudden you have to have some pizzazz. You have to be able to talk in crowds, talk to blue-collar workers, but you also have to be able to converse with CEOs."

Parsons was running out the string driving for Johnny Hayes and Leo Jackson when he got a call from the Hendrick Motorsports team. Tim Richmond, their star driver, was suffering from what everyone thought was pneumonia and he was too sick to drive. Benny Parsons got the call from crew chief Harry Hyde to replace the flamboyant Richmond in the Folgers 25 Chevrolet.

"I didn't have a contract with Johnny Hayes, and I could see that my career was winding down," said Parsons, "and that year Phil and I were going to share a car. They were going to run the 55 car the whole season, and I was going to run some races, and Phil was going to run the rest, and I'd do TV the weeks he drove.

"Harry Hyde called and asked me, 'What's your deal? Can you drive the Folgers twenty-five car?' I said to myself, 'This is a really good race car, and this is my chance to try to win some races and get out of here with a bang.' I jumped at it. Phil stayed with Leo and ran the entire series that year."

Parsons showed that with a superior car he could still run up front, when at Daytona in the second qualifier, he outran Bobby Allison and Geoff Bodine for the win. In a season when everyone was touting the Thunderbirds, Parsons took his Chevy to the front and stayed there.

"It was just very, very exciting for me to be able to do that," said Parsons. "I found me a groove that worked for me. I was able to go to the top of the racetrack in three and four and was able to get to the front. It was tremendous.

"But the most disappointing thing of the whole deal came when one of the trade papers the next week had a headline, 'Car Wins One Qualifying Race, Driver Wins the Other.' It said the twenty-five car had won my race and that Ken Schrader took an underpowered car and won the other race. I really thought I had done a terrific job in finding that groove and winning the race.

"That was their opinion, but that was disappointing. And that's one hard thing about doing TV. I never make personal comments. I don't say, 'Driver X was stupid.' I try to say, 'Here's what caused the wreck.' And there are certain times you have to point fingers when you wish you didn't have to. Most of the guys inside the garage area and I get along tremendous, but when I say something bad about somebody, that's their friend badmouthing them. It doesn't get much worse than that."

In the Daytona 500 in 1987, Parsons finished second to Bill Elliott in a race he is convinced he should have won.

"There were four or five of us competing for the win," said Parsons. "All five of us made our final pit stops in a group. I was leading the race when I went in. I came in about one hundred and fifty miles an hour trying to win the thing. I was going to show them just how good I could get down pit road. I overshot my pit by a pit and a half, so the gas man had to run down and catch me and put gas in the car, so it took a little longer to get to me, and when we took off, Elliott led, and I was second.

"Me, Elliott, Buddy Baker, Earnhardt, we all were battling. Elliott and I had lockers in them—the rear gear that locks up the wheels, so when we stood on the gas both rear tires pulled—and we were able to get out of the pits faster than the cars that didn't have them. When the other cars nailed the gas with an open gear, they'd sit there and spin the right rear tire. You could not get a grip. So Elliott and I came out two in a group because we were able to get out of the pits faster. But because I overshot my pit, I lost the race by a second and an eighth." Parsons added, "You are bringing up some bad stuff, you know that?"

"You finished second," I said.

"I know," he said, "but I didn't win."

"What was Harry's reaction?" I asked.

"He was OK with it," he said.

I asked Parsons what he recalled about Harry Hyde.

"In the movie that Tom Cruise was in [*Days of Thunder* with Robert Duvall as the Harry Hyde–like crew chief], that *was* Harry. He was stubborn, but hilarious. He was a very, very funny man. Harry was very smart and well read, and he had an opinion on everything, and he had weird theories.

"All that stuff that happened in the movies happened to Harry Hyde. Take the ice cream deal. I had crashed at Darlington, and I was out there riding around, trying to get some points. A caution came out. I asked, 'Do you want me to pit, Harry?' He said, 'Not right now.'

"The next lap went by. 'Do you want me to pit?' Harry said, 'We're eating ice cream right now. As soon as we finish, you can come by and get some gas.'

At Atlanta on March 15, 1987, Parsons finished second to 30-year-old Ricky Rudd in yet another race Parsons feels he could have won had circumstances been different and his luck a little better.

"Our radios didn't work properly," said Parsons, "so our communication was not what it should have been. We needed to make a chassis adjustment on our last pit stop. I knew about it, but I couldn't tell them."

"You couldn't drive into the pits and yell, 'Chassis adjustment'?" I asked.

"I couldn't afford to give up track position," he said.

Parsons in 1987 drove in 29 races, finishing in the top 10 nine times and earning $566,484 in purses. But he was overshadowed when the flamboyant Tim Richmond returned on June 14 from his bout with what was then thought to be pneumonia. He won the Pocono race that day and followed it up the next weekend with a win at Riverside. I asked Parsons about the Pocono race.

"It was amazing and also disappointing," he said. "I was driving the other Hendrick car, and believe it or not, my car that day was as good as Tim's, if not better. There was only one pit crew. This was not '03. This was '87, so they didn't have the pit crew I needed, so Richmond came in and got the number-one treatment, as he should have, and so the end result was that we were very lacking in the pits. And then I got far behind, and I crashed."

"And Tim won again at Riverside," I said.

"Yep," he said. "Quite something." Parsons finished third that day.

At Watkins Glen, Tim Richmond began acting very strange. I asked Parsons if he was acting weird.

"He was," he said. "He was really weird."

"What was going on?"

"I don't know, but he didn't seem right. I don't know whether he was drinking or whether it was the medicine he was on or what. We would talk, but we did not operate in the same stratosphere. We'd change clothes in the same trailer. 'Hey, Tim, how you doing?' And we'd talk about the car, but that was about it."

It rained that day, and so the race was rained out. Richmond appeared less bedraggled at Michigan, which would turn out to be his last Winston Cup appearance. He finished 29th at Michigan, the race in which he blew the engine, possibly on purpose, to end his day. Parsons ended up ninth.

"Tim never drove in another race," I said. "He just disappeared."

"He was sick," said Parsons, "and I had no idea how sick he was."

"He eventually died of AIDS," I said.

"I didn't know it at the time. In '87, we didn't know what AIDS was."

By the end of the 1987 season, Benny Parsons was ready to quit racing.

"I had all the frustration I could stand," he said. "I had a very good race car. Richmond came in and won in the car, and I didn't. I finished second at Daytona, second at Riverside, second at Atlanta, but I didn't win. I *did not* win, and that is the bottom line. I was either going to win or quit. It's very frustrating not to, so I was looking for something else. At the end of the year, I called the folks at ESPN, and I asked, 'Is there a place for me?'

"I had worked for ESPN previously, and Terry Lingner, the executive producer, said, 'We'd love to have you, but we don't have the money.' I said, 'How much money are you talking about?' He said, 'We could probably pay you thirty-five thousand a year.'

"At that time, I had some obligations I could not pay making that kind of money, so I said to myself, OK, I better find me a ride."

Parsons was hired to drive for Junie Donlavey, an old-timer who had been in the game since 1950. In 38 years of racing, Donlavey had achieved only one win, by Jody Ridley in 1981.

"Was Junie the first car owner to call you?" I asked.

"He might have been the only one," said Parsons, "and he had a sponsor willing to pay me seventy-five thousand to drive, so all of a sudden now I can meet my obligations."

The 1988 season began with the Daytona 500, a race notable for the one-two finish of Bobby Allison and his son Davey. Parsons' Ford had engine failure, and he finished 31st.

"It might have been the worst Speed Weeks of my life," said Parsons. "We had a miss that we could never find. It wouldn't clear up, wouldn't run smooth, and we never could find it."

"You didn't do well in the 125 qualifier," I said. [He finished 16th.]

"No," he said, "Didn't do well in any of it."

That year at Pocono, Bobby Allison was involved in a terrible crash that almost ended his life and left him with serious brain injuries.

"I had made a pit stop," said Parsons. "Something had happened, and when I rode by I couldn't believe the damage to his car. It was just sitting there horse-shoed, and it was really, really bad.

"I went to Allentown and saw him. Bobby didn't even know I was there."

In 27 races in 1988, Parsons had just one top-10 finish.

"We had a couple of runs," he said, "but only a couple. We were very good at Atlanta in the spring. We led the race, and then we dropped a valve. At Charlotte in the fall, we had a good car and dropped a valve. Darlington was the worst one. We had a very good race car in the Southern 500, but we ran out of tires. Nobody had any. Everyone who follows this sport knows how important tires are at Darlington, and they were worn out. There were no tires to buy. There were no tires left.

"After the season I called ESPN again and said, 'I still need a job.'

"He said, 'We've got a little bit more money, but not much.'

"'How much?'

"'We probably could come up with fifty grand.'

"I said, 'I got to do it. I can't stand this anymore.' I just couldn't stand not being able to win. Richard Petty kept going for several years after he stopped winning, and I don't know how he did it. Darrell went on for several years, and to be truthful, he was not competitive, and I don't know how he did it."

Parsons joined anchor Bob Jenkins and Ned Jarrett in the booth during the ESPN broadcasts. Then a couple of years ago, the contracts were put up for bidding, and Fox and NBC won the right to broadcast the races. Parsons now works for Turner Broadcasting and NBC.

"I am still working," said Parsons.

I asked Parsons if he had any interesting pictures that he could send me for this book. He said he didn't.

"I never kept anything," he said. "I was never interested in trophies. The enjoyment I got was in the satisfaction of doing it. That was my thrill. And when I got to the point when I was not doing it well, it became time to leave."

CHAPTER 41

JACK ROUSH GOES RACING

Robin Pemberton

When Robin Pemberton was at DiGard, Lake Speed, who was driving for the Rahmoc team, approached him to become his crew chief. After he accepted the job at Rahmoc, he didn't want to burn any bridges, so he told the people at DiGard, "I'm married. You don't have a sponsor. I got to go take care of myself."

Pemberton felt that all Speed and the Rahmoc team needed was some stability. But the day he took the job, that was the day they fired Lake Speed.

"I was out of the frying pan and into the fire again," said Pemberton. "It was as though the mess just followed me around. We went and got a string of drivers [Jody Ridley, Jim Sauter, Morgan Shepherd, and Lake Speed again]. I was making about $30,000 a year. You can afford to buy a Toyota Corolla. It wasn't too bad. They had Nationwise Auto Parts as a sponsor, and then Valvoline. Then my second year they signed Neil Bonnett.

"Neil was a good guy, real generous. Man, he was a hard driver. Christ, he drove hard. Literally, I think he drove too hard. He just drove every lap as hard as he could, but after being stuck with guys who couldn't drive, it was kind of a nice change. It was the other side of the coin. But I was kind of getting agitated, even with Neil there, with the way some of the things were going within the shop.

"I was home one day, outside mowing the lawn, and the phone rang. It was Monday. We had traveled all night somewhere, and I took Monday off. Lisa stuck her head out and said, 'The phone is for you.'

"I said, 'Whoever it is, tell them I've died and gone away. I'm not here.'

"She said, 'The guy says his name is Jack Roush. I think I know that name. Do you know him?'

"I said, 'I know who he is.'

"She said, 'He's on the phone wanting to talk to you.'

"This was July of 1987. I went into the house, and it *was* Jack Roush. He said, 'There are some people in the Ford Motor Company who you know and I know, and I'm looking to go Winston Cup racing. Would you be interested?'

"I said, 'Yeah.'

"I didn't know Jack Roush. Nope, not at all, but I felt it had to be better than what I was doing, so I told him I'd speak to him.

"Roush then called Steve Hmiel, and he asked him the same question. Steve and I got talking to each other, and we figured that out.

"Roush flew to Greensboro to see me. For starters, I was impressed that the guy had his own airplane. He had an engineering business, Roush Industries. He did a lot of engineering for all the manufacturers of aftermarket parts. He had all kinds of projects for Cadillac, Chevrolet, Ford, you name it. He was heavy. He was a lot smaller then than he is now, but he had good connections.

"His race teams were mainly SCCA and Trans Am. He had Willy T. Ribbs, Robby Gordon, and Wally Dallenbach Jr., good drivers, driving for him. It was impressive to think he was getting ready to go stock car racing.

"We talked, went our separate ways, and agreed to talk some more. I hadn't made up my mind whether to work for Jack or not.

"There was a show Dave Despain was doing on Thursday nights on ESPN, and on the show they announced that Jack Roush was going Winston Cup racing and that he was talking to Steve Hmiel and Robin Pemberton. I never saw the show. But Butch Mock and Bob Rahilly, the guys I was working for, saw it.

"It was Bristol weekend. I showed up at the racetrack on Friday, and I noticed they weren't talking to me. I didn't know what was going on. I thought, 'These guys are in a bad mood. What the hell is this all about?' I didn't say anything.

"As the day went on, friends of mine from other race teams came over and said, 'We saw that you're going to do the Jack Roush team.' I said, 'Where did you hear that?' 'Hell, it was on TV last night.' I thought to myself, 'Ah, shit.'

"Well, by Monday they fired me. Bob got all mad. He said, 'If this isn't good enough for you. . . .' And he fired me. So hell, I was out of work. And now I *have* to go to work for Jack, because it's the middle of the year, and nobody changes jobs in the middle of the year.

"So in August of 1987, I went to work for Jack Roush. We hadn't settled on a driver. Roush had also hired Steve Hmiel, and Steve and Mark Martin were pretty tight, and we hired Mark to drive. We put a deal together and we raced in '88, '89, '90, and '91.

"We had a good team. Mark drove his ass off. Steve and I worked on the cars real hard. When we were working on the car, Steve would go in one corner and watch it run, and I'd go in another corner, and we'd get together and decide on the springs and shocks, all kinds of different stuff. My brothers, Ryan and Roman, worked for me at Roush's summers. Last year [2001] Ryan worked fulltime as a mechanic."

Jack Roush was an owner who tried hard to win races. If the team had any difficulties, it was because Roush lived 600 miles away in Livonia, Michigan, and was rarely in the Charlotte race shop.

"Jack and I were like father and son. We really got along good. There were times when he fired me, and I refused to quit, and times when I wanted to quit, and he wouldn't let me go.

"We had such a love-hate relationship. One time Jack was feeling down, and I went into his office. Steve, Jack, and I were talking, and Jack said, 'Look, I have to make a change, and I'm going to fire you.'

"I said, 'Jack, no. I'm not leaving. You own this team, but this is as much mine as it is yours, and you are making a mistake, and this time I'm not going. I'm not leaving, and you're not firing me. You think about it. I'll be in the shop, and at the end of the day we'll talk about this.'

"I was mad. I got up and left. I have to say there had been other times when he should have fired me and he didn't. He had missed his opportunity. So I wasn't leaving when I didn't think I deserved it.

"Sure enough, by the end of the day it was OK. Whether he had a change of heart or other people talked to him, I don't know, but it was, 'Yeah, OK, I'm not going to fire you. Stay.' One of them deals."

Pemberton and Jack Roush remain friends to this day. They always got along better when they weren't working together.

"Jack was good about what we needed, but we suffered from the logistic nightmare of engines, which were all built in Michigan," said Pemberton. "We had to truck the engines down. Now the Roush team is big enough to send tractor trailers back and forth. Back then, we sent vans. Kids drove back and forth at night.

"We'd take engines out of the van on Monday afternoon, and they'd leave the shop Monday afternoon, and they'd be in Livonia Tuesday morning, and they'd wait until Tuesday night for other engines and send them back Wednesday to be put back into the cars to go to the race that week. It was hard at times.

"We had times when we ran good, times when we ran bad. We were learning. Mark was young and getting his start for a second time. He had tried to run Winston Cup once before.

"Mark is very quiet. His mom and dad had been divorced, and those splits affect the family members. Mark was real close to both of them. When we first started, Mark was pretty wild, but that didn't last long. Sometimes it takes a year or two to get the edges knocked off, and you kind of settle down. It was quite a learning experience for him. For all of us.

"We learned not to stay out and drink all night. I mean, we did learn those lessons.

"The team was real small, and we had small sponsors, Stroh Brewery for a few years and then Folgers coffee. Steve or Steve's wife arranged all the transportation out of the shop. A girl made all the room reservations. We were *really* small.

"We drove to all the races for a couple of years, as opposed to flying.

"We started the team thinking we were going to run fifteen races the first year, and we ended up running all of them, and that was a nightmare. We never got caught up. We had four days off between August of '87, when we started, and December of '88. It was a friggin' nightmare.

"And I was driving a hundred miles to work each day each way. Roush's shop was near Greensboro, and I was living in Charlotte. I had bought a house there when I was working for DiGard. There are four ways to drive from Charlotte to Liberty, North Carolina, but it's the same mileage any way you go: a hundred miles. You just can't get there from here.

"A couple of years we were real close to winning the championship. In '88 we sat on one pole and didn't win any races. The second year we started to come together and won Rockingham, and we won a couple races a year from then on.

"Everything was going pretty good at Roush's. You have good days and bad days, good years and bad. When in '91 Richard Petty announced he would retire at the end of the '92 season, I was invited to go over to the ceremony. I was still close to the Pettys, and so I went over there to watch Richard do his deal.

"As I got ready to leave, Kyle said, 'What are you doing next year?' I said, 'I don't know. What's going on?'

"Kyle was driving for Felix Sabates at Sabco. He asked if I'd be interested in coming over to his team. I said, 'What about Gary [Nelson, the crew chief]?' He said, 'Don't worry about Gary. He's probably going to do something else.'

"I said, 'OK, I'll talk to Felix.'

"One night I drove down to meet Felix. We met at his condo at the Charlotte Motor Speedway, and we put together a deal. Felix and I had gotten to be friends through the years, and he seemed to be a pretty friendly fellow.

"It was just time to change. It wasn't more money. With Jack, fifty percent of what you made was in bonuses. The salary was below average, but the bonuses were good. The end number was OK. Felix offered a lot more salary and an opportunity at bonuses at the top end. I thought, 'A bird in the hand.'

"Also, Jack was going to a two-car team, and I wasn't big on that. I thought it would be hard to do. If Mark had won a championship and then if he had added a car, that would have been acceptable. But to be close in the points these years and then say we're adding another car, that didn't sit right with me.

"And Kyle and I had been friends through the years.

"At the end of the year, I told Jack, 'I just have to go and do something different.'"

CHAPTER 42

AMNESIA AND RECOVERY

Susan Bonnett

NEIL BONNETT WAS RACING THROUGH HIS FOURTEENTH SEASON WHEN AT Charlotte on October 11, 1987, he blew a tire and was injured seriously for the first time. His hip was crushed.

"One time driving for the Wood Brothers at Dover, he broke his breastbone, but he never had anything as major as this," said Susan Bonnett. "I was at Charlotte with Jesse and Carolyn Cunningham, good friends who live in Lynchburg, Virginia. They had a motorhome, and they traveled to all the races. We were up on their motorhome watching the race, and I saw Neil hit the wall, and the car veered on around where it was out of our view. We did not have radios to the pits. We were listening to the radio broadcast, and they said they could not get him out of the car, but he was conscious, so I knew he was alive. I just didn't know how serious it was, because they weren't saying much on the radio, and they would not let me go through the gate—another one of their rules.

"I went to the hospital at the racetrack, and I waited until they brought him in. He looked green. He wasn't saying much, but I could see he was in terrific pain. I knew he had a broken leg, because that's what he was holding. They immediately said they were taking him to the Cabarrus County Hospital. They would not let me go in the ambulance, so the Cunninghams and I got in my rental car and followed behind.

"When we got there, they put him in intensive care. The doctor told me they were going to have to operate, but because he still had undigested food in his stomach they had to wait several hours. The doctor showed me the X-rays and said he wasn't sure about his hip, but they were probably going to put a plate and some pins in there because he had a lot of bone that was floating. It was pretty scary. Neil was in horrible pain. That was not easy to watch.

"Right off the bat, he was more worried about how long he was going to be out. He was trying to figure out what was going to happen. 'They are going to have to get another driver,' he said. The next day Dr. Wassel did the surgery. They were so good to me at the hospital. They fixed me up a room where I could stay right there.

"He crushed his femur, so he had a plate with a lag-bolt and ten screws. When they operated, he lost quite a bit of blood, and they gave him several pints. He was concerned about that because of AIDS. He had never had to take blood before. He was concerned he'd get some kind of disease.

"After surgery, he didn't wake up for three days, and then he was in such pain. He was hooked up to a morphine machine. Every so often he would press it and it would give him morphine. He was told he had to be able to do it himself, but he said, 'If I fall asleep, you mash it.'

"Several days after the surgery, he had a hematoma up in the high part of his leg. He was in so much pain, and Dr. Wassel was in surgery. We couldn't get hold of him, and even with the morphine, Neil was pulling his hair out by the handfuls. He told me, 'If they can't bring me anything, I'm going to send you out on the street to buy drugs. Either you do that, or you're going to have to roll me over to the window and throw me out.'

"I said, 'That won't help because there's a floor right underneath the window. All you will do is fall and break your other leg.'

"Neil stayed in the hospital for ten days, and he was still in pain when we left there and returned to Alabama. He lost so much weight and so much blood that he just didn't look right for a long time. He was very pale."

Bonnett missed the remainder of the 1987 season and returned for the Daytona 500 in 1988.

"He had to work out a lot in order to be able to come back," said Susan Bonnett. "He had a lot of therapy. We had home health care that came out. Neil had a gym already set up downstairs, so they showed him what to do, and they came out three or four days a week and worked with him, and he would work till it would be painful for me to watch."

When he returned, he did so with a bang, finishing fourth in the Daytona 500 in the race won by Bobby Allison, with son Davey Allison second, and Phil Parsons, Benny's baby brother, third.

"We were real concerned about his endurance," said Susan Bonnett. "He felt confident in the car's capacity, but we were not sure about his physical condition.

But he did well. He felt good after he got out. We were just ecstatic. We thought that was great."

The next race was held at Richmond, the last race ever held at the fairgrounds. Bonnett trailed by two full laps but made it up and won the race. He then flew to Australia and won a race on the other side of the world. And when he came back and raced at Rockingham, he won again, coming from 30th place to win in a Pontiac. The Rockingham win was Bonnett's 19th Winston Cup win, and it gave him the lead in the standings for the championship.

"He beat Dale Earnhardt," said Susan Bonnett. "He did. Neil was running Hoosier tires, and a lot of drivers were real upset about guys driving Hoosiers. But Neil had known the Hoosiers man for years when he was in Sportsman racing, and he always thought they were good tires. They were having problems with Goodyears, so they allowed him to use Hoosiers for two or three races. It ticked a lot of people off. I remember Neil saying something to Dale Earnhardt about it. Dale was all up in the air about those Hoosier tires. They just yan-yanned back and forth."

What began as a most promising season turned scary when Bonnett began suffering heart-attack-like symptoms.

"He would get deathly sick and his chest would hurt," said Susan Bonnett. "We thought they were heart attacks, because it would act like a heart attack. He'd get out of breath and his blood pressure would run up.

"He had an attack one night at Wilkesboro. I called Dr. Jerry Punch, because you have to keep those things private. He came and checked him. All his vital signs were OK, but his chest was hurting. Jerry gave him some nitroglycerin tablets, and they eased the pain. He said, 'You might have gallstones.' Neil told him, 'I've been tested, and they didn't find any.' He ran the race the next day.

"On Monday, we went straight to the doctor's office, and they ran tests, and this time they found them. They told him he would have to have surgery. He kept trying to get into a hospital where he could get laparoscopic surgery, but they weren't doing much of that then, and it got worse and worse. I would have to pack lunches and travel with him to the races with the things he could eat. He was a meat-and-potatoes man, so he could not eat all the things prescribed to him on the diet. After you eat lean roast beef, Jell-O, and jellybeans every day, you finally get tired of it. So he couldn't wait any longer, and in July he had to have surgery, which put him out for a bunch of races."

If 1988 wasn't good to Bonnett, it was devastating to his friend Bobby Allison, who had crashed at Pocono and almost died. When he got out of the hospital, Allison was suffering from a serious injury to the brain.

"I wasn't at Pocono, so I didn't know how serious it was," said Susan Bonnett. "I don't think Neil knew how serious until he got ready to head for home. I remember when he called me, he said it was *very* serious. He talked about Bobby having a head injury, saying it was touch-and-go, and it was so hard to believe. It was a long, long recovery for Bobby.

"Neil and I went to the rehabilitation center several times to visit him when Bobby returned home. Bobby was having a real hard time talking. It was hard for him to communicate. I felt like it taxed him so."

In 1989, his last year with Rahmoc, Bonnett's season did not include a single victory or even a top five. The car experienced a lot of motor trouble. In 1990, he returned to the Wood Brothers amid high expectations.

"He was excited about it," said Susan Bonnett. "They had taken on Citgo as a sponsor, and he got close to the top guy representing Citgo. They played golf together, and they had a good relationship, and he felt the Wood Brothers were doing all they needed to do to become a top team. He wasn't running as well as he had hoped, but he was with people he felt confidence in."

Then at Darlington on April 1, 1990, Ernie Irvan, who was hopelessly out of contention, was battling to get his lap back after a caution, and he spun and set off a wreck involving 13 cars. Bonnett's Ford was caught up in the wreckage. When they took him from the car, he didn't seem badly injured. But when he arrived at the hospital, he didn't know where he was or why he was there.

"When I first got there, Neil would look right through me," said Susan Bonnett. "It was like he didn't know me. So I knew something was wrong. He looked glassy eyed. For a while, he called me 'that woman.'

"They brought him things to smell: cinnamon, garlic, and he couldn't smell them. They brought him things to eat, and he didn't know what they were.

"After they did some tests, the doctors said, 'We're very sorry to tell you, but he's had a stroke.' I thought, 'These people don't know what they are talking about.' I said, 'Is there anyone else you can call in?' I called our doctor at home and told him what they were saying, and he said, 'They may be seeing injuries he's had in the past.' Finally, they decided he didn't have a stroke, but the doctor said, 'He has had a head injury, and it's pretty severe, and even though he's OK—doesn't have swelling—he can't remember anything.'

"He said, 'It could last a long time. It could last forever. Or it could last a short time. We have no way of knowing.'

"We had to protect him from people who came to the hospital to see him. The doctor said, 'The worst thing a person can do is say, "Do you remember me?" Because he can't remember, and he'll get upset, and it will cause other problems.'

"When they released Neil from the hospital, Dale Earnhardt's pilot flew us home. We had our doctor waiting with an ambulance when we got to Birmingham. Neil's parents and our children were waiting on us. Neil was up and walking, but he didn't recognize them or the children, and he didn't have a clue where we were going. He and Bobby had flown in and out of that part of the airport for years, but he was scared to death because he didn't have a clue where he was. When Neil walked past our doctor and didn't know him, our doctor said, 'Oh, my God, this is heartbreaking. I've never experienced this.' And it was.

"We visited a neurosurgeon in Birmingham, and he asked me, 'Does Neil normally have a temper?' I said, 'Yes, he has a terrible temper.' He said, 'Look for it to get three times as bad, because he will get frustrated. Whatever you do, don't force him into anything and keep a close watch on him.' We did that.

"When we got home, Neil didn't know where anything was. He would go out the door and start walking, and we'd have to go get him because he didn't know where he was going. It was very bad. The doctor said, 'Some things may trigger memories, but don't force him into anything.'

"My son was working on a car in the garage, and we'd take Neil out there and let him watch, because we thought this might help him remember. But he'd stand around, and when someone would drive up, he'd come running and hide, because he didn't want to have to try to figure out who it was.

"One day someone came up to him and said, 'Don't you know us?' He had a drill in his hand because David was trying to show him how to use it, and he came in the house, and he was so frustrated he drilled a hole in the kitchen countertop. The hole is still there. He went into a terrible rage, and when he would do that, he would cry, and it would take him two or three days to come out of it. It was horrible to watch. He would be so mad, and then he wouldn't know why he was mad, and he didn't understand what was happening to him. It was a tough time.

"We took him to the doctor, and he was tested. The doctor asked me, 'Have you noticed anything?'

"I said, 'I know he would never sit at the table if any of us ate fried eggs. He would make us leave, because he couldn't stand to look at them. And he would never let anyone eat blue cheese because it made him sick to smell it. But now he is eating it.' So we knew he didn't remember that he didn't eat it, couldn't stand it.

"This went on for several weeks. Then one day he was sitting in the living room when a hunting magazine came in the mail. Usually I didn't let him see those things, but the mail was laying there, and the magazine was there, and he started looking at it, and he started to put some things together. Little things started coming back. He said, 'I know I've been here.' He recognized some of the places where he and Dale Earnhardt had gone to hunt. That was how it started, and then almost every day he started remembering things. He remembered the hunting first. But for a long time he did not remember that he drove a race car."

"Tell me about the day he first remembered you," I said.

"He said he always knew he knew me and that I was someone important," she said. "He said everyone was in there, but he couldn't put them together. He knew he knew some faces, but he didn't know who they were. After he read that hunting magazine, it wasn't a week or two later when he called me by name. He was blessed. There were people who we talked to who had had this for years. I was told, 'His short-term memory will probably be terrible.' We saw that with Bobby. Before his accident, Bobby could meet you one time, and he could meet you ten years later and remember who you were. After his accident, we watched that dissipate. After Neil's accident, he never had a lot of short-term memory. There were things he never could remember."

I said to Susan Bonnett, "Bobby never could remember the Daytona 500 when he came in first and Davey came in second."

"Right," she said. "When Neil's memory started to come back, Bobby came over to see him, and Bobby could hardly talk and Neil could hardly remember, and I was sitting in the living room in between the two of them, and I was trying to speak for Bobby and think for Neil. Bobby would say, 'Hey, do you . . . ', and he'd look at me and I'd say, 'Remember,' and I'd finish talking for Bobby, and Neil would say, 'Susan, do I remember that?' And I would say, 'You remember when so and so and so and so. . . .' He'd say, 'Oh yeah.' In retrospect, it was really hilarious, but I was worn out. It wasn't funny at the time, but after Bobby left, I just had to lay on the floor and laugh."

"Did Neil suffer from depression?" I asked.

"Yes, absolutely," she said. "Very deep depression."

"What were you able to do for that?"

"Nothing," she said. "Not a thing."

"I gather he eventually remembered that he was a race car driver, but he knew he wasn't going to be able to do it," I said.

"The doctor kept telling him that it would all depend on how he recovered," she said. "He said, 'Another lick on the head would not be good.' He told Neil, 'When you damage the brain, you don't even have to hit your head. With the speeds you go, and with stopping so quickly, your body stops, but the fluid in your brain does not stop. The movement can cause damage. You have scars from the time you're born, all the little nicks and knocks you had as a child growing up that damage your brain. Those cells never regenerate. It would be a big risk for you to drive again.'

"To begin with, it wasn't hard for him not to race, because even though he had begun to remember things, he just didn't remember that he was good at racing. That took a while. The doctor told me, 'When it comes back, if it comes back, it will come back with a passion.' And of course, it did."

But before it did, Neil Bonnett recovered sufficiently to become a fine broadcaster of the Winston Cup stock car races on the Nashville Network and CBS. He was so charming and insightful that he quickly became recognized as one of the best ever to analyze the sport on TV. He even hosted his own weekly show, called *Winners*.

"Neil had done some commentating of Sportsman races," said Susan Bonnett, "so they knew he was capable of doing that. He had known Ken Squier for years, and whenever Ken did his radio show at Daytona, he would invite Neil to be a guest because he said that Neil was quick-witted and was so good on TV. Ken was in business with Fred Rheinstein, and they were the ones who approached Neil, and they did quite a few things, including the *Winners* show, in which he would go out and interview different drivers. Fred Rheinstein and the whole crew would come here every so often to film the openings and closings of the show downstairs in the house. Before Neil died, they were planning a fishing program, because Neil loved hunting and fishing. They were going to do some deep sea fishing, and it was going to be an extremely busy year for Neil."

CHAPTER 43

THE KID

Jimmy Johnson

In 1986, the Hendrick racing team fielded two cars. In 1987, it fielded four cars. Its drivers were Geoff Bodine, Darrell Waltrip, Benny Parsons, and for nine races, Tim Richmond.

"Nineteen eighty-six was as great a year as you could have," said team manager Jimmy Johnson, "and we decided if we could be successful going from one team to two, what could we do going from three to four? Well, we found out: not too good.

"Benny Parsons came in to substitute for Tim in '87, and then when Tim came back, Benny got out of the 25 red car and we put him in a green car, Folgers decaffeinated. Benny was also an extremely good race car driver. Harry was his crew chief. When Tim came back, Harry had two cars, which really taxed us. Going from two to four really taxed the engine department, and everybody else. We weren't prepared for it, and consequently we didn't do a good job for anybody. But we didn't have any choice. We backed into it. We had a sponsor who wanted to do it, a three-time Winston Cup champion [Waltrip], the best engine builder and crew chief in NASCAR [Waddell Wilson] all wanting to come together. It was a no-brainer to start that third team.

"But it's amazing how well good friends get along until they have to work together. And that's what happened between Darrell and Waddell, who were two wonderful guys. There are not two finer people to walk into the Winston Cup garage area.

"Waddell had been crew chief for Harry Ranier, and Darrell had driven for Junior [Johnson]. They were together constantly. Barbara Wilson and Stevie Waltrip were best friends. They shopped together. Those four ate dinner together almost every night. They were almost inseparable. It seemed like the perfect match. When we put the two together, and all of a sudden now when your best friend questions whether you did this right or that right, now all of a sudden your best friend is questioning your judgment, and it just didn't work. It was a very, very tense situation, and we didn't run very well."

After challenging for the championship the year before, Tim Richmond won two races in 1987, and three-time points champion Darrell Waltrip, in a constant battle with crew chief Waddell Wilson, won just one race, at Martinsville. When Jimmy Johnson saw the Waltrip-Wilson team wasn't working, he knew he had to change the chemistry.

"We brought Jeff Hammond in from Junior's," said Johnson. "We made Waddell the team manager, and we hired Jeff to be the crew chief. It was a real bad situation. Waddell eventually became crew chief for Ricky Rudd, and he had some successes there, and then he went on to work for Larry Hendrick."

The 1989 season proved more successful for Hendrick Motorsports. Darrell Waltrip won six races, Geoff Bodine one, and Kenny Schrader one. Its biggest triumph came in the Daytona 500 when Waltrip won, Schrader was second, and Bodine fourth.

"Schrader had the dominant car," said Johnson. "He could go to the front anytime he wanted to. Harry was the crew chief for Kenny, and by far they had everyone killed. There was nobody who could touch Kenny. And we ran up front all day, and Darrell, as smart a driver who ever saw behind the wheel, and Jeff Hammond, figured out how far he could go on gas, and they backed her down a little bit, and when they didn't have to make that last pit stop like everyone else, they won the race."

At the end of the 1989 season, Darrell Waltrip decided he wanted to leave Waddell Wilson and Rick Hendrick behind to start his own race team.

"Darrell wanted to do his own thing, and he had an opportunity to do it with Western Auto," said Johnson. "We had to sign a contract with Western Auto that we'd build engines for him for a couple of years, and when we agreed to do that, Western Auto said 'Fine.' At that time, Geoff Bodine also left.

"Geoff had been a fine driver for us, but Geoff didn't get much publicity because he was from New York—he wasn't one of the Good Old Boys. At that time, it was still a Southern boys' sport. Not so much today. It's only a matter of time when we will have international drivers in NASCAR. But Geoff didn't fit in with the good-old-boy, tobacco-spitting drivers."

By 1990, Hendrick Motorsports was back to a two-car team, with Ricky Rudd and Kenny Schrader behind the wheel. Waddell Wilson became Ricky's crew chief. It was a time of tranquility. I wondered whether Johnson had chosen them deliberately after the controversy surrounding Tim Richmond.

"Nah," said Johnson. "It just evolved. We wanted to find the next Tim Richmond, and we were hoping it would be Schrader or Rudd, and it just didn't turn out that way.

"Ricky is a very intense racer. That's all he wants to do, and he expects you to handle all the other stuff, which was fine with me. I have a lot of respect for Ricky Rudd. On a road course, he would kick butt. He might be quiet—he does not talk a lot, but when he says something, you better be listening. Let me tell you something, he may not be big in stature, but it would take a bad son of a gun to want to fight him. 'Cause Ricky is tough.

"I remember Ricky had announced he was going to leave, and we won at Michigan, and I came up to him in Victory Lane, and I said, 'You sure you want to leave?' And he said, 'No.' That win was a highlight with Ricky.

"And as for Kenny Schrader, I'd kill for Kenny Schrader, the finest guy who ever lived. There is no one like Kenny. About twenty years ago I heard Woody Durham, the voice of the Tarheels, talking about Al Woods, who was playing in his last home basketball game at the University of North Carolina. Woody said, 'Folks, let me tell you about Al Woods. He's the kind of guy who you want to go fishing with.' That's how I look at Kenny Schrader. He's the kind of guy you want to go fishing with. He's your friend. He'll guard your back. You never have to worry about him not being fair or honest with you. There is no positive adjective you can't use for Kenny Schrader. He wasn't in racing for the money. He could have cared less about the money.

"Kenny is now the oldest Winston Cup driver out there. He's forty-seven, and at that age, they are not going to be saying anything good about you."

In 1992, Rick Hendrick attended a Busch race at Atlanta. During the race he noticed a 20-year-old kid madly careening around the track, fighting for control of an inferior car on every turn but maintaining position near the front of the pack. Hendrick, inspired, said to himself, "I have to sign him." The 'him,' was Jeff Gordon, who had started racing in California at age 4, turned pro at 13, and who had won more than 600 sprint and Late Model races before the end of his teenage years. Jimmy Johnson became involved once Rick Hendrick decided to make the wonder boy a member of Hendrick Motorsports.

"I wasn't there the day Rick saw him at Atlanta," said Johnson. "Rick had recognized the talent. Jeff was living in an apartment [in Charlotte] with Andy Graves, who was working with Gary DeHart, and another young guy, and I called Andy and I said, 'What's your roommate doing?'

"He said, 'He hasn't done anything yet, but he's getting close. [Jack] Roush is after him.'

"I said to myself, 'Oh, hell,' and I said to Andy, 'Set up a meeting so I can meet him.' I went to the house, which was about two miles from our offices at Hendrick Motorsports.

"I went over and met with Andy and Jeff and Jeff's stepfather, John Bickford, a wonderful guy, and we just kicked around numbers. At that meeting, Jeff and John said, 'We want you to look at a guy named Ray Evernham [for crew chief.]'

"I said, 'I never heard of him.'

"He used to work for Alan Kulwicki, and now he's working as a consultant for Bill Davis," Jeff said.

"I said, 'Let me tell you about crew chiefs. If they make you happy, they make us happy. We want to make sure you team up with a crew chief you're comfortable with.'"

Johnson didn't know it, but team owner Jack Roush had the same conversation with Jeff Gordon and his stepfather. When Gordon said he wanted Evernham to be his crew chief, Roush refused. "I pick my own crew chiefs," Roush told them. It may well have been the clincher when in May 1992 Gordon signed a five-year contract to drive for Hendrick Motorsports. I asked Jimmy Johnson why he thought Gordon had signed with his team.

"For one thing," Johnson said, "we are a lot easier to deal with from a team owner/driver standpoint than some team owners. We pay decent money. Jeff could see potential, because we certainly had potential.

"The day after I met with Jeff, I interviewed Ray Evernham. Ray said, 'I don't want to be crew chief. I want to be a team manager. I want to schedule tests and be in charge of personnel.'

"I said, 'Ray, we've tried that team manager/crew chief organization, and it doesn't work.' Because we had done it with Waddell Wilson and Jeff Hammond. It creates conflicts. No one knows who is supposed to get the credit, who's going to be interviewed on TV. I said, 'We are just not going to do business that way. You're going to be crew chief, or we have to look somewhere else.'

"Ray was very calm. He said, 'Well, I can do it.' Done deal. So I signed Ray almost immediately, and, God, look what those two did together!'

"Meanwhile, we were looking for a sponsor for Jeff. We had been told by Exxon that they were going to pull out. The *Exxon Valdez* had hurt them, and they said they were getting out of racing. We needed somebody to come in and take the deck lid of all three of our cars.

"I had some indication that DuPont wanted to come in as an associate sponsor, so Rick and I flew to Wilmington, Delaware, and we met with Tom

Young and Tom Speegman of DuPont Automotive Finishes. We sat in their conference room. I had a proposal all laid out that would have given DuPont the left taillight and the top of the deck lid, worth so much, and we were going to put it on the cars of Kenny Schrader, Ricky Rudd, and our new kid, Jeff Gordon.

"We went through the whole spiel. I said, 'This is your space. You can be on all three cars. We'll give you three appearances,' and I discussed the whole nine yards.

"When I was finished, Tom Young said, 'Is there any reason you guys don't want us to be Jeff Gordon's major sponsor?'

"'Well,' Mr. Hendrick and I looked at each other. He said, 'Would you excuse us a minute?' We actually walked out of the meeting, and we bounced numbers off each other, went back in and said, 'This is the number. This is how you can be Jeff Gordon's major sponsor.'

"Mr. Young said, 'That sounds great. Do you want to draw up the contract or do you want us to do it?'

"I said, 'We'll draw it up.'

"He said, 'OK, here is our attorney's phone number. Call him and set it up.'

"We flew back high-fiving the whole way. We had finally gotten a sponsor for Jeff.

"Our attorney had the contract drawn up the next day, and our contracts are cookie-cutter—Rick Hendrick's contracts are always extremely fair to drivers and to sponsors. He filled in the blanks and sent it to DuPont's attorney.

"When the DuPont attorney got it, he called back. He said, 'We've got a problem.' My heart sank. He said, 'In the last line of the contract, it states that if it has to be litigated, it will be litigated in the state of North Carolina. This is going to have to be in Delaware.'

"I said, 'That's it?'

"'That's it.'

"I said, 'I will get the correction made, and I'll get it right out to you.'

"The next day we sent out the revised contract, and it was signed a couple of days later."

As part of the deal, Rick Hendrick agreed to use DuPont paint not only for the race cars but for all of Rick Hendrick's 90 car dealerships across the country.

"DuPont paint is used in all the body shops," said Johnson. "That's a real good incentive. And we did the same thing with our oil sponsors. When we had Exxon as a sponsor, Exxon was never interested in getting our oil business, but when we went to Valvoline, we converted every car store over to Valvoline, and then after a couple of years, we converted everything over to Quaker State, and you're talking between six- and seven-hundred thousand gallons of oil annually. So we've become a big fleet customer. And we get a heck of a deal on it, so it's good for our stores as well as good for our race team."

After Jeff Gordon signed with Hendrick Motorsports, he entered one race, the finale of the 1992 season at Atlanta. In that race, Alan Kulwicki won the racing championship in a squeaker over Bill Elliott. During the season, Kulwicki had asked Jimmy Johnson for a tour of the Hendrick Motorsports complex.

"A few hours later there was a knock on my door, and it was Alan," Johnson said. "I gave him the fifty-cent tour rather than the usual ten-cent tour. I showed him inside and out. We were nowhere compared to where we are now, but we were still a lot further than most everyone else with engineering and C&C machines, and when the tour was over I was standing outside my office beside Alan's little Thunderbird. I looked at him. His eyes were watering.

"'Are you OK?' I asked him.

"'No,' he said, 'It's scary as hell that this is what I have to race against.' And he went on to kick our butt that year. Alan was tough. Alan and Ray Evernham never got along. Ray didn't like him at all. Alan could be *very* critical."

Davey Allison, who should have won the championship, needed only to finish in the top ten, but midway through the Atlanta race Ernie Irvan cut a tire, spun, and rammed into him. Few noticed when the twenty-one-year-old Jeff Gordon had tire problems and hit the wall on the 164th lap.

Jimmy Johnson, however, was not fazed. Rather, he was impressed with his new driver and also with the preparation of his new crew chief, Ray Evernham.

"Ray was extremely prepared," said Johnson. "Not only did Ray have to build cars, he had to build a building, because we had a 10,000-foot building that was nothing but a shell with heat and air conditioning where we stored cars. There were no offices, no bathrooms, no nothing. Ray and Ed Guzzo had to go in and build the building at the same time they were trying to get race cars and motors and personnel together.

"They really did a heck of a job. They worked unbelievable hours to accomplish that, and when we went to Atlanta, we were as well prepared as anybody.

"Jeff tested well," said Johnson. "You could see the potential. I remember walking with Jeff back to the airport. This was prehelicopter days, pre-escorts, and it was quicker to walk to the airport from the racetrack than it was to drive, and as we walked over there, nobody knew who he was. I thought, 'Here's a guy with all the potential in the world, and he's so young and new to the sport, and fans don't know they are fixing to see this guy as a superstar.' And he sure turned out that way."

CHAPTER 44

DAVEY AND THE LOST CHAMPIONSHIP

Larry McReynolds

LARRY McREYNOLDS GREW UP IN BIRMINGHAM, ALABAMA. IN HIGH SCHOOL, HE helped build a street rod for his Aunt Noreen. In his spare time, McReynolds worked in a junkyard, and when the owner of the junkyard asked him if he would help him with his race car, he agreed. By 1978, the car was winning races, and he was hooked.

McReynolds saw an ad for a start-up Winston Cup team and answered it. Three weeks later, owner Bob Rogers told him to report to work on a trial basis. The team, with Don Sprouse behind the wheel, ran two Winston Cup races in 1980. When Sprouse couldn't finish races in 1981, the team hired Mike Alexander and then Tim Richmond. At Charlotte in the fall, the car was in second place when the crankshaft broke.

Rogers had no sponsor, so Richmond left, and the team got Donnie Allison and Neil Bonnett to drive for them. When Neil decided the team wasn't good enough, he left, and then Rogers folded his team.

Rogers put McReynolds in charge of auctioning off his equipment. Mark Martin and his mother bought it. The Martins hired McReynolds to be their crew chief for the 1982 season. They didn't know that he had had only a year and a half of experience. At the end of the year, Mark went to drive for J. D. Stacy.

McReynolds was offered jobs by independent owner Richard Childress in Winston-Salem and by Petty Enterprises in Level Cross. He lived in Charlotte and didn't want to commute a hundred miles each way, so he instead took a job with Raymond Beadle and the Blue Max team as a mechanic. Tim Richmond was the driver and had recommended him.

But Blue Max had financial problems. Bob Rogers was getting back into racing, and even though Rogers was setting up shop in Greenville, South Carolina, McReynolds took the job and moved there. Then Rogers ran out of money and closed his doors.

McReynolds was 23, engaged to be married, and he was living in Greenville, South Carolina, without a job. Discouraged, McReynolds felt like going back to Alabama and starting over.

Then car owner Bobby Hawkins called. He owned a race team with David Pearson behind the wheel. They ran 10 races in '83 and '84, then Hawkins and Pearson parted company. McReynolds, the only employee of Bobby Hawkins, was kept on. They hired Butch Lindley to drive the car. In April 1985, Lindley went to Bradenton, Florida, to drive in a race. He crashed and lapsed into a coma. Lindley hung on for five years until June 1990, when he died.

McReynolds hired Morgan Shepherd, and the car ran well at Charlotte in the fall, finishing seventh.

In late October 1985, Kenny Bernstein told McReynolds he wanted to go racing. Joe Ruttman was his driver, Quaker State was his sponsor, and he needed a race team. Larry was designated the crew chief. Six more men were hired to work on the cars. Morgan Shepherd was hired to replace Ruttman, and late in 1987 Ricky Rudd replaced Shepherd.

In the fall of 1990, Robert Yates asked McReynolds if he would come over to his team, and out of loyalty McReynolds said no. Then at Atlanta late in 1989, Bodine screamed at McReynolds throughout the entire race that the engine wouldn't run. On the ride home, McReynolds regretted not taking the job with Yates.

When Yates and driver Davey Allison asked him again in March 1991, he again said no, because he didn't want to take Jake Elder's job from him. A short time later, Yates called him to say that Elder had been fired. McReynolds was given one more chance to accept his offer.

This time he took it.

"It was the toughest decision I ever made in my life," said McReynolds. "Making the decision to ask my wife to marry me wasn't nearly as tough as leaving Kenny and going with Robert Yates. I had been there a long time.

"That night I called my wife and I said, 'I hate to make a premeditated call or make a rash judgment, but Linda, there is no doubt in my mind I made the best move of my life.'

"I joined Robert in March of '91, and that year we won five races, won the Winston, sat on a couple of poles, and drove to third in the points. We were in second going into the final race at Atlanta, until we had an electrical problem.

"Because we were keeping our team intact, weren't losing anybody, we hated to have to go through the winter. We wanted to go straight from Atlanta to Daytona to run the 500, because your big fear over the winter is losing your momentum.

"We came to Daytona with as much confidence as any race team could have. Davey was at the peak of his career, and Robert Yates was the car owner/engine builder. If you got the rest of it just halfway right, how could you go wrong?

MARK MARTIN
He and his
mother bought the equipment.
INTERNATIONAL
MOTORSPORTS HALL OF FAME

"In the eleven days we were at Daytona in '92, we showed how strong we were. If you can come in here and sit on the pole eight days before the 500, boy, it sets a precedent for the rest of the week and for the next two or three months really. I've seen that several times. Other years I've come to Daytona and struggled, and we carried the struggle on to the next week. I talk about momentum a lot.

"We qualified sixth, which by our standards was not great. but we got a jump start from the Busch Clash.

"The first race was the Busch Clash [now the Bud Shootout], which is a race of pole sitters from the previous year. It's the very first race of the new season. Most teams run one car in the Busch Clash and another car in the 500. They don't want to risk tearing up their good Daytona 500 cars. In '92 we wanted to get a race under our belt where we could learn about our race car, so we took a chance,

rolled the dice, and qualified our Daytona 500 car on Saturday, then ran it in the Busch Clash on Sunday. And we finished third, and we learned a lot.

"We practiced Monday, Tuesday, and Wednesday for the 125 qualifying races. The two pole winners are set in stone in the front row, and the twin 125 qualifying races on Thursday set positions three through forty-three. And if you win one of the 125s, it's a pretty good-paying race.

"In our final practice on Wednesday before the 125 miles, we wrecked our primary car in practice and had to unload the backup car. Davey was out there running in a big pack, and somebody pushed and got into us, and the car got torn up. It was in the final minutes of the last practice.

"This is where this team showed strength in its depth. We unloaded our backup car. We had tested it. It was a good race car. Practice was all but over, and I went to NASCAR and asked them if we could get just a few laps on the track. They gave me five minutes.

"We went out and made five laps. They weren't very good because we had a valve cover leaking, which wasn't a big deal because we were going to put a different engine in it anyway to run the 125-miler, but because we were using a backup car, we had to go to the rear of the field.

"Davey was the most determined individual I ever worked with in my life. You couldn't get Davey Allison down if you tried. It was almost as though the more pressure you put on him—the bigger pressure-cooker situation you put him in—the better he performed.

"Davey had a lot of confidence in himself and in the people around him. After the five practice laps, he said, 'We'll get them tomorrow. We'll be just fine.'

"Davey finished third in the 125-miler. Which put us sixth in the Daytona 500.

"We worked hard Friday and Saturday to make that car even better, and, lo and behold, we won the Daytona 500 with a backup car.

"We had a good race car. Junior Johnson had two great cars—Sterling Marlin and Bill Elliott. And Ernie Irvan was strong in the Kodak four car. That seemed to be the cream of the crop in the first two hundred and fifty miles, the first hundred laps.

"What happened, those four guys got eager to chasing the halfway money—Gatorade paid ten thousand dollars, which in '92 was a lot of money, to the car that led halfway through the race—and off turn two, a couple of them got together and caused a big wreck. We slipped through unscathed. The other three cars were torn up.

"With our strongest competition gone, we played our cool the last two hundred and fifty miles. Morgan Shepherd in the Wood Brothers car was awfully good and chased us hard the last part of the race.

"One unique thing that happened that day, about halfway through the week, one of our radios took missing. We couldn't find it. And we kind of forgot about it. With about fifteen laps to go, the radio turned up. Somebody in the grandstand, a fan, began talking to Davey on the radio. He was saying things like, 'You better go. He's coming. You better get on it.' It bent me out of shape a whole lot more than it did Davey. Same ol' Davey. No big deal. Davey Allison being the cool, calm, collected guy that he is, never let controversy bother him.

"We won the 500, and that started our season rolling. We wrecked a lot in the early part of '92, but we won a lot of races too. By early June, we had already won four races. We had won the Winston. It was wreck one week, win the next. We wrecked at Bristol, won at North Wilkesboro. We wrecked at Martinsville, we won at Talladega. The next week at the Winston in Charlotte, we figured out how to do both.

"What was unique about Robert Yates was that the very next race—whatever it was—was the most important race you were going to run. It didn't matter whether it was the 125-miler, the Bud Shootout, the Daytona 500, or the Coca-Cola World 600.

"We had this one car we called 'James Bond Double Oh Seven.' We were competitive every time we ran it. We had won several races in '91 with it.

"We won the Daytona 500 and the Winston 500 at Talladega in '92, which meant we had won the first two legs of the Winston Million. All we had to do was win the World 600 or the Southern 500 at Darlington, and we were million-dollar winners. And we had two shots at it. The way things were going, it wasn't going to be easy, but it was very possible.

"We didn't save James Bond Double Oh Seven for the World 600. The Winston was the next race, and we elected to take it there. It was going to give us a good test for the World 600.

"That night we had an OK car. It wasn't great, but we were learning. When they waved the white flag, Dale Earnhardt was leading, Kyle Petty was running second, and Davey was running a distant third. As he took the white flag, I commented to Davey, 'One more lap, Buddy. We're going to be OK. We've learned a lot tonight. We've learned things we need to do differently for next week. Let's just get this next lap in.' I figured we'd be happy taking third.

"But that wasn't Davey Allison. He didn't answer, which was not unusual in the latter part of the race. Davey was a very focused individual in that race car. Roman Pemberton, Ryan and Robin's brother, was working for us, and he was standing on the top of the toolbox, and he watched Davey go down the backstretch. I couldn't see him, and about the time we should have been in turn three, Roman turned around and clenched his fist, and I wondered to myself what was happening, but I figured it was something good. At the same time, the fans looked like they were about to rip the grandstands down.

"When I looked down at turn four, here came Davey leading the race. I wondered, 'How the hell did he do that?' What happened was Kyle and Dale got together in turn three, and Davey took advantage. Dale spun, Kyle kept his momentum, but lost enough that we got by him.

"But Kyle Petty was right with Davey, and when they crossed the start/finish line, Kyle got a good run on him, and I still to this day question whether Kyle gave Davey a little nudge that didn't need to be nudged. Obviously both were going for the win.

"After Davey and Kyle crossed the start/finish line, Davey hit the wall a ton down at the end of that dogleg going off into turn one. He was almost sitting next to the pace car down there.

"We all sprinted to him, and when I got to him, I could see Davey slumped over in the car. I thought, 'Man, he's out.' But shortly after that, he started coming to, and they got him out of the race car, but the poor James Bond Double Oh Seven was absolutely destroyed. It went to the graveyard. It was killed.

"As they were getting Davey out of the car, the racer in me came out: I kept looking at the scoreboard. They had 42 on top and 28 underneath, but I was sure we had won the race, but it was close. About the time they got Davey out of the car and put him in the ambulance, I looked at the scoreboard one more time, and they flipped the numbers. I thought, 'Yeah, at least we won the race.'

"We put Davey in the ambulance, and Bobby Allison and I got in with him, and he was starting to come to. He was still pretty foggy, but from the start of the trip to the infield center, Davey must have asked me a half a dozen times, 'What happened?' I said, 'You wrecked pretty hard, but you won the race.' And he would say, 'You're shitting me.' And he'd ask me again, 'What happened?' 'You wrecked hard, but you won the race.' 'Man, you're shitting me.' We kept this cycle going all the way to the infield care center.

"Because he was knocked out for so long, they airlifted him out of there by helicopter. He was banged up pretty bad. He still suffered from broken ribs he had sustained at Bristol and at Martinsville a couple weeks earlier.

"But Davey was right back out there the next week for the World 600. Back then, the World 600 week was real stretched out. We checked in on Tuesday, practiced Tuesday afternoon, qualified Wednesday, practiced Thursday, Friday, and Saturday, and raced on Sunday.

"On Tuesday, Davey was still hurting pretty bad. He had just gotten out of the hospital Monday morning. We had a brand new, untested race car.

"We had killed a car at Daytona, killed a car at Bristol, killed a car at Martinsville, and now we had killed a car in the Winston. We were running out of cars, fast. In fact, when we showed up on Tuesday we didn't even have a backup car on the top of the truck. They were at the shop working feverishly trying to get another car done.

"At that time, Neil Bonnett wasn't doing anything. [Neil was retired after his head injury and was a color commentator on TNN at the time.] We got Neil to come out and practice that first day.

"As the week progressed with Davey not feeling the greatest and us having a new car—we were going through what we call 'new-car blues'—we ended up fourth in the World 600. Not bad, but we didn't win the Winston Million. We still had one more shot at it in the Southern 500.

"Even with all the things that happened to us the first half of the season, it still looked like we were pretty much on track to win the driving championship. Billy Elliott was our competition. Alan Kulwicki wasn't in the picture yet.

"After that episode in Charlotte, we went on to Michigan in late June, and we went to Pocono with a lead of more than 100 points over Bill Elliott. We had a brand-new car and qualified on the outside pole. But at post-qualifying inspection, our valance was too low, and they disqualified us. We had to come back and run a second round. And we ended up starting the Pocono race twenty-fourth.

"It didn't take Davey but twenty-five laps before he was leading the race, but right past the halfway point he came in to pit under a caution. The air gun broke, and we had to go to a backup air gun, which cost us a lot of time and about twelve positions. We had been leading, and we left the pits twelfth.

"Davey went back out there. Before they restarted, I said, 'Davey, we still have ninety-something laps. We'll be OK. You just need to be patient.' He agreed totally. At Pocono, it was more than two hundred miles. That's a long way.

"The race was restarted. Darrell Waltrip was running pretty good that day. I had watched Darrell go into turn one about two laps after the restart, and as Davey went in on Darrell, Darrell pinched him up. Davey was smart enough to back off.

"They came back around, and on the next lap I saw the caution flag waving, and I could hear our spotter saying, 'Davey, are you OK? Davey, are you OK?'

"I thought, 'Man, what in the world is going on?' I said, 'Terry, what is going on?'

"He said, 'Larry, it's pretty bad.'

"What had happened, as Darrell and Davey went through the tunnel turn, Davey got under Darrell again. Darrell got a little momentum up the short sheet and hit him in the left rear quarter panel and turned him, and Davey started going across that grass sliding, and as he hit one of the access roads, it got him to barrel rolling, and he flipped about eleven times along the backstretch.

"The car just disintegrated. Davey would have been just fine, but with all the rolling his arm came out the roof, and as he went across the guardrail, it crushed his arm. I remember seeing the look on Robert Yates' face, because he was scanning the other drivers passing by on the caution. Robert heard Mark Martin make the comment, 'There is no way Davey is alive. They need to get a body bag.'

"We ran to the infield car center, and they unloaded Davey out of the ambulance. I knew then he was OK, because he looked at me. His arm was hurting him, but he was alive, and he was going to be OK.

"They took him to the hospital. There is no love lost between the Allisons and the Waltrips—you know NASCAR history—never has been. It's a battle that goes back to the '70s between Bobby and Darrell. How unique it is that Darrell and Bobby have both retired tied with wins [84, third all-time, according official NASCAR records, which overlooks Bobby's win in a Grand American Ford Mustang at Winston-Salem in 1971. If that race is counted, as it should be, Bobby has 85 victories] with the bad blood that is there.

"I couldn't help feel how unfitting it was that Darrell ended up winning the race on a fuel mileage deal. Darrell and I are best friends today. We never talked about the Pocono situation. I consider him one of my best friends, even though I disagree with what he did that day at Pocono, but that was nine years ago.

"They took Davey to the Allentown hospital, and after we got loaded up—it took us forever—we went to the hospital to check on him. Judy, his mom, met us in the lobby and said, 'He doesn't look very good. His head is very swollen.' Just from the G forces his body was going through.

"We walked into his room, and sure enough, Davey was a pitiful looking sight. His forehead was almost back up here, and his little ol' ears looked like they were way around here, but he was sitting up, and the first thing he said when we walked in that door was, 'I'm going to kill that son of a bitch. I'm going to kill him dead when I see him.'

"I said, 'No, you're not going to kill anybody. You just need to get healed up.'

"Once again we got to see the Allison determination. He was in the hospital, and they were fixing to operate on his arm and put pins in it. I said, 'Davey, what do you think here?'

"He said, 'What do you mean, what do I think? I want you all to get you all's asses on that airplane and get back to Charlotte and get my Talladega car ready, because I *will* be there, and we *will* win Talladega.'

"Davey wasn't released from the hospital until Thursday. We had hired Bobby Hillin to drive the car, and we qualified third. Our plan, which had the blessing of NASCAR, was to start Davey in the car—that was going to be a tough deal. Davey was a guy with pins in his arm. Had it not been Davey, and had Davey not been so close to the points leader—he was second to Bill Elliott by a little bit—I don't think NASCAR would have ever agreed with him starting in that race car.

"At first they wanted us to take Davey out after only one lap, which under green would have cost us a lap and destroyed our day. But we convinced them to play it by ear and let us run into the first caution.

"Davey got out there on Saturday and practiced the car. He had no strength in his right arm, so what we did, we put Velcro on his cast and Velcro on the shift lever, and we Velcroed his hand to the shift lever so he could shift for restarts and leaving the pits. He pretty much drove the car one-handed. Again, the Allison determination. Even today, when I think I can't do something, or if I can't overcome some obstacle, if I can't get something done, all I have to do is close my eyes and think about Davey, and then I say to myself, I can do *anything* if I want it bad enough.

"You know, Davey was a Christian, and he had a little saying, 'There is nothing that can't come my way that God and I can't handle together.' Race fans sent that saying to me on a little card that's sitting right on my desk today. That was Davey Allison's attitude and approach.

"Lo and behold, Davey started that race. Because Bobby Hillin had qualified the car, we had to go to the back of the field, which was probably not a bad move, and the first ten laps ran without a caution. I was thinking, 'Shoot, what are we going to do? We got to get him out of that car.' And all of a sudden, there was a little rain shower, a rain shower in the middle of July without a cloud in the sky, a little rain shower that lasted two minutes, but it was long enough for them to throw the caution so we could get Davey out and put Bobby in, and we went on to finish third and actually took the points lead back.

"We could have won the Talladega race that day. Back then, it was a four-car race, the same four cars that were strong at Daytona: two Junior Johnson Fords, Ernie Irvan in the Kodak Chevrolet, and Bobby Hillin in a Ford. Three Fords and a Chevy, but it's like I told Bobby on the radio with thirty laps to go, 'This is *not* about manufacturers. Your best friend is Ernie Irvan in that 4 car.' Because the 4 and the 28 were going to have to fight the 11 and the 22.

"We were all going to have to run one more lap and then make a green-flag pit stop with only a few laps to go to get fuel and two tires.

"I had been communicating with Tony Glover, Ernie's crew chief. We figured the 11 and 22 cars would pit, and we agreed that after one more lap, we'd both pit and maybe we'd come out in front of them.

"But when the 11 and the 22 headed for the pits, Bobby Hillin panicked, and instead of staying out and running one more lap, he hit pit road with them. Bobby left Ernie to run by himself, which Tony Glover wasn't real happy about. He said, 'What happened? You threw us in here?' I said, 'I didn't throw you in. The driver threw you in.' But it ended up working out for Ernie, who ended up winning the race. We ran third. It still was an awfully good day, but I will still go to my grave believing that the Pocono crash was the loss of our championship right there. It broke our momentum, even though we came back and still won one more race and actually took back the points lead.

"After Talladega came Watkins Glen and then Michigan in August. On Thursday before the Winston Cup race [August 15, 1992], the Busch cars were practicing and qualifying when Davey's younger brother [Clifford Allison] crashed and was killed.

"We were getting ready to go to the Charlotte airport and catch our flight to Michigan early afternoon on Thursday. We had worked at the shop that morning. Davey was already in Michigan. He had some good friends up there he always stayed with. We got word before we left that Clifford had been killed, and of course, Robert Yates and I tried to get in touch with Davey to find out what was going on.

"We got to Michigan and finally got in touch with Davey, and it was Davey who got Robert and me straightened out, because Robert and I assumed that Davey would go back to Birmingham because his brother had just been killed and that we would have to find another driver.

"We said to Davey, 'Do you want us to get Jim Sauter?' He said, 'Wait a minute, guys. Yeah, my brother was killed today, and it's killing me inside, and I'm hurting a lot, but I'm up here to do a job, and I'm going to do my job. We're going to win this race on Sunday, and then I'll go home on Monday, and we'll bury my brother.' That shows you the guts and determination and the role model that Davey Allison was.

"And don't forget, this was only a month after the Pocono crash, and he was still hurting from those injuries.

"We were at Michigan, and he would have to drive in that very corner where his brother was killed. We qualified third, and we ended up fifth in the race.

"When we got to Dover, Delaware, which was seven races from the end, we were leading Alan Kulwicki by over three hundred points. We felt that either we'd win the championship or the 11 Budweiser car with Bill Elliott would win it. But the rest of the way, I don't know who ran worse, the 11 or us. We could not find our butt with either hand. Neither team could. It was pathetic. All of a sudden, for whatever reason, we fumbled the ball every single week. In the meanwhile, ol' Alan was just coming. He wasn't winning, but he was top five, top ten, top five, top ten.

"The month of September was terrible for us. We blew up at Dover and finished forty-first. We ran terrible at Wilkesboro, which we had won in the spring. We wrecked at Martinsville. We just couldn't do anything right it seemed like.

"The month of September just destroyed us. We built a new short-track car, and we were trying to get it ready for the Phoenix race. We had won Phoenix in '91. We didn't want to have to go all the way to Phoenix to test, so we went to Richmond and tested for two days, almost six hundred laps. It was a new type of chassis that Mike Laughlin had built, a three-quarter low snout, used mainly for short tracks. We took a regular car and a low-snout, and for two days we tested at Richmond, and it wasn't two hours into the test when Davey said, 'You can put a fork in that other one. This is my race car right here for Phoenix.'

"So we went to Phoenix, won the race, and took back the points lead. But only by a handful [30 points over Kulwicki]. Going into the final race at

Atlanta, six drivers could have won the championship: Davey, Bill, Alan, and three with an outside chance, Kyle Petty, Mark Martin, and Harry Gant. It was the closest championship battle with that many drivers as had ever been.

"In order to find out what we needed to do to win the championship at Atlanta, we paid Bob Latford a fairly large sum for a big chart that told me where we needed to finish if one guy led the race the most laps and won the race.

"No matter what, we had to finish fifth, and if we led a lap, we had to finish sixth. We went to Atlanta, and once again we were beaten by inexperience. Davey was inexperienced. I was inexperienced. Robert Yates was a great car owner, and he had won championships, but he let us do our deal. He never told us what we had to do. When we went to Atlanta, we were way too overconfident and way too cocky.

"We took the same car we had won with at Phoenix. It was not the right race car to run at Atlanta. It was a flat track, but it was a short-track car, and here we went to Atlanta with it.

"We qualified seventeenth. On Saturday, we had three practices, morning, midday, and late afternoon. We ran pretty decent in the morning practice, and we were trying to play mind games with our competitors, the 11 and 7 cars. We left our car covered up during the middle practice. We went to the Ford hospitality tent and ate lunch. We should have been practicing. But we were on track to do what we needed to do on Sunday.

"On race day, we took the lead after changing two tires, and now all we had to do was finish sixth. Bill and Alan were awfully strong, and we were just OK. We were a top-ten car, but if we were to win the championship, it was not going to be by a whole lot.

"We were running sixth with one hundred and twenty-five laps to go, two-thirds of the way through the race, when Ernie Irvan, who was running right in front of us in the 4 car, blew a tire, hit the outside wall and came across—and there was nowhere for Davey to go. The car was really tore up bad.

"I remember talking to Davey on the radio. 'Get it going,' I said. 'The leaders are coming,' but he couldn't steer. His steering was bent. So we took the car to the garage area, and I know the guys weren't too pumped up about fixing it, but I said, 'Look guys, we're going to fix this race car, and we're going to finish this '92 season *on* the racetrack.' Pretty much knowing that either Alan or Bill were going to win the championship.

"We went back out there after losing sixty or seventy laps. We rode around the bottom. It made a statement about how our season had gone. Yeah, we finished third in the points, we won five races, we sat on two poles, we won the Winston, we won the Daytona 500, but we didn't accomplish what we really thought we could do, which was win the '92 Winston Cup championship."

CHAPTER 45

THE TRAGEDY OF NEIL BONNETT

Susan Bonnett

THOSE WHO KNEW NEIL BONNETT BEST UNDERSTOOD THAT HE WAS MISERABLE not to be back behind the wheel of a race car. Bobby Allison, Davey Allison, Dale Earnhardt, and car owner Richard Childress all saw this, and each in his own way did what he could to nudge a hesitant, unhappy Bonnett back into racing.

Said Susan Bonnett, "Dale Earnhardt encouraged him a lot, and he would tell me, 'There is nothing wrong with Neil except he has lost his confidence.' Which had happened even before the accident. Things hadn't been going well, and Neil was questioning himself. Davey Allison too had encouraged Neil, had him warm up his car in a couple of places, and Richard Childress also kept encouraging him."

On July 13, 1993, Neil Bonnett was at the Talladega racetrack watching his son, David, test.

"The night before Neil had flown with Davey [Allison] from New Hampshire. Davey had asked Neil what he was going to be doing, and he said they were going to Talladega, that David had a car, and they were going down there to test it. They wanted to go while nobody was there, just try it out.

"Davey said to Neil, 'I have a new helicopter. I'll fly down and meet you.'

"Davey had flown over our house a couple of times in the helicopter. Neil was pretty concerned. 'Man, he scares me,' Neil said. Supposedly, from what Neil said, it was not an easy helicopter to fly. Neil was a little bit concerned about it. He told Davey, 'We'll be there if you want to come down.'

"The next morning, I was on my way to the doctor's office. I had had my hand operated on, and I was in my car, and Davey and Red [Farmer] passed me not far from the house. They honked the horn, and I waved to them. Apparently they were headed for the airport. I didn't think about it then, but a little while later Neil called me to say Davey's helicopter had crashed at Talladega.

"I said, 'They can't be there. I just saw them.'"

Neil had been standing near where Davey was landing in a parking area of the Talladega racetrack when suddenly, mysteriously, the helicopter rose up, turned on its side, and crashed.

"It just happened so quick," said Susan Bonnett. "When Neil went running over, he didn't know who he was pulling up off the ground. He couldn't tell. He told me that Davey fell out of the helicopter, and the helicopter fell on his head. He said, 'It was horrible.'

"Neil was pretty much in shock. The whole bunch was in shock. Neil was the one who called Bobby. He told me, 'I'm going straight to the hospital.' I said, 'I will meet you there.' We stayed most of the night, and then we came home and prayed about it. We just believed he was going to make it, and then we got the call the next morning."

Davey Allison was dead, his brilliant racing career ended prematurely at age 32.

"That was a year and a few days after Clifford died at Michigan," said Susan Bonnett. "Neil was out of town somewhere, and I had heard that on the radio. I was flabbergasted. I could not believe it. Clifford's death upset my mother so bad she only lived a short while after that. It happened in June, and she died in September. We went over to the Allisons and fixed food, and it just took everything out of her. Of course, her son-in-law raced, and my son was racing. That was part of it. That just took everything out of her."

In 1993, Richard Childress and Dale Earnhardt gave Neil Bonnett the opportunity to race again. Bonnett's doctor in Birmingham was dead set against his driving. Earnhardt decided what his buddy needed was a second opinion.

"The doctor here told us it wouldn't be a good idea for Neil to get hit in the head again," said Susan Bonnett. "Neil was wanting to race again but didn't feel he had the confidence to do it. Dale said, 'There is nothing wrong with him except his confidence level.' So he took him to a well-known doctor in Charlotte and had him checked out, and NASCAR had him checked out, and they felt he was in good shape physically."

Bonnett's first race back came at Talladega, and when he went out onto the track, he began to cry, because he was so happy to be back behind the wheel of a race car. But a third of the way through the race, Bonnett's RCR Chevrolet turned sideways, became airborne, flew over the hood of Ted Musgrave's car, and crushed a chainlink fence. Miraculously, Bonnett wasn't hurt.

Said Bonnett, "That wreck wasn't near as bad as it looked."

He then entered the final race of the season, but only managed three laps before the engine quit. But Bonnett was undeterred, and when James Finch offered him a six-race deal for the 1994 season, he eagerly accepted. Country Time signed on as his sponsor.

On February 11, 1994, 47-year-old Neil Bonnett went out onto the Daytona track for the first day of practice before qualifying trials, which were to be held the following day. Shortly after noon while speeding around the track, he drove into the fourth turn, and then without warning, veered down to the safety apron before shooting up the track nearly head-on into the unyielding concrete wall. He was taken by ambulance to Halifax Medical Center, where he was pronounced dead at 1:17 P.M. He had massive head injuries. That day Susan Bonnett and a friend had left her Hueytown home at seven in the morning to drive to Daytona.

"We were driving from here to Daytona," she said. "I had never had a cell phone in the car before. My daughter had given me hers. She said, 'You don't need to be traveling without a cell phone.' I said, 'Don't call me on it, because it will scare me to death.'

"As I was nearing Tallahassee, Florida, the phone rang. It scared me and my friend who was with me. My daughter called, and I told her, 'Don't call us any more unless it's an emergency.' She just laughed. She said, 'I wanted to make sure you knew how to answer it and work it.'

"And when the next call came, that really did scare us because we told them not to call unless it was an emergency.

"James Finch called me first. He told me that Neil had been in a bad wreck in practice and wanted to know where I was. He said, 'We're going to see if we can meet you and pick you up.' But when he checked the flight time to get out to where I could get to an airport, it was going to take me the same time to drive in, so I kept driving. Of course, they didn't tell me that Neil was gone. They told me it was bad and I should get there as fast as possible.

"It was just a horrible time, stuck in the car. I wouldn't let my friend turn on the radio. I didn't want to hear anything. Then my son called, and he said, 'We'll meet you there.' He was home in Alabama.

"I said, 'How are you going to get there?'

"He said, 'James said he was sending a plane to pick us up, and we'll be there to meet you.' He sent the plane to pick up my children and Neil's parents. They knew before they left home that Neil didn't make it. But they had not told me.

"When I called the hospital back, they would direct me to a girl named Stephie, who worked for World Sports. I kept asking her, 'Is he alive?' She kept saying, 'Last we heard, he was.' She never did tell me.

"When I got about an hour from Daytona, Max Helton, the pastor with Chapel at the Track, called me. He said, 'We know you're almost here. We debated whether to tell you, but we don't want you to hear it on the radio,' and before he could say another word, I handed the phone to my friend because I knew what he was fixing to tell me.

"We were stuck in traffic, not even moving, when they met us with a police escort and took me straight on to the hospital. My family was already there. It had been a long ten-hour trip. It seemed like forever."

I said to this remarkable woman, "What was amazing to me was the patience you showed when Neil was first becoming a race driver. If you had been some other wife, my guess is you could have derailed that from the start."

"I don't know," she said. "I've always been told that two things I am are faithful and patient. If Neil were here, he probably would not agree with the second one, but yeah, I think I'm pretty patient, and I think when you love somebody totally you have to honor what they love to do.

"I might not be so patient today as I was then, because I realized I could have changed some things, but I can't go back and do that, and I won't live in the past.

"Who of us doesn't wish there are things we could change? Thank God, everything that has happened in my life has brought me to today. I'm happy. I'm healthy, and I live life abundant thanks to God. I don't know if I would have gotten here any other way."

CHAPTER 46

DEATH IN THE AIR

Larry McReynolds

In April 1993, Larry McReynolds got the answer to why Alan Kulwicki won the championship in 1992 and his Texaco/Havoline team didn't. Alan was killed in a plane crash before the Bristol race.

When Allison lost that championship to Kulwicki in 1992, McReynolds said to himself, "Davey and I have plenty of time to win more championships."

"Unfortunately, on July 13, 1993, it began to get a little bit more confusing when Davey was killed in a helicopter crash at Talladega," said McReynolds.

"Nobody I knew wanted Davey flying that thing. Davey would ask me to fly with him, and I would say, 'Davey, I will fly around the world with you in an airplane.' He was as good an airplane pilot as there was—I had flown through the middle of a lightning storm with him. But I said, 'Davey, I'm not saying you can't fly a helicopter. I know you have all the papers saying you are certified to fly it, but you have not got near enough seat time in that helicopter that I'm going to put my butt in a helicopter with you.'

"He flew around Charlotte a lot in the helicopter in which he took his courses and his certification. He'd fly to the shop. 'Come on. Let me take you to lunch in a helicopter.'

"I'd say, 'I'm not getting in a helicopter with you. I'm just not.'

"I don't know a lot about flying, but you do a lot of things in a helicopter you don't do in a plane and vice versa. I know he had a license. But with Davey Allison, if you told him you needed your book written by August, he'd have it ready in July. He put every ounce of energy and effort he had in a short time to get certified to fly a helicopter.

"He was always focused on what he was doing. There was no way Davey Allison would eat his lunch and talk to you. He would say, 'Let me eat my lunch, and *then* I will talk to you.' First focus on lunch and then focus on talking to you. That was the way he was.

"As long as everything was good and fine in that thing, he was OK. But who knows what really happened that day at Talladega? Something tells me something went wrong, and because of a lack of seat time, he couldn't respond to it."

The last race Larry McReynolds and Davey Allison ran together was at Loudon on July 11, 1993.

"We did not run very good the first part of 1993," said McReynolds. "We were struggling severely. We struggled at tracks we had dominated and run well. Yeah, we were sitting OK in the points, but we *were* struggling.

"Davey and I were even battling a little bit out of frustration, even though Davey and I were best friends. If I've ever had a best friend who I've worked with as a driver, it would be Davey Allison. His family and my family did things together. We are both devout Catholics. We had our sons baptized together. We are Alabamans, though we really didn't get to know each other until we moved to North Carolina and Davey started driving Winston Cup. We were not battling away from the racetrack, and our friendship was still strong, but we were starting to question each other a little bit. When you have the success we had, and then all of a sudden it goes away, you start questioning everything and everybody.

"We went to Loudon, New Hampshire, and we were leading with thirty laps to go—we had that same low-snout car that had won Phoenix—and a caution came out. The thing about our car, it was not very good on the short runs. It needed long runs to go, and I knew when the caution came out that we were dead in the water, and Rusty Wallace ended up winning that race, Mark Martin was second, and we finished third. But it was like we were finally starting to get this thing figured out. Here we go!

"And what made me know Davey was feeling good about it was we all flew back in the plane with Davey. He dropped us off in Charlotte and then went on to Alabama. And his dad, Bobby, was on the plane with him. It was Robert; myself; Raymond Fox; Eli Gold, the announcer; Sam Mantes, his pilot; and Bobby.

"When we got on that plane, Davey said, 'I'm going to let Dad fly up there. I'm going to sit in the back with you guys and drink a beer and enjoy our ride home.'

"You could see the confidence in him after the day we had at Loudon."

McReynolds would not see Davey Allison alive again.

"We were at our shop on Monday getting ready for Pocono, just a normal day at the shop. Every time we buckle these guys into a race car, whether for practice or qualifying or especially for the race, we don't know if it might be our last conversation with them.

McReynolds recalled a day when he saw another of his colleagues for the last time, the 2001 Daytona 500.

"I keep seeing that picture of Teresa giving Dale that extra little kiss after she gave him a kiss after he got into the car. And you just wondered whether she had a feeling it would be the last time she was going to give him a kiss. But little did I know, as we got off that airplane in Charlotte that day, that was going to be my last conversation and last time to ever see Davey.

"Because on Monday in the shop, the phone rang, and it was Bill France Jr., and I heard them page [car owner] Robert Yates to the phone, and I remember Robert turning white as a ghost.

"He said, 'It's not good. Bill France Jr. just called and wanted to know if I knew about the situation with Davey.'

"With Davey you never knew what the situation was. I wondered whether Davey had called up NASCAR and cussed them out about something or what.

"Robert said that Davey had flown to Talladega and crashed the helicopter, and it was not good. It wasn't good at all.

"Robert and I and our wives immediately flew to Birmingham, and we spent the evening there with the family, anticipating that Davey wouldn't make it. Red Farmer had flown with him that afternoon, and Red was in the hospital, but he was OK.

"Red said he had no idea what happened. He said, 'Larry, we were not five feet off the ground. We were fixing to land. It was so close to the ground I was about ready to open the door to get out. All of a sudden, the helicopter started oscillating, and it just got up further and further, and the next thing you know it was up and down on its side. I just don't know what happened.' He said, 'Davey is hurt, and he's hurt bad, and there's no way he'll make it.'

"They kept asking whether I wanted to go back to see Davey, and after talking to Red, I decided not to. If I thought it would help Davey in any way I would have, but I wanted to remember Davey Allison sitting in the back of that airplane, drinking that beer and having a good time with us, cutting up, aggravating me. I didn't want to see him hooked to tubes and wires and breathing machines just keeping him alive for whatever reason. And I'm so thankful I did that.

"In the middle of the night, early Tuesday morning, they pronounced him dead, and we flew back to Charlotte. Then we went back to Hueytown Wednesday evening with our race team. Our race team was small. Back then, we probably weren't more than twenty- five strong, but it was such a close-knit group of guys. Everybody got along, and we always supported each other. Through our struggles in '92 and into '93, you never saw anyone pointing a finger or saying, 'I told you so.' A lot like when a family loses a family member, we all brought our families over to Robert Yates' house. We gathered together, and Robert and I looked at those guys, and we said, 'What do you all want to do? Where do we want to go from here?'

"It was pretty unanimous that we didn't want to go to Pocono. We were going to bury Davey on Thursday, and we just did not feel we could go to Pocono and do a good job with a substitute driver. Because we still had a lot of tears in our eyes. Did we want to send a driver at two hundred miles an hour on a straightaway when we really weren't with the game? No, it wouldn't be fair to anyone.

"Davey would have been real pissed off knowing we didn't go to Pocono, but he wasn't the one having to deal with it. We were. So like a big family, Robert didn't make that decision. I didn't make that decision. We made it together.

"We went back to Alabama and buried Davey, and we shut the shop down until Monday morning when everyone could get themselves together.

"My wife and I have two children. I said to her, 'I just want to get away for a few days.' We went to the mountains, and nobody knew where we were. I didn't want to have to deal with anything for a few days. I wanted to be with my wife and two kids.

"I don't think you ever get it out of your system. Here it is, eight years later, and there isn't a day that goes by that I don't remember Davey. I think about him a lot. One reason was that he was such a role model to me, from his attitude toward God, his determination, his constant confidence in the people around him.

"You can't find a bad characteristic about Davey Allison."

PART IV: **THE GILDED AGE**

CHAPTER 47

RUSTY, D. J., AND BOBBY

Jimmy Makar

WHEN THE BLUE MAX TEAM DISBANDED AT THE END OF THE 1990 SEASON, RUSTY Wallace returned to drive for Roger Penske. Rusty had driven for him early in his career in the early 1980s. This time they started a new team, called Penske South. A lot of people from Blue Max went into that organization, including Jimmy Makar.

Before the end of the 1990 season, Barry Dodson left to start a new race team for Sam McMahon, so for the last four or five races, Jimmy Makar became the crew chief for Blue Max. When he left to go with Rusty Wallace and Roger Penske, he became the crew chief there.

In 1991, Wallace had limited success. He won two races and finished 10th in the points standings, not bad for an entirely new team. Makar had to go through the whole process of constructing a building, getting the machinery and equipment, and putting the whole thing together to go racing.

"Roger was a great guy to work for, but we struggled a lot trying to bring the whole thing together as far as organizing the team, and it was a bit much for me," said Makar.

"We couldn't seem to get our act together as far as getting people put in place to run certain areas of the shop, the fab shop, the mechanic shop. We all thought we could roll the Blue Max team into this organization and continue right on with a lot of success, but it just didn't work.

"Something was missing. The camaraderie, the closeness, was going away. Roger Penske was the majority partner, but Don Miller, an associate of Rusty, was a partner, and Rusty was offered a partial ownership, so he became a little more involved with ownership instead of just being the driver.

"We struggled to figure out exactly who was going to be responsible for doing what. Rusty had not been an owner/driver before, so he was trying to figure out what he was going to be part of and not a part of. We were all trying to feel our way around.

"You would have thought we could have figured it out. We had a majority owner who was a racer's racer, a man who has been successful in everything he's done, and the race car driver had won races and a championship, and the nucleus of the race team had won races and a championship, but something was missing.

"Looking back on it, we had had a good balance at Blue Max Racing. We had Raymond Beadle, the car owner, Howard Elliott, the engine builder, Barry Dodson, the crew chief, and I was the chassis guy. We had a pretty good grouping of skills, and we knew who was in charge of what.

"When we went to Penske South, some of that got out of balance. Barry went someplace else, Rusty became part owner—he started having more influence in a lot of things—it got out of balance.

"If you are the owner/driver, you don't deal with your crew the same way as if you're just the driver. And that balance got off.

"We were trying to work through the problems and get things put together, with all intentions of making the thing work, but by the middle of the season Dale Jarrett called me and told me he was going to drive for Joe Gibbs. When he asked me to come work with him, I knew I was leaving, no matter what."

Jimmy Makar is married to Dale Jarrett's sister Patty. She was a public relations representative for Skoal at U.S. Tobacco and worked with race teams with Benny Parsons and Johnny Hayes. Johnny had hired her out of school, and she worked there for 11 years.

"She was at the racetrack doing public relations work, and I was working on cars, and we got to meet at the track, got talking, and one thing led to another, and we got married, and that's how I met Dale, through Patty," said Makar.

"Dale and I got talking at the racetrack. His career was starting about the time I started dating Patty. We had talked over the years. He had had several different rides in different Cup cars struggling to get his career going. I was having pretty good success with Blue Max, winning races, winning a championship with Rusty. We had talked about it and said, 'Someday it would be neat to work together.'

"When he called and told me he was getting ready to go drive for Joe Gibbs, he didn't think I would be interested because I worked for Penske, but he wanted to give me the opportunity to talk to Joe, and I told him I would be glad to talk to Joe.

"'Things are not going great here,' I said to Dale. I told him it wouldn't hurt to listen to the guy, to hear what he had to say.

"All I knew about Joe Gibbs was that he was a professional football coach. I didn't have a clue what he had in mind. For whatever reason, I figured there was no harm in talking to him."

That week, Makar and his wife were getting ready to go on vacation to New Orleans for a few days. It was an off-weekend for racing, and they wanted a break. Joe Gibbs flew to Charlotte, and before the Makars left town, they agreed to meet Gibbs at the Sheraton Hotel near the airport in Charlotte. They sat and talked.

"At the end of the two hours, I figured right then that he was the guy I wanted to work for. We weren't talking particulars of racing. It was more his philosophy of teamwork and things like that.

"I had always in the back of my mind had an idea of how I wanted a race team to run. To me, looking back at it, a lot of race teams didn't take care of their people as well as they should have. I'm talking about the people who work in the shop, day and night. They put in a lot of hours without a lot of benefits or pay. They're kind of second-class citizens.

"My feeling was, if you treated your employees well, you could get more out of them, you could get them to work longer periods of time, you could develop long-term employee relations. I wanted to see a race team where a guy would *want* to come and work for you, where you could give him a good package, take care of him—not necessarily with a lot of money, but with benefits, small perks that make him want to stay. Perhaps a bonus program based on working for a certain length of time, where the longer you stayed, the more vested you'd become. Things like that weren't being done.

"And when I heard Joe Gibbs talking about teamwork and football players and individuals, he was saying the exact same thing I was thinking all along, that you have to take care of people, win with teamwork, win with people, give people the things I was talking about: opportunities, bonus packages, a reason to want to stay and work."

Gibbs had done just that with his football teams. He created reasons for guys to go out and excel. His philosophy was to find out what motivated people and to use those things to motivate them, thereby getting the most out of people. Gibbs wanted to create an atmosphere that would encourage people to grow and excel and do better. It fit into Makar's philosophy and what he wanted to do.

"After a couple of hours sitting and listening to him talk about how his football team was run and how he organized and how he thought people were important—not the Xs and Os, but the people—and how you needed to take care of your people—I knew right then that this guy was thinking the same way I was," said Makar. "He was a *very* successful football coach, so I knew his philosophy worked well in football. But would it work in racing?

"At least he felt the same way I did, and I thought, 'This is a perfect opportunity to create a race team the way I think a race deal should be done.' This would be my chance to see if it would work.

"Looking back on it now, a little spiritual type thing also occurred. People wonder why I left a team like Penske after the success I had with Rusty. Certainly I wonder at times too. But he was still coaching when he started the race team, and that year Joe and the Redskins won the Super Bowl.

"I had the chance to go to the game, and on Saturday before the game they held a chapel service for the football team, and I ended up giving over my life to Christ. It was a real unique experience. Looking back, I can see why I was brought to this race team. It wasn't necessarily for the racing end of it. It was to get my life straightened out. My life to that point was about racing, success, and accomplishments, and I've grown a lot as a person and realize I have my priorities in order today more than I did back then. So that was another reason I came to Joe Gibbs racing."

When Roger Penske found out that Makar was leaving at the end of the 1991 season, he decided it would be best for him to go sooner rather than later so the team could adjust to life without him. Just before he left, Rusty Wallace won the second Pocono race [on July 21, 1991]. The next Monday he went to work for Joe Gibbs.

"Dale Jarrett had not won a race when he announced he was leaving the Wood Brothers at the end of the '91 season to go and race for Joe," said Makar. "After making the announcement, then at the second race at Michigan, Dale beat Davey Allison for his first win ever. Up to that point, his career was in the growing stages.

"Gibbs Racing was a low-budget type operation. Joe didn't have a lot of money. He wasn't rich, and Interstate Batteries was a small sponsor. Basically, I had five hundred thousand dollars of parts and cars sitting in a warehouse that he had purchased from Rick Hendrick. We bought three or four cars plus used parts he had from the seventeen–car team [Western Auto with Darrell Waltrip] . . . It wasn't a whole lot to work with. And we had a pretty tight budget."

Makar had left Roger Penske's state-of-the-art race shop and his big budget for this low-budget start-up team. It was hard, but in the end, gratifying.

"As we started setting the team up, we set our priorities and goals of what we needed to make the team grow," said Makar. "We set up short-term and long-term goals.

"We started out with a lot of heart, a lot of character. We went about hiring people. The first guy I hired, David Wagner, came to work for me and helped me sort through what Joe had bought, what was good, what was bad. We threw the stuff that was no good into the garbage can. David is still with us. That's kind of neat.

"We started off renting a warehouse on Harris Boulevard in Charlotte that we converted into a race shop. It was pretty humble beginnings. We set the team up, went to work.

"I remember one of our first budget meetings. Ed Carroll, our team manager, conducted it, and when he announced that we were five hundred thousand dollars over budget, Joe freaked. He was just getting into the sport, and here he was finding out that he was already five hundred thousand dollars in debt! He got real worried, real fast. His first thoughts were, 'What did I get myself into?' And, 'How will we be able to keep this going?' It was the old joke: What's the best way to make a small fortune in racing? Start with a large fortune. I know a lot of millionaires in racing who used to be multimillionaires. It's not an easy sport to get into. You have to have a pretty large cash flow or a sponsor with a large cash flow.

"We all put our heads together. It wasn't as bad as Joe thought it was."

In 1992, the Gibbs team went to Daytona with one of Darrell Waltrip's old short-track cars, converted it, and put a body on it. It was going to be the team's backup car. They built a new car to go to the 500, and Dale ran very well in practice.

"I remember having a conversation with Joe about qualifying for the 500," said Makar. "It was the first time he had gone to Daytona, and we were talking about the unique way they qualified the cars, how they pick two cars from the time trials, and then there are two qualifying races, and then if you don't make it that way, it falls back on your qualifying time to get you in the race. Then you go to the points.

"I told him it was real important to get a good qualifying time because we weren't going to set on the pole. In explaining that to him, we really got his attention.

"He looked at me and said, 'You mean there's a chance we may not make it into the Daytona 500?'

"I said, 'Oh, yeah.' We had no points from the previous year. We either had to qualify far enough up front or do well in the 125s. If things didn't work out right, it was going to be pretty easy to go home.

"In the qualifying race, Dale was trying to pass Earnhardt for the lead, and he got into bad air coming off four, got loose and spun, and he hit the inside wall a little bit more than we wanted to fix. When Dale spun trying to pass Earnhardt, obviously our starting position went back to our qualifying lap, and we were *just* good enough to start thirty-seventh."

The Gibbs team got the backup car out and started the race in the back of the field. Jarrett went from 37th all the way to 4th and was going to the front, when there was a big wreck in the backstretch. The No. 18 Interstate Batteries car was one of 18 cars in that wreck. The Gibbs car was completely wiped out. It was Joe Gibbs' introduction to racing: Both his cars were totaled at Daytona.

"Joe never got excited," said Makar. "I think his eyes were open a little more than they had been coming in. We had run up front and tried to lead in the 125, and then in the 500 we went from the back to the front before the wreck, so I think he was encouraged. We had a pretty good race car and a pretty good race team. Even though we didn't finish, at least he knew he had a car capable of going to the front and leading.

"That first year we didn't win a race and finished nineteenth in the points. Nothing earthshattering, but we were growing."

The relationship between Joe Gibbs and Interstate Batteries blossomed. Interstate was a relatively small company, and still is. According to Jimmy Makar, 70 percent of its advertising budget is dedicated to the race team, whereas a large corporation, like Home Depot, only devotes about 10 percent of its total advertising budget to racing.

"Interstate will tell you today that their brand and product awareness is because of the race car," said Makar. "They could see how racing was making their company grow. It was a good relationship for Interstate. They were involved with Joe, who was a national celebrity, and they were able to enter the football arena and bring their brand awareness over there."

The Gibbs race car wasn't setting the world on fire as far as winning races right off the bat, but Interstate Batteries was able to use Joe Gibbs, the national football celebrity, as a spokesman while the race team was growing and improving.

"It was a good deal for everybody," said Makar.

Then in 1993, the Gibbs team, with Dale Jarrett behind the wheel and Jimmy Makar the crew chief, won the Daytona 500.

"That was a Cinderella year," said Makar. "That was the best—and the worst—thing that could have happened to us. We had a good car in the Daytona 500. We had a great rental motor program from Hendrick Motorsports the first five, six years, and we ran well."

Winning Daytona after a disastrous first year was very dramatic. Dale Jarrett beat Dale Earnhardt, who had won everything under the sun but hadn't yet won the 500. It was a huge win for Gibbs, Jarrett, and Makar, and beating Dale Earnhardt, the King of Superspeedways, made it even more special.

"Earnhardt was the one who everyone talked about him 'seeing the air,' said Makar. "Having it come down to a shootout with Dale was really special.

"I don't know if I took a breath the last three laps. My stomach was in a knot. I knew we had a good shot at it. I knew if Dale didn't make any mistakes, if he used the mirror the way he needed to—we'd win, but again, Dale didn't have a lot of experience in these situations. You had a guy behind him who had been notoriously good at Daytona for fourteen years, a guy who knew how to beat people, a guy who was always in the right place at the right time. And you had Dale Jarrett, a relative newcomer, trying to hold him off.

"I was real nervous. I worried he would make a mistake, would let Earnhardt get a run at him, that he would make the wrong move. At the time, you wondered, 'Is he going to keep the car in the right place?' But he did."

Jarrett handled the pressure like a pro. He did exactly what he needed to do. He blocked the track and didn't let Earnhardt get a run at him. He made all the right moves and was able to hold off Earnhardt. That day, Dale proved he had what it takes to be a winning superspeedway race car driver.

"Dale and I didn't talk at all those last few laps. They were all his. We were counting down the laps for him, five, four, three laps to go, and we let him have the racetrack to see and think and do his thing. We were real fortunate. It came out with us on top."

Joe Gibbs was able to get a taste of all the hard work, all the sweat , and all the blood his new sport was about. The Gibbs team added to its success with a second win at Charlotte toward the end of that season. Jimmy Makar was making good calls, the team had a good motor program with Hendrick, and, overall, the Gibbs team had a remarkable year in 1993. Jarrett led the points race for two weeks, and made a plausible run for the Cup.

"Inexperience did us in at the end of the season. We choked. We weren't ready to challenge for the championship. We ended up fourth in the points, should have by all rights finished no worse than second, but we were a second-year race team, were inexperienced and didn't have the depth and experience it took to go and be serious about challenging for the championship."

One problem with doing well is that it sets the race team up for much higher expectations than it might otherwise have had. The Gibbs team went into 1994 thinking that they had arrived, that they had everything in place, that they should be able to win races and finish high in the points. But 1994 turned out to be a reality check.

"All the little things that went right the year before went wrong in '94," said Makar. "There are a lot of things you can't explain when they happen. You have the feeling when the chemistry is there, when things are going right for you. That year, they were not. Things happened to us the year after we ran so well.

"We all were let down emotionally and mentally, and we beat ourselves up. Nobody tried to blame anybody, but nobody knew what was going on.

"I didn't do a good job as a leader of pulling everybody together and doing the things I needed to do to get through the tough times as I should have. I didn't have the experience. So we struggled. We didn't produce like we should have.

"We won a race that year, but didn't finish well in the points. We struggled really, really bad."

At the end of the 1994 season, Dale Jarrett shocked his brother-in-law and the rest of the Joe Gibbs race team by announcing he was leaving to drive for Robert Yates and replace the late Davey Allison in the No. 28 car.

"Dale had his reasons for leaving," said Makar. "We certainly had struggled. Like I said, I didn't do a good job of managing the lack of success we had. If I had to do it over again, I would have talked a lot more, been a lot more analytical. Sometimes you learn a lot more from your failures than you do from your successes."

Bobby Labonte, who replaced Dale Jarrett, was the beneficiary of Makar's experience. Makar realized that part of the problem he had with Dale Jarrett was that they didn't communicate as much as they should have. Makar made sure that he and Labonte talked to each other a lot more.

"Dale is not a big talker, and in our struggles and troubles, we never sat down and talked about it and tried to work through it," said Makar. "We both assumed it would get better, and it didn't, and so he decided to move on to the Yates team. He went first to the 28 car, replacing Davey Allison after he died. He drove that some, and then Ernie Irvan came over and drove the 28, and Dale went to the 88. It was a great opportunity for Dale. Yates has a great engine program. He's had a lot of success.

"When Dale left, I felt abandoned. I was filled with emotion. I was really feeling hurt. I never saw the situation coming. I'd have thought we'd work through it and we'd get on the other side of it. I figured Dale and I would be a team forever. We were still trying to make the race team grow. We didn't have the hard financial backing of a lot of race teams. I was trying to manage Joe's money in a way that we were not spending more than we needed to. We hadn't arrived yet as a business. We didn't have the bang-up budget where we could do everything we wanted to do. We're still not in the top group of race teams like we want to be. But it was getting better.

"When Dale left, Joe was disappointed and hurt. We all were.

"It was a tough decision for Dale to leave this organization. I always felt that Dale Jarrett was championship-caliber material as a race car driver. Like every other person, he had his weak points and things he had to work on. We all do. I always felt he had the drive, determination, and ability to get there with the right situation put together. I was hoping we could have that kind of success together. We had won races together."

When Makar set up his team, his goals were to create a successful business for Joe, put together a team with the stability to win races, and win a championship. Makar accomplished all three goals [in 2001 Bob Labonte won the championship for Gibbs and Makar], but from the start had thought that Gibbs, Makar, and Dale Jarrett would have been the team to accomplish them.

"It wasn't meant to be," said Makar.

"Things happen for a reason. Patty and I talked about this. Dale went his way to grow more as an individual and to be challenged more and to grow into a stronger person. Obviously, when he went to Robert Yates, he went in there and was beaten down pretty hard for not being Davey Allison and not being able to do the things Davey was able to do, so he went through some really, really rough times. It ended up being a great challenge and a great struggle.

"But Dale kept his head high and he got through it, and he got out the other end of it and he had great success, and he's a lot stronger person and a better person for all the struggles he went through.

"You can't look at it purely as a racing situation. Things don't happen just for racing reasons. And Dale helped us figure out what driver to get to replace him. He told me, 'Bobby Labonte is a very good race car driver. You ought to talk to him.'

"Bobby's situation with Bill Davis was going downhill. They were losing his sponsorship, and when we talked to Bobby, he was like a kid in a candy store. He was excited to go racing with us."

When Bobby Labonte joined Joe Gibbs Racing in '95, the team didn't seem to miss a beat. Labonte and Makar hit it off great from the start. Their personalities meshed. They had excellent communication, and everything felt right. The team clicked from the beginning.

"It was a really neat thing to take a really tough time and turn it into something really positive: We found a driver who would carry on right where we were trying to get with Dale," said Makar. "Black clouds can have silver linings.

"Dale went on to have success, and we were able to take Joe Gibbs Racing with Bobby and be successful. Both of us won races. Both of us won championships. We both have teams at the top of the sport. We haven't done it together, but Dale and I both were able to accomplish goals that we set ten years ago. Different places, but we both ended up in good places."

CHAPTER 48

ERNIE

Larry McReynolds

After Davey Allison's midseason death in a helicopter accident in August 1993, team owner Robert Yates and crew chief Larry McReynolds were faced with a complicated problem: where to find an equally talented replacement.

It's almost impossible to replace a top driver in the middle of the season, even when you're one of the top teams, as the Yates team was. In racing, as in life, timing is everything, and around this time, driver Ernie Irvan and the owners of the Kodak Chevy team were fussing and fighting, mostly over money. When a Ford executive asked Irvan if he would be interested in driving the No. 28 Texaco/Haviland car, Ernie jumped at the chance. As Larry McReynolds saw it, Irvan and the 28 team became an instant success.

"I had two best friends besides my wife—Robert Yates and Davey Allison," said McReynolds. "Robert and I talked a lot about who we were going to get to drive our car. Robert was being bombarded by people who wanted to drive the race car, people driving in Winston Cup, people driving Busch, people sitting in the grandstands who thought they *could* drive a race car. I don't see how he handled it mentally.

"We had a very tough situation. We had to put someone in that car, and we were headed for, of all places, Talladega, where Davey got killed, but also his home track. Those people ate, slept, and breathed Davey Allison. Who could we put in that car who could take that kind of pressure?"

The driver Robert Yates and Larry McReynolds took as a fill-in was Robby Gordon, who had ties to Texaco. Gordon had done some Indy car racing and a lot of off-road racing. He did not have a lot of Winston Cup experience, but McReynolds knew that if there is one track where you can get by without a lot of experience, it was Talladega. He and Yates figured that because Robby Gordon was a newcomer, he probably wouldn't feel the pressure that someone already in the sport would feel. Gordon qualified fourteenth. In the race his inexperience showed.

"We kept trying to get him to stay in line, but he'd say, 'I have a faster car than these guys. I'm going,'" said McReynolds. "One time, he got a little over-anxious and let the left side wheel drop below the apron, and it shot the car up the racetrack in the middle of the tri-oval, and he hit the wall hard. Fortunately, nobody hit him. The race car was tore up, but not terrible, but when the crew got the car back to the garage, Robert and I looked at each other and said, 'We don't need to fix this race car and go back out there. What's the point? Let's pack up, go home, and move forward.'"

Yates and McReynolds decided that Robby Gordon was not the long-term or short-term answer. They approached Lake Speed, a veteran driver who was driving his own car and running out of money. Lake carried some pretty good credentials. He had won Darlington, and there were other tracks where he ran well. Lake was hired to drive with the understanding that the Yates team was still looking for a full-time driver.

Lake told McReynolds, "I'm available as long as you need me."

The No. 28 car ran three races with Lake Speed, and ran well. Speed qualified fourth at Watkins Glen and was running in the top five when he missed a shift and tore up the transmission, ending his day late in the race.

At Michigan, he sat on the outside pole and finished seventh. The series moved on to Bristol. Lake hadn't run at Bristol in a while, and only qualified 21st. Bristol is a very demanding track, and toward the end of the race, the car got away from him, and he wrecked.

Darlington, a track Lake got around very well on, was next. The Yates team tested well there, and everyone was really looking forward to the Darlington race. Lake Speed never got to run it for Robert Yates.

Said Larry McReynolds, "In the meantime, Lee Morse, who was over at Ford, was starting to romance Ernie a little bit, finding out whether he'd be interested in driving that 28 car. Ernie showed a lot of interest, and right before we went to the Darlington race, we put a deal together with Ernie.

"I hated it for Lake, because he had tested well at Darlington, and he probably would have run very well, but boy, Ernie Irvan was an awesome race car driver. Back in July, I had said to Robert, 'Let's don't panic. We don't have to go out and get the first driver. I think it will come to us.' And that's exactly what happened."

When Ernie arrived at Darlington, he had not been released from his contract with the Kodak team. Larry McClure didn't release him until just minutes before the start of practice at Darlington.

"Like Davey, Ernie was a great race car driver," said McReynolds. "They both gave 110 percent every time they were in a race car. Ernie was a little more cocky. Ernie wasn't nearly as fan-friendly as Davey. Davey was probably the smarter driver. He understood his race car more. Davey could help you more to sort out the car. He needed that to be successful. Maybe Ernie was more talented than Davey. He just went out and drove whatever you gave him. He didn't care what was underneath him, didn't know what was under it, didn't know how to tell you to fix nothing. But at the end of the day, they were both great race car drivers. I was so fortunate to have been part of both their careers.

"It's so funny, the first practice at Darlington, Ernie had run a couple of times. I would kneel down in that window and talk to him, and I could feel the same relationship I had with Davey. It's like we had been working together a long time. And I'd say Davey and Ernie were the only drivers I had that relationship with. I was good friends with Dale Earnhardt and Mike Skinner, but I was closer to Davey and Ernie. With both those guys, we knew what each other was thinking. We didn't have to talk. I developed that early with Davey, and I developed it early with Ernie Irvan.

"That night when I went back to the motel, I told my wife, 'This deal with Ernie is going to be awesome.' We qualified tenth. We ran in the top five all day long. The most enjoyable thing that happened came when Dale Earnhardt was running first, and Ernie was second, and right in front of us on the straightaway, Ernie drove up underneath Dale and picked up his rear wheels off the ground. Earnhardt looked like an octopus. Ernie never said a word.

"We spun out coming onto pit road, bringing out a caution. We stayed on the lead lap and finished fifth.

"After the race, I said, 'Ernie, you kind of had Earnhardt sideways on the straightaway.'

"He said, 'Did you see it? I tried to time it where it would be right in front of you guys.' He enjoyed driving a race car. He drove it so hard.

"The next week, we went to Richmond and blew a motor early, and the next week we went to Dover and qualified on the outside pole. We had a seven- or eight- race streak where the worst we qualified was the outside pole. Ernie and I had the same approach about qualifying. To us, it was a race. We wanted to go out and win that race, which was to sit on the pole on Friday.

"After we sat on the outside pole at Dover, I couldn't wait to see Ernie practice, and, lo and behold, Ernie and Earnhardt came down into turn one and two, with Earnhardt in front and Ernie all over his rear bumper, just beating on his rear bumper going into the corner at 150 miles an hour saying, 'Move over, or I'll beat on you.'

"He wasn't doing it in a way to wreck him, and of course, Earnhardt had so much control over his race car, but Ernie was one of the few people who Dale Earnhardt didn't intimidate. If anything, maybe Ernie even intimidated Dale a little bit. Ernie didn't take nothing off of him.

"Dale hadn't intimidated Davey either. I can say I worked for two guys who Dale did not screw with mentally or physically. They'd give him back his own medicine.

"After that, we went to Martinsville and sat on the pole. Then in the race we led the thing almost all day long and got our first win with Ernie. Two things were special about that win: after we took the checkered flag, Ernie came down pit road, and I saw one guy walk out all the way to the edge of the road and give Ernie the thumbs-up, and the closer I looked, I saw it was Bobby Allison. It was hot that day, over 100 degrees, and when Ernie got to Victory Lane, he took off his uniform top, and I looked, and he had on a T-shirt that said 'In Memory of Davey Allison.' He had worn it that day under his driver's uniform.

"Ernie is a hard-core, hard-nosed, sometimes an arrogant, cocky race car driver, but the things he said that day, talking about Davey and dedicating the race to him, showed he has a heart. There was nobody whispering in his ear telling him what to say. I thought, 'On top of his being a great race car driver, this is a pretty classy guy.'"

The next week, Ernie won the pole at North Wilkesboro and finished third to Rusty Wallace in the race. The series went to Charlotte, and Ernie sat on the outside pole. In October, the Charlotte race is 500 miles, 334 laps. Irvan led all but six or seven laps that day—the only laps he didn't lead were because of pit stops.

"That was a really special win, to know we were so dominant," said McReynolds.

"We went to Phoenix and led the first half of the race, but then Mark Martin took the lead, and Ernie just could not catch him. Mark and he swapped the lead several times. Ernie had several opportunities where he could have laid into Mark and spun him, but he knew what the consequences with NASCAR would have been, and he was smart enough to say, 'The best I'm going to do today is second.' And that day is when I realized just how mature a race car driver Ernie had become. A year earlier he would have thought nothing of it to spin Mark out and just face the consequences, whether that meant tearing up his car or being penalized by NASCAR. He respected Mark and respected his own car enough not to do that.

"That was my philosophy as crew chief. I'd rather finish second than get penalized five laps for rough driving.

"In 1993, Ernie ran eight races for us and won two. We were astounded, We just never dreamed it would be this good this quick. Obviously it came together in a hurry.

"Going into 1994, we were about as high as you could carry a group. We knew we had to work hard to keep the momentum lassoed during the winter. We tried to stay focused. Fortunately, we did a pretty good job of it, because we went to Daytona, won one of the 125s, just did get beat in the 500, but finished second."

Ernie led during much of the Daytona 500. During the race, Ernie said to Larry McReynolds, "Larry, I'm getting pretty loose." He didn't dwell on it. McReynolds said, "Well, Ernie, I don't know if we're going to get a chance to adjust it." Ernie knew he had to do the best he could with what he had, and he kept fighting to stay competitive. Irvan came off turn four down in the tri-oval "just plumb sideways." He never quit trying to get that lead back. It was another confirmation, not that McReynolds needed one, of what a great race car driver Ernie Irvan really was.

"Stirling Marlin in the No. 4 Kodak car was just a little bit better than we were, and we ended up finishing second. Ernie came off four, and he tried at him one more time, and before they even got to the start/finish line, Ernie said, 'He's got me beat. I can't do nothing with him.' And even though we had had a great nine races with Ernie, that had to be hard for him, because he had left that team, and here they win the Daytona 500, but I think in his heart he knew we were going to have a lot of good times together."

If McReynolds had any worries about how Davey Allison's fans would take to Ernie, he learned that those worries were unfounded when the race team went to Talladega for the first time without their fallen hero.

"Ernie was racing in Davey's backyard for the first time, and we were concerned," said McReynolds. "We knew the Alabama/Davey Allison fans weren't the biggest Ernie Irvan fans on earth. It probably would have been true of any driver, but moreso Ernie, because Davey and Ernie had had conflicts. The diehard Davey Allison fans still accused Ernie of costing us the championship in '92.

"Robert and I talked about it before we went down there. He said, 'We don't know whether they are going to applaud us, cheer for us, scream at us, or throw chicken bones and beer cans at us.'

"I never will forget when we went out to qualify and Ernie left pit road. When the Talladega announcer said, 'The 28 Texaco/Haviland car driven by Ernie Irvan . . . ,' the fans cheered tremendously. And when Ernie sat on the pole, I thought they were going to tear the grandstands down. Robert and I looked at each other. 'Man, this is really neat,' he said. We had feared that group. They still felt Davey was a part of that car, and we still felt Davey was, and *is*, a part of that car. That's how they viewed it and why they were so happy that the car went out there and sat on the pole."

On May 15, 1994, the racing circuit traveled to Sears Point, a road course. McReynolds was once again reminded of the greatness of Ernie Irvan as he won both the pole and the race.

"I knew what an awesome road racer Ernie was," said McReynolds. "He had won in Watkins Glen in the Kodak car. He had won at Sears Point.

"We built a brand-new race car. We went to Road Atlanta and shook it down and had a close call. We were testing brakes a week before we were to leave for Sears Point, and the car got to wheel-hopping, and he spun out, but fortunately we didn't hit anything. It would have been hard to repair or replace the car in that short of time.

"I remember the practice before qualifying. Mark Martin, who is one of Ernie's close friends, is also an awesome road racer, and during practice the two were almost in competition.

"We were one of the last cars to go out and qualify, and Ernie ran a phenomenal lap, and we sat on the pole. Hoosier had a little bit better tire that day. We were on Goodyears, and so when we won, that made us feel that much better about how good our race car was.

"We were leading the race, and Geoff Bodine was second, but we had a twenty-second lead. Ernie would go through turn one, and he could see Geoff coming through the esses, and I saw that the stopwatch fell off a little bit. I said, 'Ernie, is everything OK?' He said, 'Yeah, I've been watching Geoff every lap and gauging myself off of him, making sure I pass him at the same place each lap.'

"He ran about five laps, and all of a sudden the stopwatch got faster, and just about the time I was going to ask him about it, Ernie said to me, 'It's getting faster, isn't it?' Turned out Ernie was running just as fast as he had to.

"In July, we went to Daytona. Jimmy Spencer was driving for Junior Johnson, and all of a sudden, Junior got awfully good in the restrictor-plate races. In July, the track gets awfully hot and slick, and handling becomes a big issue. One time, Ernie came on the radio and said, 'I'm running over the son of a gun in the corners, but as soon as we hit the straightaway, he pulls ahead of me four car lengths.'

"That was a telltale sign that maybe something fishy was going on there. They may not have been doing anything, but it was awfully fishy that all of a sudden Junior was as good as he was in the restrictor-plate races, especially with the horsepower we had from the Robert Yates engines.

"The next race was at Loudon, New Hampshire, and we sat on the pole. It was our fifth pole of the year. We led the race—in fact, we lapped Earnhardt on lap thirty—and we were just phenomenal. It's a 300-lap race, and on about lap

200 Ernie slowed down, and any time I saw the stopwatch slow down I would give him a few laps to see if there was a pattern. After four laps, I said, 'Ernie, is everything OK?' He said, 'Larry, the groove I've been running has changed. It's gone.' I said, 'Search around and do the best you can.'

"Fifteen laps later, all of a sudden the stopwatch sped up. I said, 'What's going on out there?' He said, 'I found me another groove.' That showed me how awesome a race car driver he was. Most of the drivers would have still been out there trying to run the same old groove, just moaning and groaning about the car.

"At the end of the race, the track was coming apart, and if you got too far onto the bottom groove, you got into what they call 'the marbles.' Ernie got too high in turns one and two, and with forty laps to go, he came down on the marbles, spun, and hit the wall.

"He came down pit road, and we tried to make repairs, but he had hit so hard he had busted the battery, and we couldn't even get the thing recranked. We had to park it. And we were nip and tuck with Earnhardt for the points. And we had lapped him that day!

"We had a good opportunity to gain a lot of points on him, but instead we crashed, and that rascal screwed around and finished second that day. Even though we finished way back in the field [Ernie was 30th], he was only a few points behind Earnhardt.

"We were not a large race team, but we were close-knit. These were the same guys who held hands and overcame the accidents of Davey, the tragedy of Davey. We worked awfully, awfully hard. We had Ray Fox Jr., Joey Knuckles, Norman Koshamishu, Doug Yates, Robert's son, who worked night and day to make more and more horsepower. You had a lot of good people. We all got along well. It was one of those good marriages among everybody, including Ernie. And if we won, we knew we had to work just as hard the next week for the next race.

"We went to Pocono in mid-July, and that was one of the races in which Hoosier had an awesome tire, and Ernie could not overcome it. Geoff Bodine won. We ran third and fourth all day long. I'd come on the radio and say, 'Ernie, you are twenty seconds behind the leader.' He'd say, 'I don't know what to tell you to do to make it better. Our car is good.' The Hoosier cars were that much better.

"We were a Goodyear contracted team, though Robert would always give us what was best for the team regardless. But that was one of those times where we knew Hoosiers were not going to be long-term, and we felt that if we worked hard the few races where the Hoosiers would be dominant, we could overcome it like we did at Sears Point. We felt we were better off fulfilling our obligation to Goodyear Tires. And Hoosier *did* go away.

"We went to Indianapolis in August of '94 to race there for the first time. A few months before the race, we had gone there to tire test for Goodyear. We went along with the 4 car with Sterling Marlin. We had an awfully good test. We went back a few weeks later and tested again. You are learning from it, but you also are doing it to help Goodyear develop a better tire, and this was a very important test, because Goodyear was in a war with Hoosiers, and they wanted to do well in the Brickyard 400.

"When we got there, Hoosier did have a little bit better tire. Rick Mast, on Hoosier tires, sat on the pole. Geoff Bodine rode on Hoosiers and had a good car that day. Fortunately, two of the best cars were on Goodyears—Jeff Gordon and Ernie.

"Qualifying we got really loose, and we were fourteenth. For us that was not good. But we worked hard on the race car the rest of the week, and when they dropped the green flag, Ernie kept marching forward.

"I had been screening the 24 car, and as the laps wound down, I heard Jeff Gordon say to Ray Evernham, 'I get real loose with someone behind me.' So as we got down to about fifteen to go, Jeff was in the first, and Ernie was right behind him, and I said, 'Ernie, I just found out some information for you. It has to do with the 24 car.'

"He said, 'I know exactly what you're talking about.' And a few laps went by, and he got Jeff really loose, and he got by him.

"We were leading with three or four laps to go, and it looked like we'd be able to hold Gordon off. But as we went down the back straightaway, we had a right front tire come apart. It tore the fender off, and we had to pit on the green, and we ended up seventeenth. Jeff Gordon won the inaugural Brickyard, and the rest is history.

"We qualified third at Watkins Glen, and Ernie and Mark Martin raced each other all day long, and I never will forget, Mark was leading, and we were second, and both of us had tires and fuel to go to the end. Track position is important at Watkins Glen, because restarts are single file. We had run about fifteen laps, and there were ten to go, and we decided to have Ernie fake out the 6 team. And if I could have gotten a better message to Ernie, we might have succeeded.

"We had no intention of pitting. We got up on the pit wall, and I held up four fingers, we held out the sign, we got all our guys in position, and all of a sudden I could see that 6 team scrambling. They didn't know what to do. Because if we pitted, they figured they'd have to pit. Steve Hmiel was talking to Mark on the radio, and we were all geared up, even though we weren't going to pit, and Ernie almost faked Mark down pit road. If Mark had committed to pit road, Ernie was going to stay on the racetrack. But at the very last moment,

Mark figured out our ruse, and they stayed out, and we stayed out, and Mark won the race, and we finished second."

The team went to Michigan in late August second in the standings, just 27 points behind Dale Earnhardt. With a dozen races to go, Robert Yates, Larry McReynolds, and Ernie Irvan were thinking realistically about winning the championship. Later, when McReynolds went to work for the No. 3 team, one of the boys told him he felt Irvan was going to beat them out.

"Going into Michigan we said, 'We have to do this week what we've done the previous sixteen weeks.' If you do your job, and if you lead races and do well, the way the system is structured the points fall in line.

"On Friday at Michigan, we were running OK, but it seemed we were struggling a little bit in qualifying. Michigan is a tricky place to qualify, because you can overdrive the corner, and if Ernie had a fault, it was overdriving a corner. He would stay on the gas too long and drive too deep, and that got the car pretty loose during qualifying.

"We qualified eighteenth, maybe the worst we ever qualified with Ernie, and as I told you, Ernie and I both were very serious about qualifying. So we were beating ourselves up pretty good as the garage closed. Ernie had his motorhome there, and Robert had his motorhome, and Robert was staying in the hotel with the team, while Doug and Doug's wife were staying in Robert's motorhome.

"Ernie and Doug were parked right next to each other, and I remember going out there and drinking a beer with them and still beating myself up. Ernie said, 'Man, don't worry about it. We're going to be just fine on Sunday. We're going to figure this Michigan qualifying deal out together.' He patted me on the back.

"I went on to the hotel, and on Saturday morning I came back to the track. Times were really fast at Michigan this time, and you always have to tighten your car to qualify, and for the race you have to free it up. Practice was real early Saturday, and I said, 'Ernie, I know we're going to be way too tight to practice. But as loose as it got yesterday, let's go ahead and leave it like it is, drop the pressure down a little on this set of tires, and let's go out and run a few laps and get you acclimated to the racetrack and then we'll work from there.'

"We had about an hour and a half practice. It started about eight Saturday morning, and it's always real smoky because of all the people in the infield, and all the motorhomes and campfires. You almost couldn't see the track except for the front straightaway.

"It's a two-mile racetrack. We got ready to practice. I was going to let him run about ten laps, and I remember giving him his lap times. We were out there with Mark Martin and two or three others, and we were getting beat pretty badly in the corners, which told me our car was too tight. I couldn't see turns one and two very well. I could see turns three and four.

"I remember seeing Mark drive away from us right in the middle of three and four. We'd run back up to him on the straightaway, then he'd pull back away from us in the middle. Ernie completed ten laps, and as he went down the front stretch, I said, 'Ernie, that is lap ten,' and I gave him his lap time. I said, 'Why don't you come on in, and we'll go to work on that thing?' He still didn't say anything, but that was Ernie. A lot of times if Ernie was going to run ten laps, he'd run an extra lap just to get an extra feel for the racetrack. And I remember seeing him cross the start/finish line, and I was standing on the top of the trailer, and Raymond Fox Jr. was standing on the fence at the top of the trailer where he could see. I saw Ernie go off into one, and I lost sight of him, and I saw Raymond waving his hands like a caution, and I asked, 'Who is it?'

"He said, 'It's us.'

"I said in the radio, 'Ernie, are you OK?' And I got no response."

CHAPTER 49

"WE NEED MORE T-SHIRTS."

Jimmy Johnson

IN FEBRUARY 1993, 21-YEAR-OLD JEFF GORDON, HELD OFF BILL ELLIOTT AND Kyle Petty to win one of the twin-125 qualifying races at Daytona. What team manager Jimmy Johnson recalls most about that day was not the victory, per se, but what it brought about—Gordon's newfound superstar status among race fans. Overnight, Jeff Gordon, the fresh-faced California wunderkind, became the sports' new heartthrob and, for many, the antidote to the Man in Black. He was the anti-Earnhardt.

"As crazy as it sounds, the thing I remember most about that day was Michelle Emser, who runs our licensing department," said Johnson. "She said to me, 'We're going to have to send back for more Jeff Gordon T-shirts.' I said, 'What?' Up to that point, revenue from souvenirs was almost nil. If we got $5,000 from a trading card company, you didn't know what to do with all that money.

"She said, 'We need more T-shirts. They are going like crazy!' Now all of a sudden we were getting income from T-shirts. 'God, you mean you can actually make money with T-shirts?' And that's what I remember most about that victory. We sent out and got more T-shirts, and after they were shipped down, they were selling as fast as we could get them on the ground. That's how instantly popular Jeff became after the win in the 125."

I said, "After that, he finished fifth in the Daytona 500, and he wrecked ten cars in the next three months."

"Seventeen cars," said Johnson, "but who's counting?" He laughed at the memory. "We burnt to the ground at Wilkesboro, and then in another race at Wilkesboro, Jeff never made it to the green flag. We hit the inside wall before we got to the green flag. We never made a tenth of a lap.

"But you know something, usually we would wreck in front, and most of those wrecks were not his fault. That first wreck at North Wilkesboro, Hut Stricklin ran into him, and we cut a tire, and it started going down, and Jeff went into the first turn, and the tire blew, and he backed into the wall and blew up and burned it to a crisp."

It took Jeff Gordon until 1994, his second season, before he won his first race. I asked Jimmy Johnson whether there was ever a moment where someone said, 'Maybe he isn't as good as we thought.'

"If there was, I cannot remember it," said Johnson. "My God, he ran real good before he wrecked at Atlanta, so you could see the star potential there, and then when he won the 125, he beat Dale Earnhardt. At that time, Jeff was considered a young kid and a weapon. He'd go out on the racetrack and practice, and everybody else would pull in to the pits—except Earnhardt, who kind of took Jeff under his wing. Dale helped him and worked with him and showed him and drafted with him, and the next thing you knew, everyone else was too."

"Why did Dale do that?" I asked.

"I guess Dale could see the kid had talent. He was just a little kid, and Dale wanted to help him for whatever reason, and he did.

"It took a while for Jeff to finally win, and one reason was that Ray Evernham had never been a crew chief, and so Ray had to learn. Ray put emphasis on being prepared, and it was only a matter of time until it all came together."

When Jeff Gordon won his first race, the Coca-Cola 600 at Charlotte in May 1994, he was 22 years old.

"Hard to believe, isn't it?" said Johnson. "He couldn't rent a car. When he came to drive for us, someone else had to rent his car for him. He was driving two hundred and twenty miles an hour on a racetrack, but he couldn't rent an Impala.

"Jeff loved Charlotte. He looked like Tim [Richmond] at Charlotte. He'd slide it right up against the wall. Jeff was a phenomenal talent, and when you watched him all day and Sunday, you knew he had a shot at it.

"Winning that Coca-Cola 600 was big. We had a suite full of sponsors. We had become very close to the DuPont people, because Tom Young and Tom Speegman were really down-to-earth wonderful guys who supported our race team even though we wrecked seventeen times. When you go out and win for them, that's pretty big.

"A lot of sponsors get nervous when you don't win right out of the box.

Tom and Tom never did. They never questioned what we were doing. Let me tell you a story about Tom Young. At Charlotte, they caught Ray using an unapproved spindle, and NASCAR fined him sixty thousand dollars. Everyone else was using the same part. We just got caught for it.

"No one had ever been fined that much. That was unheard of, and a fine of sixty thousand dollars hurt. It's a lot of money now, but it was a million dollars back then.

"I got a call a day or so later from Tom Young. I thought, 'Oh God, he's fixing to chew my butt out because we've been caught cheating.'

"He said, 'I need your address.'

"I said, 'What do you need my address for?'

"He said, 'Because we're sending you a check for thirty thousand dollars.'

"I said, 'For what?'

"He said, 'We're going to pay half that fine. We win together, and we lose together.'

"And he sent us a check for thirty thousand dollars. I'm telling you, we should give Tom Young and Tom Speegman so much credit for putting us where we are today. Without DuPont and the support those guys gave us, I don't believe you'd see Jeff Gordon quite as successful, and I know you wouldn't see us quite as successful."

Gordon's next milestone was winning the inaugural Brickyard 400 on August 6, 1994, over Ernie Irvan.

"I had never seen the Brickyard," said Johnson. "If you love baseball, it's like walking into Fenway Park or Wrigley Field or Yankee Stadium. When you get into the Brickyard, you look around at the two hundred and fifty thousand seats, and you realize the Unsers and Andrettis had raced there, and it's intimidating, scary. God, I was thinking I had died and gone to heaven. But then for us to go out and win that first race—it was incredible.

"NASCAR had set it up with the speedway that PPG was going to pay a phenomenal amount of money for every lap you led, and Jeff led quite a bit of that race. PPG is DuPont Automotive Finishes' main competitor. We were down in Victory Lane—that trophy is something to kill for—and people were screaming and hollering with cameras going off, and all of a sudden the PPG guys came up to Tom Young and asked if they could take a picture of Jeff wearing their PPG hat. And Tom said yes, which I thought was pretty big. One of Jeff's sponsors is Pepsi, and you don't see Jeff wearing a Coca-Cola hat when he wins the Coca-Cola 600.

"After the race, I was asked by a TV station what my biggest moment in racing was, and I said, 'It used to be Tim Richmond's comeback win at Pocono, but that's number two now. This *has* to be number one.'

In 1994, Hendrick Motorsports needed to find a driver to replace Ricky Rudd in the No. 5 car. Kenny Schrader walked up to Jimmy Johnson and asked him, 'Why don't you think about Terry?' meaning Terry Labonte, who had won the racing championship in 1984 but who had been running poorly of late. Until Schrader put in the good word, Labonte wasn't on Jimmy Johnson's radar.

"I had met Terry and Kim at Watkins Glen in '86, and we went to the Corning Museum together. I thought then, 'What a nice guy!' But I never thought about him ever driving for us.

"I said to Kenny, 'Terry sure hasn't been running very good,' and Kenny said, 'Trust me, he does not have as good equipment as we've got.' He gave me Terry's phone number, and I called him and asked to meet with him.

"We knew Billy Hagan wasn't going to sign him back, and Kellogg's had announced that they were getting out of racing. We met at a fast-food joint somewhere on Highway 85 in a clandestine meeting. He didn't want Hagan to know, so we met by the side of the road and we talked for no more than an hour, and the only thing Terry wanted to talk about was winning the championship and winning races. The conversation never got to money, appearances, souvenir rights. He never, never touched on it.

"I was so impressed I basically told him, 'You're our driver,' but I said, 'I'll be back with you,' because I wanted to make sure I had Mr. Hendrick's blessing. I called Rick on the way back, and I said, 'Rick, this is our guy. He's a racer. He wants to win races. He wants to win championships, and Rick, I have a tremendous amount of confidence in this guy's saying he can do it.'

"Rick said, 'I want to talk to him,' and I put them together, and a day or so later we announced we had signed him.

"We had no sponsor because Tide left to go with Ricky Rudd. Terry called and asked if we had gotten a sponsor. I said, 'I have a long list of them.'

"Terry said, 'Why don't you talk to Kellogg's?' I had assumed—you know the word *assumed* makes an ass of you and me—they were getting out of racing. Terry gave me Bill Nielsen's name and number and told me to call him.

"When I called Bill, it turned out he was not the brand person with Kellogg's, but the corporate counsel. I had never dealt with the company attorney before. The attorneys were there, but you never saw them. They picked apart your contracts.

"I told Nielsen who I was and what we wanted to do, and he said, 'That sounds like something we'd be interested in.' We discussed numbers—we weren't asking near the money then we are now. It was six and a half to seven million dollars, and I thought it was a done deal based on the numbers I had given him.

"Bill flew to Charlotte, sat down across my desk, flipped a piece of paper over, and said, 'This is what we want to do.' I looked at it, and it was nowhere near the numbers we had discussed. Not even close.

"Courteously I stood up, held out my hand to him, and I said, 'Bill, I appreciate your flying all the way here from Battle Creek, but that's not what we discussed, and obviously your objective is not to win races, and ours is, and we can't win with that, so thanks very much. Nice to meet you.'

"He said, 'Best sit back down.' I sat down, and he said, 'What's it going to take?'

"I said, 'Bill, the numbers I gave you are what it's going to take.'

He said, 'OK.'

"For the next two or three days, we had small issues. Talk about a guy who's efficient: he traveled a lot, and we would call with a two-line change in a fifteen-page contract, and Bill took his computer with him on the airplane, and he would make the change, get to a printer, and two hours later I would have it on my desk. We negotiated like that for a couple of days, and we had a contract signed.

"And that year Terry won three races, and in 1996 he won the championship."

CHAPTER 50

THE ERNIE IRVAN MIRACLE

Larry McReynolds

"As a crew chief, whenever your driver wrecks, whether it's in practice or in the race, when the driver doesn't respond, you get a really sick feeling," said Larry McReynolds, talking about the afternoon of August 19, 1994, when Ernie Irvan crashed head-on into the wall at Michigan and almost died. "A lot of times when a driver hits the wall, his earplugs will come out. It's common when he doesn't respond a few seconds later. Then he'll come back on and say, 'My radio came unplugged.'

"But I called and called and called, 'Ernie, are you OK? Ernie, are you OK?' And he wasn't responding.

"I remember seeing a really sick look on Robert's face. Robert was scanning other teams, and evidently other drivers had driven by the wreck and were saying some pretty tragic-sounding things about how hard he hit.

"Robert and I came off the trailer, and I saw Buster Auton, who drove the pace car. Whenever there is a really bad wreck, they will send the pace car and some NASCAR officials. I saw Buster run out of the NASCAR trailer in a panic.

"Robert and I ran over to Buster where the pace car sat and asked if we could go with him. He had the worst look in the world on his face. He said, 'Yeah, you-all get in.' He drove out there over at turn two, and he pulled behind the car, and I remember looking at the car thinking the car didn't look hurt so bad. We got out, and a rescue worker ran up to Robert and me and said, 'You-all don't want to go over there.'

"I walked over to the wall at turn two, maybe fifty yards behind the car, and I leaned over the wall and threw up. My best friend who drives a race car was possibly sitting there dead. I thought, 'It can't be possible.'

"Steve Peterson of NASCAR came over and said, 'He's hurt pretty bad.' He said many things, but I only picked up bits and pieces of them. I was in a state of shock. I remember them saying they were going to cut him out of the car and that some of the best doctors in the world are at Michigan, and they are going to airlift him out, but he *is* alive.

"I remember looking across and seeing a tremendous amount of blood. When you hit as hard as he hit, blood comes out of your ears and nostrils. Also, they did a trach on him in the car, and he bled from that. A little blood looks like a lot. It looked like a bucket of blood had been poured there.

"We saw the helicopter take off. Don Hawk, the president of Dale Earnhardt Incorporated, came over. Don is an ex-minister. He said, 'Is there anything we can do to help you?'

"It stood out that most of the members of the 3 team came over and said, 'Can we help you unload your backup car? Can we get it ready for you?'

"I said, 'No, don't do anything, but I can't tell you how much we appreciate it.'

"Our main concern was getting to the hospital, which was a long ways. Driving time is an hour, but it seemed like it took five hours. It was a very quiet ride. I rode and looked out the window and prayed, and what I prayed had nothing to do with racing. I said, 'Lord, don't let him suffer.' 'Cause in 1985 I had worked with a driver by the name of Butch Lindley, who had gone to Bradenton, Florida, backed into the wall, hit his head, and lay in a coma for six years. I watched what his wife and family went through. That was the illustration I used in my prayer. I know it's not fair to pray for God to take someone's life, but what I was saying to him was, 'If that's what the plan is for Ernie, if he can't be one hundred percent as a father and a husband, forget race car driving. Just don't let him do that. Take him to Heaven with you.' I had those thoughts and said those prayers as we went to the hospital.

"So many things go through your mind. It was obvious that Ernie had been hurt very bad, that his chances of living were very slim. Robert and I went off to a private room, and we said, 'We need to make a decision. We have seven or eight guys waiting at the track waiting to hear how Ernie's doing, and what are we going to do?' We asked, 'What would Ernie want us to do?' Ernie would have wanted us to go out and run on Sunday. But we decided we would not try to run that race on Sunday. No different from when Davey was killed in '93. We were in the championship hunt, but this championship hunt was with Ernie Irvan. If we could not have him on Sunday, we'd load our stuff and go home and wait from there.

"After several hours, Dr. Erlinson came into the family room. He looked at us with a very, very concerned look. He held his head down. He said, 'Right now at this hour, he has a fifteen to twenty percent chance of survival.'

"I thought, 'This just cannot be.'

"Robert and I got a ride back to the Michigan track because we were concerned about our guys. We then went back to the hospital. We paced the floor. You waited—each hour—for something to happen—one way or the other. Every time the door swung open and a doctor came through, you got up on the edge of your chair. Had something changed? And if it had, was it better or worse?

"We went to the hotel to try to sleep and in the morning went back to the hospital, but things weren't changing. Later on that afternoon, Robert and I decided to go home and figure out what to do with our race team. We had obligations to the sponsor. We had to press onward. We had to work on our future.

"We didn't run at Michigan, but the next week we ran at Bristol.

"The world of racing is a funny business. From the moment we got back to Charlotte, the phones were ringing. Anybody who had ever driven a race car was calling. It looked like Ernie would not be driving for the rest of the season. We had to figure out what was best for us.

"One call was from Kenny Wallace. He had a ride in the Busch series, and he ran a few Cup events. He said he'd race whatever races we wanted him to run. Kenny is a very upbeat guy, happy-go-lucky, doesn't get down. We thought, 'This is what we need.'

"Robert OK'ed it through the sponsor, and he got the race team together and told them. Kenny did a good job. We always qualified good. We didn't race as well as we were used to. We were to finish fourth at Martinsville, a great day. It would be Kenny's first top-five finish in Winston Cup.

"We flew home on Sunday from Michigan. We were supposed to arrive at Bristol on Friday. On Thursday, five days after the crash, I and some of the crew flew up to see Ernie. His chances for survival were getting better and better.

"It was scary going up there to see him. His wife, Kim, had said to me, 'He's in a semi-coma. His eyes are open. He'll look at you, but there's not a lot going on there.'

"I wondered what he was going to look like. My wife, Linda, and I went in, and he was holding one of his little daughter Jordan's shoes in his hand. It was like he knew we were there, but he couldn't comprehend we were there. He squeezed my hand. He'd look at us, but he was looking right through us.

"He had a lot of tubes and wires, a scary looking deal. He couldn't make any sounds because of the trach, but based on what I had heard about his condition, I thought this was looking pretty good.

"The next week was Darlington, and then came Richmond. I talked to Kim every day. Just before the Richmond race, two weeks after the accident,

Kim said, 'Larry, I have somebody who wants to talk to you.' And she put Ernie on the phone, and we talked.

"He couldn't talk a lot. He had just had the trach taken out. He had just had a tube run down his throat for two weeks. That was one of the greatest voices I ever heard. Ernie was talking. It didn't matter what he said. It was just great to hear his voice.

"A week later, I flew up with Rusty Wallace to see him. Rusty went to see him regularly. Ernie was out of intensive care, in a semiprivate room, still under nurses' care. I went up, and I couldn't believe it was the same guy I had seen two weeks earlier! It was phenomenal. Anybody on this earth who denies that there is a God, if they just knew what went on in that three-week period of time, how could you ever say there isn't a God on this earth?

"They flew him home on a medical jet the Sunday of Dover during the race. As soon as I got home from Dover that night, I went straight to the rehab center where they took him.

"When Ernie first got hurt, deep down none of us ever thought he would ever drive again, but as we saw him recover and when we knew he'd survive this, our thoughts turned back to him driving again. To me, it didn't matter whether he would drive again. What was important was that he would recover from the accident enough to be able to live a life, be a husband to Kim, a dad to Jordan. He was one of my best friends, so that was what I cared about. If he was able to race, that would be sprinkles on a sundae.

"Ernie got to where he wanted to go—to the racetrack. He wanted to be with us, but when he showed up, reporters wore him out. He got tired answering the questions, 'Can you come back? When are you going to come back?' He got burned out. He finally said, 'Guys, I've told my story a hundred times. I can't tell it anymore.'

"I remember him coming out to practice. [PR man] Brian VanDercook was his babysitter. His job was to make sure he didn't get ambushed by reporters and to make sure he didn't do things he wasn't supposed to do. It was so funny watching Ernie purposely lose Brian. Ernie wasn't supposed to climb up the ladder and go on top of the truck. And I watched poor Brian go just about bananas trying to keep up with him.

"It was hurting Ernie inside that he was back at the racetrack but wasn't able to drive, while Kenny Wallace drove the rest of the '94 season. The more Ernie recovered, the more antsy and gung-ho he got.

"We hired Dale Jarrett to come in and drive the 28 car for 1995 under the terms that Ernie was our driver, but if Ernie was able to come back during the season, he would drive a second car.

"Ernie was getting pretty headstrong by the end of '94. He said, 'I'm going to race, and if you don't want me driving your car, I'll drive someone else's.'

"We knew NASCAR was going to be very careful. We knew if we said, 'We're running Ernie in the Daytona 500,' NASCAR would not want that. They wanted to see a game plan. Dan Rivard of Ford, who is very diplomatic, told Ernie, 'We have to set up a plan. If you don't do that, it will be disastrous for everyone, but mainly for you.' Ernie wanted to know what the steps would be.

"'Step one, the doctors will have to release you to drive.' Ford has a testing ground in Naples, Florida, and Dan Rivard's plan was to go down there where they have test cars that monitor every move the driver makes. 'We'll check your reflexes down there,' Rivard told Ernie. This was step two, planned for late December.

"Ernie, Robert, Dale Jarrett, and I went to Naples for the weekend. Ernie was wearing an eye patch. Ford didn't want Ernie to feel they were singling him out, so they tested Dale first, and his reflexes were good, and then Ernie got in the car, and Dan Rivard rode with him. After they ran several laps, Dan came in smiling from ear to ear. He said, 'This cat ain't lost nothing. He's just as smooth as they come.'

"Was I surprised? Yes and no. Every time you saw Ernie, you'd say, 'He's getting better.' A week later he'd be sharper, keener.

"When we went to Daytona to test, Ernie went with us. He kept pushing us to let him get into the race car, but we knew the press would go bananas if they knew he was running at Daytona. Toward the end of the third and final day, I said to Robert Yates, 'What do you want me to do?'

"He said, 'I'm going to go to pit road. You all do what you think best.'

'I said, 'Thanks, Robert. I appreciate that.'

"We had two cars and a passenger van in a little garage we had all to ourselves. Ernie got in the van and put on one of Dale Jarrett's uniforms, and he had one of his own helmets on the truck, so he got fully clothed, and Dale got up in the van and closed the door, and Ernie came out, helmet already on, got in the race car, and went out and ran five laps, and within two laps he was running as well as Dale.

"I was scared, but I was thrilled to death. Every time he completed a lap, I went, 'Yes.' When he was done, I was relieved. Had we wrecked, God knows, they would have eaten us alive.

"That night was the All Pro banquet in Charlotte. Other teams had seen us pull the doors down to our garage, and by the time we got to the banquet, the word had spread that Ernie had gotten in the race car.

"Of course, the questions came. We kept walking around the question. I said, 'Ernie was with us, but Dale did the testing for us.' I didn't lie.

"In March of 1995, Ernie tested publicly at Darlington, a totally tricky racetrack. Ernie brought his Busch car down, and he asked Mark Martin first to shake down the car to make sure it handled right. I was a little surprised he didn't ask Dale Jarrett to do it. Dale and Ernie would have been friends, but Ernie was doing something none of us likes to do: He was watching somebody else doing his job. Ernie had accepted Dale driving the 28 car, but he wasn't thrilled about it. And so he asked Mark to shake down the car, and then Ernie got in it, and he was like a kid at Christmas. We all climbed up on the truck, and he went out and kept getting faster and faster and faster, and finally he ran a little quicker than Mark had run.

"I told Robert, 'This guy can race tomorrow and be better than ninety percent of them out there.'

"He said, 'You're right,' but he emphasized we had to follow the game plan.

"Ernie first drove in traffic at North Wilkesboro in a truck race in a truck he co-owned with Mark Simo. Robert drove up to watch Ernie in a practice test. Ernie had two trucks, and Joe Ruttman drove one, and he drove the other.

"Robert came back to the shop, and he said, 'He's as good as he ever was.'

"Finally, in the late summer of 1995, Ernie got his clearance from the doctors and from NASCAR, who wanted to see him first run in a truck on a shorter track. He went to Martinsville, and he didn't qualify because it rained. Even so, he was very upbeat about it. He said, 'It can't rain for forty days and forty nights.'

"The next week was North Wilkesboro, and he was going to run the truck race first and then the Cup race. Dale Jarrett also went. Dale wasn't setting the woods on fire qualifying. We were in the middle of the pack.

"Ernie was in the 88 car, and Dale the 28. Both cars were similar. One had a yellow 88 and the other an orange 28. I was crew chief for both cars. NASCAR was good enough to let us park the two cars close together, because we didn't have enough equipment for both cars.

"It was a challenge. That week I worked a hundred hours before that race to make sure both cars were prepared as good as we could. One group of guys worked on Dale's car and another on Ernie's car, and I went back and forth.

"Ernie went out to qualify before Dale, and when he drove onto the track at North Wilkesboro, I thought those people were going to rip the grandstand down. And when he came around and took the green flag, it got even louder. Ordinarily, the number 3 crowd hated Ernie, but when he qualified, those people were cheering just as hard in that grandstand as the Ernie Irvan fans were.

"When he finished, he was third, though he ended up sixth. I felt like the weight of the world had come off my shoulders. And everyone else on the race team felt that way too. Three cars later Dale Jarrett went out and ran two hundredths of a second off what Ernie had run. At the end of the day, I had the best night's rest I had had in a long, long time."

CHAPTER 51

THE END OF AN ERA

Mike Staley

NORTH WILKESBORO, WHICH WAS FIRST OPENED AS A 0.625-MILE DIRT TRACK IN May 1947, became a victim of NASCAR's growth and emphasis on nationalism and superspeedways. By the mid-1990s, it was clear that for NASCAR to approve dates for the new giant tracks like the ones at Loudon, New Hampshire, Texas, and Las Vegas, some of the small tracks had to be sacrificed. And so, after Enoch Staley died from a stroke in May 1995, the France family's loyalty for Staley did not extend to his family, and it quickly became clear that if Staley's family didn't take the money offered by Loudon owner Bob Bahre, they would be left owning an old track with no racing dates.

When I interviewed Mike Staley, Enoch's son, in spring 2002, his most vivid memories included the feud between Darrell Waltrip and Bobby Allison, the day a race had to be postponed because of nightcrawlers, and finally, the wrenching events that forced his mother, sisters, and him to sell the track, which today sits empty, a ghostly monument to the sport's early days.

First, Waltrip and Allison. Waltrip was particularly successful at North Wilkesboro, which he won ten times. Allison won there three times. In the late 1970s and early 1980s, the primary feud in NASCAR was between those two.

On October 14, 1979, the feud reached its low-water mark at North Wilkesboro, when the two slammed into each other on two different occasions on lap 308. Waltrip tapped Allison in turn three, sending both cars sideways. Allison's car hit the wall and was a mess, but somehow it was still driveable. After Waltrip righted himself and completed the pass in the front straightaway, Allison rammed his car into Waltrip, sending him into the wall head-on and wrecking him.

After a long pit stop, Waltrip went back out. He was 20 laps down, but he wasn't finished with Allison. He put his car right between leader Benny Parsons and Allison, who was second, in an attempt to keep Allison from winning. NASCAR officials black flagged Waltrip, who disregarded the flag. Bill Gazaway, the competition director, was so angry with Waltrip that he stormed from the control tower and personally went down and black flagged him again.

Waltrip finally drove off the track. After he and Gazaway talked, Waltrip returned, and he stayed out of Allison's way. Parsons went on to win the race, with Allison second. After the race, Waltrip accused Allison of deliberately trying to wreck him. Mike Staley watched it all with great amusement. It was Staley's greatest memory of a lifetime of memories at North Wilkesboro.

"They beat and banged each other," said Staley. "Bobby got the worst end of it. His car was torn all to pieces. No fender or hood or anything. He went back on the track, and he tried to hit Darrell again. He had to slow down to wait on him to hit him. The fans loved it. It sold a lot of tickets. Gosh, when you have a feud like that . . . I'd love to be at the race following that for ticket sales. When we had a race like that, on Monday morning all your phones light up.

"Waltrip had a natural ability, plus he had a good car—he drove for Junior. Darrell was just a super driver. He knew how to get it done.

"Bobby was a smart driver. He had a lot of stamina. He was tough too. And he was mechanically smart. He knew how to work on the car, knew what needed to be done to make it go faster."

"Tim Richmond was a little wild," he said, "but he had more natural seat-of-the-pants driving ability than I've ever seen besides Dale Earnhardt. He was the only driver I would put in the same class with Dale Earnhardt. He was that good. Dale would kid and pick at me. He was a neat guy."

One of Staley's more memorable moments was the time the North Wilkesboro race was postponed because of nightcrawlers.

"We had a lot of rain," said Staley, "and all these nightcrawlers came out of the ground in the infield, and they made the track slick. We're talking about grub worms, basically. Big, white grub worms. We had to send crews out onto the track to scoop them up in buckets. Then we took them to the dump."

The future of the North Wilkesboro track depended on the survival of Enoch Staley. As long he lived, the France family would respect and honor his special relationship with Bill France Sr. and let him keep his dates.

Then in May 1995, Enoch Staley had a stroke. Three days later, he passed away. Once Staley was dead, the vultures began to circle. It was only a matter of time before racing at North Wilkesboro would come to an end.

"With Dad gone, Mom and I were thinking, 'What's going to happen to the track?' said Mike Staley. Even if Mike didn't want to sell, he was helpless to act if the heirs of C. C. 'Jack' Combs and Charlie Combs decided to sell their fifty percent share. It was to them that Bruton Smith came first. Enoch Staley wasn't dead a month when the ink on the contract was dry. Bruton Smith paid a reported six million dollars for half interest in the North Wilkesboro track.

"The first I knew that Bruton Smith was my new partner was when he walked into the office and said, 'I'm your new partner.'

"What did you say?" I asked.

"I said, 'OK,' said Mike Staley. "What can you say?"

According to Staley, he continued running things the way he had since his dad had died. Bruton offered another $6 million to buy the other half, but the deal was for Speedway Motorsport stock, not cash, and the sellers would not be able to get rid of the stock for three years.

"Bruton wanted to pay us in stock, which we weren't too fond of," said Staley.

In December 1995, the Staleys ended up selling their stock for $8 million to Bob Bahre, the owner of the new track in Loudon, New Hampshire. Staley says he sold to Bahre because he offered him a lot more money than Bruton Smith did.

"How did you find Bahre?" I asked.

"I didn't," said Staley. "He found me. He showed up one day, walked into my office and said, 'I'm Bob Bahre. I'd like to talk to you.' He sat down and said, 'I'd like to buy your half of the track. I'll give you my top offer now. This is it. I'm going to fly to Daytona and tell Bill [France] Jr. what I did here.'

"As soon as he left, I called Bill Jr., and said, 'Who is this Bob Bahre character?' Bill told me a little bit about him. He said, 'Mike, the best way I can describer Bob Bahre to you, he's the Enoch Staley of the north.'

"I said, 'That's all you need to say.'

"After a lot of discussion, we sold. Because I didn't actually own the stock. My mother and my two sisters did.

"We gave a lot of thought to hanging on. It took a while to make a decision. It was something we didn't want to give up. But when you're forced into it, you can see what might happen if you don't sell, if you're in a partnership with a billionaire—how can you fight someone like that?

"I could see the big picture. I could see where NASCAR was going with the big cities and the big TV deals. They wanted to be in New York and Chicago and Los Angeles. I could see that coming. That was on the horizon."

The North Wilkesboro track might have stayed open if either Smith or Bahre had owned it outright. Joint ownership made it impossible after the Staleys made Bahre promise that he would not sell the track to Bruton Smith.

Bahre kept his promise. And Smith refused to sell to Bahre. The stalemate meant an end to racing at North Wilkesboro.

"Bob was all for letting me stay on and run the track and maybe run a Busch series and a truck series. At that time, we could have done that. But in order to do that, both partners had to agree, and it didn't happen," said Mike Staley. "The sole reason Bruton bought the track was to get the dates for the track he was building in Texas. I remember the day that first race was held there and our track here in North Wilkesboro was silent. It was very sad. Everybody around here felt bad about it. It was something we thought would always be there, and when something is suddenly gone. . . . Actually, on the dates when they raced in Texas, a lot of people came to the North Wilkesboro track and camped out anyway.

"The track still stands, but it's closed and locked up. There's one maintenance man who cuts the grass and keeps people from going in and vandalizing things.

"We don't own it anymore. I don't have anything to do with it. There's been talk of fixing it up, but it's all talk. It's too fast for a weekly track. And now it doesn't fit the Busch or the truck series. I don't know what you could do with it except use it for testing."

After Staley sold the track, he began a company that did trucking for Lowe's, Wal-Mart, and Payless throughout the country. After five years, he sold his interest in the firm.

Today, he is a small-time country farmer.

"I guess, more or less," he said. "I do have a farm in Burnsville. I have twelve head of cattle. I see Junior Johnson every once in a while. He's got a *big* herd of cattle. He's a gentleman farmer, as you described me, but moreso than I am."

CHAPTER 52

GROWING AND GROWING

Jimmy Johnson

JEFF GORDON BECAME THE RAGE OF WINSTON CUP RACING WHEN HE WON THE racing championship in 1995 at age 25. He went right at the reigning champ, the Intimidator, Dale Earnhardt, and more often than not beat him. At the same time, Gordon won over a legion of new race fans, especially younger women and men looking for someone to stick it to Earnhardt.

Gordon won seven races, was second four times and third five times. He won eight poles, and won $4,161,506 in purses. That year, he also snared another prize: a wife, Brooke Sealey, the current Miss Winston. Under R. J. Reynolds rules, Miss Winston was forbidden from dating any of the drivers, hence the need for secrecy. Jimmy Johnson watched as the romance blossomed.

"It was only a rumor that Jeff and Brooke were dating," said Johnson. "I knew Brooke pretty good from being with RJR. Jeff won at Charlotte, and he and I were standing side by side, and I looked at her and said, 'You are sure going to make a cute couple.'

"She said, 'What?'

"I said, 'Come on, Brooke.' She just grinned, and that was about all that was ever said. It wasn't long after that that she resigned as Miss Winston, and they did become an item.

"Jeff was fun. He liked to have a good time, but he was considerate of fans. He had been trained well by his mom and stepfather, and it showed, because he was a real gentleman. Since Tim had died, we hadn't visited Victory Lane consistently, and then all of a sudden Jeff started to win, and you had a damn good feeling when the green flag came down that that was where we were headed. It really put a big fire back in Rick Hendrick's eyes and in the engine department, and the chassis department, because we had a legitimate chance to win every race.

"And when Terry Labonte won the championship in 1996, that was the icing on the cake, because that really legitimized Hendrick Motorsports. We weren't just Jeff Gordon and Ray Evernham. It was Randy [Dorton] in the engine department, and Eddie [Gossage] in the chassis department. And when Terry won, that fired up Jeff and Ray, who said, 'That will never happen again. If there's going to be a championship won, we're going to win it.'"

Good to their word, the team of Gordon and Evernham won racing championships in 1997 and 1998.

In 1996, the budget for Hendrick Motorsports was $29.4 million. Hendrick fielded three race teams, had 160 staff members, seven engineers, a full-time aerodynamics expert, and six private planes. That was only seven years ago. According to Jimmy Johnson, that's small potatoes compared to what Hendrick Motorsports is spending today.

"We didn't have a marketing department back then," said Johnson. "I did that. Today, we have ten to twelve people in marketing. We didn't have a human resources department. I did that too. When I left [in February of 1998], we had forty people in the engine room, and today we have eighty. When I left, the chassis department had twenty, and today we have forty-two.

"Our philosophy has always been to get better, and to get better you have to spend money, and to spend money you have to earn it, from race winnings or from sponsors or from making engines for other teams. You have to keep pouring money back into buildings and into personnel and into equipment."

With the cost of running a race team going through the roof, the pressures on everyone have become enormous. Crew chiefs and crews work around the clock with very few days off during the racing season. Burnout has become much more common. Salaries are much higher than in the past, but longevity has become less common.

In 1997, Gary DeHart, crew chief for Terry Labonte, had to quit in the middle of the racing season. With Jeff Gordon and Ray Evernham on the way to winning the championship, the hard-working DeHart was unable to make it through the season.

"Gary is a winner," said Jimmy Johnson, "and Gary was under a lot of pressure. He worked himself to death. If there has ever been burnout, Gary was guilty of it. Gary worked extremely hard night and day, and it was just hard to go out and catch Jeff and Ray. Gary had gotten a taste of victory two years before, and they had beaten Jeff and Ray the year before, but here came '97, and Gary just burned out, and it took him a year to get his head back right. But I would put Gary up against anybody. He is Kyle Busch's crew chief in ARCA, and yesterday he set a track record.

"The pressure has become almost unbearable. The best crew chiefs in the world—Gary being one of them—are burning out. Jimmy Makar got off the 18 car. Jimmy is still with Joe Gibbs, but he's now the team manager. Todd Parrott in the 88 and 38, Robin Pemberton with Penske, he left and went to Petty's for a short period of time, and now he is working for the Ford Motor Company. Your life expectancy is a little bit longer than the recon guys in a war. You don't live long. When you have thirty-eight weeks of racing plus testing and the banquet, it's burnout. I don't know how they do it.

"It gets to the point that you don't love it anymore. It's not a passion when you have to sacrifice so much. The financial rewards are there. The four guys I mentioned earned a very good living, but after a while the sacrifices you have to make are not worth it."

Jimmy Johnson himself walked away. On February 28, 1998, he left Hendrick Motorsports and retired to a beach on the west coast of Florida.

"I was at the racetrack six hundred weekends," said Johnson. "It wasn't any one thing. I wanted to spend more time with my wife and family. And we had a home in Florida, and we thought that's where we wanted to be. I moved to Sarasota and worked as a consultant for two years, and at the same time helped other teams, Eel River Racing and Galaxy Motorsports, and then three years ago, Rick said, 'Come on back and help me.'" Today, Johnson is the director of special projects and vice president of Hendrick Companies.

While Jimmy Johnson was taking R&R on the Florida coast, Rick Hendrick decided to add yet another race team. This new team was another indication of Hendrick's foresight and vision. He and Jeff Gordon had signed a lifetime contract, and as part of their agreement, Hendrick agreed to become Gordon's partner in a new team. Hendrick built a new building that would house Gordon and his team and also the new team. Jeff Gordon would be the team owner of the new team. Jimmie Johnson—no relation to Jimmy Johnson—was chosen to be the driver.

"I wasn't directly involved with it," said Jimmy Johnson. "Several years ago, Ricky Hendrick, Rick's son, recommended Jimmie, and nothing happened, and then when Jeff came in, he said, 'I like Jimmie,' and they hired him." Jimmie Johnson, a motorcycle racer and a competitor on the ASA circuit, was 25 years old.

"Ken Howes, our competition director, worked closely with Brian Whitesell, a team manager who went back to day one with Ray Evernham, and Robbie Loomis to make sure the people we hired for the new team would be compatible with the guys on Gordon's team. Because you're under the same roof, eat in the same break room, you better get along. The decision was made to hire Chad Knaus. That was a good decision because Chad had worked for Ray, trained under Ray, and he's been phenomenal. As good as Jimmie is, Chad is just as good."

One of Jimmie Johnson's great advantages is that Jeff Gordon is his mentor.

"You got a guy who can walk up into a trainer and bounce things off, and he has a reason to tell you the truth. I don't think there's a driver out there who hasn't gone up to a driver and asked the question, 'What is your car doing?' And he's not sure if he's getting the skinny or not. Jimmie will get it straight."

As this book goes to press in early 2004, Jeff Gordon has gone through the heartbreak of divorce, an emotional trauma that has kept him from contending for the racing title. But in September 2003, Gordon was in sixth place behind Matt Kenseth, and it's only a matter of time before he wins another championship.

"Any time you go through a divorce and lose your soul mate, things get hairy, and it's awfully hard to concentrate on more than one thing, and if you're going to be a race car driver, distractions are not good. But Jeff is back. They better watch him. He's hungry."

I asked Jimmy Johnson whether Hendrick Motorsports is going to get any bigger.

"I don't think it will," said Johnson. "Four cup teams and a Busch team is about all you'll ever see."

"Can NASCAR grow any bigger?" I asked.

"Oh yeah," he said. "You're already seeing people like Jack Roush say he wants to have forty races a year. I don't think that's good, and I don't think anyone else does either, including Jack's guys. I don't think you'll see that, but some time—not in my lifetime—you may see NASCAR get so big that you will have a National League/American League setup. It's been discussed. A West Coast division and an East Coast division. That's way, way, way down the road. Yes, NASCAR can get a lot bigger."

CHAPTER 53

CREW CHIEF FOR THE INTIMIDATOR

Larry McReynolds

WHEN ERNIE IRVAN WON ONE OF THE TWIN 125S AT DAYTONA IN 1996, HE completed one of the greatest comebacks in the history of sports. But once he came back and began racing again, the novelty of the story quickly died out. It was movie material, but Ernie Irvan wasn't cuddly and likeable, and he went back to being just another driver when, by the end of 1996, things started to turn sour for Ernie and the Robert Yates team.

Ernie and Robert Yates' wife, Carolyn, began to fight over souvenir revenues. The fighting became so acrimonious and bitter that when Ernie won the Richmond race in September, Robert Yates didn't go to Victory Lane for fear that Carolyn would be upset.

Ernie and Texaco also began feuding, because Texaco expected Ernie to go out and sign autographs like Davey Allison used to do, and Ernie would only do it when his contract called for him to do so, and then usually half-heartedly.

There was also friction between Ernie's team and Dale Jarrett's team. Jarrett's team finished third in the points, while early in the year Ernie qualified poorly and crashed a lot, recovering the second half of the season to finish tenth in the points. Overall, it was a successful year for both teams, but the friction between the teams took its toll on team manager/crew chief Larry McReynolds until the genial McReynolds was frayed and totally worn out. As McReynolds explained it, "It was like I had two extension cords, and they weren't quite long enough to reach each other, but if I pulled them hard enough and held them, I could keep them plugged in."

Finally, after a year, his hands gave out. He couldn't hold onto those plugs any longer.

After pressure from Texaco and his wife, Carolyn, Robert Yates decided not to renew Ernie Irvan's contract at the end of the 1996 season. Around this time, Larry McReynolds was sent word that Richard Childress wanted to talk to him about coming to his team to be Dale Earnhardt's crew chief. While in Suzuki, Japan, for an exhibition NASCAR road course race, McReynolds met with Childress in a Japanese restaurant and discussed it. Childress told McReynolds that he had promoted David Smith to be Earnhardt's crew chief, but that the two "never got dialed in together." They had finished second in the points, but Childress was dissatisfied and wanted to make a change.

LARRY McREYNOLDS
His time with Dale
peaked at the 1998 Daytona 500.
NIGEL KINRADE

For McReynolds, who prized loyalty above all else, it would be the hardest decision he'd ever had to make. He was leaving the Robert Yates race team that had put him on the map, but racing had stopped being fun, and he no longer wanted to continue working there.

When McReynolds told Robert Yates what he was considering, Yates told him, "Larry, if you are not happy and not having fun, and if you have the opportunity to work for the greatest race car driver that's ever been, I cannot tell you you don't need to do that."

McReynolds took the job with Richard Childress Racing for the 1997 and 1998 seasons.

"When I took that deal," said McReynolds, "nobody's expectations were higher than my own. I'm thinking to myself, I have just left an operation where we won six races with a brand new team [Dale Jarrett] and with a guy who was just finding his way back around the racetrack [Ernie Irvan], and, man, if I can take this to Dale Earnhardt, there is no telling what we will do. No telling how many races we will win. No telling how many more championships."

Larry McReynolds had been one of the most visible and successful crew chiefs when he was offered a job to work with Dale Earnhardt, the seven-time

Winston Cup champion. But, as it turned out, it was the wrong move. Earnhardt had been seriously hurt in a crash in July 1996 at Talladega, and his injuries prevented him from returning to top form. When he stopped winning, the blame shifted onto McReynolds' shoulders, and Larry became the target of critics and fans alike.

"What I didn't realize, the reason Dale didn't win in 1996, and the reason I didn't have much success with him in 1997 and 1998, was that Dale Earnhardt was playing hurt bad. He had gotten hurt bad at Talladega in a wreck, and Ernie Irvan had been part of that wreck.

"I was still with Ernie when it happened. Ernie took a lot of heat and blame for that wreck, but I still say that it happened because Dale Earnhardt's antics backfired on him.

"Dale was strong, but Ernie was faster, and with Dale leading for three or four laps down the backstretch, Dale ran Ernie all over the backstretch. Ernie would go all the way to the grass, and Dale would go all the way to the grass to cut him off. It looked like a snake going down the backstretch.

"Finally, coming down the front stretch, Ernie got a run on Dale underneath the tri-oval, and Dale moved him down again. But there wasn't any further for Ernie to go. He was against the apron. And Ernie got into Dale's left rear, and got him upside down along the fence. Of course, everybody blamed Ernie. Ernie was wearing an eye patch, and they said, 'Ernie can't see.' But that was bull. Dale's games backfired on him. God rest his soul, but his games backfired on him. I told Richard Childress that. I told Dale that. They didn't agree with me, but I said, 'You all can blame that wreck on Ernie if you want to, but what happened was Ernie finally didn't back out. He stayed on the gas. And Dale got hurt.'

"Dale broke his sternum. He was a bummed up individual, and he was hurting for a long time, and until he finally had an operation between the '99 and 2000 seasons. He played hurt for a good two to three years.

"To give an even better understanding I had of this: Dale's girls and my girls go to school together. During the Charlotte week last October, it was on Friday, and we didn't have any on-track activity that day. Our little girls had been on a trip with the school to the Huntsville Space Camp, and we were picking them up, and the bus was running late, and I happened to see Dale sitting in his Tahoe, and I was sitting in my car, and we were by ourselves. I went over and talked to Dale, and we talked awhile about our race cars. I was with the 31, and he was driving the 3, and we were talking about how practice had gone the day before. The next thing I know we were talking about the time we had together, and Dale Earnhardt assured me and reassured me and reassured me and thanked me and blessed me over and over again for him winning the Daytona 500 in '98.

"He said, 'You know, Larry, it was so unfair to you the time you were with me, because I just never felt good. Until I had that damn operation last winter,' where they went in and fixed his neck, 'I could never get comfortable.'

"Dale used that word a lot during the time we were together. He'd say to me, 'Larry, I just ain't comfortable.' He just could not get comfortable in that race car.

"So to some degree I feel like a sacrificial lamb. But I will treasure the year and a half I spent with Dale. Dale and I did win the Daytona 500, which is something nobody else can say. I was his crew chief when we won the Daytona 500. A lot of people have said to me, 'You're the man who got him the Daytona 500,' but I didn't get him anything. Dale had come so close so many times. I just happened to be the one who was in position when everything fell into place. No flat tires. No running out of gas. No wrecks. No blown engines. No dropped valves. I just happened to be steering the ship when it all came together."

The win in the 1998 Daytona 500 was a high point in a season when very little else went right. Midway through that season, Richard Childress, car owner for drivers Dale Earnhardt and Mike Skinner, was unhappy with the performance of both cars. He decided it would be best to swap crew chiefs. Larry McReynolds, who worked with Earnhardt, would switch to Skinner's race team, and crew chief Kevin Hamlin, who worked with Skinner, would go over to Earnhardt. McReynolds recalled what was going on behind the scenes at the time.

"Dale and I became good friends," said McReynolds, "but yes, we butted heads a lot. A lot of it was over qualifying. As I've told you, I put a lot of energy and effort into qualifying. It's the way I was bred. It's the way Robert Yates taught me. It's the way Davey Allison taught me. It's the way Ernie Irvan taught me.

"Dale did not seem to worry about qualifying, and it would just kill me to know how good the equipment was, but to then go out and qualify thirty-eighth or forty-first and have to use a provisional to get in the race. I know it had to bother him, but he acted like it didn't worry him at all. And that would just kill me.

"Dale felt he could make up for it with his driving skill, and for many years that was true, but earlier in his career you could start forty-first at Charlotte and be leading by lap twenty, because there would be only ten cars in the whole garage area that could win the race. You can't do that today because the competition is too tough.

"After winning the Daytona 500 and being so dominant for a week and a half, we went to Rockingham the next week and ran terrible, needed a provisional to get into the race and ran about sixteenth, four laps down. And we ran terrible race after race after race.

"By June, Dale and I were struggling. We still were friends. I'd still go over to his motorcoach and we'd have dinner together.

"As for Dale and I, we just couldn't . . . Dale and I were too much alike. Richard Childress even told me that. One time, he said, 'The only thing I can tell you, Larry, is that you intimidated the Intimidator. You didn't just say, 'OK.' You said, 'What the hell is wrong? What are we going to do to make it better?' You wouldn't just say, like him, 'Everything will be fine.'

"The turning point: We were at Richmond, Virginia, in June. We qualified forty-first out of forty-five cars. I walked up in the lounge of the truck. Dale and Richard Childress were sitting there watching TV, and I said to Dale, 'What do you have?'

DALE AND RICHARD CHILDRESS
A winning combination.
INTERNATIONAL MOTORSPORTS HALL OF FAME

"He said, 'I don't know, Larry. The car felt good. I just didn't get back to the gas.'

"I said, 'Dale, you need to make your mind up what you want to do with the rest of your career. And I'll figure out whether I want to ride along with you or not.'

"I thought poor Richard was going to swallow his tongue. And I turned around and walked out.

"I thought to myself, 'I've screwed up. I may have cost myself my job.' But I said, 'You know what? I don't care. I'm not going to race this way.'

"I had to get it off my chest. I could not handle qualifying forty-first again. Because I can't tell you how many race cars we tore up because we started in the back of the field.

"We raced on Saturday night and ran terrible. The 31 car ran terrible. I stayed up in Richmond Saturday night with Linda and the kids. As soon as we drove from Richmond on Sunday morning, my mobile phone rang. It was Richard Childress. I had already told Linda, 'I probably screwed up today. I may have cost myself my job. But you know what? I don't care. I'm not going to race this way.' I told her what had happened.

"Richard said, 'Larry, where you at?' I said, 'I'm just leaving Richmond.'

"He said, 'Can you come by the shop on the way in? I got something I want to talk to you about.'

"I told Linda, 'He's going to fire me.'

"When I got to the shop, I learned that what he wanted to do was have his two crew chiefs swap teams. Richard Childress saw he had a great race driver in Dale Earnhardt. He had a good driver in Mike Skinner. He had a good crew chief in Larry McReynolds, had a good crew chief in Kevin Hamlin. And he's a smart man. He took a step back. He said to himself, I got Dale, who's laid back. I got Kevin, who's laid back. But I got Mike Skinner, who needs a head football coach, and I got Larry, who's one of the best crew chiefs as far as giving people guidance. I just got them mixed wrong.

"When he ran the idea by me, I said, 'Boy, I don't know.'

"He said, 'Larry, That's what I'm going to do.'

"I said, 'OK, I'll be back up here in the morning, and I'll let you know.'

"I talked to Linda about it. And Mike Skinner was begging for this change. Mike wanted me. He felt it was what he needed.

"I came back into the shop Monday morning and looked at Richard and said, 'I can't do it. Nothing against Mike Skinner, nothing against the 31 team, but I did not leave Robert Yates racing and the 28 car to go to work for the 31. I left there to work for the black number 3.'

"He said, 'But Larry, it's not working.'

"'I understand,' I said.

"'It's June,' he said. 'Just give me a few weeks, give me a few races. Just try it.'

"'OK,' I said, 'I'll try it.' And lo and behold, it appears Kevin Hamlin was what Dale Earnhardt needed, and it appears that Larry McReynolds was what Mike Skinner needed. I worked with Mike for two and a half years.

"Skinner is a hard race car driver. But he hadn't found out the fine line between what's too hard and what's not hard enough. He needed that coach.

"We immediately clicked, and Mike and I became good friends. If you gave me a magic bottle and said, 'You can rub this bottle and you get one wish, and that wish would be what you would change about Mike Skinner,' there is no question what it would be: He would take a bottle of water and I would try to look at it and say it was half full. But it don't matter how many times Mike Skinner looks at that bottle, he'll call it half empty. Whether it was the way he was brought up or the things he had to go through, when you'd fix one thing, he was going to find something else wrong. And it's been one of the things that has kept him from winning a race. I love him to death, and he is talented. If he could ever get his frame of mind in the right order, he's as talented as anybody in this garage. He's got to get a more positive attitude about things. He has to figure out that on most race days it's not a perfect world. On very few race days is it a perfect world. You've got to figure out to the best of your ability and your race teams' how to make it as close to a perfect world as you can. We came close to a couple of perfect worlds. At Atlanta, in March of 2000, no way we could lose that race. We had a fast race car all day long, led two hundred and some-thing laps. When the caution came out with thirty laps to go, our closest competition was Dale Earnhardt and Bobby Labonte. We beat everybody out of the pits with four fresh tires. The first lap we went back racing with twenty laps to go, we ran a 29.60, and Dale and Bobby were running 30.20. I thought, 'No way we can lose this race today.' And a friggin' rod broke with seventeen laps to go, and we spit the bottom out of that motor.

"If Mike Skinner can ever win that first race, I won't say others will come easy, but a lot easier than what this first one has been.

"I know when I joined Winston Cup in 1980, I didn't think I would *ever* win a Winston Cup race. It went all the way to Watkins Glen in '88, but when you finally win that first race, all those little voices that haunt you: 'Can you win a race?' 'Do you have what it takes?' 'Can you do it?' They finally go away, and I won't say the second came any easier. But then I won a second race, and a third race, and before you know it, I've won twenty-seven races.

"If Mike could win one, he'd be a different person. He might look at that bottle and say, 'Damn, she's half full.'"

After four years of working with Richard Childress Racing, Larry McReynolds had won just one race, Dale's Daytona 500 win. He also won the Motegi, Japan, exhibition race with Mike Skinner, which was special but didn't count in Winston Cup.

In 1999, McReynolds attempted to put together a deal that would have allowed him to be part owner of a race team. He joined with John Dangler, but told Dangler he would start a team only if it could attract a major sponsor.

"There are a lot of Thorne Apple Valley Meat deals out there that will promise you eleven million dollars, but when they go Chapter 11 at the end of year two, where are you?" said McReynolds. Richard Childress told him, "If you can't get a Fortune 500 company, don't do it." Dangler and McReynolds almost reeled in Tide as a sponsor, but at the last moment Tide told McReynolds they didn't want to take a chance on a new team. Two days later, however, Tide went with another brand-new team. A disappointed McReynolds threw in the towel and signed a three-year deal to return to Richard Childress for the 2000, 2001, and 2002 seasons.

Meanwhile, since 1995 McReynolds had worked for TNN as a television commentator on a part-time basis. He did commentary for Busch and truck races on Saturdays on off-weekends. The pay was excellent, he enjoyed it, and he did it very well. McReynolds had great knowledge, and he possessed an easy-going Southern charm that put viewers immediately at ease. But when NASCAR signed lucrative contracts with Fox and NBC in 2000, McReynolds figured his announcing days were over.

A month later, Fox called. At first, Fox wanted him on Saturdays on off-weekends, but then right before the Charlotte races of May 2000, he was asked to audition by doing a mock broadcast on Saturday during the Busch race. McReynolds was so insightful and folksy on TV that the Fox executives decided they wanted him as a regular.

"Shortly after the auditions," said McReynolds, "they called back, and I saw they were talking full-time. I said to myself, 'Shoot, I don't know if I want to do that.' But the more I thought about it over the month of July, I said, 'You know, this may be a once-in-a-lifetime shot.' There are crew chiefs all over the place, but to go be a broadcaster for a major network in a sport that I love. . . . If I play my cards right, I can always come back and be a crew chief again, but I may not get another opportunity to do this.

"They made me a very lucrative offer. I talked to my family about it. My kids were not crazy about it because all they had known their entire life was Dad the crew chief, and they were apprehensive. My wife, Linda, who supported everything I have done—we've been married eighteen years this October—pointed out a few more things to me, but she still said, 'Whatever makes you happy, the kids and I will support it, and we'll adapt.'

"Finally, we came together on the numbers. It was an off weekend before the Brickyard of 2000, and I thought, 'Here's what's going to be the determining factor. I'm going to sit down and talk to Richard, and if he says, "No way, you are under contract," or "If you do it, I will take you to court," that will decide it for me.'

"I didn't let Richard know this. I put it on his shoulders. I went and met with him, and I explained it, and he looked at me, and I wasn't sure what he was thinking or what he was about to say, and he said, 'Larry, I am not real happy about this. You're an integral part of this operation, especially the 31 team. But you know, if I was any kind of friend at all, and I am, there is no way I will stand in the way of your doing that. It would be crazy for me to tell you that you can't do that.'

"I considered how many times I had had to sacrifice being with my wife and three kids. Never did I get to go to my little girl's dance competition. Never did I get to go to my little boy's baseball or soccer games. Since my daughter was born, I drove for three years fifty-something miles each way, and the little girl was always asleep when I left the house and asleep when I came home. She never even knew who I was. So when I stacked in the fact that I had been doing this for twenty-something years and I was a little tired and maybe a little burned out, and I could still make really good money and have a good living and still be involved with the sport that I love so much, and yet still have the opportunity to come back and do what I do now, it was pretty much a no-brainer, and when Richard Childress gave me the green light, it was an absolute no-brainer.

"I began my broadcasting career in February scared to death. For the first time in twenty-one years, I was doing something besides being a race mechanic or crew chief. I had no idea what to expect, no idea what was going to happen, no idea about anything, but I will say it was one of the most enlightening experiences. I have had more fun in these twenty-one weeks. . . . I have not once looked back over my shoulder and questioned what I did."

When the 2001 broadcast season ended, McReynolds accepted a consulting job with Kyle Petty's race team. McReynolds, who is something of a perfectionist, wanted to make sure the racing technology didn't pass him by, that he would be up-to-date and prepared for his telecasts. Working in the garage would keep him fresh, he figured.

"Fox made it so that when we ended our broadcast at Milwaukee, I could have gone home and sat by the lake until February. I made a promise to my kids that, for the most part, their life would not change. My son just went to the beach with several of his friends for the day. At the same time, I strongly feel one of the strengths we had as a broadcast this year was the fact that myself, Jeff Hammond, and Darrell [Waltrip] had all just stepped out of the sport in November. We could explain everything that was going on. When they took the bump-stops away, we could explain what they did. When they went to shorter front springs, we knew what was going to do. We could explain it. If you're in the sport every day, it's hard enough to keep up with it. If you stand away from it, you will be lost at sea. And I want to do just as good a job as a broadcaster when we come back in February, and in two or three years I might want to go back to being a crew chief.

"I've got to be here every day. The Pettys offered me an opportunity to be a consultant to work with the 44 team and to work with all their teams, so I can keep my hand in it. Hopefully, I can help them. Hopefully, it will be a win-win situation. But I know I can't wait to get back to the broadcast booth in 2002.

"There's one other thing that contributed to my decision: I look back and reflect over my career and I don't ever question what God does. All things happen for a reason, but I look at the fact that he led me to Robert Yates and Davey Allison, and we were destined to win championships, win a lot of races, but for whatever reason—a reason I don't question—he decided on July 13, 1993, to take Davey Allison away from us. Well, we showed our strength by rebounding, putting Ernie Irvan in that car, and all of a sudden, other than missing Davey, we didn't miss a beat with our racing. We were winning races, and let me tell you something—if Ernie Irvan had not gotten hurt, and this is a bold statement I'm making, but I'm making it with confidence—Jeff Gordon would not be sitting here a three-time champion, and I don't know that Dale Earnhardt would have won his seventh championship. Ernie Irvan was going to win a bunch of races, and he was going to win championships. But unfortunately, in 1994 on a Saturday morning at Michigan in a practice session, that race car had a defective tire on the right front, and that race car hit the wall, and he was badly injured.

"So as I took the broadcast job, I was sitting in two golden opportunity situations and for whatever reason it just wasn't meant to be. It wasn't destined to pan out. So I said, 'I need this breath of fresh air that Fox is offering me.' And as long as Linda and the kids and the people I have obligations to, which was Richard Childress, as long as they support it, I'm going to do it. And when I left the broadcast booth last week, the twenty-one weeks we did, the ninety-something shows we did, I felt so fulfilled. Because as a crew chief, the way the sport has gotten, you can work till your head, arms, and legs fall off, but you're controlling about one-tenth of a percent of your destiny. Is the driver going to be in the right frame of mind? Is a lap car going to get you? Is the weather going to affect you? Is the engine going to fail you? So many things are totally out of your control. You had to live with the fact that you give it all you had, and sometimes you have to put your head down at night and say, 'Dad gum, I did all I can do, and the rest was out of my control.' And you get tired of that. You say, 'Dad gum, why can't it pay off today?'

"But as a broadcaster, I still depend on people around me, my co-broadcasters, the producers, directors, the cameramen, but also I feel as long as I dot my i's and cross my t's that I am controlling a lot more of my destiny, and not once did I leave that booth not feeling fulfilled.

"When Darrell and I were racing, we had our benchmarks. We had our qualifying sheets, we had our times, we had our race results. We knew how we stood. But as broadcasters, we look at each other and say, 'I don't know. It felt pretty good.' Everyone was always happy, and the ratings were always good, and yet I have never met a person who has a Nielsen box in his house. But I do know that everyone seems very happy. The fans are happy, NASCAR is happy, the competitors are happy, and the people we work for and sign the checks are happy, so that's a pretty good sign we need to be happy.

"We had meetings in San Francisco on Monday after the Sonoma race, and what were those meetings about? It's about what we have to work on between now and February to get better.

"We know we have to get better. We're just like a race team. We know we're only as good as the last time we were out. And we've got to keep working to get bigger and better.

"I'm going to try to be the best broadcaster who ever broadcast a race, and my goal is someday for somebody to look back and say, 'You know, ol' Larry is the John Madden of Winston Cup racing.'"

CHAPTER 54

THE 2000 CHAMPION

Jimmy Makar

WHEN DALE JARRETT LEFT THE JOE GIBBS RACING TEAM AFTER THE 1994 SEASON to drive for the Robert Yates team, team manager/crew chief Jimmy Makar was left with deep feelings of abandonment. After all, Makar was, and is, married to Dale Jarrett's sister. Blood was supposed to be thicker than water, but apparently not when a better ride appears around the corner.

Making it even harder for Makar, he had to fill not one but two drivers' seats because Gibbs had decided to add a second car to his race team. Finding one top driver was hard enough. Now Makar had to find two. To his credit, he succeeded beyond all expectations.

Makar turned to Jarrett for advice. Who did Dale think would be a worthy replacement? Jarrett suggested Bobby Labonte, Terry's younger brother. Makar had known Labonte, who hails from Corpus Christi, Texas, since Bobby started racing in the Busch series. Labonte was racing for Bill Davis when he was hired by Makar to replace Jarrett.

To find the other driver, Makar and Gibbs decided to look outside the stock car racing circuit.

"We were looking for someone a little different," said Makar. "We wanted to start a second team that would be equal to the existing team, not just a second team that was developed to create funding for the first team. We looked around the country at people who were having success in different series, USAC sprint cars and midgets, the IRL [Indy Racing League], and we came up with Tony Stewart, who had won in those cars and was just starting in IRL and having success. We felt he could make the transition over to the Cup-style cars fairly easily and quickly.

"At the time, he was under contract with Harry Ranier to go Busch racing, but the whole deal was muddled up. They weren't racing very much. We bought out his contract so he could come and sign with us. That went fairly well. There were no big issues. Harry didn't have anything going for him. He had nothing for Tony to do.

"We were very fortunate to come up with two guys like Bobby and Tony."

JIMMY MAKAR AND
JOE GIBBS WITH BOBBY LABONTE
NIGEL KINRADE

With the start of the 2000 season, Jimmy Makar fervently hoped that Bobby Labonte would be as competitive as his departed brother-in-law had been. Quickly, at Daytona, he found out that Labonte could run up front with the best of them. The 18 car was running with the leaders when on lap 134, the car made a pit stop. A tire accidentally rolled onto pit road, and as a penalty, the car had to go to the back of the lead lap. At the end, Labonte and the Interstate Batteries Pontiac finished sixth. Makar felt thrilled, and relieved.

"Before you get started with something," he said, "there is always a question in the back of your mind: Have you made the right decision? Is it going to be OK? Are we going to be competitive? Did we put a good team together? To be able to see the team being competitive early on is a very good thing. It brings a sigh of relief."

At the next race at Rockingham, the 35-year-old Labonte took the lead halfway through the race, crossing the start/finish line first ahead of Dale Earnhardt.

With the Terminator behind his car, Jimmy Makar held his breath until the end.

"Our car was fast on new tires," said Makar. "We seemed to be able to stretch a lead fairly quickly. Earnhardt was much better on a longer run. After our last pit stop, we knew we had to build a lead on new tires so he wouldn't be able to get back to us. As our tires wore down, our lead would go away.

"He didn't have the speed on the front side, but at the end of the race he was coming pretty good even though his tires were wearing down. He was catching us for sure.

"Did we have enough of a lead? Was Earnhardt going to be able to catch us? It made for an exciting race for the fans, a typical Rockingham race."

I asked Makar about what it was like to look out onto the track and see Earnhardt moving up behind his car.

"What can you say about Earnhardt?" he said. "If he's close, you have to worry about him. It was that way throughout his entire career. When I was with the Blue Max team in the 1980s, Earnhardt was the guy you had to beat. As the years went on, you knew if he was in the hunt, you had an interesting and difficult challenge. Earnhardt and Richard Childress were very good at the mental aspects of racing for a championship. Our car was often parked next to him, and Dale was always sitting there talking to us, just mentally letting you know he was there. Nothing big. Just little things. He was really good at playing with your head. It was fortunate I knew how that game was played, so it made it fun and special. It wasn't intimidating to me, because I knew it was coming. I knew how it would be. The fact alone that he had won many, many championships told you that you were racing against the best—period. It made it worthwhile."

Jeff Burton won in Las Vegas. At Atlanta, the race again came down to Labonte and Earnhardt. This time the No. 3 car won—by two feet.

"Any time we go to Atlanta," said Makar, "we felt like we had the car and the driver to beat. The Joe Gibbs team has had good success there. Whenever we don't win at Atlanta, we feel we've missed an opportunity. Some of that is mental, and some is factual. We go in with a mental advantage.

"Dale beat us by two feet. He won because NASCAR gave the Chevrolets an extended kickout on their front valence of a couple of inches. That's the only reason he won. If he hadn't had those two inches, we would have won the race."

"So it was Bill France Jr.'s fault?" I asked.

"Exactly," he said with a chuckle. "You have to blame it on somebody. The race was actually the opposite of Rockingham. We weren't as fast as Dale on brand-new tires. Our car wouldn't go very fast for four or five laps, so we had to hold on until the tires came around. Earnhardt got ahead of us a little bit, and Bobby was closing on him each lap and had a run at him on the last lap. He just came up short."

After a 13th-place finish at Darlington and a 6th-place finish at Bristol,

Labonte again finished in the top five with a 3rd-place at the Texas Motor Speedway. Dale Earnhardt Jr.—Little E, as he was called—surprised everyone by winning his first race.

"I had no idea he was that good," said Makar. "I don't think anybody really did. We thought he'd be OK. He had had limited success in the Busch series. There was no indication he'd be able to come in to Winston Cup and compete on the level he did."

Labonte was 12th at Martinsville. Talladega was next. Jeff Gordon won. Labonte was part of a 16-car wreck and finished 21st.

"We have wrecked so many times in multiple-car pileups in restrictor-plate races at Talladega and Daytona," said Makar. "We had a pretty good car that day. Typically, we hang around the back of the field waiting for the big wreck to happen in order to avoid it, and in that race the big wreck didn't happen until the latter part of the race.

"I remember the wreck came on a restart after a caution. We were in the wrong place at the wrong time. People say, 'You need to be up front all the time to stay ahead of the big wreck.' One time at Daytona, Tony was third or fourth, turned upside down, bounced off fifteen cars, and ended up on top of Bobby's car. Bobby was thirty-third, riding around in the back. So it doesn't matter where you are. When it comes to restrictor-plate racing, you become a victim of circumstances. It's absolutely out of your control. It's the main reason no one likes restrictor-plate racing."

After the Talladega pileup, Jeff Gordon was the points leader, pushing Labonte into second place. I asked Makar whether the goal at that point so early in the season was to win the driving championship.

"It's our goal every year," he said. "You start the year at Daytona with a clean sheet of paper. Going in, you're trying to win the championship. Everything we do is based on that. We can't win races every week, but the big picture to keep in mind is the championship. We built our team such that we feel we're in a position to do that, with a little bit of good fortune."

At Fontana on April 30, Labonte resumed his top-five finishes, coming in second to Jeremy Mayfield, who was driving a car that made Makar suspicious.

"There were questions about Jeremy's car being legal," said Makar. "Hehehehe. I'm thinking he had a fuel issue or a height issue. Our car was very, very good all day long. Only a couple of cars were better than we were. At the end of the race, the 12 car got two tires and we got four, and that's how we got beat. We were much better than Jeremy on the racetrack. We just ran out of time."

A week after Labonte finished 27th at Richmond, on May 12, 2000, the racing world was stunned when 19-year-old Adam Petty, son of Kyle, grandson of Richard, great-grandson of Lee, was killed at the New Hampshire International Speedway during a practice run before a Busch race. Petty had made his Winston Cup debut just six weeks earlier in Texas. His loss was felt by everyone in racing.

"Adam was a great kid," said Jimmy Makar. "He cared about people. He was fun loving. He was a good kid. He epitomized the meaning of 'a good kid.' He wasn't caught up in getting in trouble. He was very mature for a kid his age. He thought a lot about other people. He really had his head on his shoulders straight. He's the kind of kid everybody wants, and that's what made it extra hard when he died. He was in the prime of his life, and you knew he was going to be a good person and do good things throughout his lifetime. When he got cut short, that hurt. It always hurts, but that made it that much harder to understand why those things happen. It really hurt the whole racing community. The Petty family had been around racing all their lives, and this was to be the next generation coming up. It was just a real bad deal. I don't think Kyle will ever get over it."

When the 2000 season resumed, rookie Matt Kenseth won the Coca-Cola 500 at Charlotte, beating out Bobby Labonte. Dale Earnhardt Sr. was third and Little E was fourth. Kenseth, like Dale Jr. and Tony Stewart, was one of a new generation of competitive racers.

"We knew Matt well," said Makar. "When Bobby broke his shoulder in the Busch series and had to get out of the Cup car, Matt was the one we chose to get in our car. It was obvious from working with Matt that he had a lot of talent. At the time we were looking for a second driver for our team, Matt was tied up in a contract. He had a deal with Jack Roush. We talked about him. 'Let's consider Matt?' 'He's tied up with Roush.'

"For us, Charlotte is a lot like Atlanta. We feel we can win races at Charlotte any time. They don't come easy there, but they come easier. We felt we had a good understanding of the track and could win races there. Fact was, we got beat. We weren't quite good enough to beat the 17 car."

"There was a rain delay during that Charlotte race, and when NASCAR officials discovered crew members working on Jeff Gordon's car, he was penalized five laps. The No. 24 car finished the day thirty-fifth as a result of the penalty. I would have thought Jimmy Makar would have been jumping for joy at the dismal finish of a top competitor. I was wrong.

"You hate to gain an advantage because of a penalty or someone's misfortune," he said. "It's more fun to beat people straight up, with you at your best and them at their best. Even though it's a positive thing for you that helps you gain advantage, it doesn't give you a great feeling of satisfaction."

The Dover race was red-letter for the Joe Gibbs Racing team. Tony Stewart won and Bobby Labonte finished third behind Matt Kenseth. I asked Makar whether the Stewart and Labonte teams were competitive with each other, as so many race teams under the same roof are.

"When we set this thing up," said Makar, "we looked at the way other multicar teams worked and didn't work. We incorporated all the things the multicar teams did well, and we looked at negatives of the other teams and tried not to do things that way.

"We decided we wanted to create a situation where everybody would feel part of the same team. One of the biggest things we've seen on most multicar teams was that there was internal competition going on between how many teams there were, and that seemed unhealthy. It seemed to create animosity, division, between the teams. That wasn't our answer to how to make two groups of people work with one vision, with one goal in mind. We tried to create an atmosphere that was such that everybody worked on all the cars. The cars were in one building. All the mechanics would work on the green [Interstate Batteries] car in the morning and the orange [Home Depot] car in the afternoon. The cars sat across the room from each other, but the only division is the actual group of guys who go on the road and work at the racetrack. They have to be dedicated to a particular car. Other than those six or seven guys, everybody else in the shop—the fabricators, the motor guys, the mechanics—everybody works on both cars and shares in the bonus programs of both cars. Even the guys who go on the road share a percentage of the other car's winnings. So everyone benefits from both cars doing well. We all come out of the same shop. We all are on the same team. We all share in each other's triumphs and disappointments.

"My books are open books, and Greg Zipadelli [Tony Stewart's crew chief] is welcome to any information I have. I felt if it started at the top with the two crew chiefs, if we kept an open dialog with an open atmosphere and made sure we were trying to help each other all the time and not act like we were hiding things from each other, that would trickle down through the ranks of the shop. So we keep everything open. Nothing is secretive. If he beats me straight up, that's good. I just need to work a little harder."

In the June and early July races, Bobby Labonte had three top-five finishes and two finishes just under the top ten. At Pocono on July 23, he finished sixth, but he got a boost in his fight for the driving championship when Dale Earnhardt's tire came apart and he finished 23rd. For Makar, it was still too early for him to be concentrating on the championship.

"In this sport, things happen," he said. "They just do. There is no getting around it. It was one of those days when you take your gains and move forward. At this point, the championship is in the back of your mind. Each week you go to the track and try to be the best you can be and try to win a race. All year long, you think about the points, but you don't dwell on them for very long. Even halfway through the season it's way too early to worry about it. You're happy you're still competitive."

On August 5, in the Brickyard 400 at Indianapolis, Bobby Labonte outran

Rusty Wallace to win his second race of the 2000 season. Jimmy Makar knew he had the better car, knew it was just a matter of time before Wallace let Labonte get by him.

"Rusty, who was leading the race, was good," said Makar. After the last pit stop, we were behind him, and I remember talking to Bobby about our car, which was very good all day. I gave Bobby the separation between Rusty and ourselves. He knew we were catching him, and we knew we were catching him, and once we did, I felt it was just a matter for Rusty to slip and for us to get by him. It was neat to know it was late in the race and that we had a better car than the leader, that if we didn't screw up, we probably were going to be able to pass him and win the race. You don't get in that position very often, especially in a race of that magnitude.

"Bobby was in the middle of one and two, and he got on the radio, and he said, 'Uh, uh, wait a minute, got to go.' And that was when Rusty made his slip, and it allowed Bobby to pass him on the backstretch and take the lead. Once we got it, we never looked back.

"Winning at Indy was very special. I have won at Daytona, won at Charlotte, won at Indy, and it's as big as anything we have today. Even though we've only been going there for a few years, it's a very big race, one of the top three on our circuit."

The next week, Labonte finished fifth at Watkins Glen in a race won by Steve Parks. During the race, Tony Stewart and Jeff Gordon collided, and the two began cussing at each other.

"Those guys are a little bit alive," Makar said. "They have a rivalry going. They both came up through open-wheel cars, were stars, so there's a competition there."

At Michigan, in a race in which Labonte finished third, Gordon and Stewart again traded paint. This time Stewart took Gordon into the wall. There was almost a fistfight. I asked Makar if anyone was upset that Stewart had been involved in such an ugly incident.

"That's not what you want to have happen," said Makar, "but it's an emotional sport, and we know at any given moment something can trigger an emotional response like that. It's the nature of the sport, and everybody knows that. It's inevitable for emotions to come out. You just hope you can handle them in such a way that you're not detrimental to your team or sponsor. Anyone who is competitive has that emotion running through him. When you get to this level, there is an exceptional amount of pressure and emotion that goes with the territory. You know it can happen. After it's all said and done, you talk about it and try to figure out a way to keep your emotions in check. But for anyone who's passionate about what they do, it's part of it."

"So Tony wasn't sorry?" I asked.

"Tony doesn't have a lot of regrets," Makar said. "He has some. For the most part, he stands his ground and believes in what he does, and you have to be that way. If you're going to be in this sport, you better believe in yourself and not have a lot of regrets."

Rusty Wallace won the next two races, at Michigan and Bristol. Bobby Labonte finished third and fifteenth. On September 3 at Darlington, Labonte's, and Makar's, dream of a driving championship almost came to a shattering halt.

"It was Labor Day," said Makar. "We were leading in the points when at Darlington in practice during our third or fourth run we hung a throttle, and Bobby went wide open into the outside wall. I thought, 'Oh my gosh, he's hurt, and the season is over right here.'

"I was happy and surprised when he said he was OK. That was the scariest moment of 2000, thinking the season was over.

"We bounced right back, got the backup car off the truck. The 20 bunch helped us with that, and we were back on the racetrack as soon as Bobby got out of the infield care center. I don't think we even ran a lap in the backup car before we went out to qualify.

"Obviously we didn't qualify very well. We started thirty-seventh. Somehow, we came back and won the race. It was rain-shortened, and we won it on a pit stop. We went from the lowest point of the year to one of the highest when we won that race."

After a mediocre finish at Richmond, Labonte padded his lead when he finished second to Jeff Burton in the Dura Lube 300 at Loudon, New Hampshire.

"It was the only time NASCAR had us use restrictor plates away from Daytona or Talladega [in the last 20 years]," said Makar. "Adam Petty had been killed there, and Kenny Irwin, who had been close to Tony, was killed there in July. Kenny and Tony had run quite a bit in open-wheel competition. Everyone was concerned with what the problem was at Louden. Was it the racetrack? Was it the speeds? So NASCAR decided to put a restrictor plate to slow the entry speeds, so we wouldn't have a problem entering the corners. It was a unique race.

"We had a good race car that day, but we couldn't catch Burton. Bobby and Burton were the class of the field. We qualified on the pole that day. Burton was good too. They had gone to Milwaukee to test the week before with the restrictor plate on the car. We had a good car, but we were just a little bit short. Jeff was just a little bit better."

At Dover, Tony Stewart won, and when Bobby Labonte finished fourth, his lead for the championship had grown to a 249-point edge.

"It was getting more and more realistic," said Makar. At some point, you realize the races are counting down, and you have a shot at it. At this point, you're feeling the pressure. You have an idea you're going to be in the hunt, that you can win this thing. People outside the race team are saying, 'It's about over. You really have to screw up to blow it.' But I've been around long enough to know you can blow a 200-

point lead in a heartbeat. You have to keep your focus. You don't want to get caught up in the hoopla, with people trying to promote the fact you about have it clinched, because anything can happen at any time. Yeah, it's a wonderful lead to have, what everybody wants, but anything can happen in this sport. All it takes is one mistake, one problem, a crash, being at the wrong place at the wrong time."

Labonte treaded water with a 10th-place finish at Martinsville, then won the October 8 race at Charlotte. Bobby was running 6th with 25 laps to go, came in and took on four new tires, then went out and beat Jeremy Mayfield for the win, his third of the season.

"That was a huge one," said Makar. "Charlotte was always touchy at the end of the race whether to get two tires and keep track position or get four tires. We've won and lost races there both ways. We decided that four tires was the way to go. We gave up a little track position, but we made the right call. That's what makes it so much fun to do what we do. Whether your strategy works depends on what the other guy does. It's not just you. It has to fit into what everyone else does at the same time.

"As I said, we've won on two, lost on two. This time we were fortunate the four tires were the right way to go, and we were able to beat him."

At Talladega, Dale Earnhardt Sr. won when Dale Earnhardt Jr. blocked the rest of the pack behind him. Labonte finished 12th.

"Unfair?" said Makar chuckling. "Maybe. It's part of the way we have to race because of the restrictor plates. That seems to be the thing to do. If you look at the 8 and the 15, Dale Jr. and Michael [Waltrip] do it all the time. Dale Sr. lost his life doing it for Dale Jr. and Michael at Daytona the following year. It's part of the way things work, right, wrong, or indifferent. When you go into a race, there are team-mates, and you know there is a chance you're going to get ganged up on. It's one reason to have a teammate of your own."

After Rockingham, where Labonte finished 20th, Bobby had a 218-point lead. The pressure was on for the race team of the No. 18 car.

"For me," said Jimmy Makar, "the saving grace was that I had been in this posi-tion several times before. I knew what to expect, knew how to handle it much better than I would have had I not been in the situation before. I was able to convey some of that to the guys on the team."

"What do you tell them?" I asked.

"Anything and everything," he said. "Basically, to stay focused. The hardest thing is to listen to the outside information and the talk that goes on. It's so easy to let your guard down, and you can't do that. You have to stay focused, and the thing you have to do is keep doing the things you've done. You're at the end of the season, but you don't change anything. You've gotten there with a certain method and for-mula. The worst thing you can do is start doing things differently, just because you're leading the points and you have a chance to win it. That's a recipe for disaster I've seen people do in the past. They change with a couple of races to go. All through the year you say, 'The points will be what the points will be. If we go out and race to win each weekend, and we do our job, and we finish the best we can be, the points will be there.' That's what we focused on. This was no time to change.

"It's easier said than done. You have to rally your guys not to focus on the championship, but to stay focused on the race that weekend and try to be competitive."

After finishing fifth at Phoenix, Labonte needed only to finish fifth or better at Homestead to win the championship.

"Our strategy was to win the race," said Makar. "Late in the race, we were running third or fourth and had a shot to win. Tony was the guy we had to beat. We were racing hard for position, and Joe [Gibbs] came up to me during the race, and he had this look of fear in his eyes. In a panic, he said, 'We don't have to run that good. We can drop back and run fifth.'

"I said, 'Joe, we didn't come here to run fifth. We came here to win the race. We're going to try to win the race.'

"It absolutely bewildered him why we were racing as hard as we were when we were in position to win the championship just by finishing fifth.'

"It's the football coach calling running plays at the end of the game to eat up the clock," I said.

"Exactly," said Makar.

"What did Joe say?" I asked.

"What could he say?" said Makar. "He may not have liked it, but it was the attitude we took every week, and like I said, you can't change your attitude or your method of racing just because you're going for a championship. We were going to Homestead to win the race. We were not going to be happy to finish fifth."

Tony Stewart ended up winning the race, but teammate Bobby Labonte finished fourth that day, winning the 2000 racing championship for himself, Jimmy Makar, and Joe Gibbs, the first for the former winner of two Super Bowls.

"Obviously, we all felt jubilation," said Makar, "but also it took an unbelievable amount of pressure off me. The championship race was over, and I could finally let my guard down and relax. To me, it was the cumulation of nine years, when Joe and I first put this race team together. It was one of the few goals we had set that needed to be met. We wanted to be successful as a business, to win races on a competitive basis, and finally, to win the championship. This was the culmination of all those years of hard work. It was neat for us to have met all three goals that we had set out.

"It was very emotional and very rewarding. Even though I had been involved in winning a championship before, this time I was able to soak it in and watch the emotions on everyone's faces, see the way the guys handled it, the way Joe handled it. It was easier to remember. When I was part of the '89 championship, it was hard to enjoy. It was more of a relief that it was over. This time, it was fun to watch the camaraderie of our two teams, with one team winning the race and the other team winning the championship on the same day. You don't get a day like that very often. It was really unique and special to do that."

One amazing statistic stands out. In 2000, Bobby Labonte completed all but nine of the 10,167 laps that were run. It is a record that may never be broken.

"That lone statistic will forever stick in my mind as an accomplishment," said Makar. "I don't know that anyone will beat it. I am probably more proud of that accomplishment than anything, because it takes in everything: your driver, your engines, your durability, your competitiveness, week in and week out at all different racetracks. In a word, I'm very, very proud of that statistic."

When the diminutive Bobby Labonte went to hoist the huge, cumbersome driving championship trophy over his head, he tottered and almost fell over. It may have been his only slip in a season marked by consistency and excellence.

"His emotions and adrenaline were running," said Makar. "Things are happening, and when he got ready to pick the trophy up, he found himself a little off-balance and almost dropped it to the ground. It was a little awkward but fun to watch. Wouldn't that have been something dropping the trophy during the celebration! Maybe embarrassing or awkward for him, but it made for a great conversation sidebar."

CHAPTER 55

GETTING IN DEEP

Robin Pemberton

IN 1991, THE SABCO TEAM, WITH KYLE PETTY BEHIND THE WHEEL, FINISHED 31ST in the points standings. Sabco owner Felix Sabates figured the team needed a new leader. The man he chose was Robin Pemberton.

"When I started at Sabco for the 1992 season," said Pemberton, "nobody knew about any of us on the team. Nobody gave a shit about Kyle. Nobody knew who I was, nor did they know any of the guys who worked on the car. But we got along, and we all pulled together, all pulled in the same direction, and that's what made it work. The guys on the pit crew would practice every afternoon and have fun doing it. I was changing tires. I looked forward to doing it. We worked on our cars hard. It showed on the racetrack. We finished the year fifth in the points [only 123 points behind Alan Kulwicki].

"The points were a major accomplishment. The other thing that stood out was in '93 taking on the pole for the Daytona 500. Sitting on the pole for a restrictor-plate race is a team effort because that means the fabricators, the chassis guys, the engine guys, and the driver did a good job—everybody's done their job.

"That was good. And at Rockingham, which is five hundred miles and four hundred and ninety-two laps, we led four hundred and eighty-four laps. We kicked their ass so bad that day it was embarrassing. Man, we just had it going on.

"Then in '93, Alan Kulwicki was killed in a plane crash. Alan was very close to Kyle and Felix. Alan was always at our shop. We all got along great

379

together. We'd go to dinner together. Alan would go with Felix; Kyle; me; our engine builder, John Wilson. Alan was just like a team member, a good friend, and when Alan got killed, we all thought about different things. Everybody's personalities changed, and by the start of the third year we started fighting and feuding and bitching and moaning.

"It was over the usual things: The motors didn't run. The chassis weren't good. Not that any of this was true. But for some reason everything just started falling apart. As a group we said some things we shouldn't have said. We did things we shouldn't have done, and it didn't turn out the way it should have. By that third year, Felix needed to make a change, and I was the guy he had to change out.

"We went to the Coke 600 [in Charlotte] in May of 1993, and we blew a motor up. It was a holiday. We were supposed to be off, and I was in there working with only two or three other guys. We were getting some stuff caught up. Felix asked me to come in the office. He told me he had to make a change.

"I didn't argue it. A lot of stuff was going on. I was stressed out. That was fine. The sad part about it was my brothers Ryan and Roman both went to work for me at Sabco, and he fired those two guys too. He fired three Pembertons in one day. It was like, Man, this sucks.

"Looking back on it, with clearer heads the outcome would have been different."

Under Pemberton, Kyle Petty won three races and finished fifth in the championship points race in both 1992 and 1993, the team's highest finishes ever. But Pemberton and owner Felix Sabates were not getting along. Sabates blamed Pemberton for a "country-club atmosphere" on the race team, and even a plea from Kyle Petty to keep Pemberton wasn't enough to save his job.

"Felix thought we should have been doing better," said Pemberton. "We were ninth or tenth in the points, and I get fired? Like I said, things just weren't going right.

"I went home and told my wife. She was pretty upset, until she realized that I was pretty relieved over it. I spent the next eight weeks or so trying to scare up some stuff, and I really had some good things going. Don Prudhomme, the drag racer, was thinking about going stock car racing. I went and talked to him. He was at Michigan doing an autograph session during the first Michigan race up there.

"Ward Burton was driving a car out of Virginia. I talked to him. I just had a lot of things going on, but nothing solid, when I got a call from Jack Roush. He asked me, 'Do you want to come over here and work on Ted Musgrave's car?' I went and talked to him, and we came to an agreement. Steve Hmiel was still there.

"I was the crew chief, but I really didn't go there to be *over* anyone. They had already done so much. I went to be *with* the guys. I didn't want to take credit for anything they did. They had it going. They just needed a different twist.

"The first race with those guys was Loudon in '94. We led laps, could have won the race, finished in the top five. It was fine.

"We wound up sitting on the pole at Martinsville, sat on the pole at Richmond. We were doing OK. Ted and I were getting along fine. We just didn't jell. We never had confrontations. We just didn't see eye to eye. If I said, 'Left,' he'd say, 'Right.' If I said, 'Up,' he said, 'Down.' And it wasn't in a bad way. The chemistry just wasn't there. And the thing was, we needed to be one way or the other or else we weren't going to get anywhere.

"It got confusing. If he was thinking we needed to be working on the rear springs to make the car handle, I was thinking it should be the front springs. We were always at opposite ends. And it wasn't his fault, and it wasn't my fault. It was, Man, we were just two totally opposite people.

"In all the years, that had never happened to me before. I thought it was bizarre. And Teddy was getting frustrated, and I was getting frustrated.

"The best thing that came from my going there was that we were able to improve our pit crews. At Sabco, we had a very good pit crew, and when Jack hired me, Mark's crew was really struggling and so was Ted's. Jack said to me, 'I don't care what you do, but make both the pit crews better, no matter what.' So I mainly worked on the pit crews, and we did make everyone better, but they could have done it on their own. I just happened to be there at the correct time. We worked hard and tried things we hadn't been trying, practiced more than we ever practiced. I don't want anyone to read this and think I'm taking credit for *anything*. I really don't. But we did work hard, harder than they ever did before. We practiced pit stops every day for an hour, more than any team I've ever been with. But we fixed it. Everyone got better because of it. We videotaped our asses off. We went over a lot of stuff and fixed a lot of things. And that was good.

"But Ted and I were just at opposite ends. No bad thing. But I thought, 'This is just crazy.'

"I had only been there a couple of months, and I was feeling kind of frustrated. During that time, Buddy Parrott was quitting Penske. That had potential. I knew Rusty Wallace from Pontiac stuff. We never worked together. He was a driving fool, that's for sure.

"I had met Penske at the track. I had been introduced to Don Miller years before, so we'd been friends at the track and had dinner and bought each other beers in bars for years.

"At the time Buddy was leaving Penske, one afternoon I was driving home from Roush's. Back in '87, I was driving a hundred miles each way, living in Charlotte and commuting to Greensboro. And then after I moved to Greensboro, I took the job at Sabco, and for six months I was commuting the same hundred miles in the other direction, until I sold the house and moved to Charlotte.

"But when I went back to work for Jack in '95, he was still in Liberty, and I was living in Charlotte, and once again I had to drive a hundred friggin' miles to work each day! You talk about timing being everything! I was constantly skipping a gear somewhere.

"I would leave my house at five-thirty in the morning, and I would ride my Harley up to Liberty, and it was just boring as hell. I'd lock the throttle down, and I'd see how many miles I could ride no hands. I'd go sixty miles. I thought, 'You're going to fall asleep and kill yourself.' I had spent more hours on the road than some of the drivers had in the races.

"I was on my way back home from Liberty one afternoon, and the phone rang, and it was the girl from the shop. She said, 'Would you hold for Don Miller?'

"'Sure.'

"'Hey man, what are you doing?'

"'Nothing. Coming back from work. What are you doing?'

"'I want to know if you'd be interested in coming to work over here.'

"I was on my second hundred miles of the day. I was a little bit blistered. We shot the breeze, and I actually took less money to go and work for Penske. It was a good opportunity. The organization was something I thought I'd like. They had a good driver in Rusty, a good sponsor in Miller. It looked stable. It looked like they spent any kind of money they needed on their cars. And that is *very* important. If you're a hot rodder or a racer, the big thing is if they let you spend money on your car.

"You kind of watch. If you look around enough, you know if they spend money on their cars. That's the key. If they don't let you build new cars, don't let you test or go to the wind tunnel, you're in trouble. You can skimp on other stuff, but not that.

"When I worked for Petty Enterprises, they never asked a question about spending money on their cars. You could have been a million dollars over budget, and if it was on the cars, they'd go find the money somewhere. Somehow they would find it, even in the days when they didn't have enough money to do it.

"And after you come from situations like that, you see it's the better way to do things. I thought the Penske name would do something, and I just knew I wasn't going to be able to continue the commute to the Roush shop. If I stayed there, I would have to pack up and move back to Greensboro. And I wasn't going to do that. My wife had settled in and gotten a job in Charlotte, and I was living on Lake Norman, and it was hard to leave that.

"Penske was in Charlotte, nine minutes from my home. The shop is on Exit 36, and my house is off Exit 28. Don't you just hate that?

"When I took the job at Penske, everyone in the world told me I was the dumbest SOB on the face of the earth to work there. They said, 'Rusty will kill you, or you will kill him.' We were two opposites. We wouldn't get along. On and on and on. Plus, they had just come off an eight-win season under Buddy Parrott. 'Don't do it,' they said.

"I had been wrong so many times I figured eventually I was going to hit it right. I just kept thinking, 'You've been at places where you had five drivers in one year, a place where the driver didn't drive, a place where the driver drove but the motor sucked.' Man, I just felt this could be a good thing. Even though

ROBIN PEMBERTON
Daytona 1999.
NIGEL KINRADE

it was for less money, I felt I just gotta do it. I can do this and do better and make it work.

"I reported to the Penske team. My reputation was for doing well on super-speedways. I have had some success with people I surrounded myself with or was surrounded by—we did well. With Kyle we sat on the pole at Daytona and had run good at a lot of superspeedway races. Rusty's reputation was they were terrible on superspeedways—either he couldn't drive or the engines were bad or the cars were bad. The main goal was to try and fix that.

"During the first part of my first year [in 1995], my goal was to figure out how they won eight races in a year. I was sitting back and observing more than getting involved. After six months, we had won one race.

"Todd Parrott said, 'They don't know how they won them. They won them out of gas, on flat tires, or after a caution came out.' They were a good race team, but circumstances helped them win some of the races.

"Rusty was getting a little tense. It was, 'Come on, guy. Get involved here.' But it took me a while—over a year—to get in the loop, to get involved with the guys and get a hold on it. I was still trying to figure it out. Because you want to make it better. You don't want to make it worse.

"Meanwhile, good things were happening to other teams. Jeff Gordon was coming on, and Earnhardt was strong. We were taking it that first year in '95. [Wallace won two races, finished second four times, third six times, and fourth twice. He was fifth in the points standings. The year before he had been third.]

"Then in 1996 I got my hooks into it, tried to fix the Daytona problem, and we got better. We won five races that year, and I really fit in there. I'm real happy with the way it goes. We have a good race team, a good sponsor, and a lot of good things are going on.

"Rusty and I have won all kinds of different races, road courses and super-speedways. In 2000, we sat on the most poles [nine], even though Rusty didn't have a reputation for qualifying good. In 2001, we led more laps than the second- and third-place cars in the points combined. We had a really good year.

"In 2001, we were wrecked out of two races we would have been easy top-five cars. We've had a little of everything. We finished sixth in the points only because we had some DNFs."

Everything was going along fine for Robin Pemberton until the Penske team decided to add a second team. Jeremy Mayfield was chosen as the driver. Pemberton wanted to get to work immediately on staffing the team, in part to make sure that the effort wouldn't be detrimental to the Rusty Wallace team.

"I wanted to get started early," said Pemberton. "I wanted to hire some people to get them into the fold of the Penske operation. I knew we'd have some turnover, knew I'd have to weed out the people you made a mistake on, and if we got started in August, the transition would be a lot easier. And they wanted to wait. In addition, for me personally, we had done an enormous amount of testing, thirteen track tests and twenty wind tunnel dates, plus the racing, and if you add to that my having to worry about getting [a second] team ready, I was overcome. I got to thinking, 'Maybe this is pushing me to do something different.'

"At that time, a couple of people had come to me to talk about helping them with their multicar teams. I wouldn't have to be the crew chief. I could help bring younger crew chiefs along. One of those was Petty Enterprises. Petty had three cars. Their drivers were Kyle, John Andretti, and Buckshot Jones."

When Robin Pemberton was hired by Petty Enterprises in fall 2001, his job was to take an outdated organization that had won exactly three races in seventeen years and transform it into a winner. Though he knew Richard Petty had a reputation for squeezing a nickel until the buffalo screamed, he took the job because he had started his Winston Cup career working for the Pettys, and his emotional attachment to the Pettys was strong,

"Also Kyle and I had talked a number of years before when Adam was still with us, and I really liked that kid a lot. I was there when he was just a baby, and it was interesting to watch him start his career. So there was more emotion to the decision rather than a clear head as far as a business decision."

One reason the Pettys needed Pemberton was that Kyle Petty not only had to drive a car, but he was overseeing the everyday business of the race team.

"I assume you were going to take over some of that," I said to Pemberton.

"Yeah," he said, "I assumed the same thing, and did to a degree. I tried to relieve him of the day-to-day, head-to-head confrontations with people, places, building cars, testing.

"I figured Kyle would always be the owner, so you're not going to argue that part. I figured he'd drive for a couple more years, and you're not going to argue that part. If I could just get things organized from the mechanical standpoint and bring in some engineering that I knew was the wave of the future—technology I had seen when I was with Penske—I thought that would help make Petty Enterprises competitive again.

"I hired Branton Thomas, who was my track engineer at Penske. He was a young guy, a really hands-on guy who helped us with Rusty's car. I put a lot of faith in him.

"Through the middle of the summer and early fall of 2002, I worked on organizing a satellite engineer department at the engine facility at Mooresville. We were putting up facilities for shock technicians and equipment. We were going to hire several engineers and were getting going on the simulation work, which would help the picking and choosing of whatever would help the car handle better. And that seemed to be going pretty good. I had people I was hiring who I was confident working with, and I was going to pick them and move this thing forward."

"It didn't work out," I said.

"It did not work out," said Pemberton.

"What happened?" I asked.

"Kyle didn't want to let go," he said. "Kyle and whoever his confidantes were at the time didn't think this was the road to take. On December 17, 2002, Kyle brought me into his office. We were talking about a bunch of stuff, and finally he said, 'Hey look, we're not going to do this engineering thing. We don't believe it's the way to go. It's a lot of money to spend, and we don't think it's where we need to apply the resources."

"I said, 'You're kidding?'"

"He said, 'No.'

"I said, 'These people I've hired, one of them has already left his job.' I was going for the cream of the crop, and I had hired Nelson Cosgrove, who had been my head engineer at Penske Racing. He had taken leave, and he and his wife were on the way to Buffalo, where they had family, and there was no turning back. And another Penske engineer, who I'm not going to name, he was going to turn in his notice that day. I called him on the phone and said, 'Dude, the shit has hit the fan. Don't do a thing. Go be a happy employee right now.' And these guys were two of my best friends.

"Kyle said, 'If these guys are as smart as you say they are, they won't be out of work long.'

"I said, 'Kyle, you can't treat people like that. And if we aren't doing it this way, what are we doing? What's the deal?'

"He said, 'Maybe we need to rethink that.'

"I said, 'If that's the case, I'm wasting my time. Consider it rethought.' I said, 'When your name is on the door, it's your place. I'm mad. I'm upset at myself. I let my guard down. I did something emotional by coming here, and it's probably going to set me back five or six years.' Because it was December, and I had had a couple of incredible job offers during the year that I had turned down because I had a ten-year agreement with these guys. Ten years!

"I quit right there. I was pretty pissed, and I was hurt. I didn't have to leave my old position. But I was more hurt for the people who had uprooted their lives and their children to take a job.

"I was done, but we didn't tell anybody," he said. "I was in the midst of refinancing my house. I needed to pull that off, because of the interest rates. If I announced I quit, I'd have had to pull away from my new home of four years."

When Pemberton quit at Petty Enterprises, he knew he had options. He had been approached by both Ford and Dodge to run their race programs.

"Mike Eye, who builds engines for Kyle, knew I had quit. He's got a friend who has another friend in Ford. The word was out, but everyone knew to keep it quiet for a lot of reasons. For years, from my days at Penske in the '80s, I had had a relationship with Dan Davis and Greg Speck of Ford. They called and said, 'Before you do anything, talk to us.'

"In January, the guys from Dodge called, and they wanted me to do the same thing. The Dodge people are really good people. I think the world of them, like I do the Ford people. But the Pettys ran a Dodge, and I thought it would be awkward being *the* guy at Chrysler and Dodge who had to work with the Pettys. I would be open to criticism, and I didn't want to put myself in that position. If not for that, I might have taken the Dodge job, but I felt really good about the Ford people, and I took that job."

"What are your responsibilities?" I asked.

"They call it the Field Manager for Ford Racing," said Pemberton. It's a broad title, but I'm down here on Lake Norman, and I'm close to all the Ford race teams, truck, Busch, and Cup, so I'm the liaison between the factory guys and the teams.

"During the week I have my route to run, spend a day with Roush Racing, because they have five teams. I talk to their crew chiefs, hear their gripes, see if there is anything we can be doing at the factory to make things better, see if we can make better pieces. I do the same thing with Robert Yates and his group. I make the rounds of the other Ford teams, and then every Thursday through Sunday I'm on my normal schedule going to the racetrack."

I asked Pemberton about the rumor that Dale Jarrett wanted him to replace Todd Parrott as crew chief at Yates.

Pemberton chuckled to indicate that the offer had at least been bandied about.

"Yeah, that was the rumor, wasn't it?" he said. "We discussed it a little bit, but I'm obligated to Ford, and I have to respect this or I'm no better than the people who I really despise, people who don't honor their contracts.

"I'm going to do this at least for another two years. I can get in as deep as I want with the race teams just like if I was the crew chief, and the nice part about it, I don't have to worry about two or four tires on Sunday.

"The sport is going through this tremendous transition, with new rules, extra teams, and added races, and I'm trying to stand back and get a good grip on it and make sure my next move is the best move for my family and myself. The next move might be to stay here. Or I might help run one of the bigger race teams."

I said to Pemberton, "I noticed that after you left Rusty, he hasn't won a race."

"I just hate that," he said. "I think that's a shame. I really do. Rusty is still one of my very best friends. You get in one of those slumps. . . . I'd like to say it has nothing to do with me leaving. I hope next year he gets on a run and wins four races in a row. I don't think any driver deserves to go through that after being such an icon in the sport."

"But there seem to be quite a few of the veteran drivers going through this," I said. "Mark Martin, Ricky Rudd, quite a few. At a certain point, there's a turnover. New guys come in, the old guys retire."

"In a flash," said Pemberton. "When you're on top of the game, you think it's going to last forever. It's just unbelievable. All of a sudden it just happens."

CHAPTER 56

EARNHARDT'S DEATH CASTS A PALL

Jimmy Makar

THE YEAR 2001 STARTED WITH AN INCREDIBLY EXCITING RACE IN THE DAYTONA 500. Michael Waltrip, with blocking help by Dale Earnhardt, crossed the finish line first. On TV, announcer Darrell Waltrip was shedding tears of joy for his baby brother when, without warning, Earnhardt's black Chevrolet turned up the track and smashed head-on into the wall. The impact killed the great champion instantly, sending the racing world into a long period of mourning. When Jimmy Makar, crew chief for defending champion Bobby Labonte, learned of the Earnhardt tragedy, his immediate reaction was anger.

"I remember being in the middle of a pretty heated conversation," he said. "The racers were arguing with NASCAR officials about the restrictor plate issue. We told them how dangerous it is and how much we don't like it, that we needed to change it, that we needed to do something to separate out the packs, that we didn't need to be riding around in a bumblebee nest of cars waiting for a big wreck to happen. It was an ongoing discussion, and this day was no different.

"Before the race was over, we were in a big wreck. We got wrecked and taken out, so we weren't there at the end.

"We were at the airport when Zippy [Greg Zipadelli] called me. He had just heard at the track that Dale had died. I remember being angry about the whole thing. I remember it absolutely devastated me.

"Everybody has Dale Earnhardt stories. When I came South to go racing, I went to work for Robert Gee. Dale was married to Robert's daughter. Dale was struggling in the Late Model series, now the Busch series, with no money, just trying to make it. Dale would hang out in the shop. We'd spend evenings in the garage. My fondest remembrances are of Dale before he became a star. He was fun to be around. He was the guy who played the mental game with you when you were racing for the championship. For him to be the guy killed in that situation after we had been complaining about the way we had to race, that really angered me. I was a pretty angry guy, and personally I do think it took a lot out of my 2001 series. After Dale died, it didn't really matter anymore. It didn't matter. It was that devastating.

"I can't speak for Bobby, but watching him and the way he was after that, I could see that it took a huge toll on him, took a lot of drive out of him, made it very difficult to go back and race every week. It was the year we wanted to come out and defend our championship, but Dale's death took a lot of wind out of my sail and out of Bobby's and out of our team in general."

After six weeks, the No. 18 Interstate Batteries car was a distant 19th in the 2001 Winston Cup points standings.

"We had a lot of things going on where racing took a back seat. There were a lot of conversations going on, a lot of arguing and bickering. Racing was not at the forefront, and if you do not have that in front of your mind, you're not going to win.

"In addition, a major problem that year was that Goodyear had changed its tire to a new design, one that a lot of drivers hated and had a hard time getting comfortable with. Bobby spun out four or five times. We really struggled trying to get our driver comfortable on those tires. It was all the difference in the world. We had to race on those tires. So we had our emotional difficulties and tires we were struggling with."

At the California Speedway, a track where Labonte should have done well, he finished the day 22nd. It was typical.

"California, Atlanta, Charlotte, Michigan—these were tracks where we usually were at our best. All of a sudden, they became the places where we struggled the most. We had a lot of things going against us at the time."

On July 30, Labonte and the team managed to solve their tire problem, as Labonte won his first race of the year at Pocono.

"It was a long time coming," said Makar. "We finally felt we could come out of the box and win races. We got a little bit competitive again. That felt very good and took a lot of pressure off everybody."

I asked Makar how difficult it was to repeat as champion.

"It goes beyond description, because there are so many things that come with winning the championship that take your focus off the business at hand. The driver and team has to make so many personal appearances. That takes time and energy from the primary focus. That makes it much more difficult."

"You can appreciate how hard it was for Richard Petty and Dale Earnhardt to win seven championships," I said.

"Yeah," he said. "Not a lot of people can fully appreciate the magnitude of what that means and how hard that really is to do. Only a few people can do that. Most will never be able to comprehend that."

In October 2001, Jeff Burton invited Bobby Labonte and Jimmy Makar to come to New York City to visit the firemen and policemen who survived the World Trade Center disaster of September 11. Makar recalled the experience.

"We went to let the firemen and policemen know we were behind them, that the world was watching and praying for them. It was more of a pick-me-up for them than anything. We did what we could do to let them know they weren't alone.

"We visited eight fire stations, signing autographs. When we got with those folks, they took us around. We sat and listened to how many men and women were lost in each department. The personal stories were incredibly tough to hear. They were back at work, moving forward from day to day.

"Whenever we got to a station, we would be asked if we wanted to visit Ground Zero. Each time we said, 'We don't need to do that. We're here to support the guys.' All of them said the same thing, 'You ought to go.'

"After our final visit, the commanders asked us if we wanted to go, and at the last minute before going home we decided to go down there. I'm really glad we did, because it put the cap on the big picture of what really happened there. I'll never forget walking down a little side street. Everything was pretty normal, except for the dust and dirt from the debris. I turned the corner to where I could see Ground Zero, and it was surreal. There was this massive pile of twisted metal and smoke and buildings ripped wide open and parts of other buildings stuck in them, and firemen hosing everything down, and massive cranes trying to lift the debris, which was six or seven stories high.

"I grew up as a kid in New Jersey. I could see the World Trade Center from my town. The destruction was unbelievable. I cannot describe in words the smells I smelled. There was a distinct smell of sulfuric acid that hit me when I turned the corner.

"The guys in the companies were right. You had to go see this thing, and we were fortunate to be with some high-ranking officials who allowed us to get onto the rubble field. We walked up to where building five was, and while we were standing there the last company we had just left arrived for duty. They saw us, and they took us even deeper to where you could look underground. 'This is the stairwell where six people were found. . . .' We got to see the holes where people crawled to survive. We walked up the steps to where the big ball was. There was a Dunkin' Donuts store, and time had stood still: The donuts were still on the conveyor belt. It was very surreal. Guys were walking around with guns protecting the area. I told my wife, 'It was the most incredible thing I've ever seen in my life.'

"When we went back in December for the NASCAR banquet, we drove down, and it was quite a bit different. One of the policemen let us go to the viewing area for families, and the debris field was now a hole in the ground.

"It put things in perspective. To go from Earnhardt dying to the World Trade Center disaster, it didn't take away from the championship, but it sure put things in perspective for me. What's really important? What's *not* really important? That's what I took from the experience."

The No. 18 team recovered from its disastrous first half to finish sixth in the points race in 2001.

"For as horrible as the year started out, when nothing went right and it seemed things were spiraling downward, after we won at Pocono and did so well the second half, the disappointment was that had we done that well all year long, we'd have been in the hunt again. But it felt good to rally. We felt we were on the road to recovery."

The feeling didn't last very long, it turned out. To complicate matters, for the 2002 season Joe Gibbs and Jimmy Makar decided to switch from Pontiac to Chevrolet. It was a political decision, one they felt was necessary if they wanted to remain competitive.

"We were at a disadvantage with the Pontiac body style," said Makar. "We were in a minority of cars that didn't have a political voice with NASCAR. We felt we had to struggle to stay competitive because when you're a lone voice, even if you're right, it's hard to convince people. If you have half a dozen people with the same problem, you tend to get listened to a bit more. It was a struggle to get NASCAR to understand that the Pontiacs had a problem. It was a constant battle and struggle to keep the playing field level for us. So Joe and I decided we would be better off in a larger group, and we became aligned with Chevrolet. Remember, we had started with Chevrolet in '91, and we had been asked to switch to Pontiac in '97. We were just getting back to the Chevrolet side of things. It was still GM, just a different part of it. As a Pontiac, we were a bigger fish in a smaller pond, and that worked for quite some time. Things change. We were now better off as a smaller fish in a bigger pond."

Bobby Labonte managed to win a race at Martinsville in 2002, but there was constant grumbling on the team about setups and the need to make changes. Once a driver has won a championship, it's very hard for him to accept a lower status. There was discord between Bobby Labonte and Jimmy Makar. The discord grew.

"We started optimistically in 2002," said Makar, "but our ending in 2001 didn't continue in 2002. We started fumbling and struggling, and that was too much for everyone to take, and it started spiraling itself down way faster than it should have. The tolerance levels went away very fast. A lot of doubt started creeping in as far as what the problem really was. Why couldn't we be as successful as we had been in the past? There were a lot of questions."

Joe Gibbs and Jimmy Makar were faced with a tough decision. The chemistry obviously needed to be changed. Should they let Bobby Labonte go? Should Jimmy Makar quit as the crew chief?

"We do most things around here as a group," said Makar. "Joe and I had many conversations over the problem and how to fix it. Bobby was struggling. He was wondering whether it was him. Was he missing the boat on something? We decided that the best thing was for one of the two of us to do something, either him leave or me step away."

On October 1, 2002, Makar announced that he was stepping down as crew chief but would remain as Joe Gibbs' team manager. Said Makar, "The sport has changed so drastically over the last few years." Indeed it had. When Makar began the Joe Gibbs race team in 1991, he had a total of 17 employees. By 2002, the number of employees had grown to around 250.

I asked Makar what the thinking was behind his decision to step down as crew chief.

"I was wearing two hats at the shop," he said. "I always have. One being the crew chief of the 18 car. The other being the director of racing, overseeing the whole shop. In my mind, I began to wonder whether I was doing the crew chief's job well enough that we could compete. I looked across the hall at Greg, and he had one focus, and one focus only, and that was to make the 20 car work. He didn't have to worry about anything else. I wondered whether the time had come to choose one or the other.

"Something else was in the back of my mind: I had set a time frame for my leaving as crew chief. I wanted to spend more time with my family and see my kids growing up. It was going to be 2004. Bobby and I had talked about it. That was the date I had set. So the fact we were struggling and that I had made those plans suggested that the best thing to do was move the schedule forward a little quicker. I decided to bring in someone who could concentrate on the 18 car while I could focus one hundred percent on being the team manager and keeping the big picture going, and maybe we could do better that way."

I asked Makar how the move has worked out for him.

"I am thoroughly happy," he said. "I am having a lot of fun. I enjoy the new challenge. I get a chance to go out and learn things to help the race teams, and I feel I'm growing with my knowledge and how I can contribute."

I asked him if he got to spend more time with his family.

"Yeah, but not as much as I need to," he said. "I'll have twenty-eight more days off than last year. In the real world, that's not a lot, but in racing it is.

This weekend, my son, Dillon, and I got up Saturday morning and drove to the mountains and fly-fished all day. Those are the things that make it worthwhile. I remember Dale Inman telling me when he got out of the business that he didn't think anyone would make it as long as he had, just because of the pressures of the sport. He thought people's careers would get shorter and shorter, and he was right."

I mentioned that Larry McReynolds, Robin Pemberton, and he were no longer crew chiefs. He chuckled.

"Yeah," he said. "There is a big transition going on right now. The guys who have been in it quite some time are moving up into positions that are created by the sheer size of race teams. In Larry's and Robin's cases, it was a total career change. For many years, people thought crew chief was the end of the line, where you'd end up, but the sport has changed in such a way that it's no longer the end of the ladder. The size and technological advances have created positions above that."

CHAPTER 57

A LEAP INTO THE FUTURE

Larry McReynolds

LESS THAN TWO YEARS AFTER LARRY MCREYNOLDS WAS HIRED BY PETTY Enterprises in 2000 to be a consultant on Buckshot Jones' race team, Jones and the Pettys parted company. Since McReynolds was working for Jones, and Jones no longer had a steady ride, there was little for McReynolds to do. They too went their separate ways.

As it turned out, the timing was right for McReynolds. Around this time the Fox Network, where McReynolds worked full time as a broadcaster, bought the Speed Channel. The cable network began devoting more airtime to Winston Cup qualifying and "happy hour," and it created the Trackside show Friday nights. McReynolds was busier than ever covering NASCAR on TV. But even after he had become a full-time broadcaster he kept getting offers—more than 80—to run race teams.

"Ever since I stepped off the pit box at the end of the 2000 season," said McReynolds, "I've been approached by a lot of people to do a lot of things. 'Come be a part of this.' 'Come fix this.' 'Come be part-owner of this.' 'Come put this together.'

"All these people who had approached me, I just had a feeling they were hunting someone with a magic wand in their back pocket to come wave that wand over their struggling or barely surviving race team, and everything would be great and wonderful. Even though I've won twenty-three Winston

Cup races, I've also lost four-hundred-and-forty-something. So obviously I don't have a magic wand in my back pocket.

"And I never had a warm, fuzzy feeling about any of these deals."

In May 2003, McReynolds got word that a businessman by the name of Alex Meshkin wanted to speak to him about putting together a race team. McReynolds blew him off, like he had done to callers many times before. But Meshkin refused to take no for an answer, and he worked McReynolds into taking a meeting.

"I finally agreed to meet with him," said McReynolds, "and we met at the end of late May [2003], and when I first met him, I wondered, How old are you? He looked like he was still in high school."

McReynolds had reason to wonder. The kid was 23 years old. Most kids that age have barely gotten their ears wet in their chosen careers. But what McReynolds didn't know was that Alex Meshkin was one of the new breed of wunderkind dot.com millionaires—more precisely, multi-millionaires. When he was at Glenelg High School in Columbia, South Carolina, Meshkin took his college fund money, which his parents kept in stocks, and started wheeling and dealing in stocks on the Internet. The initial fund was enough to cover four years of college. Meshkin reportedly increased his holdings 25 fold.

When Alex and his brother teamed up to start an Internet company, Brian said of his baby brother, "[He] is the brain and the mouth."

Indeed, once the cherubic Alex Meshkin was able to get the wizened Larry McReynolds to sit still long enough and listen to his sales pitch, McReynolds was as good as his.

"This wasn't a deal where everything had been handed to him," said McReynolds. "He had accomplished it himself buying and selling Internet companies. He wrote some major software programs. He's a very, very smart individual."

Meshkin said that he wanted to own and be part of a race team; he wanted McReynolds to run it and that not only would he pay McReynolds a handsome salary, he'd make McReynolds part owner of the team.

"He was a huge race fan in general," said McReynolds. "He had followed the sport, and he apparently followed the race teams I was with. I guess in a small way he was a Larry McReynolds fan. So I agreed to meet with him, and we met. It didn't take me long to realize Alex could back up anything he said he could or would do. After meeting with him his enthusiasm, dedication, commitment, and desire was something that really turned me on."

What Alex Meshkin wanted to do, in corporate lingo, was "think outside the box." In their first meeting, Meshkin had told McReynolds that he wanted to start a Busch series team and one day move up to Nextel Cup racing. But when Meshkin and McReynolds agreed to meet in Costa Mesa, California, in August 2003, McReynolds was surprised to learn that they were meeting with Toyota, who had gotten permission from NASCAR to begin a race program in the Craftsman truck series.

"How we ended up meeting with the Toyota people I have not a clue," said McReynolds. "Somehow, some way, Alex got us a meeting. We met with the Toyota people, Lee White, Gary Reed, Pat Walback, and they gave us the fifty dollar tour of the Costa Mesa plant at TRD [Toyota Research and Development], but I left there saying, 'We had a really good meeting.' I felt like I gave them all the answers, but there is no way they are going to give us one of their Toyota truck deals. Even though we had myself, which carried a lot of credibility, and I had been talking with Mike Skinner about having him drive for us, Mike only said, 'Maybe I'll drive for you.' We also had a letter of intent on a building, but that's all we had.

"I knew they had seventy-five or eighty presentations come at them, everything from existing truck teams to teams from the West Coast who wanted in on the Toyota bandwagon. I said to Alex, 'There is no way they are going to give one of these programs to a start-up team. We don't even own a screwdriver.'

"Two or three weeks went by, and in early September I got a phone call from Gary Reed of Toyota. He had five or six questions he wanted answered, especially questions concerning Alex Meshkin, who nobody knew. I told Gary the same thing I had told Lee White and Pat Walback in early August, that I had investigated Alex pretty thoroughly, because I didn't know who he was, and before I put my twenty-something years of credibility on the line, I wanted to make sure who I was getting involved with. I had him checked out pretty closely, and I found no problems, no weaknesses. He was for real. As I told a lot of people, that's the only way I would have gotten involved with him regardless of how much money he gave me or how much ownership.

"Another couple weeks went by. It was mid-September, and Lee White called, and he had four or five more questions. I answered him, but I still thought there was no way they were going to give us a deal. We just don't have enough foundation, I figured."

McReynolds figured wrong. Toyota awarded franchises to seven brand-new truck race teams. Meshkin and McReynolds, operating as "Bang! Racing," got two of them.

"One night in September, my wife, Linda, and I were having dinner in a restaurant, and my phone rang. It was Lee, Gary, and Pat. They were in Lee's office on a speakerphone. They said, 'Larry, it completely goes against our philosophy, because we made a commitment that we would not do a deal with a from-scratch, start-up team, but you guys were second-to-none in enthusiasm and desire, and we are going to roll the dice, and we want you to have two of our Toyota truck teams.'

"They never told us who we had to get to drive the trucks. They said they would like us to have a winning driver from the truck series with some experience, and if he's been past champion of the series, that would be a plus. Well, that's a pretty small box."

But McReynolds, whose reputation and smarts made him a very successful crew chief and effective administrator over the years, was able to provide Toyota with two top-rated drivers who filled the criteria perfectly. He signed Mike Skinner, who had won the Craftsman Truck Series Championship in its first year in 1995, and he also signed Travis Kvapil, the 2003 truck series champ. The Toyota executives had to have been thrilled.

McReynolds and Skinner had worked together as crew chief and driver for Richard Childress until McReynolds left for broadcasting in 2000. I asked McReynolds how he was able to sign his former driver.

"Mike had been driving for Morgan-McClure until June [2003], and they went their separate ways, and Mike filled in a good part this past season for the injured Jerry Nadeau. He sat on the pole in the Richmond race. I knew Mike's future was up in the air, and I had already been talking to him, so we negotiated and got Mike to drive for us.

"As for the second team, Toyota said they'd like to see someone up-and-coming, but yet someone who wasn't straight out of Late Models, and I knew that Travis' future with the IWX team was in jeopardy, even though he would go on to win the truck championship [in 2003]. We started talking to him, and after several months, even as he was closing in on the championship, we got him hired. So I feel we have stacked the deck pretty high on drivers.

"I feel we have done a good job hiring our people. Our sport is about horsepower and aerodynamics, handling, and pit stops, but at the end of the day, it's no different from any business: It's about hiring the right people. And I feel very fortunate, because when we started this deal, we didn't even own a screwdriver, and we hadn't hired a single person, and I have handpicked every person, and we're up to twenty-three employees.

"We hired Rick Ren, Mike's crew chief. He was one of my early hires, and he's been the backbone of this operation as we put it together. He's been in the truck series a number of years and has won races. He was Travis' crew chief the first two years Travis was in the truck series. Rick is very focused. I see a lot of myself in Rick Ren. He leaves no stone unturned. He worries about everything. He dots every i and crosses the ts three times. For Travis' crew chief we hired Eric Phillips, Joe Nemecheck's brother-in-law. Eric had been with Joe for ten years, and he was crew chief for Greg Biffle the second half of this year in the Busch series when Greg ran so competitively, even winning a couple of races.

"We went out and hired an engineer from Dale Earnhardt Incorporated. We hired a good mixture of people.

"We have a budget, but Alex has committed to do whatever it takes to make this a successful operation. Today we are a week and a half from our first race. We have all our people in place. We have all our sponsorship sold—that's where Alex is an expert." Toyota Research and Development is the sponsor of Skinner's car, and Line-X, a company that makes spray-on bed liners, will sponsor Kvapil's car.

I asked Larry McReynolds whether his days will contain more than 24 hours, considering all his commitments.

"When I first met with Toyota," said McReynolds, "they asked me, 'What exactly is your role?' I said, 'I think I know how to answer that. My bread and butter is still Fox and Speed Channel, and I enjoy it very much. I signed a three-year contract extension with Fox through 2007. But with that said, I will give these two teams every ounce of energy I can give them on a daily basis as long as it doesn't shortcut my family and as long as it doesn't shortcut my broadcast work. 'Cause I hope to do broadcasting of races for twenty more years.'

"It will be a balancing act, because the commitment I've made to my family will come first. I have worked very hard at that. We were in Talladega Thursday and Friday testing, and my little six-year-old girl, Kendall, had a father-daughter dance in her grammar school Friday night, so I took a commercial flight out midday to where I could come back for that dance. I'm thankful I did."

"Is the next step for you and Alex to go to Busch or Nextel Cup?" I asked.

"I don't think we're going to get too greedy," he said. "We want to dot every i and cross every t in the truck series, make sure we've ironed out all our wrinkles, and if down the road we see some success and see an opportunity to do it right—that's the key, to do it right—we may try some Busch, may try some Cup. I want to make sure we grab this brass ring we've got today on a daily basis.

"I'm going to tell you what: this year the truck series will have all the ingredients to be more competitive and more exciting than even the Busch series. Every race will be on the Speed Channel. I'm excited. Three months ago, I was looking in the mirror and saying, 'How in the world will it ever happen? How will we make it all come together?' But today, we're there. We leave for Daytona in a little over a week. Both our teams will be in their first race.

"Are we a little behind? Sure we are. We have a brand-new manufacturer with a from-scratch engine. Are we going to go to Daytona and be dominant qualifying? Probably not. But I feel we've come together enough that we're going to be competitive, and with what I know about Toyota, and what I've seen of them in other forms of motor sports, they will be at the pinnacle of this sport, and it won't be that far down the line. They are no different from myself and Alex Meshkin. They are very committed to do whatever it takes to make this program successful."

I asked McReynolds about the strong anti-foreign feeling stirred up by NASCAR's decision to let Toyota get involved in racing. After all, since the start of NASCAR more than 50 years ago, Big Bill France was adamant that only American cars could enter a NASCAR race.

"I have received a lot of negative e-mails and feedback about NASCAR letting a foreign manufacturer into our good ole American southern-boy sport," said McReynolds, "but one of my goals, and it's also Toyota's goal, besides having a competitive and winning operation, is to educate the old-school thinking about the foreign manufacturers.

"Yes, it originated in Japan. There is still a big part of Toyota in Japan, but you know what, today there are more Toyota cars and parts and pieces built in America than there are overseas. Toyota supplies a huge number of jobs for our fellow Americans. A few months ago Toyota opened a huge assembly plant in southern Kentucky, and you know what? I've been part of this Toyota deal since August, and of the two dozen or so Toyota executives I have met, I have shaken the hand of exactly one foreign person. As far as jobs are concerned, Toyota has done a lot for Americans, and as for those people who are complaining, moaning, and groaning about Toyota getting into racing, and sending me e-mails, I'll bet if you walked into their houses, every one of them has a Mitsubishi or Sony television in their living room."

One day we may well see a Toyota winning a NASCAR Nextel Cup championship. Who knows, the rate NASCAR is growing, anything you can imagine is possible.

ACKNOWLEDGMENTS

THIS BOOK WOULD NOT HAVE BEEN POSSIBLE WITHOUT THE PERSEVERANCE of Lee Klancher, my editor at MBI Publishing. We talked off and on about working together for perhaps ten years, and it was Lee's persistence that finally made it happen. The whole experience has been pure pleasure.

During the time we have worked together, Lee and I developed a chemistry and mutual respect that has resulted in a special book that should keep the memory alive of many of NASCAR's greatest figures for a long, long time. I am very proud of this book, and I thank Lee for giving me the chance to write it.

I also want to thank Neil and Dawn Reshen, my business managers going-on seventeen years, for their support and wisdom, and to Frank Weimann, my dogged agent, as well as to all the men and women who freely gave their time and memories to fill this book. The encyclopedic Greg Fielden proofread the manuscript in an attempt to keep me as error-free as possible, and copy editor Joe Bonyata did a yeoman job in search of wayward commas and dangling participles.

As always, anything I have accomplished has been as a result of the support of my family, wife Rhonda Sonnenberg, who is still better than Eleanor Roosevelt; our son Charlie, the light of our life even after the onset of his teenage years; and to our canines, Basset Hound Doris and Mastiff Mandy. May they have a lifetime filled with rawhide and chewy bones.

Finally I wish to mark the passing of Bob Latford, who was always there whenever I needed a question answered about NASCAR history. Bob was always peacock proud of his association with stock car racing. He was a great resource and a real gentleman, and he will be sorely missed.

INDEX

INDEX